D1105992

DESIGNING FOR ECONOMICAL PRODUCTION

Designing for Economical Production

Second Edition

by

Dr. H.E. Trucks

Gordon Lewis
Editor

Rachel Subrin
Sr. Publications Administrator

Published by

Society of Manufacturing Engineers
Publications Development Department
Marketing Division
One SME Drive • P.O. Box 930
Dearborn, Michigan 48121

Designing for Economical Production

Second Edition
First Printing

Library of Congress Catalog Card Number: 86-61929
International Standard Book Number: 0-87263-249-0
Manufactured in the United States of America

Table of Contents

Preface

Since the publication of the first edition of this book, more technical advances have occurred than in any other period of time. Most sections in this book have taken this into account.

For the purposes of this book, *Designing for Economical Production*, producibility is defined as the combined effect of those elements or characteristics of a design, and the production planning for it, that enables the item described by the design to be produced and inspected in the quantity required, permitting a series of trade-offs to achieve the optimum of the least possible cost and the minimum time, while still meeting the necessary quality and performance requirements.

The key elements of the definition, analyzed independently in the paragraphs of the book, provide the fundamental factors having the greatest impact on producibility and function.

The importance and impact of producibility surfaced with the industrial mobilization occasioned by World War II. The need to re-engineer a particular design to permit ease of manufacture by multiple producers, gave testimony that problems existed. The ensuing technological explosions of materials, tooling, and manufacturing processes, coupled with the sophistication of the product to be produced, have changed that situation. Also, the emergence of new skills, technologies, and materials emphasized the need to consider producibility in the initial design phase to thereby avoid or eliminate frequently encountered design problems.

Designing for Economical Production deals with the factors that determine whether or not an item is acceptable from a producibility point of view, such as function and cost, relative machining cost, material cost, manufacturing method, cost of tolerances and surface finishes for the selected manufacturing method. Trade-off analyses to determine what manufacturing method is the most economical for the required function and quantity are discussed, in addition to the economical lot size quantity requirements for economical production.

The text includes the economical design of parts produced from non-metallic materials such as elastomers and plastics, time-proven cost reduction methods such as value engineering, and the application of this cost reduction method.

Management's role in value and cost control and planning of new programs is also featured. And finally, the producibility considerations for manual and mechanical assemblies, the basic rules for these assemblies, and the development of the industrial robot in the assembly field are illuminated. The methods described in the chapters of this book for economical production are important advantages in the world of global competition. The design engineer, manufacturing engineer, and the engineering student should study these chapters so that they can produce an economical design for economical production.

1

Metallic Materials

This chapter presents the characteristics, mechanical properties, machinability rating, cost indices, applications, weldability, and availability of commonly used metallic materials.

DEFINITIONS

Machinability rating is a percentage rating, using B1112 steel as a 100% machinable metal, and therefore rated by the number 100. A machinability rating of 137 would indicate that the metal being rated is 37% easier to machine than B1112 steel. A rating of 55 would indicate that the metal being rated is 45% harder to machine than B1112 steel.

The *cost index* is based upon the price of B1112 steel as being 100. A cost index of 155 for a given metal indicates that the given metal cost is 55% higher than the cost of B1112 steel. A cost index of 55 for a given metal indicates that the given metal cost is 45% lower than the cost of B1112 steel.

The *relative production cost* is based upon the algebraic sum of the machinability rating and the cost index for a given metal, as illustrated in *Figure 1-1*.

The following are examples of the simple math used in making the bar chart in *Figure 1-1*. First, one must remember that the machinability rating of the metallic materials is based on 100% machinability of B1112. The cost index of B1112 is based on 100. Therefore, the bar in *Figure 1-1* for B1112 is from 0 to 100. The higher the machinability rating, as shown for C1117L, the lower the cost of machining.

The relative production cost is 100 - 42 = 58. The cost index for this material is 100, therefore, there is no increase in the material cost. If the machinability rating is lower than that of B1112, the cost of machining increases. The increase of the material cost has to be added to the increase of the machining cost to achieve the relative production cost.

Example: For material C1040, the machinability rating is 64 and the cost index is 118. 100 - 64 + 18 = 54. This means that the relative production cost is 54% higher than that of B1112. The algebraic equation is simple if it is properly applied.

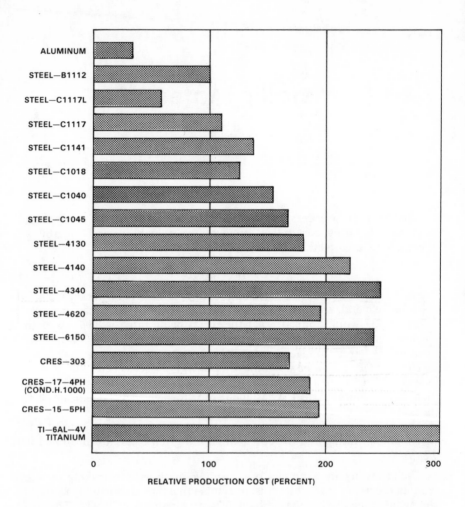

RELATIVE PRODUCTION COST (PERCENT)

Figure 1-1. Relative production cost for machined parts from various types of metallic materials.

PRACTICES

Material Selection

Materials affect manufacturing costs. This fact is illustrated in *Figure 1-1* which shows the relative costs for machining aluminum, carbon steels, alloy steels, and corrosion-resistant steels.

Although the relative cost varies with changes in shape, size, quantity, and market prices, it is a good base for comparing costs when selecting materials for a new design, or when changing from one material to another. The material selection data in *Table I-1* are helpful in selecting the best materials

2

for a specific part. Characteristics and mechanical properties of the most commonly used steels are shown in this data. For metallic materials not evaluated in *Table I-1*, the designer should consult with metallurgists who have had ample experience with these materials to ascertain the proper uses, mechanical properties, and other required data on the material selected.

Table I-1. Metallic Material Chart

FREE-MACHINING AND LOW-CARBON STEELS

B1112 Cold-rolled Steel.

Characteristics. Free-cutting; case-hardening recommended for wear resistance; not suitable for parts subject to shock, vibration, or fatigue.

Mechanical Properties. B1112 steel is not intended for use with structural parts; the mechanical properties are therefore not given here.

Machinability Rating. 100

Cost Index. 100

Application. Screw machine products; for parts where ease of machining and surface finish are of prime importance (worms, collars, screws, and shafts).

Weldability. Screw stock is not readily welded because of its high sulfur content.

Availability. Bars and rods.

C1117 Cold-finished Steel (unleaded).

Characteristics. Free-cutting; develops uniformly hard case, and a strong, tough core; carburizes without embrittlement.

Mechanical Properties. C1117 steel is not intended for use with structural parts; the mechanical properties are therefore not given here.

Machinability Rating. 90

Cost Index. 100

Application. Parts requiring greater toughness than B1112 steel (medium duty shafts, studs, pins, screws, and worms).

Weldability. Special practice required.

Availability. Cold-finished shapes.

C1117L Cold-finished Steel (leaded).

Characteristics. Same as C1117.

Mechanical Properties. Same as C1117.

Machinability Rating. 142

Cost Index. 100

Application. Same as C1117.

Weldability. Same as C1117.

Availability. Same as C1117.

C1018 Cold-finished and Hot-rolled Steel.

Characteristics. A low-carbon, open-hearth steel, having a higher manganese content than other low-carbon steels such as C1020. Because of its manganese content, C1018 is a better steel for carburized parts since it produces a harder, more uniform case.

Mechanical Properties. C1018 steel is not intended for use with structural parts; the mechanical properties are therefore not given here.

Machinability Rating. 76

Cost Index. 100

Table I-1. Metallic Material Chart (*Continued*)

Application. Parts requiring high surface hardening and soft cores, such as gears, king pins, chain pins, ratchets, and dogs.

Weldability. Easily welded by all welding processes.

Availability. Cold-finished and hot-rolled shapes.

MEDIUM CARBON STEELS

C1141 Hot-rolled Steel.

Characteristics. This is a medium-carbon, manganese, open-hearth steel. Strength characteristics are high in the as-rolled condition. Greater hardness and strength can be obtained through heat treatment. Machinability is good due to the addition of sulfur.

Mechanical Properties. Tensile strength (as-rolled), 95,000 psi (655 MPa); yield strength (as-rolled), 56,000 psi (390 MPa); elongation in 2 inches, 25%.

Machinability Rating. 70

Cost Index. 106

Application. This grade is used in applications where good machinability combined with high strength is required, i.e., axles, studs, bolts, shafts, and tie-rods.

Weldability. Not readily weldable because of its high carbon, manganese, and sulfur content. Gas or arc welding can be performed provided the area to be welded is preheated. Stress relieving after welding is recommended.

Availability. Hot-rolled bars.

C1040 Cold-finished and Hot-rolled Bars.

Characteristics. This is a medium-carbon, open-hearth steel; tough and ductile; wear and shock resistant. It has good hardenability but relatively high distortion, therefore, small and intricate sections must be heat treated with care.

Mechanical Properties. Tensile strength: cold-finished, 110,000 psi (760 MPa); hot-rolled, 93,000 psi (640 MPa); yield strength: cold-finished, 83,000 psi (572 MPa); hot-rolled, 59,000 psi (407 MPa); elongation in 2 inches, cold-finished, 22%; hot-rolled, 27%.

Machinability Rating. 64

Cost Index. 118

Application. Parts requiring greater strength than can be obtained from the lower carbon steels (shafts, machinery parts, large gears, forgings, and pump shafts).

Weldability. Not readily welded.

Availability. Cold-finished, hot-rolled bars, and forged stock.

C1045 Cold-finished, Hot-rolled Bars and Forgings.

Characteristics. This steel is similar in characteristics, mechanical properties, applications, weldability, and availability to C1040 steel. Higher mechanical properties and hardness can be obtained in the heat treated condition due to the slight increase in carbon, but the machinability is decreased.

Mechanical Properties. Similar to C1040.

Machinability Rating. 55

Cost Index. 121

Application. Similar to C1040.

Weldability. Similar to C1040.

Availability. Similar to C1040.

4

Table I-1. Metallic Material Chart (*Continued*)

ALLOY STEELS

4130 Steel: Chrome-Molybdenum (for aircraft applications).

Characteristics. Manufactured by the electric furnace process, this grade meets the rigid standards of the aircraft industry. The greatest care is taken throughout its processing to insure against the presence of injurious defects. This steel is suitable for fabrication of parts subject to magnetic particle inspection.

Mechanical Properties. The minimum mechanical properties in condition F (quenched and tempered) are: tensile strength, 125,000 psi (862 MPa); yield strength, 100,000 psi (690 MPa); elongation in 2 inches, 17%.

Machinability Rating. 60

Cost Index. 138

Application. This material is intended for general use in the manufacturing of various aircraft and missile parts.

Weldability. Weldable by all procedures, but preheating is sometimes necessary for heavy sections or parts having wide variations in thickness.

Heat Treatment. Parts can be heat treated to about 200,000 psi (1379 MPa). Avoid the use of cross sections over one inch.

Availability. Bars, rods, and forgings, in the following physical conditions: (A) as-forged, (B) as-rolled, (C) annealed, (D) normalized, (E) normalized and tempered, and (F) quenched and tempered.

4140 Steel: Chrome-Molybdenum (for aircraft applications).

Characteristics. This oil-hardening alloy steel is manufactured by the same process and rigid standards as those required for the 4130 steel. This is a high-strength steel which has high resistance to wear and fatigue. Suitable for large sections and can be deep hardened. Good for parts of varying thicknesses, and responds well to simple normalizing treatment or flame hardening. Has high impact strength when fully heat treated, but is difficult to forge or roll.

Mechanical Properties. The minimum mechanical properties in condition F (quenched and tempered) are: tensile strength, 150,000 psi (1034 MPa); yield strength, 120,000 psi (828 MPa); elongation in 2 inches, 17%.

Machinability Rating. 57

Cost Index. 138

Application. This material is intended for general use in the manufacture of various aircraft parts (cams, cylinders, rollers, gears, pins, and spline drives).

Weldability. Weldable by all procedures. However, preheating is sometimes necessary for heavy sections or parts having wide variations in thickness.

Heat Treatment. Parts can be heat treated to 200,000 psi (1379 MPa).

Availability. All standard mill forms in the following physical conditions: (B) as-rolled, (C) annealed, (D) normalized, (E) normalized and tempered, and (F) quenched and tempered.

4340 Steel: Chromium-Nickel-Molybdenum (for aircraft applications).

Characteristics. This steel is a deep-hardening grade manufactured by the electric furnace process to meet the rigid standards of the aircraft industry. The greatest care is taken throughout the processing to insure against the presence of injurious defects. It has high hardenability and high strength for the medium-carbon range, and develops combinations of ductility and strength in heavy sections. 4340 is an oil-hardening grade steel, with a maximum hardness of R_c 55. For better machinability, it should be used in the annealed or normalized condition.

Table I-1. Metallic Material Chart (*Continued*)

Mechanical Properties. The minimum mechanical properties in condition F (quenched and tempered) are: tensile strength, 150,000 psi (1034 MPa); yield strength, 130,000 psi (896 MPa); elongation in 2 inches, 14%.

Machinability Rating. 52

Cost Index. 193

Application. This material is intended for use in the manufacture of highly stressed aircraft and missile parts requiring good hardenability.

Weldability. Weldable by oxyacetylene, inert arc, and electrical resistance methods.

Heat Treatment. Parts can be heat treated to a maximum hardness of R_c 55 (284,000 psi) (1960 MPa).

Availability. All standard mill forms in the following conditions: (A) as-forged, (B) as-rolled, (C) annealed, (D) normalized, (E) normalized and tempered, and (F) quenched and tempered.

4620 Steel, Nickel-Molybdenum, Aircraft Quality, Carburizing.

Characteristics. This is a carburizing grade of alloy steel, manufactured by the electric furnace process to meet aircraft industry standards. It is the best of the carburizing steels, having outstanding uniformity of case and response to heat treatment. It is relatively free from distortion during quenching, has excellent toughness at high hardness, and high fatigue resistance. For better machinability, it should also be used in the annealed or normalized condition.

Mechanical Properties. Tensile strength, 82,000 psi (565 MPa); yield strength, 55,000 psi (380 MPa); elongation in 2 inches, 30%.

Machinability Rating. 58

Cost Index. 154

Application. Carburized parts, automatic screw machine parts, gears, cams, splines, bushings, rollers.

Weldability. Weldable by all procedures.

Heat Treatment. Parts can be heat treated to R_c 32-48.

Availability. All standard mill forms in the following conditions: (A) as-forged, (B) as-rolled, (C) annealed, (D) normalized, and (E) normalized and tempered.

6150 Steel: Chrome-Vanadium (aircraft quality).

Characteristics. This chrome-vanadium steel is manufactured by the electric furnace process to meet aircraft industry standards. It has high strength, high fatigue resistance, high shock resistance, and high wear resistance; excellent ductility; little heat-distortion; fine grain structure. Unless annealed before machining, it has poor machinability.

Mechanical Properties. The following properties are for 6150 steel in the annealed condition: tensile strength, 103,000 psi (710 MPa); yield strength, 70,000 psi (482 MPa); elongation in 2 inches, 27%.

Machinability Rating (annealed). 50

Cost Index. 191

Application. Parts with varying thicknesses; springs subject to high temperatures, high stress, and impact; parts requiring high strength and resistance to impact.

Weldability. Weldable by all procedures.

Heat Treatment. This steel can be heat treated to a maximum hardness of R_c 58.

Availability. All standard mill forms in the following conditions: (A) as-forged, (B) as-rolled, (C) annealed, (D) normalized, and (E) normalized and tempered.

Table I-1. Metallic Material Chart (*Continued*)

CORROSION-RESISTANT STEELS

---

303 Corrosion-resistant Free-machining Steel.

Characteristics. Type 303 is 18-8 chromium-nickel corrosion-resisting steel, modified by the addition of sulfur and phosphorus, to improve machinability and nonseizing properties. It is the most readily machinable of all the chromium-nickel grades, and has a good corrosion resistance. It is nonmagnetic in the annealed condition, but slightly magnetic when cold-worked, and not hardenable by heat treatment. Tensile strength and hardness can be increased by cold working. It is manufactured by the electric furnace process. Other types of 303 chromium-nickel steels to which elements have been added to improve machining and nonseizing characteristics are available.

Mechanical Properties. In practice, annealed bars will average as follows: tensile strength, hot-rolled and annealed, 90,000 psi (620 MPa); cold-finished and annealed, 100,000 psi (690 MPa); yield strength, hot-rolled and annealed, 35,000 psi (240 MPa); cold-finished and annealed, 60,000 psi (414 MPa); elongation in 2 inches, hot-rolled and annealed, 50%; cold-finished and annealed, 40%.

Machinability Rating. 65

Cost Index. 130

Application. Used almost exclusively for parts requiring machining, grinding, or polishing, and good corrosion-resistance. Its nonseizing and nongalling properties make it ideal for moving parts. Being an austenitic steel, it is useful where low magnetic permeability is required.

Weldability. Not recommended. If welding is required, the designer should consult a welding expert for proper welding procedures.

Availability. This steel is available in all mill shapes, either hot-rolled and annealed or cold-finished and annealed.

17-4PH Precipitation-hardening, Corrosion-resisting Steel.

Characteristics. This is a chromium-nickel grade of corrosion-resisting steel that can be hardened by a single, low temperature, precipitation-hardening heat treatment. The strength and corrosion-resisting properties of 17-4PH steel hold up well in service temperatures up to 800° F (427° C). This material machines well, has excellent welding characteristics, forges easily, and has excellent castability. The combination of excellent mechanical and processing properties makes this grade adaptable to a wide variety of applications.

Mechanical Properties. AMS 5643 requires the following mechanical properties after precipitation heat treatment at 900° F (482° C). Tensile strength, 180,000 to 215,000 psi (1240 to 1480 MPa); yield strength, 165,000 psi (1137 MPa); elongation in 2 inches, 10%.

Machinability Rating. Cast material, heat treated to H1000, and bar stock, heat treated to H1050 are rated at 60.

Cost Index. 146

Application. Used where high strength and good corrosion-resistance are required, as well as in applications requiring high fatigue strength and good resistance to galling, seizing, and stress corrosion. Suitable for intricate parts which require machining and welding, and for parts where distortion in conventional steel heat treatment is a problem. It is an excellent forging and casting material.

Weldability. Readily weldable by all of the commercial processes. Preheating or postheating practices used for standard, hardenable corrosion-resisting grades are not required.

Heat Treatment. This is a precipitation-hardening steel. The wrought and cast material should be heat treated as outlined in MIL-H-6875.

7

Table I-1. Metallic Material Chart (*Continued*)

Availability. This material is available in the standard, wrought shapes, flats, and forged billets.

15-5PH Precipitating-hardening, Corrosion-resisting Steel.

Characteristics, and *Mechanical Properties* are in general, somewhat similar to 17-4PH. It is used mainly where high stress corrosion can be encountered.

Machinability Rating. Machinability for heat treated material is rated at 55.

Cost Index. 150

Application. Used where high strength and good corrosion-resistance are required. Stress corrosion resistance is better than that of 17-4PH, and is used as a replacement for 17-4PH where high stress corrosion can be encountered.

Weldability. Readily weldable by arc and resistance techniques used for stainless steels in general.

Heat Treatment. This is a precipitation-hardening steel. The wrought cast and forged material should be heat treated as outlined by the manufacturer or by the requirement of the latest MIL standard.

Availability. This material is available in bars, forged billets, plates, and sheet.

Titanium-base Alloy Grade TI-6AL-4V.

Characteristics. This alloy is often called the workhorse grade of titanium. The TI-6AL-4V composition comes as close to being a general purpose grade as possible in titanium.

Mechanical Properties. Tensile strength-annealed bar: 130,000 psi (897 MPa); yield strength, 120,000 psi (830 MPa); elongation in 2 inches, 10%; reduction in area, 20%. Solution treated aged bar and forgings: tensile strength, 150,000 psi (1034 MPa); yield strength, 140,000 psi (965 MPa); elongation in 2 inches, 8%; reduction in area, 20%. Strengthening heat treatments for this alloy are predicted on the retention of the high temperature beta phase to room temperature for subsequent controlled decomposition during aging. Thus, a high temperature solution treatment operation is followed by a lower temperature aging treatment.

Machinability Rating. The machinability rating of this alloy for bars and forgings in the solution treated aged condition is rated at 50.

Cost Index. 350

Weldability. The welding of this alloy by either the TIG or MIG process can be performed when material is in the annealed, the solution treated, or the fully aged condition, and may be with or without filler wire. Where maximum joint ductility is desired, commercially pure filler wire is frequently used.

Availability. This alloy is available in bars, forged billets, sheet, strip, and plate.

Aluminum. *Table I-2* lists the most commonly used aluminum alloys in the metalworking industry. For other aluminum alloys, their typical characteristics, and applications, the designer should seek the advice of an aluminum fabricator.

Low-carbon Steels. The mechanical properties of the low-carbon steels are not given in the steel selection data, since these steels are not intended to be used for structural parts.

The low-carbon and free-machining steels should be used only for overall economy and only where they can be used in a nonstructural application.

Alloy Steels. In general, an alloy steel should be selected when one or several of the following properties are required:

Table I-2. Aluminum Alloy Material Selection Chart

Alloys and Temper	Resistance to Corrosion		Workability (Cold)	Machinability	Brazability	Weldability			Typical Application
	General Stress	Corrosion Cracking				Gas	Ark Resistance	Spot and Seam	
2024-0	—	—	—	D	D	D	D	D	Screw machine products and aircraft structure
2024-T3	D	C	C	B	D	C	B	B	
2024-T4	D	C	C	B	D	C	B	B	
2024-T6	D	B	C	B	D	D	C	B	
5052-0	A	A	A	D	C	A	A	B	Sheet metal work and hydraulic tubes
5052-H32	A	A	B	D	C	A	A	A	
5052-H34	A	A	B	C	C	A	A	A	
5052-H36	A	A	C	C	C	A	A	A	
5052-H38	A	A	C	C	C	A	A	A	
6061-0	B	A	A	D	A	A	A	B	Heavy duty structural requirements, good corrosion resistance
6061-T4	B	B	B	C	A	A	A	A	
6061-T6	B	A	C	C	A	A	A	A	
7075-0	—	—	—	D	D	D	C	B	Aircraft and other structures
17075-T6	C	C	D	B	D	D	C	B	

- Better response to heat treatment as indicated by greater hardness.
- Less distortion from heat treatment.
- Greater strength.
- Impact strength.
- Fatigue strength.
- Shock resistance.
- Wear resistance.
- Ductility.

Ratings *A* through *D*, as shown in *Table I-2*, are relative in decreasing order of merit. For weldability and brazability, ratings *A* through *D* are relative but defined as follows:

A — Generally weldable by all commercial procedures and methods.

B — Weldable with special techniques or for specific applications which justify preliminary trials and testing to develop welding procedure and performance.

C — Limited weldability because of crack sensitivity or loss in resistance to corrosion and loss of mechanical properties.

D — No commonly used welding methods have been developed.

The machinability comparison of aluminum alloys and B1112 steel has not been established, but aluminum is known to machine 3 to 4 times faster than B1112 steel.

The cost index of aluminum alloys is based on cubic inch per pound compared to B1112 steel. This indicates that there is about 68% less cost in machining aluminum alloys as compared to B1112 steel.

2

Machining

GENERAL DESIGN RULES

Because of the highly competitive nature of most manufacturing businesses, the question of finding ways to reduce cost is ever present. A good starting point for cost reduction is in the design of the product. The design engineer should always keep in mind the possible alternatives available in making designs. It is often impossible to determine the best alternatives without a careful analysis of the probable production cost. Designing for function, interchangeability, quality, and economy requires a careful study of tolerances, surface finishes, processes, materials, and equipment.

To assure sound and economical design from a producibility standpoint, careful consideration of the following general design rules—both separately and together—is of paramount importance. The order of importance may vary according to design requirements, or factors, but the overall importance always remains the same.

- **Seek simplicity.** Design for maximum simplicity in functional and physical characteristics.
- **Determine the best production method.** Seek the help of the manufacturing engineer to design for the most economical production methods available with consideration for inherent producibility limitations.
- **Analyze materials.** Select materials that will lend themselves to low-cost production as well as to design requirements.
- **Minimize production steps.** Design for the minimum number of separate operations in machining, finishing, forming, molding, casting, fabrication, and assembly.
- **Eliminate fixturing and handling problems.** Design for ease of locating, setting up, and holding parts.
- **Employ maximum acceptable tolerances and finishes.** Specify surface roughness and accuracy no greater than that which is commensurate with the type of part or mechanism being designed, and the production method or methods contemplated.

Tolerances on finish and dimensions play an important part in the final achievement or absence of practical production design.

11

A comprehensive study of the principles of interchangeability is essential for a thorough understanding and full appreciation of low-cost production techniques. Interchangeability is the key to successful production regardless of quantity. Details of all parts should be surveyed carefully to assure not only inexpensive processing but also rapid, easy assembly and maintenance. It must be remembered that each production method has a well-established level of precision which can be maintained in continuous production without exceeding normal basic cost.

Economic manufacturing does not just happen. It starts with design and considers practical limits of machine tools, processes, tolerances, and finishes. The production tolerances for various machining operations, and cost curves for tolerances and surface roughness, show that it is important to analyze the tolerance structure and surface roughness to produce a functional, economical design.

DIMENSIONAL TOLERANCES AND SURFACE ROUGHNESS

Neither dimensional tolerances nor surface roughness should be specified to limits of accuracy closer than those which the actual function or design necessitate. This is done to assure the advantages of lowest possible cost and fastest possible production.

Figure 2-1 provides, at a glance, a general relationship of actual dimensional tolerance to surface roughness by indicating a range of accuracy for each processing method.

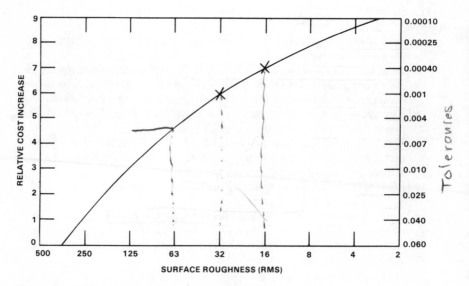

Figure 2-1. Relationship between tolerance and finish.

12

With *Figure 2-1* it is obvious that there must be some relationship between surface roughness and dimensional accuracy. It is not feasible to expect to hold a tolerance of 0.0001 (0.0025) on a part which is to be machined to an average roughness of 125 μin. rms (3.2 μm rms). Likewise, a finish of 10 to 15 μin. (0.25 to 0.38 μm) for a surface which is merely intended to provide proper size for locating for subsequent operations cannot be justified. A 40 to 60 μin. (1.0 to 1.5 μm) finish would be satisfactory, and would cost at least 50 to 60% less.

Besides showing the relationship between surface finish and roughness, *Figure 2-1* shows the relative cost increase as tolerances and surface roughness become finer. If a part is machined to a tolerance of ±0.0004 in. (±0.010 mm), the chart indicates a finish of 16 μin. rms (0.4 μm rms) at a cost factor of seven. If the tolerance is increased to ±0.001 in. (±0.025 mm), the chart indicates a finish of 32 μin. rms (0.8 μm rms) at a cost factor of six. This is a 14.3% decrease in cost.

Figure 2-2 indicates the tolerance range of general machining processes. As can be seen, various processes overlap. This is due to the ranges and sizes which the various processes can handle.

For example, it would be rather difficult to handle a 20-in. (500-mm) diameter hone, and therefore other processes should be used to hold a tolerance of ±0.0015 (±0.0381 mm), as indicated in *Figure 2-2*. Similarly, one does not build a 20-in. (508 mm) diameter drill only to use a boring tool to finish the inside diameter. The figure shows only the tolerance that can be held within the limits of the process.

| RANGE OF SIZES | | TOLERANCES ± | | | | | | | | |
FROM	THROUGH									
0.000	0.599	0.00015	0.0002	0.0003	0.0005	0.0008	0.0012	0.002	0.003	0.005
0.600	0.999	0.00015	0.00025	0.0004	0.0006	0.001	0.0015	0.0025	0.004	0.006
1.000	1.499	0.0002	0.0003	0.0005	0.0008	0.0012	0.002	0.003	0.005	0.008
1.500	2.799	0.00025	0.0004	0.0006	0.001	0.0015	0.0025	0.004	0.006	0.010
2.800	4.499	0.0003	0.0005	0.0008	0.0012	0.002	0.003	0.005	0.008	0.012
4.500	7.799	0.0004	0.0006	0.001	0.0015	0.0025	0.004	0.006	0.010	0.015
7.800	13.599	0.0005	0.0008	0.0012	0.002	0.003	0.005	0.008	0.012	0.020
13.600	20.999	0.0006	0.001	0.0015	0.0025	0.004	0.006	0.010	0.015	0.025

LAPPING & HONING
GRINDING, DIAMOND TURNING, BORING
BROACHING
REAMING
TURNING, BORING, SLOTTING, PLANING, & SHAPING
MILLING
DRILLING

Figure 2-2. Tolerance ranges of machining processes.

SURFACE FINISH

Process

Without needing to know how to operate a particular machine to attain the desired degree of surface roughness, there are certain aspects of all these methods which should be understood by the design engineer. Knowledge of facts such as degree of roughness obtained by any operation, and the economics of attaining a smoother surface with each operation, will aid in deciding just which surface roughness to specify.

In general, *surface roughness* is defined as the average deviation expressed in microinches from the mean surface. Some may use the root-mean-square average deviation, and others the arithmetic average deviation. Although the two averages described are not mathematically equivalent, agreement exists that the difference between them is negligible, and the term *average* is universal. The mean surface is located in such a way that the volume of peaks above the surface cross-section exactly equals the volume of valleys below it.

Advantages and Limitations

As an aid for understanding the applications of various surface finishes, the following list describes some typical examples and their usage. *Figure 2-3* shows the range of surface finishes produced by various processes.

4-microinch rms (0.1 micrometer). This surface results from processes which produce mirror-like surfaces, free from tool grinding or visible marks of any kind. The finish is used on rolls for roller bearings subject to heavy loads, for packings and rings that slide across the direction of the finish grain, and for tool components. Because of the high cost, this finish is used only when essential.

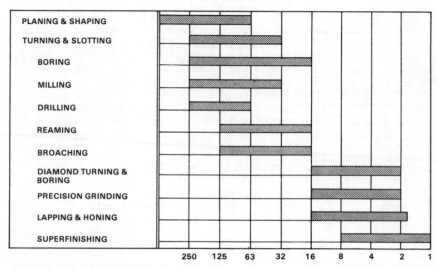

Figure 2-3. Surface roughness (μ in.-rms).

8-microinch rms (0.2 micrometer). This surface results from processes which produce close tolerance, scratch-free surfaces. The finish is used for the interior surface of hydraulic struts, for hydraulic cylinders, pistons and piston rods for O-ring packings, for journals operating in plain bearings, for cam faces, for raceways, and for rolls of antifriction bearings when loads are normal. This finish is normally used only when coarser finishes are known to be inadequate.

16-microinch rms (0.4 micrometer). This surface results from processes which produce a finish that is essential in those applications where surface finish is of primary importance for proper functioning. The finish is used for rapidly rotating shaft bearings, for heavily loaded bearings, for rolls in bearings of ordinary commercial grades, for hydraulic applications, for static sealing rings, for the bottom of sealing-ring grooves, for journals operating in plain bearings, and for extreme tension members.

32-microinch rms (0.8 micrometer). This surface results from processes which produce a fine machine finish. The finish is normally found on parts subject to stress concentrations and vibrations, for brake drums, broached holes, gear teeth, and other precision machined parts.

63-microinch rms (1.6 micrometer). This surface results from processes which produce a high-quality, smooth machine finish—as smooth a finish as can be economically produced by turning and milling without subsequent operations, and can be produced on a surface grinder. This finish is suitable for ordinary bearings, for ordinary machine parts where fairly close dimensional tolerances must be held, and for highly stressed parts that are not subject to severe stress reversals.

125-microinch rms (3.2 micrometer). This surface results from high-grade machine work where high speeds, fine feeds, light cuts, and sharp cutters are used to produce a smooth machine finish. It may also be produced by all methods of direct machining under proper conditions. The finish should not be used on sliding surfaces, but can be used for rough bearing surfaces where loads are light and infrequent, or for moderately stressed machine parts which require moderately close fits.

250-microinch rms (6.4 micrometer). This surface results from average machine operations using medium feeds. The appearance of this finish is not objectionable, and can be used on noncritical component surfaces, and for mounting surfaces for brackets.

THE RELATIONSHIP OF CLOSE TOLERANCES AND FINE FINISHES TO PRODUCTION COST

As can be seen in *Figure 1-1* material cost and material machinability ratings show the relative production cost of a product. The percent cost increase as related to fabrication requirement is dependent upon the tooling and equipment used for the fabrication of a part.

Figure 2-4 shows how the cost increase due to fabrication requirements is related to the tolerances and surface roughness shown for the part.

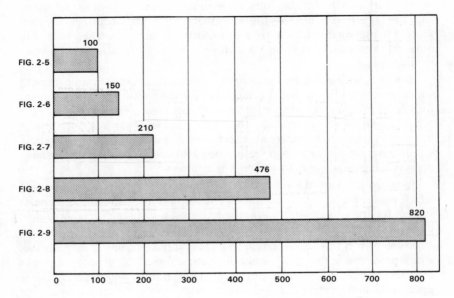

Figure 2-4. Percent cost increase as related to fabrication requirements.

Figures 2-5 through *2-9* show the percent increase due to these requirements. *Figure 2-5*, a plain shaft turned and cut off to tolerances, is based
on 100%.

A careful analysis should be made as to the design requirements, the
economy of the type of tooling, and equipment used to fabricate the part.
There is seen, therefore, a direct relationship between production cost and
tolerances and surface requirements.

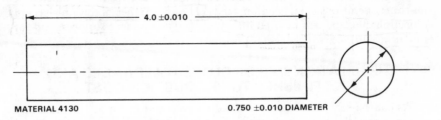

Figure 2-5. Shaft—straight turning and cutoff.

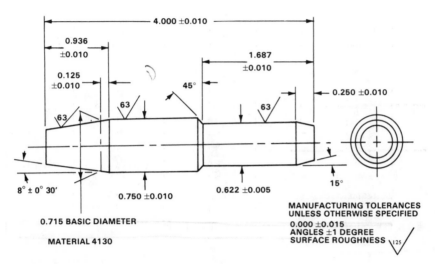

4.000 ±0.010

0.936 ±0.010

1.687 ±0.010

0.125 ±0.010

45°

0.250 ±0.010

63

63

63

15°

8° ± 0° 30'

0.750 ±0.010

0.622 ±0.005

0.715 BASIC DIAMETER

MATERIAL 4130

**MANUFACTURING TOLERANCES
UNLESS OTHERWISE SPECIFIED**
0.000 ±0.015
ANGLES ±1 DEGREE
SURFACE ROUGHNESS 125

Figure 2-6. Shaft—turning, forming, and cutoff.

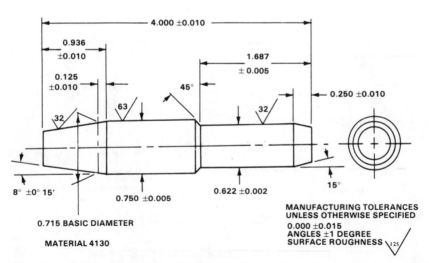

4.000 ±0.010

0.936 ±0.010

1.687 ± 0.005

0.125 ±0.010

45°

0.250 ±0.010

32

63

32

15°

8° ±0° 15'

0.750 ±0.005

0.622 ±0.002

0.715 BASIC DIAMETER

MATERIAL 4130

**MANUFACTURING TOLERANCES
UNLESS OTHERWISE SPECIFIED**
0.000 ±0.015
ANGLES ±1 DEGREE
SURFACE ROUGHNESS 125

Figure 2-7. Shaft—turning, forming, and cutoff to a closer tolerance than
Figure 2-6.

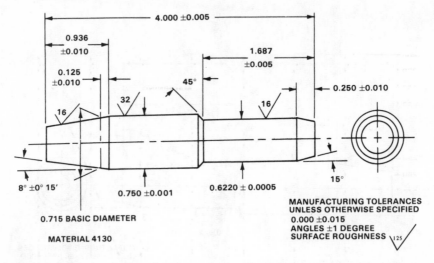

Figure 2-8. Shaft—turning, forming, cutoff, and grinding.

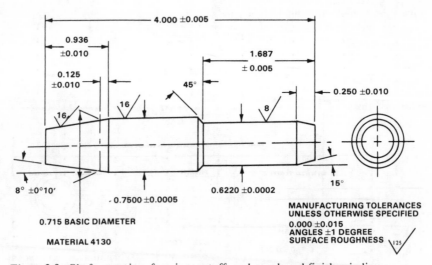

Figure 2-9. Shaft—turning, forming, cutoff, and rough and finish grinding.

Cost savings can be realized by establishing tolerances and finish requirements that are in agreement with part functions. *Figure 2-10* shows the additional machining operation necessary to produce close tolerances and their relative finish. As can be seen from the chart in *Figure 2-10*, tolerances of less than ±0.001 (±.0254) require additional operations, and this increases the cost of the product.

18

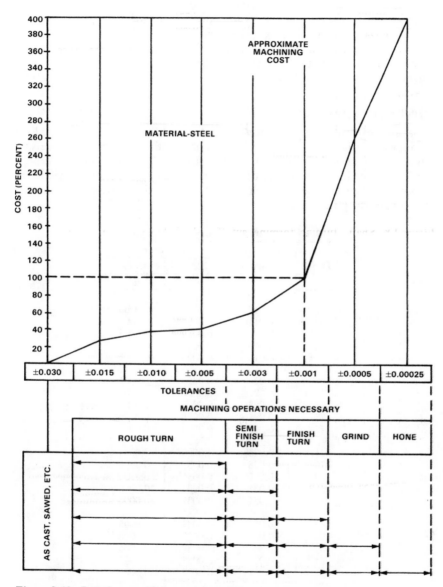

Figure 2-10. Relative machining cost based on tolerances.

DRILLING

Drilling, the simplest of all machining operations, can be expensive if the tolerances and the depth of holes are not carefully analyzed. Modern computer numerical control (CNC) and numerical control (NC) equipment and improved tooling and cutting tool material have made it possible to reduce the cost of drilling, but the designer must be careful to use drill hole dimension and depth of hole callouts that are within normal tolerance limits as functionally required.

Drill Hole Tolerances

Standard drill hole tolerances shown in *Table II-1* should be used for economical drilling operations. If functional requirements make it necessary to use hole tolerances closer than shown in *Table II-1*, additional operations such as gundrilling, reaming, boring, grinding, and/or honing are needed to reproduce these tolerances. Each of these additional operations will increase the cost of the hole or holes.

Table II-1. Drill Hole Sizes and Tolerances

Drill	Size	Tolerance	
		Plus	Minus
	in.	in.	in.
80	0.0135	0.0023	0.0005
79	0.0145	0.0024	0.0005
1/64	0.0156	0.0025	0.0005
78	0.016	0.0025	0.0005
77	0.018	0.0026	0.0005
76	0.020	0.0027	0.0005
75	0.021	0.0027	0.0005
74	0.0225	0.0028	0.0005
73	0.024	0.0028	0.0005
72	0.025	0.0029	0.0005
71	0.026	0.0029	0.0005
70	0.028	0.003	0.0005
69	0.0292	0.003	0.0005
68	0.031	0.0031	0.0005
1/32	0.0312	0.0031	0.0005
67	0.032	0.0031	0.0005
66	0.033	0.0032	0.0005
65	0.035	0.0032	0.0005
64	0.036	0.0033	0.0005
63	0.037	0.0033	0.0005
62	0.038	0.0033	0.0005
61	0.039	0.0033	0.0005
60	0.040	0.0034	0.0005
59	0.041	0.0034	0.001
58	0.042	0.0034	0.001

Table II-1. Drill Hole Sizes and Tolerances (*Continued*)

Drill	Size	Tolerance	
		Plus	Minus
	in.	in.	in.
57	0.043	0.0035	0.001
56	0.0465	0.0035	0.001
3/64	0.0469	0.0036	0.001
55	0.052	0.0037	0.001
54	0.055	0.0038	0.001
53	0.0595	0.0039	0.001
1/16	0.0625	0.0039	0.001
52	0.0635	0.0039	0.001
51	0.067	0.004	0.001
50	0.070	0.0041	0.001
49	0.073	0.0041	0.001
48	0.076	0.0042	0.001
5/64	0.0781	0.0042	0.001
47	0.0785	0.0042	0.001
46	0.081	0.0043	0.001
45	0.082	0.0043	0.001
44	0.086	0.0044	0.001
43	0.089	0.0044	0.001
42	0.0935	0.0045	0.001
3/32	0.0938	0.0045	0.001
41	0.096	0.0045	0.001
40	0.098	0.0046	0.001
39	0.0995	0.0046	0.001
38	0.1015	0.0046	0.001
37	0.104	0.0047	0.001
36	0.1065	0.0047	0.001
7/64	0.1094	0.0047	0.001
35	0.110	0.0047	0.001
34	0.111	0.0048	0.001
33	0.113	0.0048	0.001
32	0.116	0.0048	0.001
31	0.120	0.0049	0.001
1/8	0.125	0.005	0.001
30	0.1285	0.005	0.001
29	0.136	0.0051	0.001
28	0.1405	0.0052	0.001
9/64	0.1406	0.0052	0.001
27	0.144	0.0052	0.001
26	0.147	0.0052	0.001
25	0.1495	0.0053	0.001

Table II-1. Drill Hole Sizes and Tolerances (*Continued*)

Drill	Size	Tolerance	
		Plus	Minus
	in.	in.	in.
24	0.152	0.0053	0.001
23	0.154	0.0053	0.001
5/32	0.1562	0.0053	0.001
22	0.157	0.0053	0.001
21	0.159	0.0054	0.001
20	0.161	0.0054	0.001
19	0.166	0.0055	0.001
18	0.1695	0.0055	0.001
11/64	0.1719	0.0055	0.001
17	0.173	0.0055	0.001
16	0.177	0.0056	0.001
15	0.180	0.0056	0.001
14	0.182	0.0056	0.001
13	0.185	0.0057	0.001
3/16	0.1875	0.0057	0.001
12	0.189	0.0057	0.001
11	0.191	0.0057	0.001
10	0.1935	0.0057	0.001
9	0.196	0.0058	0.001
8	0.199	0.0058	0.001
7	0.201	0.0058	0.001
13/64	0.2031	0.0058	0.001
6.	0.204	0.0058	0.001
5	0.2055	0.0059	0.001
4	0.209	0.0059	0.001
3	0.213	0.0059	0.001
7/32	0.2188	0.006	0.001
2	0.221	0.006	0.001
1	0.228	0.0061	0.001
A	0.234	0.0061	0.001
15/64	0.2344	0.0061	0.001
B	0.238	0.0061	0.001
C	0.242	0.0062	0.001
D	0.246	0.0062	0.001
1/4	0.250	0.0063	0.001
F	0.257	0.0063	0.001
G	0.261	0.0063	0.001
17/64	0.2656	0.0064	0.001
H	0.266	0.0064	0.001
I	0.272	0.0064	0.001

Table II-1. Drill Hole Sizes and Tolerances (*Continued*)

Drill	Size	Tolerance	
		Plus	Minus
	in.	in.	in.
J	0.277	0.0065	0.002
K	0.281	0.0065	0.002
9/32	0.2812	0.0065	0.002
L	0.290	0.0066	0.002
M	0.295	0.0066	0.002
19/64	0.2969	0.0066	0.002
N	0.302	0.0067	0.002
5/16	0.3125	0.0067	0.002
O	0.316	0.0068	0.002
P	0.323	0.0068	0.002
21/64	0.3281	0.0068	0.002
Q	0.332	0.0069	0.002
R	0.339	0.0069	0.002
11/32	0.3438	0.007	0.002
S	0.348	0.007	0.002
T	0.358	0.0071	0.002
23/64	0.3594	0.0071	0.002
U	0.368	0.0072	0.002
3/8	0.375	0.0072	0.002
V	0.377	0.0072	0.002
W	0.386	0.0072	0.002
25/64	0.3906	0.0073	0.002
X	0.397	0.0073	0.002
Y	0.404	0.0073	0.002
13/32	0.4062	0.0074	0.002
Z	0.413	0.0074	0.002
27/64	0.4219	0.0075	0.002
7/16	0.4375	0.0075	0.002
29/64	0.4531	0.0076	0.002
15/32	0.4688	0.0077	0.002
31/64	0.4844	0.0078	0.002
1/2	0.500	0.0079	0.002
33/64	0.5156	0.008	0.002
17/32	0.5312	0.0081	0.002
35/64	0.5469	0.0081	0.002
9/16	0.5625	0.0082	0.002
37/64	0.5781	0.0083	0.002
19/32	0.59375	0.0084	0.002
39/64	0.6094	0.0084	0.002
5/8	0.625	0.0085	0.002

Table II-1. Drill Hole Sizes and Tolerances (*Continued*)

Drill	Size	Tolerance	
		Plus	Minus
	in.	in.	in.
41/64	0.6406	0.0086	0.002
21/32	0.65625	0.0086	0.002
43/64	0.6719	0.0087	0.002
11/16	0.6875	0.0088	0.002
45/64	0.7031	0.0088	0.002
23/32	0.7188	0.0089	0.002
47/64	0.7344	0.009	0.002
3/4	0.750	0.009	0.002
49/64	0.7656	0.0091	0.003
25/32	0.7812	0.0092	0.003
51/64	0.7969	0.0092	0.003
13/16	0.8125	0.0093	0.003
53/64	0.8281	0.0093	0.003
27/32	0.8438	0.0094	0.003
55/64	0.8594	0.0095	0.003
7/8	0.875	0.0095	0.003
57/64	0.8906	0.0096	0.003
29/32	0.9062	0.0096	0.003
59/64	0.9219	0.0097	0.003
15/16	0.9375	0.0097	0.003
61/64	0.9531	0.0098	0.003
31/32	0.9688	0.0098	0.003
1	1.000	0.010	0.003

Hole Depth vs. Cost

The depth of the hole is another cost factor to be taken into consideration. *Figure 2-11* shows the effect of hole depth on drilling cost. The cost curve is based on standard equipment, and shows that the cost of a drilled hole increases proportionately to its depth only where the depth becomes three times the diameter. Beyond this depth, the cost increases more rapidly than by equal increments of depth. The dotted line is shown to emphasize the accelerated cost.

True Position Hole Tolerances

Another factor of cost increase is the location tolerance of holes. If the method of true position tolerancing is used, it should be carefully analyzed. *Figure 2-12* illustrates the cost increase as true position tolerances become tighter.

True position tolerances for hole patterns that must match with mating holes for good assembly are shown in *Tables II-2* and *II-3*. These tolerances

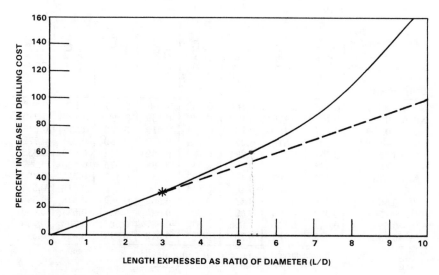

Figure 2-11. Cost comparison of drilled holes as affected by depth. (*Courtesy*, ASME)

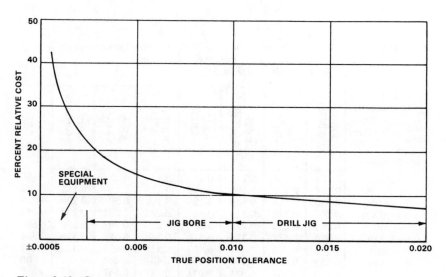

Figure 2-12. Cost vs. true position tolerance.

Table II-2. Clearance Hole Sizes for Mating Multiple Hole Patterns in a Fixed Condition Based on True Position Tolerances.
(*Formula*: Hole Size = 2 T.P. + S)*

True Position (S) (Diameter) Max. & Equiv. Screw Rect. or Bolt Tol. Body Diameter	0.005 (± 0.0018)	0.010 (± 0.0035)	0.015 (± 0.0053)	0.020 (± 0.007)	0.025 (± 0.009)	0.030 (± 0.0106)	0.035 (± 0.012)	0.040 (± 0.014)
No. 4—0.112	0.125	0.136	0.144	0.152	0.166†	0.173†	0.182†	0.193†
No. 6—0.138	0.149	0.159	0.169	0.180	0.189	0.199†	0.209†	0.219†
No. 8—0.164	0.177	0.185	0.196	0.204	0.219	0.228	0.234†	0.246†
No. 10—0.190	0.201	0.213	0.221	0.234	0.242	0.250	0.261	0.272†
1/4—0.250	0.261	0.272	0.281	0.290	0.302	0.312	0.323	0.332
5/16—0.312	0.323	0.332	0.344	0.358	0.368	0.375	0.386	0.397
3/8—0.375	0.386	0.397	0.406	0.422	0.437	0.437	0.453	0.469
7/16—0.437	0.453	0.469	0.469	0.484	0.500	0.500	0.516	0.531
1/2—0.500	0.516	0.531	0.531	0.547	0.562	0.562	0.578	0.594
9/16—0.562	0.578	0.594	0.594	0.609	0.625	0.625	0.641	0.656
5/8—0.625	0.641	0.656	0.656	0.672	0.687	0.687	0.703	0.719
3/4—0.750	0.766	0.781	0.781	0.797	0.812	0.812	0.828	0.844

* Hole size given is the next largest drill size to the required hole.
† Requires washers to assure proper seating of the screw head.

Table II-3. Clearance Hole Sizes for Mating Multiple Hole Patterns in a Floating Condition Based on True Position Tolerances.
(*Formula*: Hole Size = T.P. + S)*

True Position (S) (Diameter) Max. & Equiv. Screw Rect. or Bolt Tol. Body Diameter	0.015 (± 0.0053)	0.020 (± 0.007)	0.025 (± 0.009)	0.030 (± 0.0106)	0.035 (± 0.012)	0.040 (± 0.014)	0.045 (± 0.016)	0.050 (± 0.0176)
No. 4—0.112	0.128	0.136	0.140	0.144	0.147	0.152	0.157	0.166
No. 6—0.138	0.154	0.159	0.166	0.169	0.173	0.180	0.185	0.189
No. 8—0.164	0.180	0.185	0.189	0.196	0.199	0.204	0.209	0.219
No. 10—0.190	0.205	0.213	0.219	0.221	0.228	0.234	0.238	0.242
1/4—0.250	0.266	0.272	0.277	0.281	0.290	0.290	0.295	0.302
5/16—0.312	0.328	0.332	0.339	0.344	0.348	0.358	0.358	0.368
3/8—0.375	0.391	0.397	0.404	0.406	0.413	0.422	0.422	0.437
7/16—0.437	0.453	0.469	0.469	0.469	0.484	0.484	0.484	0.500
1/2—0.500	0.516	0.531	0.531	0.531	0.547	0.547	0.547	0.562
9/16—0.562	0.578	0.594	0.594	0.594	0.609	0.609	0.609	0.625
5/8—0.625	0.641	0.656	0.656	0.656	0.672	0.672	0.672	0.687
3/4—0.750	0.766	0.781	0.781	0.781	0.797	0.797	0.797	0.812

* Hole size given is the next largest drill size to the required hole.

are based on standard drill sizes and hole tolerances. Rectangular toleranced hole pattern calculations and charts must take into consideration the difference of a two-hole pattern versus three or more patterns for a given size fastener. By using the method of true position tolerancing, the same size hole can be used for one or any number of holes.

These tables list the clearance holes for the fixed condition and floating condition that provide a no-interference, no-clearance fit (at worst case condition) for hole patterns of mating parts which are toleranced using true position.

True position tolerancing is the preferred method of controlling the location of holes with respect to other holes. The placement of dimensions is not as difficult in this system as in the coordinate system, since there is no tolerance buildup. Therefore, datums may more readily be selected to reduce calculations. However, functional datums must be selected that are more accurate than the tolerances used for dimensions based from these datums. This will require the use of a datum hole in lieu of an untrue surface or formed sheet metal flanges.

By using this system, fewer parts are rejected when holes are out of tolerance. Parts with clearance holes may have their centers outside the specific zone and still be acceptable. This is possible because interchangeable calculations are made using the smallest hole possible. If the hole checks in excess of its minimum size, this additional factor can be added to the true position diameter for that hole.

The selections of datums (starting base for dimensions) must be located from the same matching surface or hole if perfect alignment is required. If two surfaces are to be flush after assembly, or if two holes are to be matched perfectly for insertion of a dowel, the use of matching datums is good practice for true position toleranced dimensions.

Since we are only dealing with holes for fixed and floating conditions, it is advisable that the design engineer study the method of true position tolerancing as outlined in USASI Y14.5, since this standard has become mandatory for all military drawings. A fixed condition is where one matching member has studs, pins, and countersunk holes, while the other matching member has clearance holes. (See *Figure 2-13*.) A floating condition (*Figure 3-14*) is one where both members have clearance holes, or one member could have a floating nut; the amount of float being the same as the amount of clearance in the clearance hole.

For a better understanding of the method of true position tolerancing, the book *Fundamentals of Position Tolerance* is highly recommended.

Drill Depth for Tapped Holes

There are two classifications for tapped holes: the open or through hole, and the closed or blind hole. When blind holes cannot be avoided in design, the depth of perfect thread should not exceed two times the thread diameter. The depth of the drilled hole should be the depth of the perfect thread plus the K factor. (See *Figure 2-15*.) Use a bottom tap-chamfer (1 to 1-½ threads)

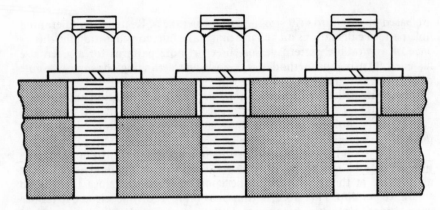

Figure 2-13. Fixed condition.

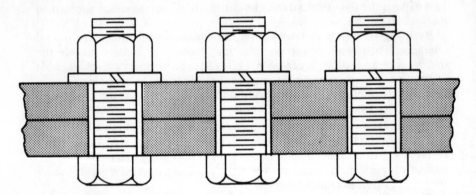

Figure 2-14. Floating condition.

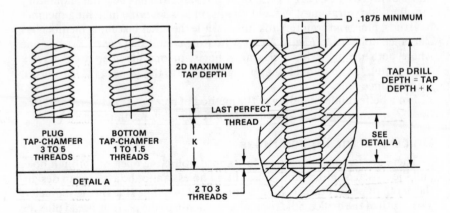

Figure 2-15. Drill depth.

28

only where the depth of the hole prohibits using a plug tap-chamfer (3 to 5 threads).

Adequate clearance, which can be determined from *Tables II-4* and *II-5*, is required between the ends of the thread and the drilled hole to produce the maximum number of perfect threads. Drill depth must be specified to permit tapping in this order of preference—first plug tapping and then bottom tapping.

In *Tables II-4* and *II-5*, drill depth equals the desired tap depth plus K. Factor K is a minimum dimension and should be exceeded wherever possible.

Example. To determine the drill depth (not diameter) for a ¼-28-UNF tapped hole, using a plug tap for 0.31 tap depth, the K dimension will be 0.28. (See *Table II-4*.) The drill depth will be 0.31 + 0.28 = 0.59 for a ¼-28-UNF tapped hole with 0.31 perfect threads. Therefore, a plug tap can be used to complete the tapping operation.

Example. To determine the drill depth (not diameter) for a 10-24 UNC-2B tapped hole, using a plug tap for 0.25 tap depth, the K dimension will be 0.33. (See *Table II-4*.) The drill depth will be 0.25 + 0.33 = 0.58 for a 10-24 UNC-2B tapped hole with 0.25 perfect threads. Therefore, a plug tap can be used to complete the tapping operation.

Table II-4. Drill Depth For Blind Tapped Holes—Fine Thread

UNF Thread Designation	K Dimension	
	Plug Tap 1st Choice	Bottom Tap 2nd Choice
0—80 UNF	0.10	0.06
1—72 UNF	0.11	0.06
2—64 UNF	0.12	0.07
3—56 UNF	0.14	0.08
4—48 UNF	0.17	0.09
5—44 UNF	0.18	0.10
6—40 UNF	0.20	0.11
8—36 UNF	0.22	0.13
10—32 UNF	0.25	0.14
12—28 UNF	0.28	0.16
1/4—28 UNF	0.28	0.16
5/16—24 UNF	0.33	0.19
3/8—24 UNF	0.33	0.19
7/16—20 UNF	0.40	0.23
1/2—20 UNF	0.40	0.23
9/16—18 UNF	0.44	0.25
5/8—18 UNF	0.44	0.25
3/4—16 UNF	0.50	0.28
7/8—14 UNF	0.57	0.32
1—12 UNF	0.67	0.37
1-1/8—12 UNF	0.67	0.37
1-1/4—12 UNF	0.67	0.37
1-3/8—12 UNF	0.67	0.37
1-1/2—12 UNF	0.67	0.37

Table II-5. Drill Depth For Blind Tapped Holes—Coarse Thread

UNC Thread Designation	K Dimension	
	Plug Tap 1st Choice	Bottom Tap 2nd Choice
1—64 UNC	0.12	0.07
2—56 UNC	0.14	0.08
3—48 UNC	0.17	0.09
4—40 UNC	0.20	0.11
5—40 UNC	0.20	0.11
6—32 UNC	0.25	0.14
8—32 UNC	0.25	0.14
→10—24 UNC	0.33	0.19
12—24 UNC	0.33	0.19
1/4—20 UNC	0.40	0.23
5/16—18 UNC	0.44	0.25
3/8—16 UNC	0.50	0.28
7/16—4 UNC	0.57	0.32
1/2—13 UNC	0.62	0.35
9/16—12 UNC	0.67	0.37
5/8—11 UNC	0.73	0.41
3/4—10 UNC	0.80	0.45
7/8—9 UNC	0.89	0.50
1—8 UNC	1.00	0.56

Gundrilling, Reaming, and Boring

Economical tolerances for holes produced by gundrilling, reaming, or boring, are as follows:

Gundrilling	±0.0005 in. (±0.013 mm)
Reaming (under 0.5-inch diameter) (12.7 mm)	±0.0003 in. (±0.007 mm)
Reaming (over 0.5- to 1-inch diameter) (12.7 to 25.4 mm)	±0.0005 in. (±0.013 mm)
Reaming (over 1-inch diameter) (25.4 mm)	±0.001 in. (±0.025 mm)
Boring Machines (up to 12-inch diameter) (30.5 mm)	±0.001 in. (±0.025 mm)
Boring Machines (up to 12-inch diameter) (30.5 mm) spacing	±0.001 in. (±0.025 mm)
Boring Machines (up to 12-inch diameter) (30.5 mm) alignment	±0.001 in. (±0.025 mm)
Boring Machines (production), small holes diameter	±0.0002 in. (±0.005 mm)
alignment	±0.0001 in. (±0.002 mm)
spacing	±0.0005 in. (±0.013 mm)
depth of blind holes	±0.003 in. (±0.076 mm)

TURNING

Plain turning operations constitute one of the primary machining operations employed in the manufacturing of parts.

The engine lathe, one of the oldest metal removal machines, has a number of useful and highly desirable attributes. Today, these lathes are used primarily in small shops where smaller quantities rather than large production runs are encountered.

The engine lathe has been replaced in today's production shops by modern NC slant bed lathes for precision turning. The tolerances of a part machined on an engine lathe in the past depended primarily on the skill of the operator. With today's modern NC lathes, tolerances of ±0.001 (±0.02) on the diameter can be held. Length tolerances of steps, shoulder-to-shoulder, can be held to ±0.002 (±0.05), but wherever possible, these tolerances should be held to ±0.002 (±0.05) on diameter and to ±0.005 (±0.127) on length and shoulder for greater economy.

In today's modern production shop, the design engineer must work with the manufacturing engineer in order to design the product and related parts to tolerances and finishes that can be achieved with the production equipment available for economical production.

Machine controls play a vital part in improving manufacturing productivity and enhancing workpiece quality. While the basic configurations of many machine tools such as lathes, turret lathes, automatic screw machines, tracer lathes, and swiss automatic lathes have not changed in recent years, the advent of numerical control, computer numerical control, direct numerical control, and adaptive control have spurred significant changes in methods and costs. Technological developments within the electronics industry have stimulated evolutionary changes in machine controls.

New generations of machine controls come into existence, but the fundamental goals remain constant: the elimination of errors normally associated with manual control, high repeatability and increased quality-assurance measures, faster workpiece processing, greater control flexibility, less waste and paperwork, and improved management of the production process. In short, improved productivity remains the justification for machine controls.

Turret Lathes

Production machining equipment must be evaluated now, more than ever before, in terms of ability to repeat accurately and rapidly. Applying this criterion for establishing the production qualification of a specific method, the turret lathe merits a high rating.

A natural outgrowth of the well-known engine lathe, the turret lathe can handle either bar or chucking work. Although adapted to produce parts in quantities too limited to be economically produced on an automatic screw machine, the turret lathe is primarily suited for parts not within screw machine capacity.

In designing for low quantities such as 100 or 200 parts, it is most economical to use the standard turret lathe. However, when a modern NC or CNC

31

turret lathe is used, production quantities such as 500 or 1000 parts become economical quantities. In achieving the optimum tolerances possible on the turret lathe, the designer should strive for a minimum of operations.

Tolerances. A minimum tolerance of ±0.002 in. (±0.05 mm) on diameters can be held, but this requires a rough cut and a finish cut. On parts suitable for the use of a single-cutter roller turner piloted on a cut being made on a previously turned surface, tolerances of ±0.001 in. (±0.02 mm) can be held in normal setups.

In normal setups, concentricity can be held within 0.002 in. (0.05 mm) TIR if diameters are formed from the cross slide; and can be held within 0.004 in. (0.10 mm) TIR between hole and outside diameter.

Length and Depth. Standard stop equipment can be expected to hold ±0.002 in. (±0.05 mm) on length; but wherever possible, depth and length should be specified as ±0.005 in. (±0.13 mm) or greater for economy.

Hole Tolerances. Drilled hole tolerances should be those indicated in *Table II-1*. A tolerance of ±0.001 (±0.02) can be held in ordinary reaming operations. For hole tolerances closer than those shown in *Table II-1*, a reaming or boring operation must be added. Each of these additional operations will increase the cost of the part.

The following are the economical tolerances for these operations:

Reaming:	Up to 0.5-inch (12.7 mm) diameter	±0.0005 in. (±0.013 mm)
	Over 0.5-inch to 1-inch (12.7 to 25.4 mm) diameter	±0.001 in. (±0.25 mm)
	Over 1-inch (25.4 mm) diameter	±0.0015 in. (±0.04 mm)
Boring:	For boring up to 1-inch (25.4 mm) diameter	±0.0003 in. (±0.076 mm)
	Over 1-inch to 1.5-inch (25.4 to 38.1 mm) diameter	±0.0005 in. (±0.013 mm)

Depending upon the type of material being cut, surface roughness on turret lathes will be about 60 μin. rms (1.5 μm rms) or less. Surface patterns depend upon type of tooling and cuts employed.

Pitch and lead accuracy of threads can usually be held to that required by a Class 3 fit, as set up by the National Screw Thread Commission.

For quantities too small for economical machining on the automatic screw machine, the turret lathe becomes one of the most universal machines in today's machine shop.

Automatic Screw Machines

Generally, automatic screw machines fall into several categories: single-spindle automatics, multiple-spindle automatics, and automatic chucking machines. Originally designed for rapid, automatic production of screws and similar threaded parts, the automatic screw machine has long since exceeded the confines of this narrow field, and today plays a vital role in the mass production of a variety of precision parts.

Quantities play an important part in the economy of the parts machined on the automatic screw machine. Quantities less than 1000 parts may be more economical to set up on the turret lathe than on the automatic screw machine. The cost of the parts machined can be reduced if the minimum economical lot size is calculated and the proper machine is selected for these quantities.

Tolerances. The following are the economical tolerances that can be held on automatic screw machines—and the designer should design parts with these tolerances in mind. Closer tolerances can be held with special tooling, but at higher cost, and should be avoided wherever possible.

Diameters and length of steps formed from the cross slide are: up to 1 in. (25.4 mm), ±0.002 (±0.05 mm); over 1 in. to 2 in. (25.4 to 50.8 mm), ±0.003 (±0.08 mm); and over 2 in. (50.8 mm), ± 0.005 in. (±0.13 mm).

Concentricity. 0.002-in. (0.05-mm) TIR on diameters; and 0.004-in. (0.10-mm) TIR between hole and diameter.

Hole Tolerances. Drilled hole tolerances are indicated in *Table II-1*. For hole tolerances closer than shown in this table, additional operations must be added, and this will increase the cost of the part.

Automatic Tracer Lathes

Since surface roughness depends greatly upon material turned, tooling, and feeds and speeds employed, minimum tolerances that can be held on automatic tracer lathes are not necessarily the most economical tolerances.

In some cases, tolerances of ±0.002 in. (±0.05 mm) are held in continuous production using but one cut. Groove width can be held to ±0.005 in. (±0.13 mm) on some parts. Bores and single-point finishes can be held to ±0.0005 (±0.013 mm). On high-production runs where maximum output is desirable, a minimum tolerance of ±0.005 (±0.13 mm) is economical on both diameter and length of turn. Concentricities can be held to as close as 0.002 (0.05 mm) TIR.

Swiss Automatic Lathes

Swiss automatics are designed primarily for the machining of small, slender parts requiring extreme accuracy and fine finishes.

In designing these parts for electronic equipment and instruments to be run on a Swiss automatic, it is important that the proper stock size be used. Centerless ground or polished stock held to ±0.0003 (±0.007 mm) is costly, but obtaining accuracy without additional operation usually warrants such a cost increase. Size, accuracy, and fine finish are dependent to a large extent upon the accuracy of the stock.

Tolerances on diameters can be held to ±0.0003 in. (±0.007 mm). Turned length of shoulder locations can be held to ±0.0005 (±0.013 mm). For maximum economy, a tolerance of ±0.005 (±0.13 mm) should be specified on shoulder length or steps.

Surface finish can be held as fine as 10-μin. (.254 μm) rms, but 32-μin. (0.82 μm) rms is a more economical range.

Concentricity of 0.0005 in. (0.013 mm) TIR is not uncommon, but 0.001 in. (0.025 mm) TIR is more economical. If concentricity and diameter tolerances can be used in the economical range, cost can be reduced considerably by the use of cold drawn material.

PRODUCTION MILLING

With the exceptions of turning and drilling, milling is undoubtedly the most widely used method of removing metal. Well suited and readily adapted to the economical production of any quantity of parts, the almost unlimited versatility of the milling process merits the attention and consideration of designers seriously concerned with the manufacture of their product.

Tolerances. As in any other process, parts that have to be milled should be designed with economical tolerances that can be achieved in production milling. If the part is designed with tolerances finer than necessary, additional operations will have to be added to achieve these tolerances—and this will increase the cost of the part.

Tolerances for shell milling are ±0.001 in. (0.025 mm); step milling ±.002 in. (0.05 mm); keyway cutting ±0.002 in. (0.05 mm); and end milling ±0.003 in. (0.08 mm).

Figure 2-16 illustrates the effect of surface finish and dimensional tolerances on face milling costs. With a tolerance under ±0.002 in. (±0.05 mm), there is a 40% difference in cost between machining to 63 μ in. (1.6 μm) and 125 μ in. (3.2 μm). At 125 μ in. (3.2 μm), the cost of ±0.002-in. (±0.05 mm) tolerance and under is 110 more than at ±0.002 in. (±0.05 mm) and over. At 63 μin. (1.6 μm) there is a 110% difference, and at 45 μin. (1.2 μm) there is a 100% difference.

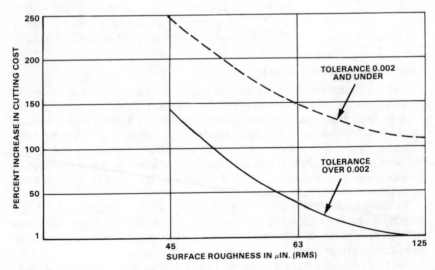

Figure 2-16. Cost comparison of milled surfaces. (*Courtesy*, ASME)

PRODUCTION GRINDING

Production grinding is one of the most widely used methods of finishing parts to extremely close tolerances and fine surface finishes. Currently, there are grinders for almost every type of grinding operation. Particular design features of a part dictate to a large degree the type of grinding machine required. Where processing costs are excessive, parts redesigned to utilize a less expensive, higher output grinding method may be well worthwhile. For example, wherever possible, the production economy of rotary surface and centerless grinding should be taken advantage of by proper design consideration.

Although grinding is usually considered a finishing operation, it is often employed as a complete machining process on work which can be ground down from rough condition without being turned or otherwise machined. Thus, many types of forgings and other parts are finished completely with the grinding wheel at appreciable savings of time and expense. Conditions that would control this practice would be the total amount of stock to be removed, the general shape of the piece, and the type of machines available.

Classes of grinding machines include the following: cylindrical grinders, centerless grinders, internal grinders, surface grinders, rotary surface grinders, and tool and cutter grinders.

The cylindrical and centerless grinders are for straight cylindrical or taper work; thus splines, shafts, and similar parts are ground on cylindrical machines, either of the common-center type or the centerless machine.

Thread grinders are used for grinding precision threads for thread gages, and threads on precision parts where the concentricity between the diameter of the shaft and the pitch diameter of the thread must be held to close tolerances.

The internal grinders are used for grinding of precision holes, cylinder bores, and similar operations where bores of all kinds are to be finished.

The surface grinders are for finishing all kinds of flat work, or work with plain surfaces which may be operated upon either by the edge of a wheel or by the face of a grinding wheel. These machines may have reciprocating or rotating tables.

Various specialized types of grinding machines are built for different classes of work, such as crankshaft grinders (for cylindrical surfaces); precision bench grinders for tool work; chucking and hole grinders for finishing flat faces and the bore of a piece held in a chuck; belt grinders with flat abrasive belts for flat work of suitable form and dimensions; and special cylindrical grinders that are capable of holding tolerances of ±0.000050 in. (±0.00127 mm).

Production Grinding Tolerances

Today's modern grinding equipment can grind parts for various operations to the following tolerances:

Diameters	±0.00025 in.
	(±0.0064 mm)

35

Holes (using automatic sizing devices)	±0.00025 in.
	(±0.0064 mm)
Squareness to shoulders and runout	±0.00025 in.
	(±0.0064 mm)

For Centerless Grinding:

Diameters and parallelism	±0.0001 in.
	(±0.0025 mm)
Concentricity of stepped diameters	±0.00025 in.
	(±0.0064 mm)

For Surface Grinding (Reciprocating Table):

Flatness	±0.0002 in.
	(±0.005 mm)
Size	±0.0003 in.
	(±0.008 mm)

For Surface Grinding (Rotary Table):

Flatness	±0.0002 in.
	(±0.005 mm)
Thickness	±0.001 in.
	(±0.025 mm)

EFFECTS OF TOLERANCES AND SURFACE ROUGHNESS ON CYLINDRICAL GRINDING COST

Figure 2-17 shows cylindrical grinding costs, exposing a nonuniform cost behavior pattern. The 40-μin. (1.02 μm) quality line shows definite breaking points at 0.0005 in. (0.013 mm) and at 0.00025 in. (0.006 mm) tolerance. The line shows a minor cost rise between 0.001 in. and 0.0005 in. (0.025 and

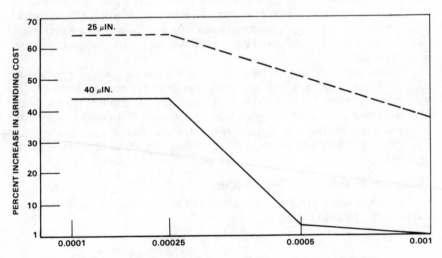

Figure 2-17. Cost comparison of cylindrical grinding. (*Courtesy*, ASME)

0.013 mm) tolerances, followed by an abrupt rise between the 0.0005 in. and 0.00025 in. (0.013 and 0.0064 mm) tolerances, and then leveling off at 0.00025 in. (0.064 mm). The cost at 0.0001 and 0.00025 in. (0.0025 and 0.0064 mm) tolerances is apparently the same.

The 25-μin. (0.64-μm) surface rises from 37% at 0.001 in. (0.025 mm) to 65% at 0.00025 in. (0.0064 mm), and then levels off. The break may be explained by the peculiarities of the machine and the skill level of the grinding operator.

Cost will vary according to the type of machine used, its condition, how it is mounted, the abrasive wheel, the speeds, the coolant, the material, and the coolant filter, as well as the skill of the operator.

Centerless Grinding Costs

The chart shown in *Figure 2-18* demonstrates the possibility of incorporating quality features other than surface roughness or tolerance. The difference between the two curves is governed by the design of the part.

To gain the benefit of the high-production, low-cost "through-feed" method on the centerless grinder, the ground diameter must be the largest dimension on the part. Should such a design be impractical, the design engineer should select a tolerance for the resulting "in-feed" method to minimize cost.

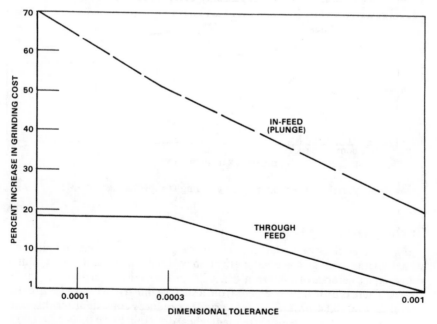

Figure 2-18. Centerless grinding cost. (*Courtesy*, ASME)

37

In plunge grinding, the use of duplex wheels for grinding two diameters simultaneously increases the rate of output.

Hydraulic operation and automatic size control are among the newer features of many grinders today.

Internal Grinding Costs

There are many factors that govern the cost of internal grinding such as stock left in the hole for grinding, tolerances, finishes, gaging cost, and dial adjusting cost—all of which make up the total grinding cost.

Where pieces are ground in large quantities, and stock and heat-treating conditions are carefully controlled, less stock may be left in order to reduce the cost of grinding.

Figure 2-19 illustrates how certain elements influence cost behavior in internal grinding. It shows that, although cost is increased by tighter tolerances, even greater cost increases result from increased gaging and dial-readjusting time due to tighter tolerances.

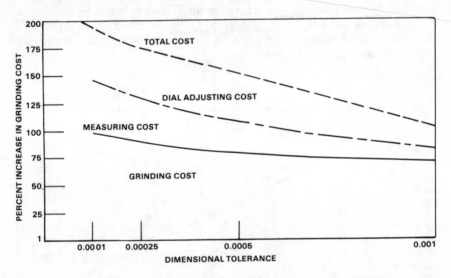

Figure 2-19. Variables affecting internal grinding cost. (*Courtesy*, ASME)

Surface Grinding Costs

Figure 2-20 illustrates that in reciprocating surface grinding, the dimensional tolerance range has greater effect on cost than does the surface quality range. At a tolerance of ±0.001 in. (±0.025 mm), cost rises sharply on all three curves. There is little improvement from a surface finish of 63 μin. (1.6 μm) to one of 25 μin. (0.64 μm). A surface grinder produces consistent results, but closer tolerances require more frequent wheel dressing. For ±0.0002 (±0.005 mm) tolerances, very light passes of the wheel must be made.

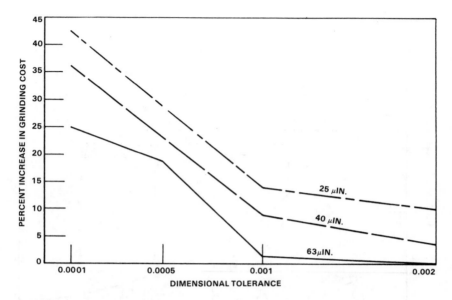

Figure 2-20. Effects of tolerances and surface grinding cost. (*Courtesy*, ASME)

Rotary Surface Grinding Costs

Figure 2-21 shows a cost comparison on rotary surface grinding, and demonstrates that cost is not always severely affected by quality variations. The cost increase over the whole tolerance range is 15%—by far the smallest of all illustrations. Yet, even here, more than half the cost increase occurs between tolerances of ±0.001 in. and 0.0005 in. (0.025 and 0.013 mm).

The cost curves on the various grinding operations show the importance of keeping tolerances in the economical range.

Table II-6 shows the production and precision tolerances for various grinding operations. The production tolerances can be held without difficulty—but are not always the most economical. Precision tolerances can also be held, but they too are costly.

DETERMINING ECONOMICAL PRODUCTION LOT SIZE DEFINITION

An economical lot size is the quantity of an item released for production at a given time, based upon the practical consideration of the effect of quantity on both tangible and intangible cost.

No matter how well designed a product is, its manufacture can be costly if it is not produced in economical quantities. That this is axiomatic is well documented by the experience of many companies working on government contracts calling for relatively small production quantities. The economical lot size is determined by such factors as yearly requirement, setup and tooling

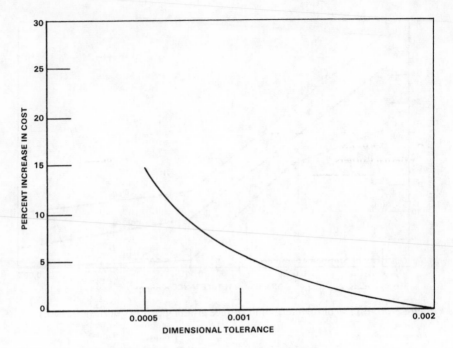

Figure 2-21. Effects of tolerances on rotary surface grinding cost.
(*Courtesy, ASME*)

cost, average inventory per year, cost of carrying inventory, selection and availability of equipment, material cost, and an allowance for contingencies, such as design changes, after a certain quantity has been produced. These quantities must be determined prior to production release because they are critical to determining the type of machine to be used.

The Standard Approach. The production quantities, as opposed to economic production quantities, may be determined in a number of ways. Standard practice on the part of some manufacturing engineers is to base their production quantity determination on three known factors: setup time in minutes, standard machining time in minutes, and an efficiency factor—usually 10% of the machining time. The formula for determining the production quantity based upon the setup and the unit standard is:

$$Q = \frac{S}{(T)+(K)} \tag{1}$$

where:

Q = Production quantity
S = Setup time in minutes
T = Standard machining time in minutes
K = Efficiency factor (usually 10% of machining time)

40

Table II-6. Production Grinding Tolerances

Grinding Operation	Tolerances Plus or Minus	
	Production	Precision
Cylindrical Grinding		
Diameters	0.00025	0.00001
Shoulders:		
Shoulder to Shoulder	0.00025	0.0005
Traverse Grinding to a Shoulder	0.002	0.001
Corners and Radii:		
External Corners	Sharp	
Internal Corner Radii	0.005	0.0025
Spherical Sections (Oscillating Grinders)		
Diameters	0.00015	
Location of Centers	0.001	
Centerless Grinding		
Diameters and Parallelism	0.0001	0.000025
Roundness	0.000012	
Concentricity of Stepped Diameters	0.00025	0.0001
Thread Grinding		
Lead Error (inch per inch)	0.00025	0.00001
Pitch Diameter	0.0005	0.0002
Roundness	0.00025	
Concentricity (Thread Form with OD)	0.0005	
Grooves (width)	0.001	
Surface Grinding		
Reciprocating Table Grinder:		
Flatness	0.0002	0.00015
Thickness	0.0003	0.00015
Rotary Table Grinder:		
Flatness	0.0002	0.0001
Parallelism	0.0002	0.00005
Thickness	0.001	0.0002
Internal Grinding		
Holes (Using Automatic Sizing Devices)	0.00025	0.00005
Face Runout (Squareness of Shoulder to Bore)	0.00025	0.00005

For example:

$$S = 60 \text{ minutes}$$
$$T = 2.5 \text{ minutes}$$
$$K = 10\%$$
$$Q = \frac{60}{2.5 + .25} = \frac{60}{2.75} = 22$$

The setup quantity in this case is 22 parts. While this formula can be, and is used by many manufacturing engineers, it does not take into consideration all factors needed to make an accurate determination of economical production quantities.

Truth in Manufacturing. Basic formulas for determining economical production quantities are derived by first establishing total cost per production quantity for the major factors which affect cost. The point of minimum cost can then be determined by setting to zero the first derivative with respect to the economical production quantity.

For items that are machined and processed in a relatively short period of time, moved into storage or inventory for a short time, and then consumed at a constant rate, the longest setup time and only an inventory should be used for setting the economical production quantity.

For items that are machined or assembled and then moved into inventory until used, the setup cost per assembly, the inventory cost per dollar per year, and the total cost per item or assembly must be used to determine the economical production quantities. Thus two formulas are required. The basic Formula (2) is expressed as:

$$Q = \sqrt{\frac{2RS}{C}} \tag{2}$$

It is derived from the quantity formula:

$$E = \frac{Q}{2} C + \frac{R}{Q} S$$

Where:

E = Measure of effectiveness in dollars (total incremental cost)

$(R/2)C$ = Inventory cost

S_t = $(R/Q)S$ = Total setup cost

S = Setup cost in dollars

I = Cost of carrying inventory

For $(Q/2C)$,

C = Annual incremental cost in dollars associated with inventory (based on dollars per year per unit of inventory)

R = Yearly requirements

Q = Minimum economical production quantity

Since the average inventory level is $Q/2$, and the inventory cost per unit is C, the annual incremental cost associated with inventory is $(Q/2)C$. The total annual incremental cost due to setups is $(R/Q)S$. Equation (2) is minimized by taking the first derivative of E, with respect to economical production quantity (Q), and equating it to zero.

Solving for Q:

$$\frac{dE}{dQ} = -\frac{RS}{Q^2} + \frac{C}{2} = 0 \tag{3}$$

$$Q^2 = \frac{2RS}{C}$$

$$Q = \sqrt{\frac{2RS}{C}}$$

This formula gives the value Q that yields the minimum incremental cost. Using this formula, Q can be calculated for any value of I, R, or S. Once the minimum economical quantity has been established, the setup cost and the inventory cost are equal, as seen in *Figure 2-22*. For any quantity less than the minimum, the cost curve climbs quickly. For any quantity greater than the minimum, the cost increase is not as rapid. From an economy standpoint, then, the production quantity should never be less than the minimum quantity Q.

The curve plotted in *Figure 2-22* is obtained from the basic formula Equation (2) with the following numerical substitutions. The inventory cost and hourly rate for setup cost will change with the economy and location of the producer.

Yearly requirement R = 1000
Setup time S = 3 hours
Inventory cost C = \$0.17

Setup cost, based on an \$8.50 hourly rate, thus equals 3 x \$8.50 or \$25.50. If each setup cost is \$25.50, the total annual incremental cost due to setup is:

$$\frac{R}{Q} S = \frac{1000 \times 25.50}{Q} = \frac{25,500}{Q}$$

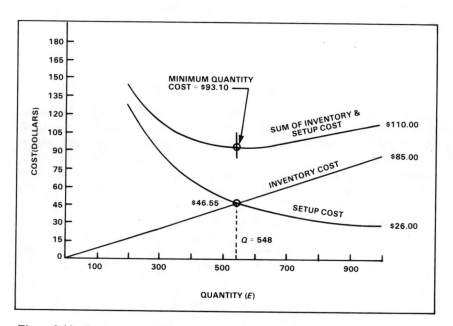

Figure 2-22. Determination of minimum economical quantity using Formula (2).

43

The annual incremental cost associated with inventory cost is:

$$\frac{Q}{2} C = \frac{Q}{2} (0.17) = \$0.085Q \tag{4}$$

$$Q = \sqrt{\frac{2 \times 1000 \times 25.50}{0.17}} = 548$$

The minimum economical production quantity is $Q = 548$, and:

$$I = \frac{Q}{2} C = 0.085Q = 0.085 \times 548$$

$$= \$46.57$$

$$S_t = \frac{R}{2} S$$

$$= \frac{25,500}{Q} = \frac{25,500}{548}$$

$$= \$46.53$$

E = Measure of effectiveness
I = Cost of carrying inventory
S_t = Total setup cost

$$E = I + S_t$$

$$= \$93.10$$

$$E = \$46.57 + \$46.53 = \$93.10$$

The difference in the inventory and setup costs (\$46.57 and \$46.53) results from rounding off the economic quantity to 548. In Formula (5) the total cost of the part is added in order to arrive at the total inventory cost, and is expressed:

$$Q = \sqrt{\frac{2RS}{CpI}} \tag{5}$$

This is derived from the quantity cost formula:

$$Y = \frac{RS}{Q} + \frac{QCpI}{2} + CpR \tag{6}$$

where:

Y = Yearly cost of making the part
RS/Q = Setup cost
$QCpI/2$ = Total inventory cost

S = Setup cost in dollars
I = Cost of carrying inventory
R = Yearly requirement
Q = Minimum economical production quantity
Cp = Cost of making part (exclusive of setup) and 2 is the conversion factor for average inventory.

In this instance, the equation is minimized by taking the first derivative of Y, with respect to economical production quantity (Q), and equating it to zero. Then solving for Q:

$$\frac{dy}{dQ} = -\frac{RS}{Q^2} + \frac{CpI}{2} + 0 = 0 \tag{7}$$

$$Q^2 = \frac{2RS}{CpI}$$

$$Q = \sqrt{\frac{2RS}{CpI}}$$

Since these parts are in storage for a given length of time before being used, the cost of the parts is increased because of the money invested in parts and the cost of storage space. In this case, Formula (5) should be used to determine the minimum economical production quantity (Q). From the break-even curves plotted in *Figure 2-23*, the minimum economical quantity is determined to be 2450 parts. In this example, the yearly requirement is 10,000 and the inventory level is $Q/2$. Thus:

$$Q = \sqrt{\frac{2RS}{CpI}} \tag{8}$$

where:

R = 10,000
S = \$25.50
Cp = \$0.50
I = \$0.17

then,

$$Q = \sqrt{\frac{2 \times 10,000 \times 25.50}{0.50 \times 0.17}} = 2450$$

Y = Total yearly cost

$$= \frac{RS}{Q} + \frac{QCpI}{2} + CpR = \frac{10,000 \times 25.50}{2450}$$

$$= \$104.08 + \frac{2450}{2} \times 0.085 + \$5000.00$$

$$= \$5208.00 \text{ (rounded off).}$$

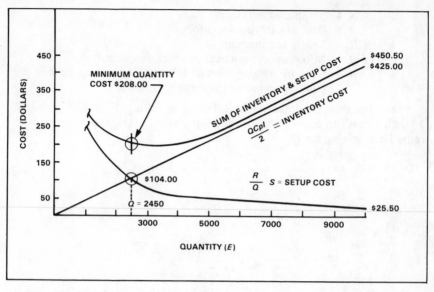

Figure 2-23. Curves plotted using sample data substituted into Formula (5). Note that in both *Figures 2-23* and *2-24*, setup cost and inventory cost are equal when the most economical number of parts is made.

If the total amount of 10,000 parts is run in one setup, and put into inventory, the cost increase due to inventory cost would be $242.50. Since Y = $25.50 + 425.00 + 5000 = $5,450.50, the cost reduction by using the minimum economical quantity is: $5450.50 - $5208 = $242.50. On the other hand, if less than the minimum economical quantity is run, then the cost would increase due to the added setup cost.

The setup cost and the inventory cost are equal when the most economical number of parts is made. Generally this is called the *minimum economical production quantity*.

If production is such that the parts are consumed at a steady rate, a chart can be made to show the minimum economical quantity, based on Formula (2). This eliminates the calculations needed to determine the quantities to be released. However, if the manufacturing engineer uses Formula (5) with the use of a computer, the minimum production quantities can be calculated with ease.

3

Castings

This chapter presents the design aspects of sand, permanent mold castings, diecastings, and investment castings.

DEFINITIONS

Sand castings are created by pouring molten metal into a cavity of desired shape made from sand.

Permanent mold castings are made by pouring (without pressure) molten metal into a permanent mold (die) made of metal (iron, steel, or bronze).

Diecasting is the forcing of metal, in a highly viscous state, under air or hydraulic pressure, into a closed metal die.

Investment casting is making a wax, plastic, or even a frozen mercury pattern from a die, surrounding (investing) it with a wet refractory material, melting or burning out the pattern after the investment material has dried and set, and finally pouring molten metal into the cavity.

Chill marks are surface marks left by special mold material which aid in cooling the casting surface it contacts.

A *gate* is the end of the runner in a mold where molten metal enters the casting or mold cavity.

A *riser* is a reservoir of molten metal which is used to compensate for internal contraction of the casting as it solidifies. Also called *feeder* or *feeder head*, depending upon its usage.

A *vent* is a small opening in a mold or core to facilitate escape of gases.

Projected area is the area projected, in square inches, by viewing the casting normal to the parting line at the parting line.

PRACTICES

Castings play an important part in the economics of missile, aircraft, automotive, and other product designs. In order to obtain economical and functional castings for the fewest dollars, designers should have a knowledge of sound casting practices that will enable them to design castings which are practical from the foundry and manufacturing standpoints. Good casting design requires special attention to the following fundamental rules:

47

- Determine the best casting method suited for the design of the product.
- Determine the mechanical and physical requirements of the part.
- Determine the best alloys for these requirements.
- Keep tolerances and finishes within the range of the selected casting method.
- Determine if it is more economical to drill certain holes and machine surfaces that would require a high cost of molding or die tooling.
- Locate tooling points in such a manner that they will not fall on the parting line of the casting, since the mismatch on the parting line will not be a good locating point for machining.

A wide latitude of design is offered by the use of an approved casting method. The following factors, which are common to all casting processes, should also be considered.

- Both simple and complex shapes may be cast.
- Machining, forming, and joining requirements may be reduced.
- Parts can be produced on a volume basis.
- A wide choice of alloys are available.
- A reduction of generated scrap can be realized.
- Cost of inspection and quality control may be reduced.

Certain design limitations that should be observed are when certain structural limitations are characteristic of casting processes; and the cost of pattern or die, rough castings, and subsequent machining operations must be considered when selecting the casting process.

The selection of the proper casting process is mainly dependent upon consideration of the following variables: complexity of the shape, cost of pattern or die, quantity of parts required, surface finish required, tolerances required, cost of machining, strength, weight, and choice of material.

Since the choice of casting process, tolerances, surface finishes, and complexity play an important role in obtaining economical castings, *Table III-1* will assist designers in selecting the most economical casting design for their products.

Break-even Formula

If a casting can be produced by more than one process, it is often advisable to calculate the break-even point. In other words, the designer should determine the quantity at which it is more economical to change from one process to another—or if one method should be used throughout the entire production run.

The simple formula for these calculations can be used to compare any casting or other production process.

$$X = \frac{T - t}{P - p} \quad \text{where } X = \text{Break-even point}$$

T = Tooling cost of method number 1
t = Tooling cost of method number 2
P = Per piece cost of method number 1
p = Per piece cost of method number 2.

48

Table III-1. General Comparison of Alloy Castings*

Property or Characteristic	Sand	Permanent Mold	Die	Plaster or Investment
Strength	A	A	B	A
Structural density	B	A	C	A
Reproducibility	C	B	A	B
Pressure tightness	B	A	C	A
Cost per piece*	C	B	A	D
Production rate*	C	B	A	D
Flexibility as to alloys	A	B	C	A
Tolerances	D	C	A	B
Design flexibility	A	B	C	A
Size limitation	A	B	B	C
Surface finish	C	B	A	A
Time to obtain tooling	A	B	B	B
Pattern or mold cost	A	B	C	B
Thin sections	C	B	A	A
Freedom from porosity	B	B	D	A
Structural uniformity between pieces	B	B	D	A

(Ratings A, B, C, and D indicate relative advantages; A is best.)
* Although this rating covers the majority of castings in the case of multiple patterns or mold cavities, sand, or permanent mold may take preeminence.

Figure 3-1. Circuit board holder casting.
(*Courtesy*, General Dynamics, Pomona Division)

49

Example. A circuit board holder casting (*Figure 3-1*), could only be produced by the diecasting or investment casting method, due to tolerances and the complexity of the casting. To determine the method that should be used for an economical casting, the preceding break-even formula was applied. It proved that for the production quantity required (1000 parts), the diecasting becomes more economical over 115 parts. The double check chart and the graph in *Figure 3-2* prove the break-even quantity to be correct.

Break-even Computation

Die Casting: *Investment Casting:*

Tooling cost	=	$13,000.00	$7000.00
Casting cost	=	+ $18.00	+ $70.00
Total	=	$13,018.00	$7070.00

$$X = \frac{13,000.00 - 7000.00}{70.00 - 18.00} = \frac{6000.00}{52.00} = 115 \text{ parts}$$

Die Casting:

$$\text{Total piece cost} = \frac{\text{Tooling cost}}{\text{Total run}} + \text{piece cost}$$

$$= \frac{\$13,000.00}{115} + \$18.00 = \$131.00$$

Investment Casting:

$$\text{Total piece cost} = \frac{\text{Tooling cost}}{\text{Total run}} + \text{piece cost}$$

$$= \frac{\$7000.00}{115} + \$70.00 = \$131.00$$

SAND CASTINGS

Sand castings are considered the most flexible of the casting methods. A major advantage is their availability in almost limitless shapes and in extreme complexities. They can be both large or small—although there is a practical limit as to just how small. The casting process itself is not recommended for thin sections. However, when moderate quantities of a part are required, sand castings can be relatively inexpensive, despite the additional labor required.

Sand Processes

Sand casting is any of the molding processes where a sand aggregate is used to make the mold. Whatever metal is poured into sand molds, the product may be called a sand casting. However, there are several major variations of the sand molding process and these should be considered.

Green sand casting derives its name from the fact that the mold formed from sand is not treated after forming, i.e., it is used "green". A plastic

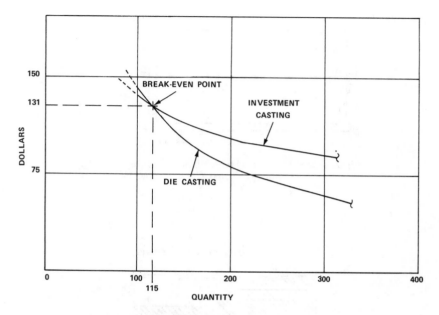

Figure 3-2. Break-even curve.

mixture of selected sand, clay, and water is compacted around a reusable pattern of wood, plaster, or metal. Sufficient strength is developed in the compacted mold to retain the desired shape of the part during pattern removal and pouring of the molten metal. The strength of the mold is obtained primarily by the presence of water and clay.

Dry sand casting is basically the same as green sand molding except that sufficient strength is developed in the mold by altering the molding mixture and baking to remove the present liquid. The advantages of dry sand molding are greater strength in the mold and the elimination of casting difficulties inherent when moisture is present during the pouring of molten metal.

The sequence in *Figure 3-3* illustrates the sand casting process. The mold is formed in an open box called a *flask* (*Figure 3-3a*). This box is divided into two halves so that the mold can be parted to remove the pattern. The plane where the flask parts is called the *parting line*. The two halves of the flask are called the *cope* and the *drag*. The drag is the bottom half, and the cope is the top half.

A sand mold is formed around a pattern. The pattern looks very much like the desired casting, but is slightly oversize to compensate for shrinkage. Often, additional oversize areas are added to provide metal for machining (*Figure 3-3b*). This is called a *machining allowance*.

On vertical surfaces that rub against the mold when the pattern is withdrawn, a taper is added to provide a slight clearance during pattern withdrawal. This allowance is called *draft* (*Figure 3-3c*). To provide allowances,

51

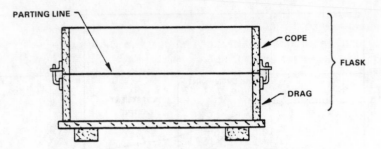

Figure 3-3a. Flask (box) which holds sand-clay mixture. (*Courtesy*, Xerox Corporation)

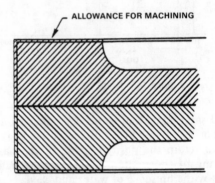

Figure 3-3b. Pattern. (*Courtesy*, Xerox Corporation)

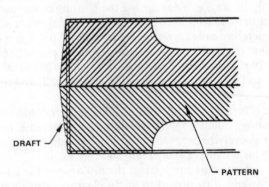

Figure 3-3c. Pattern showing taper. (*Courtesy*, Xerox Corporation)

the pattern is made larger than the desired casting. The three types of allowance are shrinkage allowance, machining allowance, and draft.

If cores are required to form interior surfaces in the casting, the pattern will be made with projections called *core prints* (*Figure 3-3d*). Corresponding projections formed on cores permit exact location of the core in the mold cavity.

Like the mold, the pattern will usually be made in two sections, unless the casing is to have a large, flat surface. Registration runs (*Figure 3-3e*) are used to ensure accurate alignment of the two pattern halves. The half of the pattern that is to be molded in the drag half of the mold is placed upside down, on a molding board (*Figure 3-3f*). The drag half of the flask is placed upside down around it.

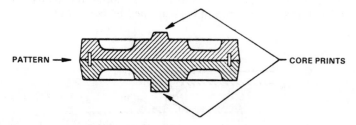

Figure 3-3d. Pattern showing core prints. (*Courtesy*, Xerox Corporation)

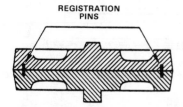

Figure 3-3e. Pattern showing registration pins. (*Courtesy*, Xerox Corporation)

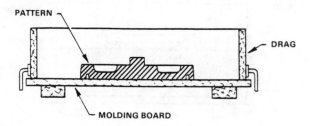

Figure 3-3f. Pattern placed in drag side of flask. (*Courtesy*, Xerox Corporation)

53

Next, the drag is filled with the prepared sand-clay mixture, which is packed firmly around the pattern by ramming (*Figure 3-3g*). Then the drag is turned over and the board removed. The top half of the pattern is placed on the bottom half, and aligned with the registration pins. The other half of the flask, the cope, is then placed on the drag (*Figure 3-3h*).

The cope is then filled with sand and rammed in the same way the drag was. A gating system is needed to get the metal into the mold cavity. A vertical channel called the *sprue* is cut into the sand at this stage of mold making (*Figure 3-3i*).

The mold can then be parted and the pattern removed. The gating system is completed by cutting in the short horizontal channel, called a *runner*. If required to compensate for shrinkage, one or more riser(s) can be cut into the mold at this time (*Figure 3-3j*).

The core is set in place, then the mold is closed and ready for casting (*Figure 3-3k*). If a core is used, it is positioned by core prints.

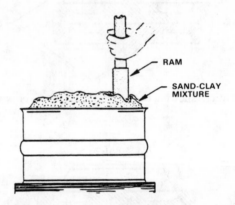

Figure 3-3g. Packing sand-clay mixture into drag. (*Courtesy*, Xerox Corporation)

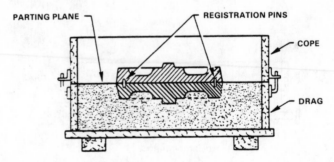

Figure 3-3h. Pattern half put together. (*Courtesy*, Xerox Corporation)

54

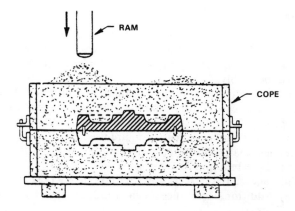

Figure 3-3i. Cope is filled with sand. (*Courtesy*, Xerox Corporation)

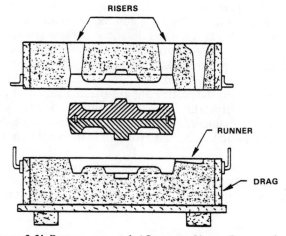

Figure 3-3j. Pattern removed. (*Courtesy*, Xerox Corporation)

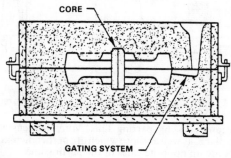

Figure 3-3k. Mold is ready for casting. (*Courtesy*, Xerox Corporation)

Tolerances

The values shown here represent normal production practice at the most economical level. Greater accuracy involving extra close work or care in production should be specified only when and where necessary, since additional cost will be involved.

The following are the minimum tolerances for economical sand-casting design. These tolerances are for aluminum, copper, magnesium alloys, and beryllium copper. An additional 0.005 in. (0.13 mm) should be added when malleable irons, cast steels, and cast iron are used.

Tolerances, less than those noted, may be obtained at additional cost, and by machining to the required dimensions.

Linear Tolerances. Basic tolerances up to six inches (152 mm) are ±0.030 in. (±0.7 mm). Additional tolerance for each additional inch over six inches is ±0.003 (±0.07 mm).

Parting Line Tolerances. Parting line tolerances are additional tolerances that must be added to the linear tolerances on all dimensions which cross or emanate from the parting line of the casting. *Figure 3-4* illustrates those dimensions that cross the parting line and require both the linear tolerance and the parting line tolerance. The tolerances in *Table III-2* reflect only the variations caused by expansion and contraction of the mold itself, the metal during solidification, patternmaking tolerances, and vibration of the pattern during its removal from the mold.

Dimensions crossing the parting line are affected not only by all the above factors, but by the hydrostatic pressure of the fluid metal itself, which acts as a hydraulic fluid in a cylinder, attempting to force the mold halves apart. In sand, this pressure usually causes the top half of the mold to sag from its own weight.

To make allowance for this additional variation, the tolerances given in *Table III-2* must be added to the applicable linear tolerances and then the combined tolerance applied to those dimensions that cross the parting line.

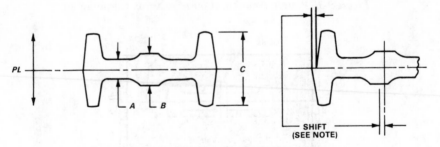

Figure 3-4. Dimensions crossing parting line. *Note:* Dimensions parallel to the parting plane, as well as those which are perpendicular, are affected if the surfaces are on opposite sides of the parting line.
(*Courtesy*, the Aluminum Association)

Table III-2. Parting Line Tolerances

Additional Tolerances (inch)	
Projected Area (sq in.)	Sand Mold
Up to 10	± 0.020
Over 10 to 49	± 0.035
Over 50 to 99	± 0.045
Over 100 to 249	± 0.060
Over 250 to 500*	± 0.090

* Over 500 consult foundry. (*Courtesy*, the Aluminum Association)

Additional tolerances, in the case of cores or moving mold parts, are shown in *Table III-3*.

Core Location Tolerances. The use of cores enhances the design flexibility of sand castings by allowing a hole or undercut to be produced in the surface of a casting, perpendicular to the parting plane.

Since cores are separate from the sand mold, there must be a clearance allowance for placement or movement. Such allowances create an added variation in the dimensions of the surface produced by the core, to a surface produced by the mold. The amount of this additional tolerance shown in *Table III-3* is governed by the projected area of the core. *Figure 3-5* shows dimensions affected by a moving core. The tolerances in *Table III-3* are to be added to the linear tolerances. However, dimensions within the area of a single core need not have the core location tolerances added; only the linear tolerance would apply.

Table III-3. Core Location Tolerances

Additional Tolerances (inch)	
Projected Area (sq in.)	Sand Mold Sand Core
Up to 10	± 0.020
Over 10 to 42	± 0.035
Over 50 to 99	± 0.045
Over 100 to 499	± 0.060
Over 500 to 1000*	± 0.090

* Over 1000 consult foundry. (*Courtesy*, the Aluminum Association)

Example. The dimensions shown in *Figure 3-5* must have the following tolerances applied:

A — Linear.
B — Linear and parting line (*Table III-2*).
C — Linear.
D — Linear and core location (*Table III-3*).
E — Linear and core location.

Figure 3-6 indicates the cost increases as the tolerances decrease. The curve is an average cost curve with size and quantities not considered.

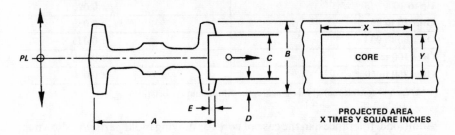

Figure 3-5. Dimensions affected by moving cores.
(*Courtesy*, the Aluminum Association)

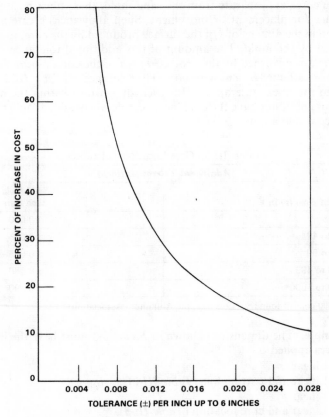

Figure 3-6. Sand casting tolerances and cost comparison.

Draft Requirements

Adding draft to a part being machined is standard practice among foundries today. What this entails is actually adding metal to the casting—thereby increasing its size and weight.

It is not required to show draft on the pictorial presentation of the drawing. (See *Figure 3-7*.) However, if it would add clarity, the draft should be shown, and preferably exaggerated.

A dimension pertaining to a surface requiring draft is measured at one point on that surface only. Draft will increase or decrease such dimensions. *Figure 3-8* shows what takes place when draft is applied. Dimension A is increased to A_1 and dimension B is decreased to B_1.

Draft may be removed (eliminating material rather than adding) if desired for clearance purposes, but must be specified on the drawing. (See *Figure 3-9*.) The best method to ensure clearance, however, would be to specify that the draft be held within the dimensional tolerance.

As a general rule, draft is added in holes to effectively reduce the hole size from the base diameter. Therefore, should the designer require that a hole be enlarged rather than reduced, one must so specify as stated above. (See *Figure 3-10*.) Once again, the best method is to specify that the draft be held within the hole tolerance. The amount of draft is governed by the length of wall (L), and is shown in *Table III-4*.

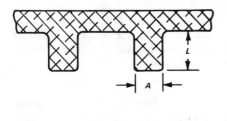

Figure 3-7. Draft not shown.

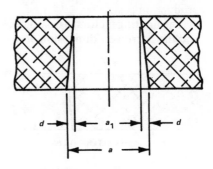

Figure 3-8. Results of additive draft.

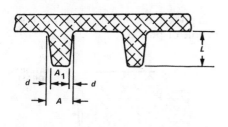

Figure 3-9. Results of removal draft.

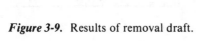

Figure 3-10. Draft in cored hole.

59

Table III-4. Draft Angles for Sand Casting Walls

Wall Depth (inch)	Draft Angle	Draft (inch)
0.1	17°	0.030
0.2	9°	0.030
0.3	6°	0.030
0.4	4° 30'	0.030
0.5	3° 30'	0.030
1.0	1° 45'	0.030
1.5	1° 30'	0.039
2.0	1° 15'	0.044
2.5	1°	0.044
3.0	1°	0.052
3.5	1°	0.061
4.0	1°	0.069
4.5	1°	0.077
5.0	1°	0.087
6.0	1°	0.104
7.0	1°	0.122
8.0	1°	0.139
9.0	1°	0.156
10.0	1°	0.174

The direction in which draft is applied is governed by the location of the parting line, and will be at the foundry's option unless otherwise specified. (See *Figure 3-11*.)

When a parting line interrupts a surface to which draft is applied, the amount of draft to be added will be determined by the longer portion of surface to be drawn. Drafts will be applied to the remainder of the surface to provide a match at the parting line. (See *Figure 3-12*.)

Holes and Pockets

Holes and pockets in sand castings may be produced either by incorporating them as integral features of the pattern equipment (sand mold)—provided that size limitations, draft requirements, and direction of draw are satisfactory—or by inserting separately made sand cores. These sand cores can give a flexibility of design to the pattern equipment, but generally at a higher production cost.

The limiting factors in casting holes and pockets are depth, degree of draft, and the narrowest dimension across the hole or pocket.

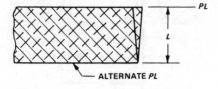

Figure 3-11. Draft from parting line.

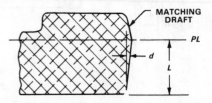

Figure 3-12. Draft blending.

Surface Finish

Cast surface finish requirements (excluding areas of gating, risers, fillets, and parting lines) are: 250-μin. (6.4 μm) rms for nonferrous metals, and up to 500 μin. (12.8 μm) rms for ferrous metals.

PERMANENT MOLD CASTINGS

Although enhanced quality plays a significant role in selecting the permanent mold process, the economy of the process itself is usually the primary basis of selection. The cost of the mold and the accessory equipment is higher than that of the patterns used in sand castings. However, where the number of castings required is sufficient to justify the initial tooling cost, permanent mold castings are usually more economical than sand castings because of the higher production rates and the generally lower labor skill required. Further economics are often found in the opportunity to design to a smaller casting weight. Major savings are frequently possible because of the decrease in machining costs permitted by closer dimensional tolerances.

Permanent mold castings must be, in general, of simple design. Some complexity is possible, however, by using sand cores with steel molds.

The most common alloying materials are aluminum, copper-based, and magnesium. Permanent mold castings are usually dense grained, and have better surface finishes than sand castings.

Processes

Permanent molds are usually made of cast iron, although some are coated with graphite, depending on what material will be cast. Cast iron molds are used for casting nonferrous alloys, which are not as hot in the molten state as steel or cast iron. For casting steel, a high heat resistant die steel is used, and coated with graphite or ceramic to extend mold life. Unlike sand or investment castings, permanent mold castings, do not require a pattern. Instead, the mold cavity is machined in a block of iron in two halves (*Figure 3-13*).

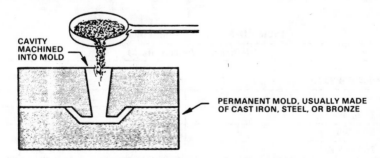

Figure 3-13. The permanent mold cavity is machined in two halves. (*Courtesy*, Xerox Corporation)

Advantages and Limitations

The advantages of permanent mold castings are:

- Good surface finish.
- Good metallurgical grain structure, 0-20% stronger than sand.
- Good dimensional accuracy.
- Rapid production rate.
- Low scrap loss.
- Low porosity (less than diecasting).
- More machining allowance than with diecasting; better for extensive machining.

The limitations include higher tooling costs and longer lead time than sand or plaster processes; more limited shape, size, and intricacy than with investment process. In addition, parts cannot be produced with wall thickness less than 0.094 in. (2.4 mm). (See *Table III-25*.) Also, tolerances are not as good as with the die or investment processes.

Tolerances

Solid die tolerances for aluminum and magnesium alloys are ±0.015 in. (0.38 mm) for the first inch or less, and ±0.002 in. (0.05 mm) for each additional inch. With copper-based alloys, tolerances are ±0.015 in. (±0.38 mm) for the first inch or less, and ±0.005 in. (±0.13 mm) is the solid die tolerance for each additional inch.

The tolerances represent normal production capability at the most economical level. Closer tolerances should be specified only when absolutely necessary, to produce greater accuracy or finish. More liberal tolerance values can be specified, where practical, to further reduce production cost.

Parting Line Tolerances. Those dimensions occurring across the moving part of a mold and across parting line dimensions cannot be held as close as those in one of the machined cavities of the mold. An additional tolerance must be allowed for such dimensions. The tolerances to be added are given in *Table III-5*. Additional tolerances, in the case of cores or moving parts, are shown in *Table III-6*.

Table III-5. Parting Line Tolerances

Additional Tolerances (inch)	
Projected Area (sq in.)	Permanent Mold
Up to 10	± 0.010
Over 10 to 49	± 0.015
Over 50 to 99	± 0.020
Over 100 to 249	± 0.025
Over 250 to 500*	± 0.030

* Over 500 consult foundry. (*Courtesy*, the Aluminum Association)

Table III-6. Core Location Tolerances

Projected Area (sq in.)	PM to Sand Core	PM to Metal Core
Additional Tolerances (inch)		
Up to 10	± 0.015	± 0.010
Over 10 to 49	± 0.025	± 0.015
Over 50 to 99	± 0.030	± 0.015
Over 100 to 499	± 0.040	± 0.022
Over 500 to 1000*	± 0.060	± 0.032

* Over 1000 consult foundry. (*Courtesy*, the Aluminum Association)

Holes and pockets in permanent mold castings are preferably produced by steel cores which are incorporated in the mold design so that they can be withdrawn manually or mechanically during the casting cycle. Such cores require draft for withdrawal.

Sand cores may be used where normal draft cannot be tolerated, or where internal chambers which do not permit withdrawal of steel cores are required. Thus modified, the process is known as *semipermanent molding*. In special circumstances, steel cores may be collapsed and removed in sections to accomplish a result which is similar to that of the semipermanent mold process. In such cases, consultation with the foundry is advisable.

Table III-7 gives desired values for core depths and draft in relation to diameters. *Figure 3-14* illustrates typical holes and pockets used in permanent castings.

The parting line tolerances and core location tolerances are to be added to the applicable linear tolerances in the same way sand casting tolerances are added to the applicable linear tolerances. Tolerances shown for permanent mold castings are economical tolerances, and should be used whenever possible. Closer tolerances are possible—but at higher cost, as indicated by the cost curve in *Figure 3-15*.

Table III-7. Limiting Factors for Permanent Mold Casting Holes and Pockets

Type of Core	Base Hole Diameter or Minimum Dimensions of Pocket (inch)				
	0.25	0.50	1.00	2.00	4.00
	Maximum Depth (inch)				
Permanent	0.25	1.00	2.00	4.00	8.00
Sand	0.0	0.50	2.00	4.00	8.00
	Draft Required Per Side (deg)				
Permanent	10	5	3	3	3
Sand	*Use Data in Table III-8*				

(*Courtesy*, the Aluminum Association)

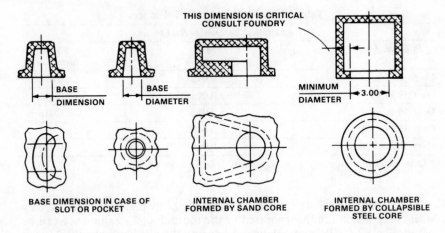

BASE DIMENSION

BASE DIAMETER

THIS DIMENSION IS CRITICAL
CONSULT FOUNDRY

MINIMUM DIAMETER ◄3.00►

BASE DIMENSION IN CASE OF
SLOT OR POCKET

INTERNAL CHAMBER
FORMED BY SAND CORE

INTERNAL CHAMBER
FORMED BY COLLAPSIBLE
STEEL CORE

Figure 3-14. Holes and pockets. (*Courtesy*, the Aluminum Association)

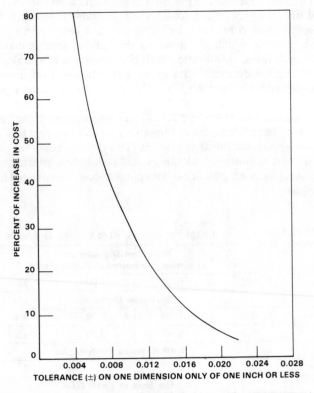

Figure 3-15. Permanent mold casting tolerances and cost comparison.

64

Draft Requirements

Draft angles for permanent mold castings are required to remove the casting from the mold. *Table III-8* indicates the amount of draft required for the various depths of walls. Draft angles for cores are shown in *Table III-7*. Draft angles for sand cores should be taken from *Table III-8*.

DIECASTING

Diecastings offer closer dimensional tolerances than any production casting process producing comparable results. As in any other casting design, tolerances should be held to a minimum only on dimensions which so require.

Simple forms that are easily cut into the die blocks help to minimize die cost, but it is entirely possible to make complex forms when they are necessary. Parts having external undercuts or projections on side walls often require slides that materially increase the die costs.

Along with significant savings in the amount of metal actually used, diecasting offers other advantages—such as more uniform wall sections—all of which offset the extra cost, or effect a net economy in the overall cost of the part. This is especially true when large quantities are involved, as a small saving per diecasting may fully justify a more expensive die. However, as in any casting design, the designer must analyze the design, as to quantity and cost of machining, if other methods are used to fabricate the part. If the quantity is low and the die cost is high, it is perhaps better and more economical to use other fabrication methods.

Casting Processes

In hot-chamber die casting, metal alloys that melt at lower temperatures, such as zinc, are cast. In this process, the injection cylinder is immersed in a

Table III-8. Draft Angles for Walls of Permanent Mold Castings

Wall Depth (inch)	Draft Angle (deg)	Draft (inch)
0.125	10	0.022
0.250	8	0.035
0.312	8	0.044
0.437	7	0.054
0.500	7	0.061
0.625	6	0.066
0.750	6	0.079
0.812	6	0.085
0.937	6	0.098
1.000	6	0.105
1.500	5	0.131
2.000	4	0.140
2.500	4	0.175
3.000	3-1/2	0.183
3.500	3-1/2	0.213
4.000	3-1/2	0.244
4.500	3-1/2	0.274
5.000	3-1/2	0.305

reservoir of molten metal. With each stroke of the plunger, sufficient metal to fill the die cavity is drawn into the injection cylinder and then forced from it into the die cavity (*Figure 3-16*).

Cold-chamber die casting is used for metals that melt at higher temperatures, such as aluminum and copper. A quantity of metal sufficient to fill the die cavity is ladled through the pouring slot into the shot chamber (*Figure 3-17*). That metal is then forced into the die by the plunger.

Design Justification

When considering the use of a diecasting, the designer must first consider the merits and limitations of the casting process, and the end product.

Merits:

* Most dimensions can be held within limits so close that little or no machining is required.

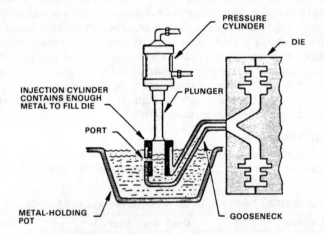

Figure 3-16. Hot-chamber die casting.

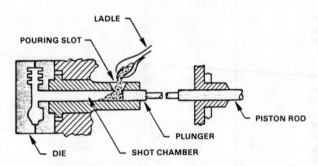

Figure 3-17. Cold-chamber die casting.

66

- Surfaces, as diecast, are smoother than most other types of castings.
- Most holes can be cored—sometimes as small as 0.093-in. (2.4-mm) diameter. Coring is usually done to tap drill size.
- Thousands of diecastings can be produced by the same die, and usually without significant change in the dimensions of parts produced.
- Diecastings can have more complex shapes and thinner walls than most other types of castings.
- Material cost is usually low, primarily because the diecasting process permits use of thinner sections.
- Inserts of other materials are readily diecast in place.
- A fairly wide choice of aluminum, zinc, and magnesium alloys are available for use. New alloys are being considered for future use.

Limitations:
- Only nonferrous alloys are used, and the range of these is narrower than for other casting processes.
- Cores involving undercuts are limited in their application.
- Diecastings are subject to some porosity, which usually occurs in the area of the heaviest section. This porosity, however, can be confined to locations where its presence is not significant, or may be held within required limits. If not controlled, machining will expose porosity which will create a defect.

Before choosing a diecasting, the designer should question whether dimensional requirements will permit any other casting method to be used; and if another casting method is used, whether the cost of machining will offset the total cost of a diecasting. The designer should also question whether the diecasting will give the proper strength requirement.

Design Considerations

Designs with diecastings are almost unlimited. However, to achieve the maximum benefit from diecasting methods, it is necessary to observe certain rules for design. The following rules will help the designer avoid costly and difficult die design.

Because permanent steel dies are used, it is obvious that the design of a diecast part must reflect many of the same characteristic design limitations found in the design of a permanent mold casting part.

Maximum simplicity in design will achieve the lowest possible die cost, and consequently, part cost. However, the greater the quantities produced, the greater the opportunities to utilize complex die designs to cost advantage by eliminating machining and other subsequent production operations.

Figures 3-18 and *3-19* illustrate, by comparison, correct and incorrect diecasting designs.

Rules for Design

As in any other casting design, certain rules must be followed to get economical and functional diecastings. Rules for the design of any diecasting

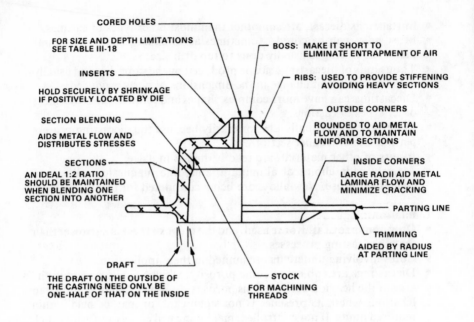

CORED HOLES

FOR SIZE AND DEPTH LIMITATIONS
SEE TABLE III-18

INSERTS

HOLD SECURELY BY SHRINKAGE
IF POSITIVELY LOCATED BY DIE

SECTION BLENDING

AIDS METAL FLOW AND
DISTRIBUTES STRESSES

SECTIONS

AN IDEAL 1:2 RATIO
SHOULD BE MAINTAINED
WHEN BLENDING ONE
SECTION INTO ANOTHER

DRAFT

THE DRAFT ON THE OUTSIDE OF
THE CASTING NEED ONLY BE
ONE-HALF OF THAT ON THE INSIDE

BOSS: MAKE IT SHORT TO
ELIMINATE ENTRAPMENT OF AIR

RIBS: USED TO PROVIDE STIFFENING
AVOIDING HEAVY SECTIONS

OUTSIDE CORNERS

ROUNDED TO AID METAL
FLOW AND TO MAINTAIN
UNIFORM SECTIONS

INSIDE CORNERS

LARGE RADII AID METAL
LAMINAR FLOW AND
MINIMIZE CRACKING

PARTING LINE

TRIMMING

AIDED BY RADIUS
AT PARTING LINE

STOCK

FOR MACHINING
THREADS

Figure 3-18. Correct design considerations.

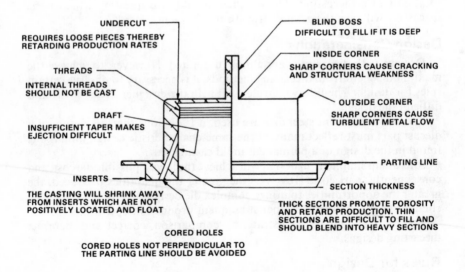

UNDERCUT

REQUIRES LOOSE PIECES THEREBY
RETARDING PRODUCTION RATES

THREADS

INTERNAL THREADS
SHOULD NOT BE CAST

DRAFT

INSUFFICIENT TAPER MAKES
EJECTION DIFFICULT

INSERTS

THE CASTING WILL SHRINK AWAY
FROM INSERTS WHICH ARE NOT
POSITIVELY LOCATED AND FLOAT

CORED HOLES

CORED HOLES NOT PERPENDICULAR TO
THE PARTING LINE SHOULD BE AVOIDED

BLIND BOSS
DIFFICULT TO FILL IF IT IS DEEP

INSIDE CORNER

SHARP CORNERS CAUSE CRACKING
AND STRUCTURAL WEAKNESS

OUTSIDE CORNER

SHARP CORNERS CAUSE
TURBULENT METAL FLOW

PARTING LINE

SECTION THICKNESS

THICK SECTIONS PROMOTE POROSITY
AND RETARD PRODUCTION. THIN
SECTIONS ARE DIFFICULT TO FILL AND
SHOULD BLEND INTO HEAVY SECTIONS

Figure 3-19. Incorrect design considerations.

68

must be somewhat general in character, and subject to many exceptions. It is possible in some instances, however, to formulate guidelines indicating what is desirable in such a design and what should be avoided. This is especially true when the objective is to produce a satisfactory product at a minimum cost.

The following rules are intended merely as a guide to the designer. There are exceptions, and there are cases in which other considerations outweigh the advantages that may be attained by following a particular rule. However, where the rules can be followed, either costs are likely to be lowered or better diecastings will result, or both.

- Keep overall dimensions as small, and weight as low, as possible.
- Specify sections as thin as can be diecast readily and still provide adequate strength and stiffness. Use of ribs can frequently aid in attaining maximum strength with minimum weight.
- Keep sections as uniform as possible. When sections must be varied, make the transitions gradually to avoid stress concentrations.
- Avoid nonessential projections and keep shapes as simple as other requirements permit.
- Coring of holes should only be specified where holes can be cored without undue die cost. Many times it is more economical to drill small holes in sections less than 0.19-in. (4.8-mm) thick.
- Provide fillets at all inside corners, and avoid sharp outside corners, unless deviation from this practice is warranted by some special considerations.
- Explore all design innovations which may eliminate any recessed or undercut portions in the direction of core or die travel. Recessed and undercut portions can be formed only with expensive dies, which usually have a shorter die life because of their complexity.
- Design so that flash removal costs are minimized.
- Avoid the use of loose pieces unless there is assurance that they will allow a net savings in cost or other compensating benefits.

There are many other rules that can be followed in making an economical design, and it is best to check with a competent diecaster for suggested changes that may lower the cost and improve the diecasting.

Parting Lines. To eliminate as much die sinking as possible, the *parting line*—the area where the die halves separate—should be established on a single plane parallel to the surface of greatest length. This also permits ejection of the part over the shortest possible distance; a feature which facilitates production of satisfactory castings. Die parting should never be such that a feather edge is left on one half.

Establishment of the proper plane of parting may often depend upon design features, diecasting machine used, die operation, tolerances, and metal soundness.

It is often desirable to visualize final design results to determine the problems which result from the normal flash which occurs at the parting line. Seldom should the parting be established at sharp-cornered or complex contours; it is much simpler to trim flash if the outline is smooth and uniform. Only where a part can be completed in one-half of a die, or where final machining operations can be utilized for flash removal, should sharp-edged parting be considered.

Frequently, a bead or rounded edge can be used at the parting line. Such a design makes flash removal a simple, neat operation.

When costly die slides and movable cores can be avoided by use of irregular or joggled parting lines, deviation from the rule of flat parting can often be highly economical in die cost and/or production time. It is advisable therefore, to carefully analyze the design to determine the most economical way to part the casting.

Draft. Provide sufficient draft on side walls and cores to assure removal of the diecasting from the die without distortion.

Dimensions. Keep overall dimensions small, and weight as low as possible. (*Table III-9* shows approximate dimensional and weight limits.) However, dimensional tolerances should never be closer than necessary. The data in *Table III-9* applies to average conditions. For exceptional conditions, variations such as larger castings, closer dimensional limits, and thinner sections may be feasible.

Tolerances

The closest tolerances can be held on portions of the item which formed with a solid portion of the die. Dimensions across the parting line require additional tolerances. Before a design is started, a thorough analysis of the tolerance structure should be made. *Figure 3-20* indicates that the cost increases as tolerances decrease. The curve is an average cost curve. Size and quantities are not considered.

Table III-9. Approximate Dimensional and Weight Limits for Diecasting in Different Alloys

Type of Alloy (Base Metal)	Zinc	Aluminum	Magne-sium	Copper
Maximum weight of casting (lb)	35	20	10	5
Minimum wall thickness of large castings over 2 lb (inches)	0.050	0.080	0.080	0.090
Minimum wall thickness of small castings up to 2 lb	0.025	0.050	0.050	0.050
Minimum variation per inch of diameter or length from drawing dimensions over 1 inch	0.0015	0.0015	0.0015	0.002
Cast threads, maximum number per inch external	24	24	16	10
Cored holes, minimum diameter, inch	0.094	0.125	0.125	0.250
Minimum draft on cores inch per inch of length or diameter	0.005	0.010	0.010	0.020
Minimum draft on side walls inch per inch of depth	0.007	0.015	0.010	0.020

Note: Larger variations may be anticipated across die partings or where slide or core fits are involved. These variations depend to a considerable degree on core length, although smaller cores than indicated here are rarely used. (*Courtesy*, the American Die Casting Institute Inc.)

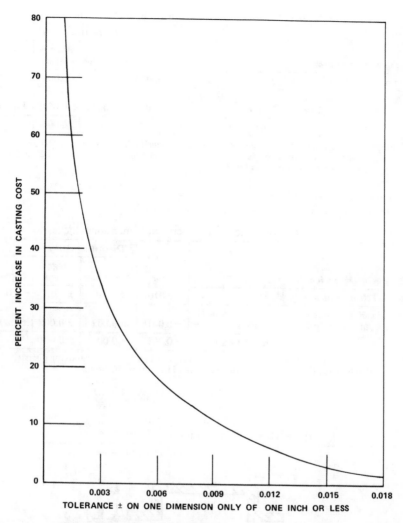

Figure 3-20. Diecasting tolerances and cost comparison.

Linear Dimension Tolerances. Cast linear dimension tolerances on the length or width are the values shown in *Table III-10* or *Table III-11*. These tolerances must be increased where the parting line of the die, or moving die part, affects the length or width dimensions (see *Table III-12*). *Table III-10* shows the tolerances for critical dimensions, while *Table III-11* shows the tolerances for noncritical dimensions. For the most economical design, tolerances shown in *Table III-11* should be used, but if the design requires critical dimensions in some areas, then a combination of both tolerances should be used.

71

Table III-10. Tolerances for Critical Dimensions (Inches)

Length of Dimension		Diecasting Alloy			
		Zinc	Aluminum	Magne-sium	Copper
Basic Tolerance up to 1 Inch		± 0.003	± 0.004	± 0.004	± 0.007
Additional Tolerance for each Additional Inch of Length	Over 1 Inch to 12 Inches	± 0.001	± 0.0015	± 0.0015	± 0.002
	Over 12 Inches	± 0.001	± 0.001	± 0.001	—

Example: An aluminum diecasting on a 4.000 inch dimension has a tolerance of ±0.0085 inch, if the dimension is not affected by a parting line or moving die part. (*Courtesy*, the American Die Casting Institute Inc.)

Table III-11. Tolerances for Noncritical Dimensions (Inches)

Length of Dimension		Diecasting Alloy			
		Zinc	Aluminum	Magne-sium	Copper
Basic Tolerance up to 1 Inch		± 0.010	± 0.010	± 0.010	± 0.014
Additional Tolerance for each Additional Inch of Length	Over 1 Inch to 12 Inches	± 0.0015	± 0.002	± 0.002	± 0.003
	Over 12 Inches	± 0.001	± 0.001	± 0.001	—

Note: The tolerances shown above must be modified in a parting line or moving die part affects dimensions. (*Courtesy*, the American Die Casting Institute)

Table III-12. Parting Line Tolerances (Inches)

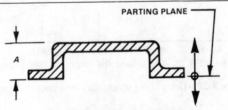

A = LINEAR DIMENSION AFFECTED

Projected Area of Diecasting.	Diecasting Alloy			
	Zinc	Aluminum	Magnesium	Copper
Up to 50 sq in.	± 0.004	± 0.005	± 0.005	± 0.005
50 to 100 sq in.	± 0.006	± 0.008	± 0.008	—
100 to 200 sq in.	± 0.008	± 0.012	± 0.012	—
200 to 300 sq in.	± 0.012	± 0.015	± 0.015	—

(*Courtesy*, the American Die Casting Institute Inc.)

Parting Line Tolerances. The parting plane may be critical where tight tolerances are desirable without recourse to additional finishing operations. It is often desirable to locate tight tolerance portions so that they will be produced in the solid portion of one-half of the die, rather than between the two halves.

Parting line tolerances (*Table III-12*), in addition to linear dimension tolerances, must be provided when the parting line affects a linear dimension.

Moving Die Part Tolerances. Moving die part tolerances (*Table III-13*), must be added to the linear dimension tolerances and parting line tolerances when a moving die part affects a linear dimension.

In this case, the projected area in square inches is that portion of the diecasting which is affected by the moving die part.

Angularity (Parallelism and Perpendicularity) Tolerances. Angularity refers to the angular departure from the designed relationship between the elements of a diecasting. The angular accuracy of a casting is affected by numerous factors including the size of the diecasting, the strength and rigidity of the diecasting die and die parts under conditions of high heat and pressure, positioning of moving die members, and distortion during handling of the diecasting.

Angularity tolerances for plane surfaces (all alloys) vary with the length of the surface on the diecasting and the relative location of these surfaces in the casting die cavity. *Figure 3-21* shows the angularity tolerances of various surfaces measured from a datum plane.

Angularity tolerances for cored holes (all alloys) must take into consideration the fact that cores used in dies to form holes bend after prolonged exposure to thermal and mechanical stresses.

Table III-13. Additional Tolerances (Inch) for Moving Die Part

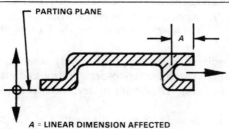

A = LINEAR DIMENSION AFFECTED

Projected Area of Diecasting Portion	Diecasting Alloy			
	Zinc	Aluminum	Magnesium	Copper
Up to 10 sq. inches	± 0.004	± 0.005	± 0.005	± 0.010
10 to 20 sq. inches	± 0.006	± 0.008	± 0.008	—
20 to 50 sq. inches	± 0.008	± 0.012	± 0.012	—
50 to 100 sq. inches	± 0.012	± 0.015	± 0.015	—

(*Courtesy*, the American Die Casting Institute Inc.)

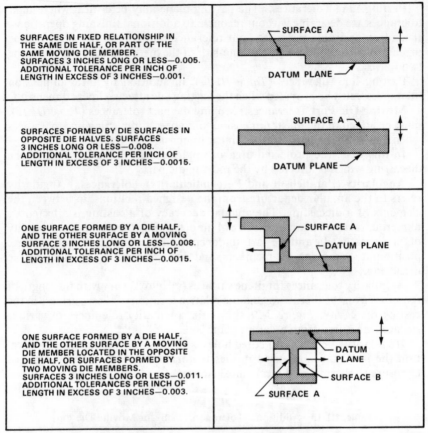

SURFACES IN FIXED RELATIONSHIP IN THE SAME DIE HALF, OR PART OF THE SAME MOVING DIE MEMBER. SURFACES 3 INCHES LONG OR LESS—0.005. ADDITIONAL TOLERANCE PER INCH OF LENGTH IN EXCESS OF 3 INCHES—0.001.	
SURFACES FORMED BY DIE SURFACES IN OPPOSITE DIE HALVES. SURFACES 3 INCHES LONG OR LESS—0.008. ADDITIONAL TOLERANCE PER INCH OF LENGTH IN EXCESS OF 3 INCHES—0.0015.	
ONE SURFACE FORMED BY A DIE HALF, AND THE OTHER SURFACE BY A MOVING SURFACE 3 INCHES LONG OR LESS—0.008. ADDITIONAL TOLERANCE PER INCH OF LENGTH IN EXCESS OF 3 INCHES—0.0015.	
ONE SURFACE FORMED BY A DIE HALF, AND THE OTHER SURFACE BY A MOVING DIE MEMBER LOCATED IN THE OPPOSITE DIE HALF, OR SURFACES FORMED BY TWO MOVING DIE MEMBERS. SURFACES 3 INCHES LONG OR LESS—0.011. ADDITIONAL TOLERANCES PER INCH OF LENGTH IN EXCESS OF 3 INCHES—0.003.	

Figure 3-21. Angularity tolerances for plane surfaces.
(*Courtesy*, the American Die Casting Institute)

The alignment tolerances are applicable only when proportions of the cored holes conform to the diameter-to-depth ratios and draft requirements. The values shown in *Table III-14* refer to deviation from the normal axis of the cored hole.

If a cored hole is 0.5-in. (12.7-mm) diameter and 1.5-in. (38-mm) deep, alignment of the hole will deviate from its normal axis 0.0075 in. (0.19 mm) maximum.

Explanation. The hole is less than 3-in. (76-mm) deep. Therefore, formula 0.010 D/M will apply. The hole depth (D) is 1.5-in. (38-mm). The maximum depth (M) for a 0.5-in. (12.7-mm) hole is 2-in. (50.8-mm). Therefore: (0.010 x 1.5)/2 = 0.0075 (0.19 mm).

If a hole is one inch (25.4 mm) in diameter and 5-in. (12.7-cm) deep, alignment of the hole will deviate from its normal axis by a 0.016 in. (0.4 mm) maximum.

Table III-14. Angularity Tolerances (Deviation from Normal) for Cored Holes (All Alloys)

Minimum Tolerance—Any Hole	0.005 inch
Tolerance for Holes 3 Inches or Less in Depth	$\dfrac{0.010\,D}{M}$ D = Depth of Hole M = Maximum Depth in Table III-18
Tolerance for Holes Greater than 3 Inches in Depth	0.010 plus 0.003 per Inch of Depth over 3 Inches.

(*Courtesy*, the American Die Casting Institute Inc.)

Explanation. The hole is more than 3-in. (76-mm) deep, therefore the total deviation will include 0.010 in. (0.25 mm) for the first 3 in. (76 mm), and 0.003 in. (0.07 mm) for each inch (25.4 mm) over 3 in. (76 mm). In this case, 0.006 in. (0.15 mm) equals 0.016 in. (0.4 mm).

Diecasting Tolerances for Aluminum Alloys. The average production tolerances which can be maintained with aluminum diecastings are given in *Table III-15* and *Figures 3-22* and *3-23*.

Table III-15. Average Production Tolerances (Using Aluminum Diecasting)

Dimensions	Tolerance for Dimension of one inch or less	Add this amount for each additional inch	Illustration
A. Dimensions between cores in one die half.	±0.005	±0.0015	Fig. 3-22a and b
B. Dimensions between cores opposite die halves.	±0.015	±0.0015	Fig. 3-22a and b
C. Dimensions between moving cores parallel to the parting line and on one side of die half.	±0.005	±0.0005	Fig. 3-22a and c
D. Dimension between moving cores opposite of one die half and between moving core, and parting line of one die half.	±0.015	±0.002	Fig. 3-22c
E. Dimension between moving cores at right angles to each other in the same die half.	±0.010	±0.001	Fig. 3-22b
F. Dimension between lower side of part and moving core parallel to parting line.	±0.010	±0.001	Fig. 3-22a
G. Dimension across parting line measuring depth of cores in two die halves.	±0.010	±0.0015	Fig. 3-22a
H. Dimensions between fixed points in opposite die halves (space).	±0.006 0.000	±0.0008	Fig. 3-23a

Table III-15. Average Production Tolerances (*Continued*)

Dimensions	Tolerance for Dimension of one inch or less	Add this amount for each additional inch	Illustration
I. Dimensions between fixed points in opposite die halves (misalignment).	± 0.004	± 0.0008	Fig. 3-23*b*
J. Dimensions between a moving core and a fixed location in the same die half.	± 0.002	± 0.0008	Fig. 3-23*c*
K. Dimensions between a moving core and a fixed location in opposite die halves (misalignment).	± 0.008	± 0.0008	Fig. 3-23*c*
L. Dimensions between a moving core and a fixed location in the same die half (space).	± 0.002	± 0.0008	Fig. 3-23*d*
M. Dimensions between a moving core and a fixed location in opposite die halves (space).	± 0.008 − 0.002	± 0.0008	Fig. 3-23*d*
N. Dimensions between centers of moving cores located in opposite die halves.	+ 0.006 − 0.003	± 0.0008	Fig. 3-23*e*
O. Dimensions between locations of moving cores located in opposite halves.	± 0.008	± 0.0008	Fig. 3-23*f*
P. Dimensions between locations of opposed moving cores in the same die half.	+ 0.010 − 0.002	± 0.0008	Fig. 3-23*g*
Q. Dimensions between moving cores located at right angles to one another in the same die half.	+ 0.008 − 0.004	± 0.0008	Fig. 3-23*h*
R,S. Dimensions between moving cores located in opposite die halves taken parallel (R) and at right angles (S) to the plane of the parting line.	+ 0.006 (R) + 0.010 − 0.003 (S)	± 0.0008 ± 0.0008	Fig. 3-23*i*
T. Dimensions between locations of opposed moving cores in opposite die halves.	± 0.007	± 0.0008	Fig. 3-23*j*
U,V. Dimensions between a moving core and a fixed location in the same (U) or opposite (V) die halves.	± 0.008 (U) + 0.006 − 0.002 (V)	± 0.0008 ± 0.0008	Fig. 3-23*k*
W. Possible variation due to warpage and other factors between two identical dimensions taken between different core plains across the die parting line.		Variations for each inch between the pairs of locations (W) ± 0.0008	Fig. 3-23*l*

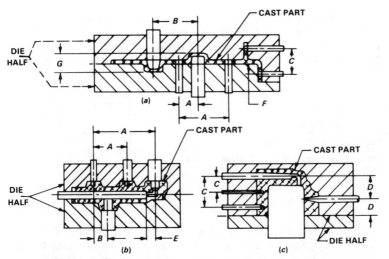

Figure 3-22. Dimensions between cores and die halves.

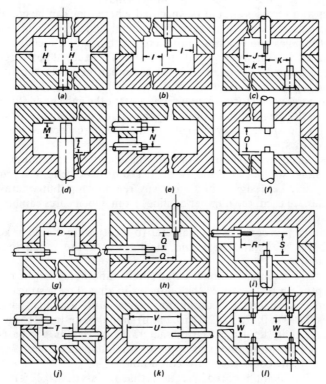

Figure 3-23. Dimensions between cores and die halves.

Flatness Tolerances. The normal as-cast flatness tolerances that can be expected when the casting is measured on a surface table with a feeler gage are given in *Table III-16*. These dimensions are based on the maximum diameter of a circular surface or the maximum diagonal of a rectangular surface.

Table III-16. As-Cast Flatness Tolerances

Dimensions of Diecasting	All Alloys
Basic Tolerance up to 3 Inches	0.008
Additional Tolerances for each Additional inch	0.003

(*Courtesy*, the American Die Casting Institute Inc.)

CORING

Coring is widely employed to assist in attaining uniformity of sections, as well as in providing holes. Use of cores as metal savers, and to provide uniform walls in a casting, assures maximum economy in design. The use of cores also eliminates heavy portions which are inherently subject to shrink-porosity, which in turn, reduces overall strength.

Holes and recesses should be specified where they can be cored without undue die costs, and where savings in metal and overall cost will result. Design the holes and recesses so that core withdrawal is facilitated to avoid complicated die construction and operation. Where cored holes are required, they should not be so small that the cores can be easily bent or broken. Frequent replacement of cores can substantially increase cost.

Fixed cores which form an integral part of the die halves and that have axes parallel to the die motion are least expensive and produce the most accurate results. It is possible, however, to utilize movable core pieces which slide on or within the dies.

Large, deep holes should normally be cored for maximum economy. Smaller holes should, as a rule, be drilled to provide better economy.

Holes may be designed in almost any relationship, but where multiple-cavity dies are used, the number of slides from which cores can be applied is distinctly limited.

For maximum core life, the diameter-to-length ratio should be kept small. Large cores withstand heat and mechanical abuse much longer than small ones.

Generally, circular or noncircular cored blind holes can be designed to have depths up to five times the diameter in zinc-alloy castings; and up to three times the diameter in aluminum, magnesium, or copper-base alloys.

Holes 0.093 to 0.125 in. (2.4 to 3.2 mm) should be designed to have a depth no greater than 1.5 times the diameter. These depths are based on the minimum draft allowable, and apply to minimum-size holes. *Table III-17* shows the draft requirements for cored holes.

Holes should not be cored in sections that are less than 0.125-in. (3.2-mm) thick when the hole is located parallel to the thin dimension.

Table III-17. Draft Requirements for Cored Holes

Alloy	Depth of Cored Hole	Draft Angle*	Draft (inch)
Aluminum	0.060 to 0.080	9° 30'	0.012 to 0.013
	>0.080 to 0.100	9°	0.014 to 0.015
	>0.100 to 0.200	7°	0.016 to 0.022
	>0.200 to 0.300	6°	0.023 to 0.027
	>0.300 to 0.400	5°	0.028 to 0.031
	>0.400 to 0.500	4°	0.032 to 0.034
	>0.500 to 0.600	3° 45'	0.035 to 0.038
	>0.600 to 0.800	3° 30'	0.039 to 0.042
	>0.800 to 1.000	3° 15'	0.043 to 0.050
	>1.000 to 2.000	2° 30'	0.051 to 0.065
	>2.000 to 3.000	2°	0.066 to 0.083
Copper	0.060 to 0.080	12°	0.014 to 0.016
	>0.080 to 0.100	11°	0.017 to 0.018
	>0.100 to 0.200	8°	0.019 to 0.026
	>0.200 to 0.300	7°	0.027 to 0.032
	>0.300 to 0.400	6°	0.033 to 0.038
	>0.400 to 0.500	5°	0.039 to 0.41
	>0.500 to 0.600	4° 30'	0.042 to 0.046
	>0.600 to 0.800	4°	0.047 to 0.053
	>0.800 to 1.00	3° 30'	0.054 to 0.059
	>1.000 to 2.000	3°	0.060 to 0.082
	>2.000 to 3.000	2°	0.083 to 0.100
Magnesium	0.060 to 0.800	8° 30'	0.010 to 0.011
	>0.080 to 0.100	7°	0.012 to 0.013
	>0.100 to 0.200	6°	0.014 to 0.018
	>0.200 to 0.300	5°	0.019 to 0.022
	>0.300 to 0.400	4° 30'	0.023 to 0.026
	>0.400 to 0.500	3° 30'	0.027 to 0.029
	>0.500 to 0.600	3° 15'	0.030 to 0.032
	>0.600 to 0.800	3°	0.033 to 0.037
	>0.800 to 1.000	2° 30'	0.038 to 0.041
	>1.000 to 2.000	2°	0.042 to 0.059
	>2.000 to 3.000	1° 45'	0.060 to 0.100
Zinc	0.060 to 0.080	6° 15'	0.007 to 0.008
	>0.080 to 0.100	6°	0.009 to 0.010
	>0.100 to 0.200	4° 30'	0.011 to 0.013
	>0.200 to 0.300	3° 15'	0.014 to 0.016
	>0.300 to 0.400	3°	0.017 to 0.018
	>0.400 to 0.500	2° 45'	0.019 to 0.020
	>0.500 to 0.600	2° 30'	0.021 to 0.023
	>0.600 to 0.800	2°	0.024 to 0.026
	>0.800 to 1.000	1° 45'	0.027 to 0.030
	>1.000 to 2.000	1° 30'	0.031 to 0.041
	>2.000 to 3.000	1° 15'	0.042 to 0.051

* Draft angle given indicates total draft.

The maximum depth for cored holes, as related to diameter, is shown in *Table III-18*. The values shown for hole depths are subject to draft requirements.

Table III-18. Cored Hole Depths

Alloy	Diameter of Hole (inch)								
	1/8	5/32	3/16	1/4	3/8	1/2	5/8	3/4	1
	Maximum Depth (inch)								
Zinc	3/8	9/16	3/4	1	1-1/2	2	3-1/8	4-1/2	6
Aluminum*	5/16	1/2	5/8	1	1-1/2	2	3-1/8	4-1/2	6
Magnesium*	5/16	1/2	5/8	1	1-1/2	2	3-1/8	4-1/2	6
Copper				1/2	1	1-1/4	2	3-1/2	5

* For cores larger than one inch in diameter, the maximum diameter-depth ratio will be 1:6.
(*Courtesy*, the American Die Casting Institute Inc.)

Cored Holes for Tapping

Holes required for tapping necessitate values for draft and depth other than the optimum values for cored hole production at the most economic level. However, casting holes for subsequent tapping is, in general, more economical than drilling.

When required, cored holes in zinc, magnesium, and aluminum diecastings may be tapped without removing the draft by drilling. Recommended sizes for tapping are based upon allowing 75% of full depth of thread at the bottom or small end of the cored hole, and 60% at the top or large end of the cored hole.

Dimensions for cored holes for tapping are given in *Table III-19*.

Example. Cored holes for tapping a 10-32 thread, 0.380 in. (9.6-mm) maximum depth, should *not* be dimensioned 0.159 in. $^{+0.005}_{-0.002}$ (4 mm $^{+0.13}_{-0.05}$), but should be within the draft angle tolerances 0.165—0.159 in. (4.2—4.0 mm). This is based on 75% of full depth of the thread of the bottom or small end of the cored hole, and 60% at the top or large end of the cored hole.

DRAFT ANGLES

To assure ready removal of castings from the dies, draft is required for all portions which are substantially normal to the parting line, or parallel to the line of die movement. The same is true for cores or slides. Typical draft values normally employed for various materials are tabulated in *Table III-20*. Minimum values are shown in the table, but where function and design permit, greater drafts should be allowed.

Generous drafts extend die life considerably by eliminating the natural core and die wear to a great extent. The poorer the bearing qualities of the metal, the more important a generous draft becomes. Relatively large draft permits easier withdrawal, eliminates possible distortion in removal, and assures the best surface quality obtainable.

For rib thicknesses of 0.125 in. (3 mm) or greater, a minimum draft of 3° (0.052 rad) is desirable. When narrower ribs are necessary, as much as 15° (0.261 rad) of draft per side may be required.

The general practice is to show draft, wherever draft is needed, as a part of the drawing. However, it is recommended that a note be added to show the

80

Table III-19. Dimensions of Cored Holes for Tapping

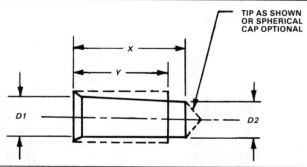

	Hole Diameters†		Maximum Threaded Depth of Hole	Maximum Depth of Cored Hole
Tap Size	D1	D2	Y	X
6-40 NF	0.119	0.114	0.208	0.270
6-32 NC	0.113	0.107	0.162	0.240
8-36 NF*	0.142	0.134	0.321	0.390
8-32 NC*	0.140	0.133	0.307	0.385
10-32 NF	0.165	0.159	0.380	0.458
10-24 NC	0.158	0.150	0.380	0.482
12-28 NF	0.188	0.181	0.432	0.519
12-24 NC	0.184	0.176	0.432	0.534
1/4-28 NF	0.222	0.215	0.500	0.587
1/4-20 NC	0.211	0.201	0.500	0.625
5/16-24 NF	0.280	0.272	0.625	0.727
5/16-18 NC	0.269	0.259	0.625	0.762
3/8-24 NF	0.343	0.334	0.750	0.852
3/8-16 NC	0.326	0.314	0.750	0.906
7/16-20 NF	0.398	0.388	0.875	1.000
7/16-14 NC	0.382	0.368	0.875	1.053
1/2-20 NF	0.461	0.451	1.000	1.125
1/2-13 NC	0.440	0.425	1.000	1.192
9/16-18 NF	0.519	0.508	1.125	1.262
9/16-12 NC	0.497	0.481	1.125	1.333
5/8-18 NF	0.582	0.571	1.250	1.387
5/8-11 NC	0.554	0.536	1.250	1.497
3/4-16 NF	0.701	0.689	1.500	1.656
3/4-10 NC	0.672	0.652	1.500	1.750
7/8-14 NF	0.819	0.804	1.750	1.928
7/8-9 NC	0.789	0.767	1.750	2.027
1-14 NF	0.944	0.929	2.000	2.178
1-8 NC	0.903	0.878	2.000	2.312

* Minimum size recommended for aluminum or magnesium alloys.
† These dimensions are subject to ±0.375 inch or smaller diameters and ±0.003 inch tolerances for larger diameters. (*Courtesy*, the American Die Casting Institute Inc.)

required amount of draft and the direction of the draft from the parting line. Where the direction of draft is not critical, the supplier should be allowed to place the draft to facilitate production.

Table III-20. Draft Angles for Walls

Alloy	Depth of Wall	Draft Angle	Draft (inch)
Aluminum	0.010	18°	0.003
	0.020	13°	0.004
	0.030 to 0.050	9°	0.005 to 0.008
	>0.050 to 0.080	8°	0.007 to 0.011
	>0.080 to 0.100	6°	0.008 to 0.010
	>0.100 to 0.300	4°	0.007 to 0.021
	>0.300 to 0.600	3°	0.016 to 0.031
	>0.600 to 1.000	2° 30′	0.026 to 0.043
	>1.000 to 1.300	2°	0.035 to 0.045
	>1.300 to 2.000	1° 30′	0.034 to 0.052
	>2.000 to 3.000	1°	0.035 to 0.052
Copper	0.010	20°	0.004
	0.020	16°	0.006
	0.030 to 0.050	12°	0.006 to 0.010
	>0.050 to 0.080	9°	0.008 to 0.012
	>0.080 to 0.100	7°	0.010 to 0.012
	>0.100 to 0.300	5°	0.009 to 0.026
	>0.300 to 0.600	3°	0.015 to 0.037
	>0.600 to 1.300	2°	0.021 to 0.045
	>1.300 to 2.000	1° 30′	0.034 to 0.052
Magnesium	0.010	15°	0.003
	0.020	11°	0.004
	0.030 to 0.050	7°	0.004 to 0.006
	>0.050 to 0.080	5°	0.004 to 0.007
	>0.080 to 0.100	4°	0.005 to 0.007
	>0.100 to 0.300	2° 30′	0.004 to 0.013
	>0.300 to 0.600	2°	0.010 to 0.021
	>0.600 to 1.300	1° 30′	0.015 to 0.034
	>1.300 to 2.000	1°	0.022 to 0.034
Zinc	0.010	11°	0.002
	0.020	8°	0.003
	0.030 to 0.050	6°	0.003 to 0.005
	>0.050 to 0.080	5°	0.004 to 0.007
	>0.080 to 0.100	4°	0.006 to 0.007
	>0.100 to 0.300	3°	0.005 to 0.015
	>0.300 to 0.600	2°	0.010 to 0.021
	>0.600 to 1.300	1° 30′	0.016 to 0.034
	>1.300 to 2.000	1°	0.023 to 0.035

When dimensioning holes, the minimum hole size should be shown, with the draft added to the hole size. If draft must be within dimensional tolerances of the hole, tolerances should conform to standard draft requirements for holes, as shown in *Table III-17*.

Draft Requirements for Walls

The values shown in *Table III-20* represent normal production practices at the most economical levels. Greater accuracy involving extra close work or care in production should be specified only when and where it is necessary.

All diecasting walls, which normally are vertical to the parting plane of the diecasting die, require draft or taper. This draft is not constant. It will vary with the alloy used and with the depth of the walls, as indicated in *Table III-20*. The draft shown in the table is for draft on inside walls. Draft required on outside walls is one-half that required on inside walls.

Special Case

Occasionally there is a requirement to cast containers with no draft on the outside walls. The design for such an item requires special dimensioning. *Figure 3-24* shows the correct dimensioning practices.

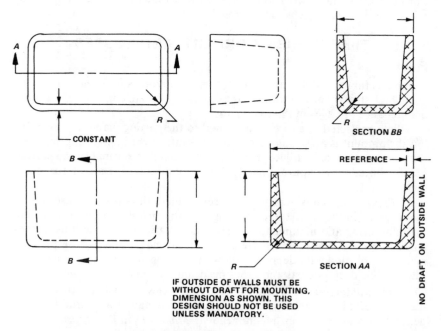

Figure 3-24. Dimensional walls of containers.

WALL SECTIONS

Uniformity of wall thickness is extremely important in the design of any casting to avoid undue shrinkage and warpage variations. Where walls must vary, gradual blending should be used to make satisfactory transitions. A good rule is to make the length of tapered sections greater than four times the difference in wall thickness.

To permit the most rapid cooling and hence the most rapid casting cycle, the lightest wall feasible is generally recommended. Extremely heavy walls usually result in voids and porosity.

In general, the walls of diecastings should fall within the practical range of 0.0625 to 0.3125 in. (1.6 to 7.9 mm). The limits of wall dimensions generally feasible in diecastings of various alloys are shown in *Table III-9*.

Where concentrations of metal such as bosses or heavy ribs are used, the unequal shrinkage compared with that of adjacent thin walls results in some shrinkage on the wall surface. The shrink marks may be undesirable, and in cases where the metal volume cannot be reduced, the shrinkage can often be masked by low ribbing or low-relief designs.

Large, plain, flat surfaces should be avoided wherever a perfect, unblemished area is desired. To eliminate the cost of rejects from natural imperfections in such surfaces, it is recommended that they be crowned, curved, or broken up by beads, steps, or low relief.

FILLETS, RIBS, CORNERS, AND BOSSES

Fillets

Intersecting metal surfaces which form junctions should have fillets to avoid high stress concentrations in the diecasting, and to control and facilitate maintenance of edges in the casting die.

Fillets projected in a direction normal to the parting plane require draft, but the amount is always governed by the draft of the intersecting surfaces. Draft in corners, or in fillets projecting in a direction normal to the parting plane, should have approximately 1.5 the amount of draft of the intersecting walls.

In *Figure 3-25*, consideration has been given to the stresses of use, and to the stresses induced in the diecastings by the process, as well as to die manufacturing and maintenance costs. The notations with the illustrations cover fillets on corners which are projected normal to the parting plane in diecasting of moderate depth. Shallow diecastings may have much smaller fillets, while deep pockets and other inside corners may have larger fillets.

Fillets will facilitate the flow of metal in the dies and will lengthen the die life considerably. To avoid overlarge fillets which may create shrink-voids, a general formula has been recommended: *Make the radius approximately equal to one-third the sum of two adjacent wall thicknesses. With magnesium diecastings, however, an exception exists and generally, fillet radii should be equal to the sections joined.*

Ribs

Ribs are used to increase the stiffness of, or add strength to, a diecasting. Further, they assist in making sound diecastings. Ribs are sometimes misused and can be a detriment if working stresses are concentrated by their use, or if stresses at the edges of the ribs are high. See *Figure 3-26* for recommended applications of ribs to a diecasting.

Corners

Sharply squared corners projecting in a direction normal to the parting plane may cause chipped edges when withdrawing the diecasting from the die.

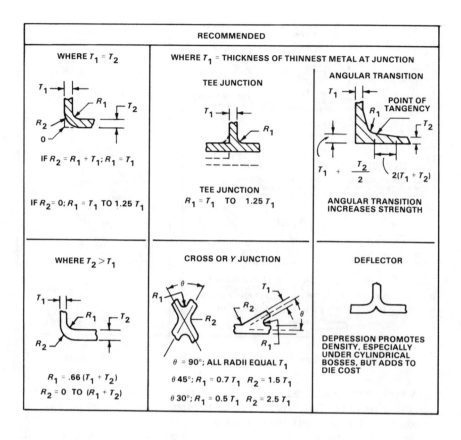

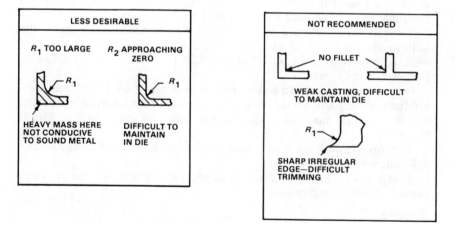

Figure 3-25. Fillets. (*Courtesy*, the American Die Casting Institute)

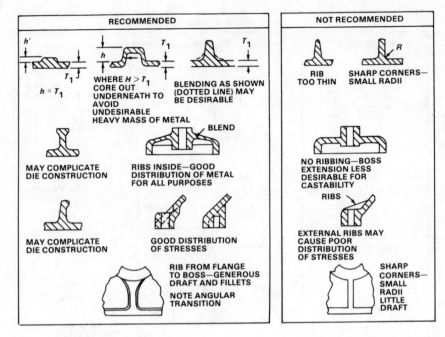

Figure 3-26. Ribs. (*Courtesy,* the American Die Casting Institute)

However, sharply squared corners may be used in locations where die construction permits. This type of corner is often mandatory at parting line locations and at die block intersections.

Normally, corners of diecastings should have radii to prevent early die failure, to reduce the probability of nicking the edge of the diecasting in handling, and to minimize material handling for personnel.

Wherever possible, outside corner radii of parts should match inside fillet radii to maintain uniformity of sections. If sharp outside corners must be used, a minimum radius of 0.015 in. (0.38 mm) should be specified for purposes of economy.

Because it is difficult to sink a sharp corner into a die (other than those produced at the parting line), it is recommended that such corners be rounded to 0.0625 in. (1.6 mm) radius and that the radius never be less than 0.03 in. (0.8 mm).

The top edges of ribs and webs should be generous, and a full radius is desirable wherever possible.

Sharp inside corners in diecastings (outside corners in dies) are detrimental. Fillets should be used.

Bosses

Since the lightest possible walls are desirable in diecasting design, it is usually necessary to provide bosses or hubs at points in the part where

86

fasteners are to be used or where mating parts are to be positioned. Minimum practical wall sections should be used, and reinforcing ribs can be employed together with the bosses where additional strength and rigidity are desired.

Wherever possible, all bosses should be on the same side of the casting to aid adherence to one die-half for ejection.

Where bosses must be inclined at an angle to the parting line or major surface of the part, design should be such that it allows forming by the solid die. If this procedure creates a boss with a large base, the major portion should be cored to maintain a uniform wall throughout. (See *Figure 3-27.*)

Ejector Pins

Metal cooling in the die tends to exert considerable shrink-force against parts of the die which resist the shrinkage. Location and magnitude of this shrinkage stress in the diecasting determines the quantity, location, and size of ejector pins. The diecasting design must consider the location of these pins, and the effect of the resulting ejector marks on the appearance and function of the diecasting. Normally, ejector pin locations are left to the discretion of the diecasting supplier, but are subject to design requirements.

Marks on diecastings resulting from ejector pins should be allowed to vary from the adjoining surface by some reasonable amount. It is best to specify that the marks be either raised or depressed, depending on the results desired, by some maximum limit, and by further specifying the adjoining surface as the origin. For example: *Ejector pin marks shall be 0.000 to 0.030 (0 to 0.8 mm) below the surface.* These ejector pin marks are surrounded by a flash of metal which need not be removed if it will not interfere with the end use of the diecasting. Where it does interfere, the supplier will normally crush or flatten the flash.

Note: Complete removal of ejector pin marks and flash by machining or hand-scraping operations should be specified only when requirements justify the expense involved in the extra operation or operations which will be necessary.

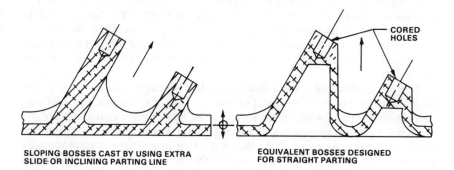

SLOPING BOSSES CAST BY USING EXTRA
SLIDE·OR INCLINING PARTING LINE

EQUIVALENT BOSSES DESIGNED
FOR STRAIGHT PARTING

Figure 3-27. Design modification for bosses at an angle to parting line.

Machining

Design the diecasting so that a minimum of machining will be required. Allow sufficient metal to clean up properly where machining is specified, but not so much as to require cuts of unnecessary depth.

Surface Quality

The smoothness of the surface on a diecasting depends greatly upon the type of metal cast and especially on its melting temperature.

When aluminum and magnesium alloys are used, surface roughnesses in commercial runs of castings range from 125 to approximately 250 μin. (3.2 to 6.0 μm). Smoother surfaces can be achieved by additional operations such as vapor honing—but at additional cost.

INVESTMENT CASTING

Investment casting has become an established foundry method complementary to, and competing with, machinings as well as other foundry processes. Investment castings generally are more expensive to cast than other castings, but as an end product they can be more economical, since little if any machining will be required.

One of the reasons for the high cost of investment castings is that the designer often has a tendency to use tight tolerances on all dimensions. When analyzing the design for economical use, the designer might find that some tolerances can be increased which could reduce the overall cost of the casting. Also, recent improvements in technology have lowered costs, and have markedly improved product quality, making investment castings practical for many applications formerly beyond their scope.

When the acceptance of complex shapes, the tooling costs, the economical tolerances, and the wide choice of metals that can be cast are taken into consideration, investment castings sometimes can be more economical than any other method for fabricating a part.

Experienced users of investment castings take maximum advantage of the process by specifying practical dimensional tolerances (economical as well as functional).

Used properly, investment castings offer new freedom of design and new areas of economy. The time to decide when a part is suitable for investment casting or any other casting method is when the part is still on the drawing board. While it is easy to modify the design of a machine part for investment casting, it is even easier to design the part to be investment cast from the ground up.

Generally speaking, the designer can follow the same basic design rules for an investment casting that would be followed for any other casting method. The designer must know when to specify the investment casting method.

Deciding to use an investment casting is easy when a part is so complex or the alloy so difficult to machine that any other process is not economically feasible. An investment casting should also be considered when it proves more economical than making the same part by stamping, forging, diecasting, or any other low-cost, mass-production method.

It is more economical to investment cast a part when the machining operations can be reduced or eliminated, or when internal contours or configurations are impossible to machine. This generally holds true, unless the part is made from various pieces and assembled by soldering, brazing, or welding, or when the quantity is small and the design is likely to change.

Processes

Investment casting utilizes ceramic molds. These molds are formed by pouring a slurry of refractory material around the pattern, held firmly in a flask (*Figure 3-28a*). After preliminary drying, the mold is placed in an oven. The wax or plastic pattern melts, leaving the mold cavity empty (*Figure 3-28b*).

The pattern for this investment molding process was melted out of the mold. Hence it is an expendable (last wax process) pattern. The expendable pattern is formed by injecting wax or plastic into a metal die. See *Figure 3-28c*.

A separate pattern is made for each investment casting required. A single sprue and runner can be attached to feed several patterns. Such an assembly is

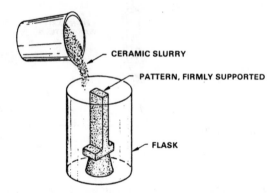

Figure 3-28a. Pouring ceramic mold. (*Courtesy*, Xerox Corporation)

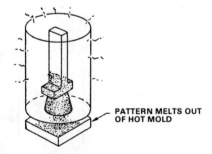

Figure 3-28b. Heating mold to remove pattern (lost wax process). (*Courtesy*, Xerox Corporation)

89

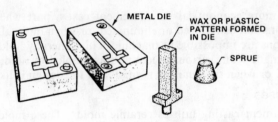

Figure 3-28c. Patterns produced in metal die. (*Courtesy*, Xerox Corporation)

called a tree of patterns (*Figure 3-28d*). The investment mold is then fired at high temperatures; while it is still hot, molten metal is poured into the mold and then it freezes (*Figure 3-28e*).

The mold is then broken away from the casting during shakeout, and the sprue is removed to complete the casting process. See *Figures 3-28f* and *3-28g*.

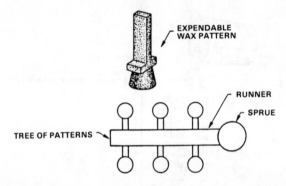

Figure 3-28d. Wax or plastic pattern. (*Courtesy*, Xerox Corporation)

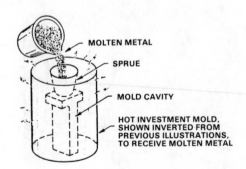

Figure 3-28e. Pouring molten metal. (*Courtesy*, Xerox Corporation)

90

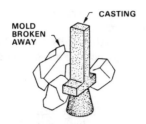 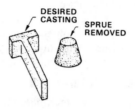

Figure 3-28f. Ceramic mold is broken away. (*Courtesy*, Xerox Corporation)

Figure 3-28g. Ceramic mold is broken away. (*Courtesy*, Xerox Corporation)

Advantages and Limitations

The advantages of investment castings are:
- Parts that are produced by expensive machining or by other casting processes can be economically cast.
- Low volume; good for experimental or short run production.
- Very little porosity, good strength.
- Draft requirement is less than with other processes.
- Intricate shapes can be molded.

The limitations are that initial production tooling cost is high and the maximum size is usually less than 10 lb (4.5 kg).

Basic Design Rules

In designing for an investment casting, the following basic design rules must be observed:
- Never hesitate to choose the best metal or alloy for the job. The amount of money saved by using lower grade metal is minimal. Complete freedom in alloy selection is one of the greatest advantages in using an investment casting.
- Surface finishes should be no better than the process can produce; 125 μin. (3.2 μm) rms for ferrous castings, and 63 to 100 μin. (1.6 to 2.5 μm) rms for nonferrous castings.
- If surfaces and tolerances are critical, allow enough extra metal to let the cutting tool get below the somewhat abrasive casting surface. Allow 0.010 in. (0.25 mm) for the grinding operation, or 0.030 in. (0.8 mm) for machining if warpage or out-of-roundness is not involved.
- Knurling designs should be simplified for tooling economy.
- Curved and blended contours allow better design than straight lines and abrupt angles, and usually involve less cost. Nevertheless, if the part function requires the latter type of design, the part can be investment cast, but usually at a higher cost.
- The depth of blind holes should be limited to about two times the diameter. The length of through holes should not exceed six times the diameter.

- Particular care should be given to the design and use of cores. Simplified internal core design can save expensive tooling.
- Avoid heavy sections and uneven thicknesses on thin walls. For certain dimensions, tapered cylinder walls are advantageous in an investment casting design.

Design Tolerances

It must be remembered that in designing for investment castings, as well as for other methods, the *design must be for the process*. For dimensions that are not critical, generous casting tolerances will result in the lowest possible production costs. *Figure 3-29* indicates that relative costs increase as tolerances decrease. Recommended design tolerances are given in *Table III-21* and, if used in combination, they can result in a more economical part.

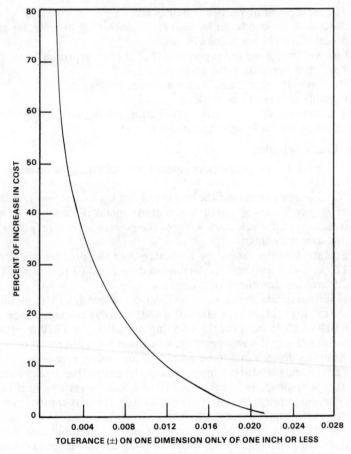

Figure 3-29. Investment casting cost vs. tolerances.

Table III-21. Length and Width Tolerances for Investment Casting

Length or Width (inch)	Maximum Tolerance (per inch)	Economical Tolerance (per inch)
5/8 or less	± 0.003	± 0.010
1	± 0.005	± 0.010
2	± 0.010	± 0.020
3	± 0.015	± 0.030
4 or over	± 0.020	± 0.040

Straightness Tolerances. When parts are long and thin, the finish castings have to be mechanically straightened. *Table III-22* lists both the as-cast and straightened tolerances full-indicator readings (FIR) for various lengths.

Flatness Tolerances. Mechanical straightening is required to eliminate bow, twist, and waviness in typical flat sections. While the tolerances given in *Table III-23* are for rectangular castings, they can be applied to any flat piece regardless of its irregular shape.

Parallel Tolerances. Parallel tolerances should be applied to the as-cast conditions. However, if closer tolerances are needed, they can be achieved by straightening, though at a higher cost. *Table III-24* gives tolerances between sections.

Radii Tolerances. Radius tolerance is generally held at ±0.015 in. (±0.4 mm), although, if necessary this can be reduced to ±0.005 in. (±0.13 mm), but at a higher cost. For best results and lowest cost, allow as generous a radius as possible, and avoid sharp corners. Minimum economical section thicknesses of various casting processes as shown in *Table III-25* should be used in designing for castings. Thinner sections increase cost due to higher rejection rates.

Table III-22. Investment Casting Straightness Tolerances

Length (inch)	FIR As-cast (inch)	FIR Straightened (inch)
2 or less	0.010	0.005
2 to 4	0.015	0.010
4 to 6	0.020	0.010
over 6	0.030	0.015

Table III-23. Investment Casting Flatness Tolerances

Length (inch)	FIR As-cast (inch)	FIR Straightened (inch)
1	± 0.008	± 0.004
2	± 0.016	± 0.006
3	± 0.020	± 0.008
4	± 0.025	± 0.010
6	± 0.030	± 0.015

93

Table III-24. Investment Casting Parallel Tolerances

Distance Between Sections (inch)	FIR As-cast	FIR As-straightened
1/16	± 0.003	± 0.003
1/8	± 0.003	± 0.003
1/4	± 0.003	± 0.003
1/2	± 0.005	± 0.004
3/4	± 0.006	± 0.004
1	± 0.007	±0.005
1-1/2	± 0.010	±0.007

Table III-25. Minimum Economical Section Thickness (Inches)

Sand Casting		Investment Casting	
Aluminum Alloy	Thickness	Aluminum Alloy	Thickness
Area up to 4 in.^{2}	0.125	Area up to 4 in.^{2}	0.050
Area up to 10 in.^{2}	0.150	Area up to 10 in.^{2}	0.060
Area up to 20 in.^{2}	0.188	Area up to 20 in.^{2}	0.070
Area over 20 in.^{2}	0.250	Area over 20 in.^{2}	0.100
Steel and Magnesium		*Stainless Steel*	
Area up to 4 in.^{2}	0.156	Area up to 4 in.^{2}	0.060
Area up to 10 in.^{2}	0.188	Area up to 10 in.^{2}	0.080
Area up to 20 in.^{2}	0.250	Area up to 20 in.^{2}	0.100
Area over 20 in.^{2}	0.312	Area over 20 in.^{2}	0.120
Permanent Mold Casting		*Die Casting*	
Aluminum Alloy		*Aluminum Alloy*	
Area up to 4 in.^{2}	0.094	Area up to 4 in.^{2}	0.040
Area up to 10 in.^{2}	0.125	Area up to 10 in.^{2}	0.060
Area up to 20 in.^{2}	0.156	Area up to 20 in.^{2}	0.080
Area over 20 in.^{2}	0.188	Area over 20 in.^{2}	0.100

In designing for a casting as for any manufacturing process, tolerances play a vital role in economical production. If the tolerances are less than those indicated for the process, there will be higher rejection rates and an increased cost of the product. *Figure 3-30* shows the percent increase in casting cost.

RECOMMENDATIONS FOR PROCUREMENT OF ECONOMICAL CASTINGS DESIGNED FOR A PROCESS

For competitive, budgetary, and scheduling purposes, castings must be designed for a specific process. This can be affected by a reference to dimensional and geometric parameters that are state-of-the-art. The potential basis for this design and procurement section is derived from General Dynamics' Engineering Research Report GDC-EER-1388.

Casting vendors—even the best—are inclined to be highly optimistic about

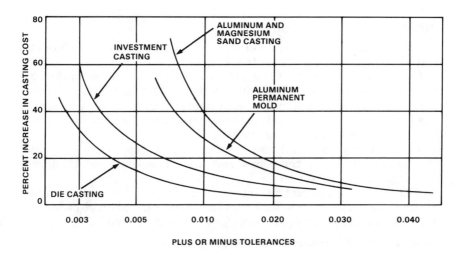

Figure 3-30. Increased cost due to rejection rates.

their capability and schedules for achieving the necessary precision. This is apparently the result of their sensing schedule demands that experience has shown will result in selling deviations and will thereby achieve the necessary prolonged development.

It is more practical (less overall cost and faster procurement) to obtain castings that require some minimal machining, than to require castings with tight tolerances on every dimension.

Engineering changes should only be made when an analysis shows that the design cannot be cast economically. A system of communication should be implemented so that there will be no confusion by the vendor.

The acceptance of out-of-tolerance castings should involve consultation with the manufacturing engineer and design engineer. The out-of-tolerance casting has to be analyzed to determine that it will not cause difficulty in machining with the standard tooling. If approved, the time standard and shop schedule should be adjusted accordingly for an accurate production schedule and equitable time standards.

The casting industry is continuing its recent rapid improvement in precision and metallurgical aspects of castings. New and super-strength aluminum alloys such as high quality titanium castings as large as 75 lb are being cast. However, the manufacturing engineer must analyze the additional cost of the new alloys, the high precision, and other advantages that might be offered by the foundries. If the analysis shows the production quantity does not warrant the additional cost, then the design engineer should redesign the casting to allow additional machining and simplicity of the part.

Adequate metallurgical consultation in the procurement of complex, high-strength precision castings could avoid unnecessary schedule delays and extra cost.

Predesign Considerations

If it is decided that a casting is the most economical way to produce the part, the designer should ask the following questions:

- Is the design such that in the case of a sand casting, the pattern can be adapted for economical molding by standard methods?
- Can gates, risers, and chills be positioned properly to ensure soundness?
- Could the section size and configuration cause undue stress in the mold and consequent tearing or cracking?
- Can directional solidification be established and controlled, or should the part be cast in component parts and the separate castings joined together by mechanical means?

If not, then, the inherent advantages of the casting process are not fully realized. The proper engineering balance can be determined only by knowing and applying minimum requirements for good foundry practice.

Designing for Minimum Casting Stresses

External cracking or tearing in the mold may be caused by influences external to the casting or by inherent characteristics. The only external influence of importance in sand, permanent, die, and investment castings is the effect of the mold or die which may restrain normal contraction and cause cracks, tears, or warpage. Stresses can be reduced by proper mold or die design or by part design reconsiderations.

If the casting is large and complex in shape, it may prove desirable to cast two or more sections and weld the parts together. Small tie bars are sometimes used to prevent tearing in critical areas and in straight members. Tie bars also are used to prevent warpage before or during heat treatment.

Stresses arising from inherent conditions are those due strictly to design or those peculiar to the composition of the metal. Thin sections of castings cool and contract much faster than thick members. If such members cool and shrink, they are restrained by larger, slower cooling sections. The small members may either tear to relieve stresses or deform plastically without tearing; if they do not tear, warpage occurs when the larger members contract away from the extended smaller parts.

Tearing may even develop in straight bars which are unrestrained at the ends. As the section cools and contracts, enough resistance may be developed from friction between mold and metal to rupture the casting. If the bar is uniform in cross-section, no particular region of weakness will develop and the bar will not tear because solidification and contraction occur uniformly across the section. However, if another member is joined to the straight bar, a hot spot is formed and the solidification pattern is conducive to hot tearing.

Metal composition influences tearing tendencies in at least three ways by:

- the inherent strength and ductility at critical temperatures.
- the existence and extent of solid transformations; most metals have their atoms in a close-packed arrangement in the solid; their molar volumes increase by several percent on melting.
- the presence of impurities at grain boundaries.

96

Unnecessary bulk and weight were outlawed from every part used by the aircraft and missile industry long ago, since it is well known that strength does not increase proportionally with mass. The demand for light weight with maximum performance and strength has spread throughout the commercial industries.

More exacting requirements from customers and keen competition from many other fabrication processes and materials should serve as a warning to designers and producers of aluminum castings that excessive bulk and weight will increase the cost of their products. Designers must achieve strength by configuration of the part rather than by mass.

In addition, the foundryman must control the process to produce castings having mechanical properties and quality expected by the designer to meet the strength requirements. Casting processes have reached an advanced state of development. It is no longer difficult to achieve high quality in a well-designed casting produced in a well-equipped and properly managed foundry.

Calculating Service Stresses

Many casting designers recommend using analytical stress analysis to make certain that castings will have adequate strength. It should be noted, however, that mathematical stress analyses of complex designs are not too reliable. Stress calculations derived from this method usually will accurately predict the performance of an uncomplicated casting in service. If the stress analysis of a well-designed casting has been accurately made but the casting fails in structural test, the fault may lie in production; process techniques or control were not good enough to achieve the level of quality which the designer can realistically expect with his or her calculations and, therefore, use as the basis for the design.

Unfortunately, structural failures are often corrected by beefing up the part, a practice which adds unnecessary weight to the casting. Designers who use analytical techniques often can demonstrate that heavy parts are not always necessary to carry heavy loads; proper location and sizing of ribs and gussets usually provide the extra strength required.

For determining stresses in more complex shapes, experimental methods rather than theoretical mathematical analyses are frequently used. The brittle lacquer photoelastic and strain gage techniques are some of the methods used.

Designing for Directional Solidification

It has been established that temperature gradients in solidifying castings must be favorably controlled if sound economical castings are to be made. The design engineer is largely responsible for the relative ease or difficulty in what can be done by the foundryman; design can be such that adequate directional progressive solidification cannot be attained. In that case, rejection rates are high and the cost of the casting is higher than estimated, schedules fall behind—adding to extra inspection time. It is therefore essential that the casting be redesigned.

The main design considerations which influence directional solidification are:

Heavy Sections Cannot be Fed Through Light Sections. Various members or component parts of castings are joined in various ways (*Figure 3-31*). The *T* section is selected to represent the series. By inscribing circles as in *Figure 3-32*, it is easy to determine that the region depicted by circle *D* is a larger mass of metal than those of circles *A*, *B*, or *C*. This means that under normal conditions of cooling, metal at the center of the *D* region is a hot spot, the last to solidify. When it is not convenient, economical, or even possible to place a riser at this point, it is necessary to rely on chilling, coring, or reducing the section.

The designer should attempt to limit junctions to as few as possible and to select the least difficult. The *L* joint in *Figure 3-31*, for example, is less troublesome and easier to treat than the *Y* or *V* sections; the *L* section is easier to correct by design alone than any others. Sometimes it is impossible to limit the number of junctions except by casting in segments and joining these together later by welding or with fasteners.

If Possible, Sections Should Taper Toward Risers. The importance of this principle has been established. Some compromise must often be made with ideal conditions to meet weight and cost requirements. Within reason, the castings' soundness obtained by natural solidification is proportional to the degree of tapering allowed. *Figure 3-33* illustrates the design of a valve casting. One half is drawn to illustrate the usual situation in which no attempt has been made to enhance feeding by natural methods; the other half is correctly designed.

Figure 3-31. Basic forms of casting junctions.
(*Courtesy*, General Dynamics)

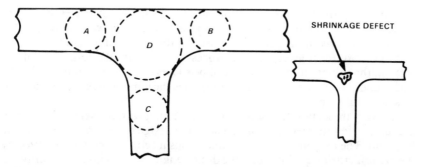

Figure 3-32. Location of a hot spot in a casting junction can be determined by inscribing circles. (*Courtesy*, General Dynamics)

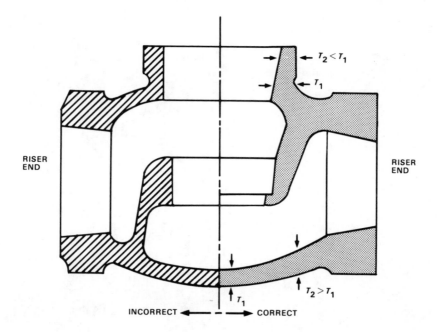

Figure 3-33. A casting designed for controlled directional solidification. Note tapering of section in the correct design (T = thickness). (*Courtesy*, General Dynamics)

Design for Metal Flow

Minimum section thicknesses for castings are principally a function of metal composition. Recommended minimum section thickness for the various casting processes and alloys are shown in *Table III-25*. Unnecessarily heavy sections increase the problem of feeding. Excessively thin walls increase foundry scrap from misruns and cold shuts. This in turn increases the cost of the casting. The minimum section thickness which can be cast economically, as shown in *Table III-25*, should be used in the design of a casting.

In general, for a given casting process, the smaller the total area of the section, the thinner it may be and still be successfully cast. Additionally, the gating and risering system largely determines the minimum section which can be successfully poured.

It is very important that a production meeting with the selected foundry, manufacturing engineering, purchasing, and design engineering departments be set up. The recommendations made at this meeting should be analyzed by the manufacturing engineer and the design engineer, with no casting drawing released to the foundry until the accepted changes are incorporated for economical and practical castings.

4

Forgings

This chapter defines forgings, and discusses forging types, materials, design, and production economy.

DEFINITIONS

Forging is a forming process that involves plastic flow of a metal under pressure at some predetermined temperature range. At elevated temperature, the process is known as *hot forging*; at room temperature, it is known as *cold forging*.

TYPES OF FORGING PRACTICES

General Considerations

Some of the advantages and disadvantages of forgings are listed below.
Advantages:
- High ultimate strength
- Controlled grain flow
- Uniform density of grain structure
- Low machining cost
- Wide range of shapes, sizes, and materials.

Disadvantages:
- High die cost when only a small quantity is desired
- Difficulties in meeting requirements such as draft, radii, and thickness, on unmachined surfaces.

Hot Forging

This process involves the forming of a metal at a predetermined elevated temperature which renders the metal into a workable plastic state.

The shaping of a hot forging is caused by impact (striking) or pressing (squeezing) forces. When hot metal is forged, displacement usually occurs at temperatures above those required for recrystallization, thus forming the part with less internal stress.

There are several methods of hot forgings in use, namely: Smith (flat die) forging, drop (impact) forging, press forging, and machine (upset) forging.

Smith Forging. Smith, or flat die, forging is done with flat dies and simple hand tools, using either press or impact pressure to form the metal while in a plastic state. This is usually done with steam hammers, but small forgings are sometimes produced with motor-driven helve hammers or pneumatic hammers.

This type of forging is used principally when the quantity desired is too small to justify the expense of impression dies, and when it is more economical to machine the part from a rough forging than from bar stock.

Drop Forging. Drop, or impact, forgings are formed by impact pressure from either gravity drop hammers or direct-powered drop hammers.

The parts are formed from pressure between impression dies, one of which is on the hammer face and the other on the anvil. The pressure is applied intermittently and the plastic metal is gradually formed into shape.

This is the most common of the forging processes. It is a high-production process adaptable to all materials except high-strength magnesium alloys. The equipment cost is low, but the die maintenance required is high. Parts produced by this method have wide tolerances.

Press Forging. Press forging is similar to drop forging, with the main distinction being that press forging employs squeezing pressure rather than impact pressure. The process is usually done on mechanical or hydraulic presses with impression dies which contain mechanical ejectors to knock the work out of the die after the stroke is completed. (This is also called closed die forging.)

Press forgings can produce a part by a single blow rather than by repeated blows as in drop forging. Although this process is adaptable to all materials, it is most commonly used in producing aluminum or magnesium parts.

The parts produced by press forging can have close tolerances as well as thin webs, and low or no-draft angles as in no-draft forgings.

Machine Forging. Machine, or upset, forging is limited to producing symmetrical parts, but of any variety of size and material. Upsetting increases the cross-sectional area of the part by squeezing the metal between the dies and striking it with a heading tool. Machine forging is done on a horizontal, double-acting press known as an *upsetter*. This produces the part with no flash, and thus eliminates machining.

Machine forging is particularly adaptable to mass production of identical parts. It can handle all materials and is probably the best forging operation for high production rates.

APPLICATION AND LIMITATIONS

The design engineer should know the limitations as well as the advantages of forging, to fully realize the benefits of this form of metalworking.

There are many instances when forgings are impractical. These cases include when materials to be used are not adaptable to effective forging; when part design is incompatible with forging; and when it might be more economical or more efficient to do it another way.

Generally speaking, there are three areas to consider before producing a part by forging or any other way: materials; part size and shape; production factors.

METALLURGICAL ADVANTAGES OF FORGINGS

According to the Forging Industry Association, listed below are several metallurgical advantages of forgings.

- Forgings have proved to have a high degree of statistical reliability in service. The forging method may not always be the most economical method for producing a required geometry, therefore an analysis should be made by the design engineer and/or the manufacturing engineer as to the most economical production method. This may be machining from raw stock or machining from a suitable casting for the product, but the history of material forming has demonstrated that a forging has the highest level of reliability and combination of mechanical properties.
- The combination of controlled deformation and proper heat treatment allows the precise engineering of mechanical properties for a particular service situation.
- Defects in a forging are at a minimum. Internal flaws are rare. In reality, forgings constitute an inspection process, contributing to its reliability. The workpiece is heated, squeezed, bent, and stretched. Internal defects are sealed up and healed.
- The geometric shape is preserved in a metal die, insuring increased uniformity, both dimensionally and structurally. The latter in turn gives more uniform response to heat treatment.
- Forgings provide superior fracture toughness or resistance to unstable propagation of a flaw.

MATERIALS

There are distinctive characteristics in each group of ferrous and nonferrous metals. Different metals respond differently to forging.

The amount of deformation a metal can be subjected to without exhibiting adverse effects must be considered in the selection of forging methods, the selection of forging equipment, and the die design.

Costs are affected by the kind of material selected and by the type of forging to be used with that material. The following materials are ranked in order of increasing forging difficulty:

1. Aluminum alloys
2. Magnesium forging alloys
3. Copper alloys
4. Carbon and alloy steels
5. Martensitic and ferritic stainless steels
6. Maraging steels
7. Austenitic stainless steel
8. Nickel alloys
9. Semiaustenitic pH stainless steels

10. Titanium alloys
11. Iron-based superalloys
12. Cobalt-based superalloys
13. Columbium alloys
14. Tantalum alloys
15. Molybdenum alloys
16. Nickel-based superalloys
17. Tungsten alloys
18. Beryllium.

Table IV-1 describes the typical applications of the materials listed, courtesy of the Forging Industry Association.

Table IV-1. Typical Applications

ALUMINUM AND ALUMINUM ALLOYS

Aluminum Association Designation

1100	Heat exchangers, pressure and storage tanks, chemical equipment
2024	Heavy-duty forgings, aircraft fittings, structural members, wheels
2018	Jet engine impellers and compressor rings
2218	Aircraft engine cylinder heads and pistons
2618	Aircraft engine parts
5456	Aircraft landing gear parts, marine superstructures, overhead cranes, pressure vessels
6061	Truck wheels, hardware, flanges and fittings, high-strength and corrosion-resistant applications
7075	Aircraft structural components

MAGNESIUM FORGING ALLOYS

ASTM Number

AZ31B, AZ31C	Aircraft and missile parts, ordnance vehicles,
AZ80A	Auto and truck parts, electronic equipment, materials handling equipment, wheels
ZK60A	High strength, heat treatable, widely used as forging alloy

COPPER ALLOYS

CDA Number

162 Cadmium Copper	Pole line hardware, electrical conductors
172 Beryllium Copper	High strength components, marine parts, bearings, cams, electrical contacts, valves, fasteners, gears
268 270 Yellow Brass	Fasteners, plumbing accessories

Table IV-1. Typical Applications (*Continued*)

CARBON AND ALLOY STEELS

AISI Number

1006 to 1015	These grades are low-carbon steels used for relatively low-strength applications, and also where cold formability is a primary requirement. AISI 1015 is a popular carburizing steel.
1010 to 1015	These grades are used in the automotive industry and for farm implements.
1016 to 1030	These grades are medium low-carbon steels with modest strength and are commonly known as carburizing or case-hardening grades.
1033 to 1052	These grades are medium carbon steels used for applications requiring higher mechanical properties, and are often further hardened or strengthened by heat treatment or by cold work.
1055 to 1095	These grades are high carbon steels used for applications requiring high strength and hardness, and are usually heat treated after forging.
1117 to 1119	These grades are used for applications where good machining is needed.
1132 to 1151	These grades have characteristics similar to carbon steels of the same carbon levels, but provide better machinability and good response to heat treatment.

AISI Grade

1340	Auto and farm implements: axle shafts, output shafts, transmission gears, and bolts.
4063	Leaf and coil springs; hand tools.
4130 to 4150	Auto connecting rods, gears and shafts, bearings and bearing races.
4320 to 4340	Heavy-duty high strength parts: gears, bearing races, aircraft parts, shafts, heavy forgings.
4620	Auto shafts, gears, and bearings.
4815 to 4820	Heavy-duty gears, rock bits, pump parts tools, and special bearings.

All other hardening grades from 5140 to 9255 are used for heavy-duty forgings for the automotive and aircraft industries.

MARTENSITIC AND FERRITIC STAINLESS STEELS

These steels are the AISI 400 series grades, and are mainly used for forgings such as turbine wheels and blades, and highly stressed temperature-resistant parts, such as steam and gas turbine buckets.

Other applications are for parts that require good corrosion resistance, such as parts for food and chemical processing equipment.

Table IV-1. Typical Applications (*Continued*)

MARAGING STEELS

Grade

200	These steels are used for parts requiring high strength-
250	to-weight ratio and toughness such as: missile motor
18 Ni 7 Co Mo	cases, aircraft structural and landing gear parts.
300	
18 Ni 9 Co Mo	

AUSTENITIC STAINLESS STEELS

The 200 and 300 AISI types of austenitic stainless steels are used for parts subject to severe corrosion service, high temperature applications, and parts used for cryogenic applications and chemical equipment.

These are but a few of the materials that are recommended for forging applications. However, if the analysis shows that a forging is the economical production method for the product, the design engineer and the manufacturing engineer must select the proper material for the design requirements. If the part is not a structural part, then one of the economical low or medium carbon steels should be used for better forging and machining abilities.

When the aluminum alloys are suitable, then the suitable alloy for the design should be used. For structural requirements or wear-resistant requirements, an alloy steel should be used. If high temperatures and corrosion resistance are functional requirements, then a stainless or nickel-based superalloy should be used.

PART SIZE AND SHAPE (DESIGN CONSIDERATIONS)

All of the materials shown in the preceding list are applicable for forging. However, in designing for forging from titanium, the designer must remember that titanium is an extremely active element that readily combines with other elements when heated to the forging range. A hard oxide coating forms on the surface during forging. Since this coating must be removed either by cleaning or machining, it is presently impossible to design for precision forgings in titanium.

Draft Angles

Draft angle is the most important shape problem to be considered in designing a part to be forged. *Tables IV-2* and *IV-3* list some of the recommended draft angles to use. Since the actual draft angle is basically a function of the location of the die parting line, it is recommended that draft angles be used for producibility and sound economical design.

The column headings over *Table IV-2* lists three types of forgings: precision, conventional, and blocker. A *precision* forging denotes closer than

Table IV-2. Recommended Draft Angles for Closed Die Forgings

Material Forged	Precision (deg)	Conventional (deg)	Blocker (deg)
Aluminum	0—1	3—5	5—10
Magnesium	0—1	3—5	5—10
Steel	—	7—10	10—15
Titanium	—	7—10	10—15

(*Courtesy*, John I. Thompson & Company)

Table IV-3. Conversion Chart for Draft Dimensions *(X)* for Standard Draft Angles (Θ)

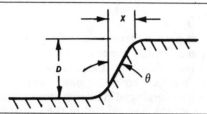

Depth of Draft D (inch)	Draft Angle (θ)				
	1 (deg)	3 (deg)	5 (deg)	7 (deg)	10 (deg)
0.0312	0.0005	0.0016	0.0027	0.0038	0.0055
0.0625	0.0011	0.0033	0.0055	0.0077	0.0110
0.0937	0.0016	0.0049	0.0080	0.0015	0.0165
0.1250	0.0022	0.0066	0.0109	0.0150	0.0220
0.1875	0.0033	0.0098	0.0160	0.0230	0.0330
0.2500	0.0044	0.0130	0.0220	0.0310	0.0440
0.3125	0.0055	0.0160	0.0270	0.0380	0.0550
0.3750	0.0065	0.0200	0.0330	0.0460	0.0660
0.4375	0.0075	0.0230	0.0380	0.0540	0.0770
0.5000	0.0087	0.0260	0.0440	0.0610	0.0880
0.6250	0.0110	0.0330	0.0550	0.0770	0.1100
0.7500	0.0130	0.0390	0.0660	0.0920	0.1320
0.8750	0.0150	0.0460	0.0770	0.1070	0.1540
1.0000	0.0170	0.0520	0.0870	0.1230	0.1760

normal tolerances. It may also involve a more intricate forging design than a conventional type, and may include smaller fillet radii, smaller corner radii, smaller draft angles, and thinner webs and ribs.

The higher cost of a precision forging, including increased cost of dies, must be justified in the reduced machining required for its end use.

The *conventional* forging is the most common of all die forging types. A conventional forging normally requires only partial final machining, with the blocking operation required prior to finishing operations. It is more intricate in configuration than a blocker type forging, having proportionately lighter sections, sharper details, and closer tolerances. It is therefore more difficult to forge.

A *blocker type* forging is an end product and should not be confused with a blocker forging which is a preliminary shape requiring a subsequent finishing die operation to attain its final shape. This particular forging has large fillet and corner radii and thick webs and ribs, so that it can be produced only in a set of finishing dies. It generally requires machining on all surfaces.

Economics may dictate a blocker type design if quantity requirements are limited or if the finish part tolerances necessitate complete machining.

The designer must evaluate cost differences between conventional and blocker type forgings. A conventional forging has a higher die cost but will be lighter than the blocker type and will also require much less machining. Only a cost comparison by the designer can determine which type of forging will give the lower total cost.

No-draft Forging

No-draft forgings permit zero draft angle, thin webs and flanges, and improved accuracy and finishes. Since no draft, and in some cases minimum draft, is used in this type of forging, it is possible to make this forging from a machine drawing rather than from a forging drawing.

In addition, no-draft forgings differ from precision or conventional types of forgings in the draftless feature, and in the relatively high vertical wall height-to-width ratio which requires specialized diemaking and forging facilities.

No-draft forging requires the least amount of machining of any forging type, a fact that may offset generally higher forging and die costs. However, a no-draft forging can be difficult to make due to especially close design proportions and tolerances.

Since the no-draft process is subject to tolerances, those shown in *Table IV-4* should be considered good commercial practice.

Any of these tolerances can be held more closely by expensive and elaborate tooling, but this should not be considered unless production quantities are high and there is assurance that highly dependable tooling can be built.

Fillet radii from web to flanges, ribs, and bosses, should be as large as possible, with minimum radii not under 0.125 in. (3.2 mm).

All corner radii should be called out with an optional sharp corner. A general note stating that corner radii should be ±0.060 in. (±1.5 mm) is

Table IV-4. No-draft Forging Tolerances

Wall Thickness	±0.015
Rib thickness	±0.010
Web thickness	±0.020
Location to point on part	±0.015
Length and width tolerances	
Up to 10 inches	±0.015
10 to 18 inches	±0.020
18 to 24 inches	±0.030
24 to 30 inches	±0.035

common practice. This permits sharp corners at parting lines and optional radii in areas within the tooling where stress concentrations and thermal stresses might cause cracks.

Parting Line

The line of separation between the upper and lower parts of a closed-die set is called the *parting line*. It is usually established through the maximum periphery of the forged part. It may be straight or irregular, but it must be designated on all forging drawings.

The parting line position can measurably affect the initial cost and ultimate wear of dies, the ease of forging, the grain flow, related mechanical properties, and the machining requirements for the finish part.

Strive for Maximum Periphery. It is preferable to place the parting line around the largest periphery of the forging. It is easier to force metal laterally in a spreading action than it is to fill deep, narrow die impressions.

Use Flat-sided Forgings. Flat-sided forgings present an opportunity to reduce die costs, since the only machining required is in the lower block. The upper block is a completely flat surface. This simplifies production by eliminating the possibility of mismatch between the upper and lower impressions.

Limit the Inclination of the Parting Line. Forgings in which the parting lines are inclined to the forging planes may present difficulties in trimming if the inclinations are too great. It is generally good practice to limit the inclination to no more than 75° (1.3 rad) out of parallel with the forging plane, and thereby avoid raggedly trimmed edges.

Corner and Fillet Radii

Corner and fillet radii are of prime importance in forging. Basically, dimensions are determined from height/depth ratios. As a rule, radii should be as large as possible. *Figures 4-1* through *4-4* show some typical minimum values of corner and fillet radii. The resistance to deformation of the superalloys is much greater than that of the aluminum alloys. Thus, if the design parameters dictate the need for a more difficult to forge material, larger radii would be required.

Webs and Ribs

When designing the webs and ribs of a forging, consideration must be given to the fact that the thinner the cross section, the faster it cools. Often a tapered web or a punched-out opening in the web facilitates forging in that it permits a thicker section to be forged. *Figure 4-5* and *Table IV-5* present minimum web thicknesses and total areas which can be readily forged. *Figure 4-6* shows the minimum forgeable rib thickness.

TOLERANCES

Tolerances are another of the vitally important factors to be considered when designing for forging. Since tolerance limits are determined basically by the future purpose and use of the part, it is impossible to give specific limits at

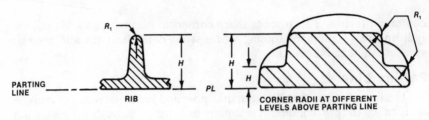

Height (inch)		Forging Types			
From	To	Precision R_1	Close Tolerance R_1	Conventional R_1	Blocker R_1
0.00	0.50	0.03	0.06	0.06	0.12
0.50	1.00	0.04	0.08	0.09	0.18
1.00	1.50	0.05	0.10	0.12	0.25
1.50	2.00	0.06	0.12	0.18	0.37
2.00	2.50	0.07	0.14	0.25	0.50
2.50	3.00	0.08	0.16	0.31	0.62

Figure 4-1. Minimum forged rib and corner radii.
(*Courtesy*, John I. Thompson & Company)

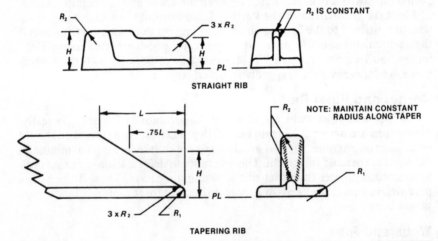

STRAIGHT RIB

TAPERING RIB

Height (inch)		Forging Types			
From	To	Precision R_2	Close Tolerance R_2	Conventional R_2	Blocker R_2
0.00	0.50	0.09	0.18	0.18	0.37
0.50	1.00	0.12	0.24	0.25	0.50
1.00	1.50	0.15	0.30	0.37	0.75
1.50	2.00	0.18	0.36	0.50	1.00
2.00	2.50	0.21	0.42	0.62	1.25
2.50	3.00	0.24	0.48	0.75	1.50

Figure 4-2. Minimum forged rib end radii.
(*Courtesy*, John I. Thompson & Company)

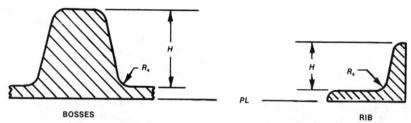

BOSSES   PL   RIB

Height (inch)		Forging Types			
From	To	Precision R_4	Close Tolerance R_4	Conventional R_4	Blocker R_4
0.00	0.50	0.06	0.06	0.12	0.18
0.50	1.00	0.06	0.10	0.22	0.25
1.00	1.50	0.08	0.15	0.31	0.37
1.50	2.00	0.10	0.20	0.40	0.50
2.00	2.50	0.12	0.25	0.50	0.62
2.50	3.00	0.15	0.30	0.59	0.75

Figure 4-3. Minimum forged fillet radii (unconfined).
(*Courtesy*, John I. Thompson & Company)

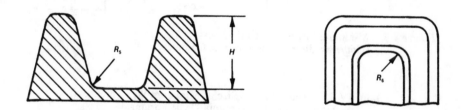

NOTE: R_6 (VERTICAL FILLET) MUST BE EQUAL TO OR LARGER THAN R_5.

Height (inch)		Forging Types			
From	To	Precision R_5	Close Tolerance R_5	Conventional R_5	Blocker R_5
0.00	0.50	0.06	0.10	0.12	0.25
0.50	1.00	0.06	0.20	0.25	0.37
1.00	1.50	0.08	0.30	0.37	0.50
1.50	2.00	0.10	0.40	0.50	0.75
2.00	2.50	0.12	0.50	0.62	1.00
2.50	3.00	0.15	0.60	0.75	1.25

Figure 4-4. Minimum forged fillet radii (confined).
(*Courtesy*, John I. Thompson & Company)

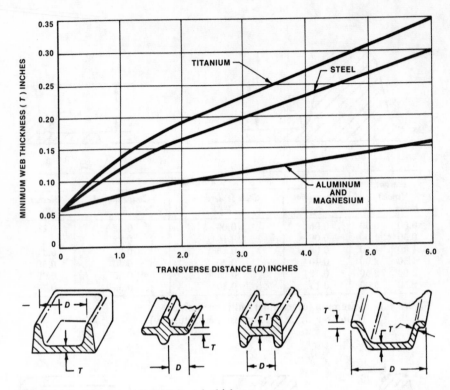

Figure 4-5. Minimum forgeable web thickness.
(*Courtesy*, John I. Thompson & Company)

Table IV-5. Recommended Size of Minimum Web Thickness
(Precision or Conventional-Type Forgings)

Within Average Width (inch)	*Within Total Area (sq. in.)*	*Thickness (inch)*
3	10	0.09
4	30	0.12
6	60	0.16
8	100	0.19
11	200	0.25
14	350	0.31
18	550	0.37
22	850	0.44
26	1200	0.50
34	2000	0.62
41	3000	0.75
47	4000	1.25
52	5000	2.00

Note: Use the larger web thickness when width and area are not on the same line.

(*Courtesy*, Forging Division of the Aluminum Association)

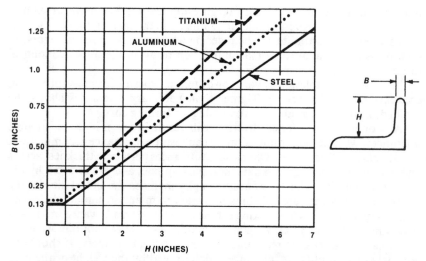

Figure 4-6. Minimum forgeable rib thickness (unconfined).
(*Courtesy*, John I. Thompson & Company)

this point. Rather, limitations of forging processes are presented so that the designer may, upon investigation, determine for oneself which one will conform to the design limits required. With this information, the designer may adjust the plan to be within forging limitations, or determine where finish machining is required to complete the manufacturing process of the part.

How Dimensional Accuracy is Influenced by Design

A forging's proportions have a great deal to do with its dimensional accuracy. Shrinkage, warpage, and other deviations can usually be anticipated, and their effects minimized, by appropriate design precautions.

Shrinkage is the dimensional contraction that occurs when a forging cools to room temperature after removal from the die. The amount of shrinkage depends on the temperature of the part as it comes from the die and the material's coefficient of thermal expansion.

By providing a simple, well-proportioned shape, conventional forging tolerances, and ample fillets, the designer can be assured that the average forged part will be within its dimensional and straightness tolerance.

Suggested Die Forging Tolerances

The tolerances listed in the following tables are for general application. When produced to meet these limits, most die forgings combine reasonable tooling costs and piece cost with adequate dimensional accuracy. In individual cases, however, tolerances smaller than those indicated may be justified.

Certain dimensions often require close limits to suit fixtures used in subsequent processing, to assure clearance for mating parts, or to satisfy other conditions stemming from a forging application. The designer should, when changes are desired in tolerance values, make an estimate of the cost increase. Such an estimate will help decide whether very close tolerances, or such measures as additional machining, will result in the most economical forging.

In most cases, tolerances vary for different types of forgings (precision, conventional, and blocker). Tighter than necessary tolerances should be avoided, as these invariably result in a higher forging cost.

A properly dimensioned drawing will result in the minimum possible tolerances, whereas poor dimensioning can result in tolerance accumulation.

Die-closure Tolerances. Die-closure tolerances pertain to thickness across and perpendicular to the fundamental parting line, and are affected by the closing of the dies. This tolerance normally includes the initial die sinking limits, the subsequent die polishing necessary to maintain smooth die cavity surfaces in production (correcting for die wear), and an allowance for deflection (which creates a thickening at the middle, especially with thin webs).

Table IV-6 shows the recommended die closure tolerances. It should be noted that the applicable tolerance is determined by the weight or the plan area of the forging—whichever is greater.

Dimensional Tolerances. Dimensional tolerances (sometimes called width and length tolerances) usually apply to dimensions essentially parallel to the fundamental parting line. They also apply to all dimensions not otherwise covered by die closure tolerances.

Dimensional tolerances consist of two factors—a shrinkage tolerance and an allowance per surface. The shrinkage tolerance is solely for the oversize or undersize variations that may occur because of shrinkage differences. The per surface allowance is a plus material amount on the forging, which is frequently called *die wear allowance*.

This allowance includes the die sinking limits, die wear, and die dress-outs, and it results in larger outside dimensions and smaller inside dimensions.

Table IV-6. Suggested Die-closure Tolerances

Weight in Pounds (within)	Plan Area in Sq. In. (within)	Precision Type (inch)	Conventional Type (inch)	Blocker Type (inch)
1/2	10	+0.020 − 0.010	+0.020 − 0.010	+0.032 − 0.016
1/2 to 1	30	+0.020 − 0.010	+0.032 − 0.016	+0.047 − 0.031
1 to 5	100	+0.031 − 0.010	+0.047 − 0.016	+0.062 − 0.031
5 to 20	400	+0.047 − 0.016	+0.062 − 0.031	+0.093 − 0.062
20 to 50	750	+0.062 − 0.016	+0.093 − 0.031	+0.125 − 0.062
50 to 100	1000	+0.093 − 0.016	+0.125 − 0.031	+0.187 − 0.062
100 to 200	2000	+0.125 − 0.016	+0.187 − 0.031	+0.250 − 0.062
200 to 500	3500		+0.250 − 0.031	+0.375 − 0.062
500 Up	5000			+0.500 − 0.062

Note: Use the larger tolerance when weight and plan area are not on the same line.
(*Courtesy*, Forging Division of the Aluminum Association)

Dimensional tolerances in *Table IV-7* depend both on the size and type of dimensions. The individual dimensions may be affected by shrinkage only or by both shrinkage and die wear. Center dimensions are affected only by shrinkage. Dimensions from a centerline to a surface are affected by both shrinkage and die wear allowance.

Mismatch Tolerances. Mismatch tolerance is the maximum shift or misalignment variation allowed between the two die halves at, and parallel to, the parting line. The features on one side of the forging are slightly out of line with

Table IV-7. Width and Length Tolerances for Forgings

Dimensions (inch)	Aluminum and Magnesium		
	Width and Length		
	External		Internal
0 to 8	+ 0.030 − 0.015		+ 0.015 − 0.030
8 to 12	+ 0.045 − 0.020		+ 0.020 − 0.045
12 to 16	+ 0.060 − 0.025		+ 0.025 − 0.060
16 to 20	+ 0.075 − 0.030		+ 0.030 − 0.075
20 to 24	+ 0.090 − 0.040		+ 0.040 − 0.090
24 to 28	+ 0.105 − 0.050		+ 0.050 − 0.105
28 to 32	+ 0.120 − 0.060		+ 0.060 − 0.120
32 to 36	+ 0.135 − 0.070		− 0.060 − 0.135
36 to 40	+ 0.150 − 0.080		+ 0.080 − 0.150
Add Per Inch	+ 0.004 − 0.002		+ 0.002 − 0.004

Dimensions (inch)	Titanium	
	Tolerance Width and Length	
0 to 6	± 0.032	
6 to 8	± 0.040	
8 to 10	± 0.050	
10 to 18	± 0.062	
18 to 24	± 0.078	
24 to 30	± 0.093	
30 to 60	± 0.109	

(*Courtesy*, John I. Thompson & Company)

Table IV-7. Width and Length Tolerances for Forgings (*Continued*)

Steel

Dimensions (inch)	Width and Length	
	External	*Internal*
0 to 5	+0.030 −0.015	+0.015 −0.030
5 to 10	+0.045 −0.015	+0.015 −0.045
10 to 15	+0.060 −0.030	+0.030 −0.060
15 to 20	+0.075 −0.030	+0.030 −0.075
20 to 25	+0.090 −0.045	+0.045 −0.090
25 to 30	+0.105 −0.045	+0.045 −0.105
30 to 35	+0.120 −0.060	+0.060 −0.120
35 to 40	+0.135 −0.060	+0.060 −0.135
40 to 45	+0.150 −0.075	+0.075 −0.150
45 to 50	+0.165 −0.075	+0.075 −0.165
50 to 55	+0.180 −0.090	+0.090 −0.180
55 to 60	+0.195 −0.090	+0.090 −0.195
60 to 65	+0.210 −0.105	+0.105 −0.210
65 to 70	+0.225 −0.105	+0.105 −0.225
70 to 75	+0.240 −0.120	+0.120 −0.240
75 to 80	+0.255 −0.120	+0.120 −0.255

(*Courtesy*, John I. Thompson & Company)

those on the other side because of this shift. Mismatching is caused when forging forces are parallel to the forging plane.

Mismatch tolerances are applied separately from, and independently of, all other tolerances. They depend on the weight or overall length of the forging, whichever is greater, as indicated in *Table IV-8*.

Table IV-8. Suggested Mismatch Tolerances

Approximate Forging Weight (lb)	Overall Length in Inches (within)	Precision Type (inch)	Conventional and Blocker Type (inch)
0 to 1	10	0.010	0.015
1 to 5	17	0.015	0.020
5 to 20	25	0.020	0.030
20 to 50	50	0.030	0.045
50 to 100	75	0.045	0.060
100 to 200	100	0.060	0.080
200 to 500	150		0.100
500 Up	250		0.120

Note: Use the larger tolerance when weight and overall length are not on the same line.

(*Courtesy*, Forging Division of the Aluminum Association)

Straightness Tolerances. Straightness tolerance, a deviation generally applicable to flat surfaces, is a total indicator reading (TIR) limit. On a continuous flat surface, it is the total maximum deviation from a plane surface. On noncontinuous surfaces, the deviation is a total flatness relationship of all parallel surfaces, but it does not include the step tolerance that may exist between any two surfaces, nor is it applicable to any surface that is inclined to the major surfaces being measured.

Contoured or tapered surfaces are not covered by the specified straightness tolerance, but must be within the specified dimensional tolerances, which should also be large enough to allow for warpage existing at these areas. On cylindrical forgings, the straightness tolerance is applicable to the axis of the part.

Straightness tolerances are measured separately from, and independently of, all other tolerances. Warpage in a forging, caused by differential cooling of varying sections, occurs both after the hot forging operation, and after heat treating—especially during the quenching operation. The overall length of the forging determines the amount of straightness tolerance, as shown in *Table IV-9*.

Table IV-9. Suggested Straightness Tolerances

Overall Length in Inches (within)	Aluminum Magnesium (TIR)	Steel Titanium (TIR)
10	0.015	0.020
20	0.030	0.035
30	0.045	0.055
40	0.060	0.070
50	0.075	0.085
60	0.090	0.105
90	0.120	0.135
150	0.180	0.200
Over 150	0.250	0.300

Although the straightness tolerance is independent of, and, in addition to all other tolerances, it may be difficult or even impossible to measure separately from other tolerance deviations because of part configuration. This applies particularly to ring, tubular, and contoured shape forgings. However, the straightness tolerance must be considered and an allowance made for it. On such shapes, a 0.0015-in. (0.04-mm) total tolerance per inch of dimension should be added to the dimension tolerance for aluminum and magnesium forgings. For titanium and steel, the additional tolerance should be 0.003 in. (0.07 mm). This is an allowance for the straightness deviation.

On ring-type and tubular-type forgings, this larger tolerance would be applicable only to the diameters, with the additional straightness allowance allowed for possible ovality. The general straightness tolerance would otherwise apply to the flat surfaces. Ovality is permissible even though the drawing omits any mention of it. Ovality must not exceed the diametral tolerance limits, however.

Thickness Tolerances. Thickness tolerances apply to the web thickness of a forging, and are independent of the length and width tolerance. To obtain minimum web thickness as shown in *Figure 4-5* and *Table IV-5*, the plus tolerance should be applied. For heavier web thickness, the plus and minus tolerance should be applied as shown in *Table IV-10*.

Draft Angle Tolerances. Draft angle tolerances (*Table IV-11*) are the permissible variations from the specified draft angles.

Angular Tolerances. Standard angular tolerance applies to angle dimensions other than draft angles. This tolerance is ±0.5° (0.0087 rad) for aluminum and magnesium, and ±1° (0.0174 rad) for steel and titanium. This tolerance is also applicable to unspecified but implied 90° (1.57 rad) angles.

Radii Tolerances. Standard tolerances for both corner and fillet radii are ±0.03 in. (±0.7 mm) on dimensions up to ±0.30 in. (±7.6 mm), and ±10% on dimensions over 0.30 in. (7.6 mm).

Surface Roughness. Die forgings for aluminum and magnesium are normally supplied with clean etched surfaces and are within 250 μin. (6.4 μm) rms. Smoother surfaces are possible, but at higher cost. Forgings for steel and titanium are usually supplied within a roughness rating of 500 μin. (12.8μm) rms.

Out-of-round Tolerances. The out-of-round tolerance is the allowable roundness or ovality deviation from a perfect circle. Generally, it is expressed as a TIR tolerance, which requires that the actual diameter must fall within two concentric circles with a total difference equal to the tolerance. When specified as a radial tolerance, it defines the space allowable radially between two concentric circles. Any such deviation must fall within the diametral tolerances.

Concentricity Tolerances. Concentricity tolerance is the maximum eccentricity from the true axis between two or more diameters or features. It expresses the allowable diametral zone about the true axis or the TIR limit. The drawing should specify the diameter or feature to which the concentricity tolerance applies, and the diameter or feature establishing the datum axis.

118

Table IV-10. Thickness Tolerances

Steel Forgings

Forging Weight (lb)	Thickness Tolerance (inch)	Forging Weight (lb)	Thickness Tolerance (inch)
0 to 5	+0.030 −0.015	132 to 160	+0.080 −0.032
5 to 15	+0.033 −0.015	160 to 190	+0.087 −0.040
15 to 25	+0.038 −0.015	190 to 240	+0.095 −0.040
25 to 40	+0.043 −0.015	240 to 290	+0.105 −0.055
40 to 55	+0.048 −0.020	290 to 345	+0.120 −0.055
55 to 80	+0.055 −0.020	345 to 400	+0.135 −0.075
80 to 105	+0.065 −0.020	Over 400	+0.150 −0.075
105 to 132	+0.072 −0.032		

Aluminum and Magnesium			Titanium	
0 to 1	0 to 1	+0.030 −0.015	0 to 1	+0.030 −0.015
1 to 4	1 to 3	+0.045 −0.030	1 to 8	+0.040 −0.020
4 to 17	3 to 11	+0.060 −0.030	8 to 24	+0.055 −0.030
17 to 24	11 to 16	+0.075 −0.030	24 to 44	+0.070 −0.035
24 to 50	61 to 33	+0.090 −0.030	44 to 64	+0.085 −0.045
50 to 100	33 to 67	+0.125 −0.045	64 to 89	+0.110 −0.050
100 to 250	67 to 170	+0.185 −0.060	89 to 119	+0.150 −0.060
250 and up	170 and up	+0.250 −0.060	119 to 150	+0.175 −0.075

(*Courtesy*, John I. Thompson & Company)

Any such deviation must fall within the dimensional tolerances for the diameters of the feature.

Since the out-of-round and concentricity tolerances fall within the diametral and dimensional tolerances, ample finish allowance for machining should be added. This will permit the use of greater tolerances.

Table IV-11. Draft Angle Tolerances		
Draft Angle (deg)	Depth of Draft Angle (inch)	Tolerance (deg)
Up to 3	Up to 1.00	1/2
	Over 1.00 To 3.00	1
3 and Over	Up to 1.00	1
	Over 1.00 To 3.00	1-3/4

(*Courtesy*, Forging Division of the Aluminum Association)

Finish Allowances for Machining

A designer must be familiar with both the magnitude and the application of the tolerances required on a forging to determine the necessary amount of finish allowance on the machined surface. The relationship of a dimension to the parting line determines which tolerances affect accuracy. (See *Figure 4-7*.)

Surfaces parallel to the parting line are affected by the die closure and straightness tolerances. Surfaces perpendicular to the parting line are affected by dimensional, straightness, and mismatch tolerances. Only the adverse effect of these tolerances need be considered, and this amount should be added to a minimum clean up allowance on each surface to assure satisfactory machining. The minimum machining allowance is arbitrary and varies from 0.060 to 0.25 in. (1.5 to 6.4 mm) on large forgings.

Initial Machining Setup

To lessen any possibly adverse effect of forging tolerances, the designer must know how the forging will be positioned in the initial machining setup. For example, a forging fixtured on one side of the parting line is not affected by either the mismatch tolerance or the minus die closure tolerance on that side. These same tolerances do affect the opposite side of the parting line, however, and must be considered.

Not knowing how a forging is to be fixtured makes it necessary to allow the full machining allowance for the adverse forging tolerances on both sides of the parting line. The preceding example further illustrates the growing practice of showing tooling points on drawings or using such means of indicating the machining fixture points.

PRODUCTION ECONOMY

Maximum economy in production is usually achieved by reducing design to the simplest possible shapes and forms consistent with functional requirements. Die costs for average forgings vary roughly with the rectangular area which encloses the plan of the part. Straight or angular parting lines are far more economical than curved ones. Intricate or nonuniform shapes parallel

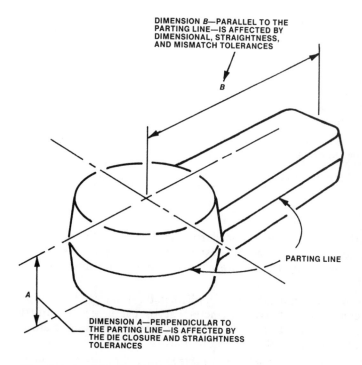

DIMENSION *B*—PARALLEL TO THE
PARTING LINE—IS AFFECTED BY
DIMENSIONAL, STRAIGHTNESS,
AND MISMATCH TOLERANCES

B

PARTING LINE

A

DIMENSION *A*—PERPENDICULAR TO
THE PARTING LINE—IS AFFECTED BY
THE DIE CLOSURE AND STRAIGHTNESS
TOLERANCES

Figure 4-7.   Relationship of a dimension to the parting line.
(*Courtesy*, Forging Division of the Aluminum Association)

to the parting line are often difficult to produce. Maximum permissible tolerances should be indicated. Wherever possible, the economical tolerances shown in the tables should be used.

Forging dies are machined to the low limits specified for the part, and when the impression is worn to the high limits, the die must be either resunk or scrapped. It follows that wide tolerances extend die life considerably, especially with tougher alloy steels.

In comparing metal fabrication processes, a cost analysis usually calls for consideration of the investment in special purpose tools such as dies, jigs, and fixtures that will be required to produce each of the alternative designs of a manufactured part.

Since the economy of proposed special purpose tools depends upon the number of units on which they are to be used, it is often helpful to examine the behavior of unit costs as a function of total units to be produced.

Forgings vs. Machining from Bar Stock

In the design of a product to be produced in limited quantities, the designer must consider relative costs, as indicated in *Table IV-12*, to deter-

Table IV-12. Relative Costs, Machining vs. Forging

Items	Part from Bar Stock	Part by Forging
Investment in Tooling		
Forging Die	—	$3263.00
Drill Jig	$450.00	405.00
Milling Fixture	720.00	180.00
Direct Material Cost per Piece	2.07	2.03
Setup Cost Per Lot		
Forging Die Setup	—	$72.00
Machine Setup	$33.75	18.00
Direct Labor Cost per Piece	2.88	0.79

mine if the part should be designed to be machined from bar stock or designed to be made from a forging. The most important differences for making the bar stock versus forging decision are in the tooling costs and direct labor costs per piece.

The designer must determine whether the total production of forged pieces can assure that savings in increment cost per piece will justify the extra tooling investment. The possibility of frequent design changes must also be considered in making that determination.

Representative calculations in *Table IV-13* and *Figure 4-8* in this example show that it will be more economical to design a given part as a forging and then have it machined if the total production is 1500 parts or more. Unit costs shown in *Table IV-13* for the given part were computed for production from 200 to 4000 units.

The curves shown in *Figure 4-8* are based on the assumption that total production is a multiple of the lot size of 200. Using this assumption, setup costs may be treated as variable costs per unit of $0.17 and $0.45, respectively, and break-even point calculations may be made as follows:

Table IV-13. Calculation of Unit Cost of Alternate Designs

	Part Machined From Bar Stock			Forging		
	Quantity					
Total Production	400	2000	4000	400	2000	4000
Tooling Cost	$1170	$1170	$1170	$3848	$3848	$3848
Setup Cost	68	338	675	180	900	1800
Direct Material Cost	828	4140	8280	810	4050	8100
Direct Labor Cost	1152	5760	11520	315	1575	3150
Total Cost	$3218	$11408	$21645	$5153	$10373	$16898
Comparative Unit Cost	$8.05	$5.70	$5.41	$12.88	$5.19	$4.22

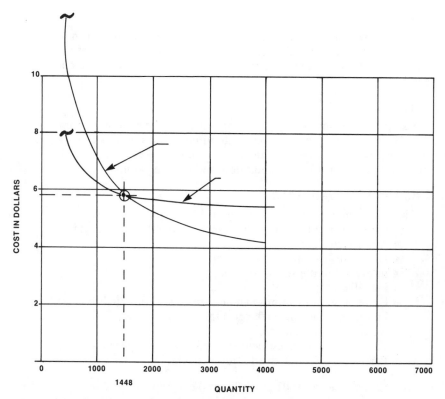

Figure 4-8. Comparative unit cost of alternative design of a manufactured product in relation to total production.

Break-even point calculations:
$1170 + ($2.07 + 0.17 + 2.88) X = $3848 + ($2.03 + 0.45 + 0.79) X

To find the value of X:

3848 - 1170 = 2678   (2.07 + 0.17 + 2.88) = 5.12
5.12 - 3.27 X = 1.85 X   (2.03 + 0.45 + 0.79) = 3.27
X = 2678 ÷ 1.85 = 1448 parts

Proof for X:
$1170 + (5.12) 1448 = 8582
$3848 + (3.27) 1448 = 8582

ORBITAL FORGING PROCESS

Many forging methods have been developed to produce better and more economical forgings. One of the methods that has an economic advantage over conventional forgings is the *orbital forging process*. This process is a breakthrough in cold forming.

123

Application

Tests show that cold forming with an orbiting die allows the production of workpieces having very different shapes such as discs, all types of rings, discs with thin hubs, bevel gears, chain wheels, thin spur gears, and ratchet clutch components.

Materials

Using this method of metalforming, parts can be produced from various metallic materials, such as copper, aluminum alloys, brass alloys, and steel with low carbon content. In the case of alloyed steel, material should be induction heated for better metal flow and forming ability.

Economic Advantages

The economic advantages of using orbital forgings include:
- Superior part accuracy—tolerances to 0.001 in. (0.02 mm)
- Almost no flash
- Better surface finish—no oxidation or scale
- Improved part strength—better grain flow
- Less die wear
- Extremely thin sections can be formed without die breakage
- Lateral displacement (flanges) up to 30% greater
- No lubrication required
- Far lower press investment (meaning less cost per hour)
- Part accuracy reduces additional machining.

Note: Tolerances to 0.001 in. (0.02 mm) can be held on some dimensions, however, a functional tolerance should be used for greater economy.

Orbital forgings differ from standard conventional forgings in that the hydraulic ram is under constant pressure against the upper rocking die. This creates line contact on the part and lets material flow into a predetermined die cavity with pressures many times greater than conventional cold forming equipment.

Four different motions of upper die are available to produce a wide range of part configurations. From a single slug of material to a finished part, this process is repeated on an average of three to six times per minute.

124

5

Extrusions

This chapter defines extrusion, and discusses extrusion types, materials, design considerations, and extrusion tolerances.

DEFINITIONS

Extrusion is a plastic forming process usually done hot, but in some instances cold. It differs basically from forging in that the extruded shape has either a constant cross section or the same type of cross section with a tapered effect along its length. Because of its severe metalworking characteristics, extrusion provides fiber-oriented and fine-grained wrought products. An extrusion is a product whose configuration is formed by first confining a billet of the material to be formed, sometimes with heat applied. A ram is then used to force the material through a die opening in much the same manner that toothpaste is squeezed from a tube. The emerging extrusion, traveling in the same direction as the ram, takes on a cross-sectional shape identical to that of the die opening.

PRACTICES

Types of Extrusion

Extrusion equipment is in one of two categories of machinery—impact or press. Within either of these categories, extrusions can be made by the direct method in the manner described above, or by the inverse method, whereby the extrusion travels backwards along the outside or inside of the pressure ram. A limitation of the inverse method is that the available length of the ram precludes the extrusion of very long pieces.

Direct Extrusion. A direct extrusion is made in the manner previously described.

Stepped Extrusion. A stepped extrusion can be made with two or more different cross sections. This is accomplished by interrupting the extrusion process and changing dies. The principal advantage in stepped extrusion is a reduction in the need to remove excess metal by machining or chemical milling. (See *Figure 5-1.*)

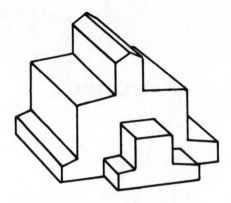

Figure 5-1. Stepped extrusion.

Dies for stepped extrusions are split into two segments for ease of removal. Because these dies have lower stability, the cross-sectional dimensional tolerances of stepped extrusions are greater than those of normal extrusions. Accordingly, it is good practice to allow additional tolerances for machining.

It may be necessary to vary the allowable design stresses on stepped extrusions because of differences in cross-sectional areas and thicknesses.

Before designing for a stepped extrusion, the designer should compare the cost of a stepped extrusion and its finish machining to the cost of a part machined from a billet or machined from a direct extrusion.

Coextrusion. A coextrusion results when two different alloys are extruded together to form a composite part. (See *Figure 5-2.*) Alclad tubing is an example of a coextrusion. In this instance, a clad layer of one aluminum alloy can be placed inside, outside, or on both sides of a core alloy of another composition.

Figure 5-2. Coextrusion.

Cold Extrusion. There are two methods of cold extrusion: impact extrusion and the Hooker process. Aluminum, tin, copper alloys, and steel are worked by these two extrusion methods.

Aluminum alloys are well adapted to cold extrusion. The low strength, ductile alloys such as 1100 and 3003 are easier to extrude. When higher mechanical properties are required in the final product, heat treatable grades are used. However, extrusions from these grades are more susceptible to defects—such as laps or cracks—than those extruded from the lower strength alloys.

Impact Extrusion. There are three variants of the impact extrusion process as depicted in *Figure 5-3:*

- Forward, or direct, wherein the metal flows in the same direction as the applied force.
- Backward, or indirect, wherein the metal flow is opposite to the applied force, or back over the punch.
- Opposed, wherein the metal is forced to flow simultaneously with, and opposite to, the direction of applied force.

It is possible to form a part with any combination of inside and outside shapes plus splines, or bottoms with bosses. *Figure 5-4* shows some commonly extruded sections.

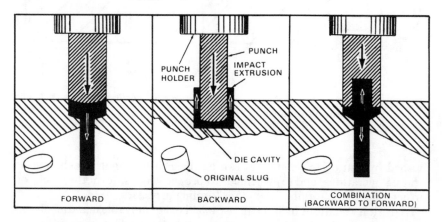

Figure 5-3. Impact extrusion process. (*Courtesy*, Xerox Corporation)

Hooker Process. A cupped blank is used in this process as shown in *Figure 5-5.* The blank is placed in the die, the punch enters, and pressure causes the metal to flow between the nose of the punch and the land of the die. Both large and small tubings and cups can be extruded to considerable length and extreme thinness if required.

An extruded product may be placed in general classes according to the finish required. These classes are divided into those parts which (1) can be

127

Figure 5-4. Common extruded sections. (*Courtesy*, McGraw-Hill Book Company)

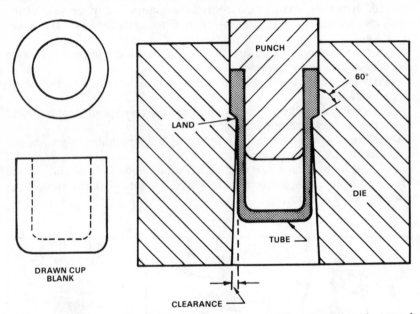

Figure 5-5. Hooker process for extrusion causes a thick-walled cup to be extruded or drawn over a land in the die.
(*Courtesy*, McGraw-Hill Book Company)

finished by cutting to length, (2) can be finished by simple machining or forming operations, and (3) when cut to proper lengths, form the stock for further machining, forging, and other forming processes.

Extrusion variations include the use of a fixed or movable mandrel placed in the center of the die opening so that a tubular product (tapered, if the mandrel is tapered and movable) is formed between the die and mandrel; the use of a fixed, multimandrel type die—called a *port hole die*—primarily for products which have more than one longitudinal chamber.

ADVANTAGES AND LIMITATIONS

Advantages:

- The exact placement of metal where it is needed, thereby utilizing the quantity of metal to maximum advantage, and providing maximum structural and mechanical properties.

128

- Extensive plastic working which produces a dense and homogeneous product, free from porosity, and having favorable grain flow characteristics.
- Easy production of sharp corners.
- Easy production of reentrant angles.
- Elimination of rough edges and burrs.
- Incorporation of controlled twist in parts.
- Efficient production of large diameter, thin walled tubular products having excellent concentricity and tolerance characteristics.
- Application of changing section thicknesses.
- Consolidation into a single extrusion of several individually fabricated pieces.
- Lowering the machinery costs with attendant savings in wasted material.
- Relatively economic die design as compared with forging and some drawing methods, thus allowing good application to short production runs and to design revisions.

Limitations:
- Dimensional tolerances are not as close as in machining.
- For certain applications, size is limited according to die and press capacities.
- Warpage and distortion require subsequent correction operations.
- Certain sizes and shapes have limited applications in steels and titanium.

MATERIALS

Aluminum and aluminum alloys, copper and copper alloys, low-carbon and medium-carbon steels, and stainless steels are the metals most commonly cold extruded. These materials are listed in the order of decreasing extrudability.

Most of the austenitic stainless steels, martensitic stainless steels, ferritic stainless steels, and carbon steels are cold or hot extruded. AISI alloy steels, tool steels, nickel-base alloys, high-temperature and specialty alloys, and titanium and titanium alloys are hot extruded. Choosing an alloy and the correct cross-sectional design is of utmost concern.

Aluminum Alloys

The most widely alloys used are the aluminum alloys, and they are as follows:

Alloy EC. A nonheat treatable alloy that is easily extruded. The ultimate and yield properties are extremely low. This alloy is used chiefly in the manufacture of bus bars. Because of its high aluminum purity, it can also be used where atmospheric conditions would corrode other alloys.

Alloy 1100. Also a nonheat treatable alloy. This alloy is easily extruded and has superior finishing characteristics. It is used for appliance trim and decorative parts. It is also extruded as hollows for use in the refrigeration and heat transfer industries.

Alloy 3003. Another nonheat treatable alloy with superior strength to both EC and 1100 alloys. It has extremely good finishing characteristics. Because of its excellent extrudability, brazability, weldability, plus heat transfer qualities, it is used in radiator cores and air conditioning equipment.

Alloy 6061. This alloy is available in various heat treated tempers. It can obtain tensile and yield strengths of over 40,000 psi (276 MPa). This is the hardest to extrude of the more common alloys. It is a structural alloy that is rarely used as a decorative trim because of the die liner and pick-up that hamper polishing and anodizing finishes. The machining of 6061 is very good and is one of the most widely used alloys for machine parts.

Alloy 6063. This is the all-purpose alloy of the extrusion industry. It is readily extrudable and heat treatable. It has extremely good formability, finishing, machining, weldability, and corrosion resistant characteristics. Tensile and yield strengths of 35,000 psi (241 MPa) and 31,000 psi (215 MPa) are possible in the T-6 condition. 6063 alloy is used in both structural shapes and decorative parts.

Alloy 6463. This alloy has the same basic characteristics as 6063 alloy, however, the high copper and low iron content make it ideal for achieving chrome-like finishes by polishing and brite dip anodizing. This alloy is used in the furniture and appliance industries.

Other popular alloys include the *2000, 5000,* and *7000 alloys.* The 2000 series is used mainly in aircraft and missile work due to its high strength qualities. The 5000 series is used mainly in the marine industry due to its high resistance to corrosion, and the 7000 alloys, also known as the super alloys, are used whenever maximum strengths are required. The relatively poor extrudability of these alloys makes it difficult to extrude complex shapes.

Finishing Extrusions

This is a guide to help the designer in the selection of an alloy for an economical low-cost extrusion. For a finish part, the designer must also select the proper finish required for the extruded part. Aluminum extrusions and their wide variety of finishes offer the designer a panorama of choices for any particular shape. Many technical papers have been written and published about finishing aluminum. This chapter adds a clear, comprehensive study of the extrusion design in its relation to these finishes.

The most common methods of finishing aluminum extrusions are anodizing, brushing, sanding, polishing, tumble deburring, painting, silk screening, and wood graining. These finishes may be combined with the natural contours of the aluminum shape to achieve a contrasting beauty of design and purpose.

Care should be taken in the design of the extrusion to allow the maximum benefits for finishing. Flutes, reeds, scallops, and other serrations may be used to break up a wide, unfinished surface and eliminate costly brushing, sanding, or polishing. These may be spaced intermittently and height and depth varied to form contrasting light reflecting appearances. Areas that are exposed, but inaccessible to buffing wheels are especially suited for this purpose.

Indicating exposed surfaces and occasional secondary surfaces where the part will receive further finishing is important in the manufacture of the extrusion die and subsequent handling of material. More material has been ruined because of this fact and subsequent improper packing than any other factor.

Specific alloys are recommended for different types of finishes. The two most common alloys used for finished parts are 6063 and 6463 aluminum. These alloys are identical in mechanical and physical properties. The 6063 alloy is generally used for matte or satin finishes. It is not recommended for polished or bright finishes because of its tendency to show extrusion heat lines or white streaks when bright dip anodized. The alloy of choice for any bright finish due to its high copper and low iron content is 6463. The 6061 alloy is a poor choice for any critically finished part due to the watermarks and selective etching which are characteristic of this alloy.

New straight line polishing equipment gives a uniform finish that was not possible until recently. High-speed buffs, automatic polishing compound applicators and specially designed polishing boards have been especially instrumental in giving the aluminum a high polish comparable to a chrome finish.

Anodizing

Anodizing forms a hard, protective coating to retard the natural oxidizing tendency of aluminum and protects the surface from scratches and handling marks. This coating also acts as an insulator against the natural conductivity of aluminum. When electrical conductivity is required, these parts must be spot-faced after anodizing.

After anodizing and prior to sealing, the material may be dyed virtually any color imaginable. Most anodizers have a standard color line available at all times, with special colors available upon request. A slight variation in color ranges (highs and lows) can be expected on various runs and will appear more noticeable on dark colors. While these ranges are stringently controlled, it is recommended that parts used in close proximity to each other be taken from the same runs.

Anodizing finishes other than hard coating are limited to indoor use with the exception of clear satin with a thickness of 0.0004 in. (0.01 mm) and organic brass-colored anodizing. These two finishes will withstand the normal inclemencies of weather and ultraviolet sunlight exposure.

As a point of fact, anodizing costs for a particular shape can normally be expected to increase for darker color ranges. This is due to the rework that can be expected for darker colors.

There are many other decorative processes available, such as silk screening, wood graining, embossing, roping, and painting. The designer should, before calling for a particular decorative finish, consult with the extruder as to the economy of the finish. There may be other finishes that give the same results at a lower cost.

With the addition of new techniques and applications, the aluminum extruder and finisher helps to meet the demands that industry and consumer have come to expect. However, function and low cost are the most important factors in the selection of extrusions, the alloys, and the surface finishes required.

Work Hardening of Metals When Cold Extruded

Metals are work hardened when deformed at temperatures below their recrystallization temperatures. This can be an advantage if the service requirements of a part allow its use in the as-extruded condition. (Under some conditions, heat treatment of the extruded part may not be required.)

Workhardening, however, raises the ratio of yield strength to tensile strength while lowering ductility. Therefore, when several severe cold extrusions follow one another, ductility must be restored between operations by annealing. The effect of cold extrusion on the hardness across a section of extruded metal varies directly with the extrusion ratio. An increase in extrusion ratio results in a corresponding increase in the amount of cold deformation.

Effect of Composition and Condition on Extrudability of Steel

Extrudability of steel decreases with increasing carbon or alloy content. Extrudability is also affected by greater hardness. Free-machining additives such as sulfur or lead, and the nonmetallic inclusions—particularly the slilicate type—are also detrimental to extrudability.

Carbon Content. It is common practice to cold extrude steels containing up to 0.45% carbon. Steels with even higher carbon content have also been successfully extruded. However, it is advisable to use steels of the lowest carbon content that will meet service requirements.

Alloy Content. For a given carbon content, most alloy steels are harder than plain carbon steels and therefore more difficult to extrude. Further, most alloy steels workharden more rapidly than carbon steels of the same carbon content, and therefore require intermediate annealing. As a rule, low-carbon stainless steels are more difficult to extrude than plain low-carbon steels.

Hardness. The softer a steel, the easier it is to extrude. Steels that have been spheroidize-annealed are in their softest condition and are thus preferred for extrusion. However, any operations that precede the extrusion process—such as machining the billet for its proper size or follow extrusion—may make it impractical to have the steel in its softest condition. Extremely soft steels have poor machinability, and thus, for practical reasons, extrudability is sometimes sacrificed. Annealing techniques that produce a pearlitic structure, with a corresponding increase in hardness, are ideal for many extrusions in which machinability is important.

Free-machining Steel. These steels contain additives such as lead and sulfur, and are not preferred for cold extrusions. Since cold extrusions require little if any machining, there is less need for free-machining additives than if

132

the part were to be produced entirely by machining. Free-machining steels have been extruded successfully, but for practical purposes these should be avoided.

DESIGN CONSIDERATIONS

General

Although the extrusion process is capable of producing a wide variety of configurations, certain limitations exist due to die design characteristics and other manufacturing factors—all of which should be considered in designing an extruded section for optimum economy and maximum efficiency.

As in all design problems, the first step entails the establishment of the basic function of the section. This step includes consideration of the most important requirements, such as strength, decorative characteristics, machinability, formability, resistance to corrosion, weldability, and other fundamental characteristics. Usually a combination of several of these characteristics is desired, with selection of one or two as more critical than the others.

Just as important as the choice of proper alloy is the selection of correct structural design. Here also, the flexibility allowed by the extrusion process makes it possible to design to exact values and requirements without undue concern for the restrictions imposed by other less flexible processes.

Almost any component with a constant cross section may be a candidate for the extrusion process. Factors which generally govern the characteristics of extrusion design are configuration to accomplish the desired function, and distribution of metal for necessary mechanical properties at maximum production economy. These basic variables, applied to conventional strength and design formulas, provide the most desirable structural and economical cross section.

Although the extrusion process imposes few restrictions, effective designing depends on an understanding of the extrusion ratio, the part size, the shapes than can be extruded most efficiently, and the limitations imposed by die configuration as it affects metal flow.

Extrusion Ratio. The extrusion ratio is determined by dividing the original area undergoing deformation by the final deformed area. Because volume remains constant during extrusion, this ratio may also be calculated by increase in length. An extrusion ratio of 5:1 indicates that the length has increased by a factor of five.

The metal being extruded has a substantial effect on the maximum practical ratio. Most common extrusion ratios for aluminum range between 15:1 and 50:1. Extrusion ratios below 15:1 are seldom used because insufficient hot working is provided to impart satisfactory mechanical properties to the extrusion. Extrusion ratios for low-carbon steels are approximately 5:1 and for stainless steel, 3.5:1.

Low extrusion ratios are sometimes used for purposes of intermediate extrusion, a process in which billets are preextruded to a given diameter prior to final extrusion. Intermediate extrusion can be accomplished in several successive stages and is applicable to mandrel type extrusion. Progressive extrusion is helpful in cases where prolonged working of the metal during a single cycle may result in cooling and workhardening of the billet. Therefore, following each successive extrusion cycle, the partially extruded billet is stress-relieved and then reheated to extrusion temperature for the next cycle.

Progressive extrusion cannot be accomplished where porthole dies are used. The reason is that the metal flow is separated into several streams through the holes in a porthole die, and the mandrel cannot be extracted until the operation has been completed.

Part Size. In general, extrusion size is limited by available press capacities. The overall size of an extruded section is determined by the *circumscribing circle.* This is the smallest circle that will completely enclose the cross section of the shape. The cross section is also determined primarily by the size of the extrusion die insert and the back-up tools that resist the extrusion forces.

The maximum circumscribing circle for aluminum, magnesium, copper, and copper alloys is approximately 12 in. (305 mm), but some of the new presses have increased the maximum circle to 27 in. (685.8 mm). The maximum circumscribing circle for alloy steel and stainless steel is 5.375 in. (136.5 mm), and for carbon and titanium—6.5 in. (165.1 mm). *Figure 5-6* illustrates how the circumscribing circle encloses the section.

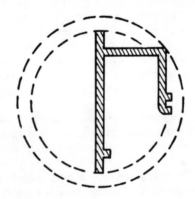

Figure 5-6. Extrusion size is measured by the circumscribing diameter enclosing the section.

As the circumscribing circle (CCD) increases, the pressure required to extrude a given alloy and shape increases. Wall thickness must usually be increased to permit the metal to flow through the die and, therefore, die cost increases. *Figure 5-7* shows a typical extruded section. Some of the important factors to consider when extruding will now be examined in greater detail.

Length. Extruded shapes can be straightened in lengths up to 60 ft (18.29 m). To go beyond this length imposes certain heat treating restrictions that are not feasible or economical. Steel sections up to 24 ft (7.31 m) can be

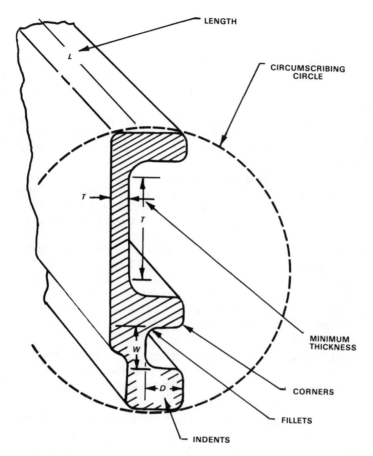

Figure 5-7. Typical extruded section. (*Courtesy*, ITT Harper, Inc.)

deglassed and heat treated. Maximum product weight per foot (0.305 m) of extruded shape is 20 lb (9.07 kg) for aluminum and 15 lb (6.8 kg) for steel.

Minimum Size. This factor is determined by the cross-sectional area, and the resistance of a given material to deformation and other factors at a given temperature. The minimum cross section is not less than 0.10 in.^{2} (65 mm^2) for aluminum and not less than 0.50 in.^{2} (322.6 mm^2) for steel.

Minimum Thickness. A problem often posed by the designer concerns the minimum thickness to be achieved in extruding a section of given overall dimensions. Thickness limitations are based on the size of the cross section since, when the diameter of the circumscribing circle is large, it becomes increasingly difficult to force the metal through thin sections in the die, especially if the shape has adjacent thick and thin sections.

As a general rule, a thicker wall is required as the size of the section increases. This is true because friction of the metal against die surfaces on

135

large cross sections having thin walls may exceed the pressures that dies and presses can exert. This occurs because the pressure required to force metal through a narrow die cavity is greater than that required for a wider cavity. From the standpoint of straightening, the wall should also be strong enough to assure that the extrusion will maintain its contour during its manufacture and use.

Thickness limitations also depend on other important factors, such as flow or yield strength of the particular metal or alloy extruded. This, in turn, is determined by the alloy composition. Other important factors include the extrusion ratio.

Thickness of extrusions generally range from 0.050 in. (1.27 mm) to several inches for aluminum alloys, although thinner sections have been extruded. The minimum production thickness for steel is 0.180 in. (4.6 mm). Some of the low-carbon steels have been extruded with a wall thickness of 0.125 in. (3.2 mm).

A common ratio of thickness to width for aluminum and magnesium extrusions is 8.0-in. (203-mm) width to 0.10-in. (2.5-mm) thickness. For steel and steel alloys, the ratio is about 2.50-in. (63-mm) width to 0.180-in. (4.6-mm) thickness. *Table V-1* lists some guidelines for minimum thickness of aluminum alloy extrusions. It should be emphasized that these are *only* guidelines. The extruder should be consulted for advice on minimum thickness of a specific section.

Corner and Fillet Radii. Corners can be sharp on aluminum and magnesium alloys. For steel extrusion, normal production radii are 0.062 in. (1.6 mm). Fillets should be 0.030 in. (0.8 mm) minimum for aluminum and magnesium. Normal production radii for steel extrusions are 0.250 in. (6 mm).

Indents. Depth of indents should be no greater than the width of the indent.

Part Complexity. The complexity of an extruded shape is usually measured in two ways: shape and shape factor.

Shape classifications, in the order of generally increasing production and die costs, are listed below and illustrated in *Figure 5-8*. They are:

- Solids
- Semihollow—Class 1
- Semihollow—Class 2
- Hollow—Class 1
- Hollow—Class 2
- Hollow—Class 3.

Thus, extrusion costs per pound (kg) are lowest for the solid shapes and highest for the complex Class 3 hollow shapes (several internal voids).

Figures 5-9 and *5-10* illustrate two factors which should be considered when designing for an extrusion.

Within any given classification, the second measure of complexity is the shape factor. This is the amount of surface generated per pound (kg) of metal extruded. Shape factor is determined by the perimeter of the cross section in inches divided by the weight of the extrusion in pounds per lineal foot (kg per

Table V-1. Guidelines for Minimum Section Thickness

	Minimum Section Thickness					
	Aluminum Alloy Numbers					
	1060 1100 3003	6060	6063	2014 5086 5454	2024 7001 / 2219 7075 / 5083 7079 / 7178	
CCD in Inches	Thickness					Shapes
0.5 to 2	0.040	0.040	0.040	0.040	0.040	Solid and
2 to 3	0.045	0.045	0.045	0.050	0.050	Semihollow
3 to 4	0.050	0.050	0.050	0.050	0.062	Shapes, Rods,
5 to 6	0.062	0.062	0.062	0.078	0.094	and Bars.
6 to 7	0.078	0.078	0.078	0.094	0.109	
7 to 8	0.094	0.094	0.094	0.109	0.125	
8 to 10	0.109	0.109	0.109	0.125	0.156	
1.25 to 3	0.062	0.050	0.062	—	—	Class 1
2 to 4	0.094	0.050	0.062	—	—	Hollow Shapes*
4 to 5	0.109	0.062	0.062	0.156	0.205	
5 to 6	0.125	0.062	0.078	0.188	0.281	
6 to 7	0.156	0.078	0.094	0.219	0.312	
7 to 8	0.188	0.094	0.125	0.250	0.375	
8 to 9	0.219	0.125	0.156	0.218	0.438	
9 to 10	0.250	0.156	0.188	0.312	0.500	
0.5 to 1	0.062	0.050	0.062	—	—	Classes
1 to 2	0.062	0.055	0.062	—	—	2 and 3
2 to 3	0.078	0.062	0.078	—	—	Hollow
3 to 4	0.094	0.078	0.094	—	—	Shapes†
4 to 5	0.109	0.094	0.109	—	—	
5 to 6	0.125	0.109	0.125	—	—	
6 to 7	0.156	0.125	0.156	—	—	
7 to 8	0.188	0.156	0.188	—	—	
8 to 10	0.250	0.188	0.250	—	—	

* Minimum inside diameter is one-half the circumscribing diameter, but never under one inch for alloys in the first three columns, or under two inches for alloys in the last two columns.

† Minimum hole size for all alloys is 0.110 in.^{2} in an area 0.375 in. in diameter.

meter). An extrusion cost generally can be expected to increase as the shape factor increases.

Shape classifications illustrated in *Figure 5-8* are defined as follows:

Solid extruded shape: Any extruded shape other than semihollow or hollow.

Class 1. A semihollow extruded shape of two voids or less in which the area of two voids and the surrounding metal thickness is symmetrical about the centerline of the gap.

Class 2. Any semihollow extruded shape other than Class 1.

Hollow extruded shape: An extruded shape is termed hollow if a part of its wall section forms a complete hollow. Further subdivision follows:

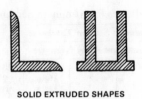

SOLID EXTRUDED SHAPES

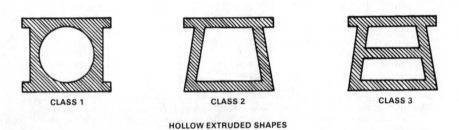

HOLLOW EXTRUDED SHAPES

Figure 5-8. Extruded shape classifications.

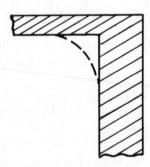

Figure 5-9. Avoid sharp fillets between thick and thin transitions.

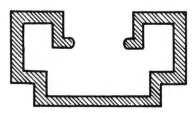

Figure 5-10. Semihollow shapes should have a wide channel opening for stability of the die tongue.

Class 1. A hollow extruded shape whose void is round and one inch (25.4 mm) or more in diameter, and whose weight is equally distributed on opposite sides of two or more equally spaced axes.

Class 2. Any hollow extruded shape other than Class 1, which does not exceed a 5-in. (127-mm) diameter circumscribing circle, and has a single void of not less than 0.375-in. (9.5-mm) diameter or 0.110-in.^{2} (71-mm^2) area.

Class 3. Any hollow extruded shape other than Class 1 or 2. Note that a hollow extrusion whose wall is of uniform thickness, and whose cross section is completely sectional, and is round, square, rectangular, hexagonal, octagonal, or elliptical, with sharp or rounded corners, is termed *extruded tubing.*

TOLERANCES

Some general tolerance indications for extruded aluminum shapes are shown in *Tables V-2* and *V-3.* For tolerances not shown, the designer should use standard tolerances developed by the Aluminum Association. The standard tolerances are contained in the association's publication *Aluminum Standards and Data,* and the USA Standard H35.2, "Aluminum Mill Products, Dimensional Tolerances for."

Tolerances for Steel Extrusions

Cross-sectional Dimensions.

Specified Dimensions	*Tolerances*
Under 1.00 in. (25.4 mm), inclusive	±0.020 in. (0.5 mm)
Over 1.00 in. to 3.00 in. (25.4 to 76 mm), inclusive	±0.031 in. (0.78 mm)
Over 3.00 in. to 4.38 in. (76 to 111 mm), inclusive	±0.046 in. (1.17 mm)

Corners. In normal practice all corners have a radius tolerance of 0.062 in. (1.6-mm), unless otherwise specified.

Fillets. In normal practice all fillets have 0.062-in. (1.6-mm) radius tolerance, unless otherwise specified.

Angles. Angles of extruded solid shapes have a tolerance of ±2° (±0.0349 rad) from the designated angle, unless otherwise specified.

Table V-2. Cross-sectional Dimension Tolerances (Standard Tolerances/Structural Aluminum Shapes)

Shapes	Nominal Dimensions	Tolerances* Allowable Deviation from Nominal Dimension	
		Width or Depth less than 8 Inches	Width or Depth 8 to 15 Inches
I-BEAMS	t Thickness	±2-1/2%, ±0.010 min	±3%, ±0.015 min
	b Flange Width	+4%	+4%
	d Depth	+3/32, −1/16	±2-1/2%, ±1/4 min
H-BEAMS	t Thickness	±2-1/2%, ±0.010 min	±3%, ±0.015 min
	b Flange Width	+4%	±4%, ±1/4 min
	d Depth	±2-1/2%, ±1/16 min	±3%, ±1/4 min
CHANNELS	t Thickness	±2-1/2%, 0.010 min	±3%, ±0.015 min
	b Flange Width	+4%	±4%
	d Depth	+3/32, −1/16	±2-1/2%, ±1/4 min

Table V-2. Cross-sectional Dimension Tolerances (*Continued*)
(*Courtesy*, The Aluminum Association Drafting Standards, Aluminum Extruded and Tubular Products)

Shapes	Nominal Dimensions		Tolerances* Allowable Deviation from Nominal Dimension	
			Width or Depth less than 8 inches	Width or Depth 8 to 15 Inches
ANGLES	t	Thickness	±2-1/2%, ±.010 min	±2-1/2%, ±.015 min
	b	Flange Width	±2-1/2%, ±1/16 min	±2-1/2%, ±3/16 min
TEES	t	Thickness	±2-1/2%, ±.010 min	±2-1/2%, ±.015 min
	b	Flange Width	±4%	±4%
	d	Stem Height	±2-1/2%, ±1/16 imn	±2-1/2%, ±1/4 min
ZEES	t	Thickness	±2-1/2%, ±.010 min	±2-1/2%, ±.015 min
	b	Flange Width	±2-1/2%, ±1/16 min	±2-1/2%, ±3/32 min
	d	Depth	±2-1/2%, ±1/16 min	±2-1/2%, ±1/4 min

* Depth tolerance applies only at web. Depth across other points is controlled by angularity tolerance.

141

Table V-3. General Shape Tolerances

Type of Tolerance	Dimensions to Which Tolerance Applies	Tolerance (plus and minus)
Straightness	Circumscribing circle diam. up through 1.499 inch	0.05 inch per foot for minimum thickness up through 0.094 inch 0.0125 inch per foot for minimum thickness 0.095 inch and up.
	1.5 inch and up	0.0125 inch per foot
Twist	Circumscribing circle diam. up through 1.499 inch	1° per foot
	1.50–2.99 inch	1/2° per foot; 5° total
	3.0 inch and up	1/4° per foot; 3° total
Contour	Deviation from specified	0.005 inch per inch of chord width (0.005 inch minimum)
Corner and Fillet Radii	Sharp corners	0.0156 inch
	Radius up through 0.197 inch	0.0312 inch
	Specified radius 0.188 inch and up	10 percent
Angles	Minimum leg thickness: Under 0.188 inch	2°
	0.188 to 0.750 inch	1-1/2°
	0.750 inch to solid	1°
Flatness		0.004 inch per inch of width (0.004 inch minimum)
Surface Roughness	Section thickness: up through 0.063 inch	Maximum depth of defect: 0.0015 inch
	0.064–0.125 inch	0.002 inch
	0.126–0.188 inch	0.0025 inch
	0.189–0.250 inch	0.003 inch
	0.251 inch and up	0.004 inch

(*Courtesy*, John I. Thompson & Company)

Tolerances for Impact Extrusions

Wall thickness tolerances are from ±0.001 to ±0.005 in. (±0.02 to ±0.13 mm) for relatively thin wall, low-strength alloy, cylindrical shapes of moderate size, but they may be as large as ±0.010 to ±0.015 in. (±0.25 to ±0.38 mm) for large parts of high-strength alloy. Wall thickness tolerances for rectangular shells range from ±0.005 to 0.015 in. (±0.13 to ±0.38 mm) depending on size, alloy, and nominal wall thickness.

Diameter tolerances typically range from ±0.001 in. (±0.025 mm) for small parts to ±0.010 to ±0.015 in. (±0.25 to ±0.38 mm) for large high-strength alloy parts.

Table V-4 indicates some of the economical tolerances for cylindrical parts. Closer tolerances at higher cost can be achieved by centerless grinding

Table V-4. Tolerances for Impact Extrusions

Diameter in Inches	Tolerances in Inches (plus or minus)		
	Outside Diameter	Inside Diameter	Bottom Thickness
Up to 0.750	0.001	0.002	0.007
0.750 to 1.500	0.003	0.004	0.010
1.500 to 1.750	0.005	0.006	0.012
1.750 to 2.000	0.006	0.007	0.012
2.000 to 2.500	0.007	0.008	0.012
2.500 to 3.500	0.009	0.010	0.015
3.500 to 4.000	0.010	0.011	0.015
4.000 to 4.500	0.011	0.012	0.015
4.500 to 5.000	0.014	0.015	0.015
5.000 to 6.000	0.020	0.020	0.015

the impacts. Dimensional tolerances in the forged part (the bottom) of the extrusion are influenced by many variables, but ±0.005 to 0.015 in. (±0.13 to ±0.38 mm) is typical. Variation of extruded length usually requires a separate trimming operation.

FASTENING AND ASSEMBLY TECHNIQUES FOR EXTRUSIONS

Aluminum extrusions are continuously showing their flexibility in the reduction and elimination of mechanical fasteners needed to assemble component parts.

Some of the chief extrusion design features have been accomplished by dove tail assemblies, ball and socket details, key slots, screw bosses, simulated screw slots, V-notching, and snap fits that will not become unhinged. Both the dovetail (*Figure 5-11*) and the ball socket type of fastening allow slip fits between mating parts over either short or long lengths. However, accumulated straightness and twist tolerances limit the effectiveness on extremely long sections because of the metal binding tendencies.

Figure 5-11. Jointing components. (*Courtesy*, Xerox Corporation)

These details should never be toleranced, but only designated as mating slip fits over a specified length. The slip fit can be be controlled when both sections are supplied at the same time. With a slip fit (*Figure 5-12*), adjustments can be made to counter tolerance accumulations.

With the *hinge fit* (*Figure 5-13*), larger assembly can be made up by the hinge fitting smaller extrusions together.

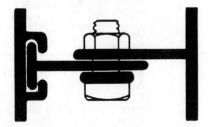

Figure 5-12. Slip fit. (*Courtesy*, Xerox Corporation)

HINGE FIT

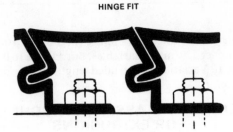

Figure 5-13. Hinge fit. (*Courtesy*, Xerox Corporation)

Key slots are used primarily for joining mitered sections where the method of closure is best hidden for decorative purposes and where the unit structural stresses are minimal. This is the principal choice of fastening used in the picture frame industry where many unique corner keys have been designed to afford better finish corner assemblies.

Screw bosses perform the simple function of accepting self-threading screws and have been modified in recent years to include raised areas that allow for major and minor diameter for ease of insertion while not sacrificing holding power. (See *Figure 5-14.*) This fastener can save a machining operation in connecting parts.

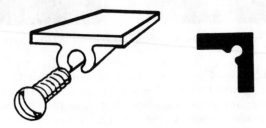

Figure 5-14. Extruded screw bosses. (*Courtesy*, Xerox Corporation)

144

Extruded simulated *screw slots* offer the designer the option of fastening screws in either direction and allow a latitude of movement for joining tightly toleranced prepunched or drilled parts to the extrusion without fear of tolerance buildup and hole interference. V-notching is the designer's choice for sections, that will not require disassembly once assembled.

The one-way *snap fit* is specifically utilized by those designers who require an assembly without any mechanical fasteners. *Snap fits* (*Figure 5-15*) leave exposed surfaces of assemblies uncluttered. Before the designer uses a method of fastening an extrusion to another extrusion, he or she should consult with the extruder and the manufacturing engineer to determine the most economical method of assembly.

Mechanical fasteners are convenient because they allow for easy assembly and disassembly, adjustment, and maintenance. Slots, holes, and threads for mechanical fasteners can be extruded as integral features of a shape. When ordering a thread fit (*Figure 5-16*), supply the extruder with complete fastener details or a sample of the fastener itself for inspection purposes.

Nut retainers (*Figure 5-17*) or *T-slots* retain nut or bolt heads.

The adjustable locking connectors and restrained nut connectors (*Figure 5-18*) give adjustment to the joining of parts.

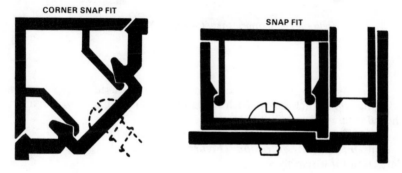

Figure 5-15. Snap fits. (*Courtesy*, Xerox Corporation)

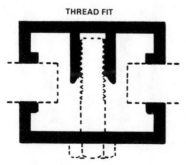

Figure 5-16. Thread fit. (*Courtesy*, Xerox Corporation)

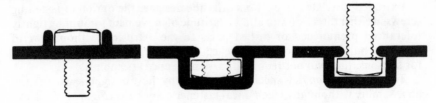

Figure 5-17. Nut retainers. (*Courtesy*, Xerox Corporation)

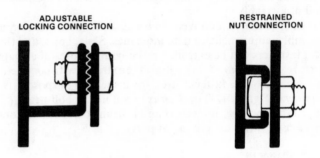

ADJUSTABLE
LOCKING CONNECTION

RESTRAINED
NUT CONNECTION

Figure 5-18. Connectors (*Courtesy*, Xerox Corporation)

Figure 5-19 shows various examples of lap joints used for positioning or building larger enclosures. With the lap-lock joints, *A* is moved in and up, then *B* is inserted to lock the joint.

Figure 5-20 is an example of a cylindrical sliding fit.

With *interlocking extrusions* (*Figure 5-21*), flat locking edges require less deflection for assembly.

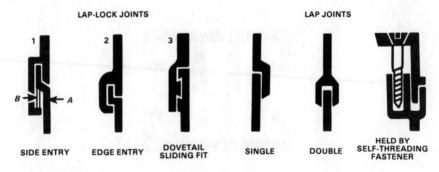

LAP-LOCK JOINTS   LAP JOINTS

1   2   3

B ➤   ◄ A

SIDE ENTRY   EDGE ENTRY   DOVETAIL
SLIDING FIT   SINGLE   DOUBLE   HELD BY
SELF-THREADING
FASTENER

Figure 5-19. Extrusion joining methods. (*Courtesy*, Xerox Corporation)

146

Figure 5-20. Cylindrical sliding fit. (*Courtesy*, Xerox Corporation)

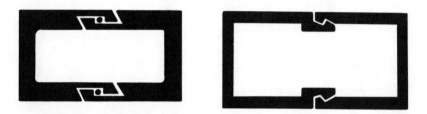

Figure 5-21. Interlocking extrusions. (*Courtesy*, Xerox Corporation)

6

Metalstamping and Forming

This chapter discusses metal stamping and forming, materials, design considerations, and tolerances.

DEFINITIONS

Stamping is passing a cold sheet or strip of metal through a pair of dies to cut it to a predetermined size and shape.

Forming is stressing metal beyond its yield point and thus producing a permanent dimensional change and desired shape.

A *press brake*, sometimes called a *power brake*, is a mechanical press with a long bed and a relatively short stroke. This press is used to produce long and narrow sheet metal or plate parts, and to fill voids in production capabilities between stamping and forming.

Spinning is forming a disc of sheet metal into conical, hemispherical, or cylindrical shapes.

PRACTICES

All metal stamping operations can be classed as either cutting or forming. Cutting operations are those in which the metal is completely sheared by stressing it beyond its ultimate strength. Forming operations are those in which the metal is stressed beyond the yield point and permanently deformed.

A stamped part is shallow-formed and involves little or no change in the thickness of the metal. Parts that are deep-formed are considered to be drawn parts.

Stamping is a mass production process, and quantity is the key to its effective usage. Generally, if a product can be designed as a stamping, it can be produced in large quantities at a lower cost than by any other process.

To consider stamping as practical only in mass production applications is erroneous, however. Some short-run stampings can produce as few as a hundred parts in competition with other processes. The minimum quantity for economical production by stamping is determined by the design of the part.

149

STAMPING OPERATIONS

Cutting

Cutting operations are designed to change the outline of the edges of the part, or cut holes in the interior of the part. These operations include blanking, shearing, parting, notching, lancing, slitting, punching, and piercing.

Blanking. Blanking is the cutting of shapes from sheet stock, either to produce finished parts or to perform the first stage in a forming operation. If size is important, the die is made to size, and clearance is taken off the punch. If the blank is very large in relation to the metal thickness, curvature of the sheet may cause measurable inaccuracy in the blank even though the tools are accurate.

Since the blank follows the shape of the punch, it is possible to form a shallow shape simultaneously with blanking; if the face of the punch has a convex contour, the metal is stretched to that shape before shearing occurs.

In blanking, the pressure required depends upon the strength of the stock and the depth of penetration before shearing occurs; it is inversely proportional to the stock hardness.

Blanking Costs. Since the blank contour and intricacy determines die cost, simple blank contours should be used whenever possible. It may be less expensive to build a component from several simple parts than to make an intricate part.

Straight-sided blanks with corner radii are less expensive than blanks with square corners. Sharply pointed corners are even worse than square corners in reducing tool life. Narrow slots also reduce tool life and increase the cost of blanking.

In making a blanking layout, an attempt should be made to get the greatest number of blanks for a given area. To facilitate bending, the direction of the grain must be carefully considered. The greatest saving results when the blank can be cut from standard width material, and sometimes a small design change facilitates the use of such material.

Some of the factors which can save stock and increase production—and should therefore be considered in designing for blanking—are illustrated in *Figures 6-1, 6-2,* and *6-3.*

Shearing, Parting, and Notching. Shearing and notching operations differ from blanking in that they set up unbalanced lateral forces which make it difficult to control dimensions. In the parting operation, lateral forces are in balance, thus allowing closer dimensional control than in shearing.

Parting and shearing are both used to separate a part from raw stock. Shearing generally produces no scrap while the parting operation does produce some scrap.

Notching is blanking along an edge, which is to say that only part of the punch periphery is cutting. Because of the unbalanced forces incidental to notching, the part tends to move away from the punch, making it difficult to control dimensions as accurately as can be done with blanking. Since notches

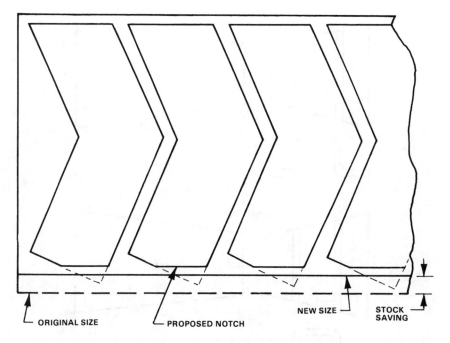

NEW SIZE ──┐ **STOCK SAVING** ──┐

└─ **ORIGINAL SIZE**   └─ **PROPOSED NOTCH**

Figure 6-1. Arrangement of parts for blanking must be carefully studied. Nesting or slight redesign can reduce scrap losses. (*Courtesy*, Reinhold Publications)

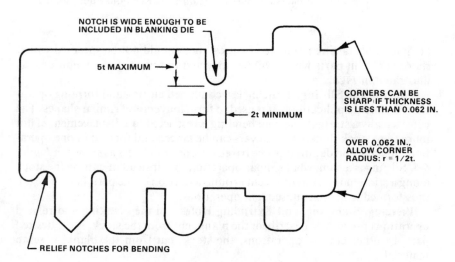

NOTCH IS WIDE ENOUGH TO BE INCLUDED IN BLANKING DIE

5t MAXIMUM ──▶

2t MINIMUM

CORNERS CAN BE SHARP IF THICKNESS IS LESS THAN 0.062 IN.

OVER 0.062 IN., ALLOW CORNER RADIUS: $r = 1/2t$.

└─ RELIEF NOTCHES FOR BENDING

Figure 6-2. Attention to contour details will produce the best part at the lowest cost. (*Courtesy*, Reinhold Publications)

151

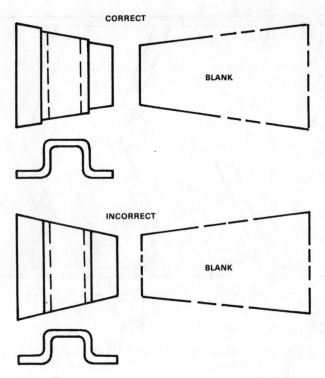

Figure 6-3. For economical operation, parts should be designed to permit straight edges on flat blanks, if possible. (*Courtesy,* Reinhold Publications)

are potential starting points for failures, they should not be specified with a sharp vertex in parts which will be subjected to severe stress conditions, as illustrated in *Figure 6-4*.

Lancing and Slitting. Lancing is a combined cutting and forming operation of limited applications. It is used to form louvers and similar shapes. The cut is usually a straight line, and bending is restricted to a displacement of not more than stock thickness. Louvers can be lanced and formed in one operation. Spacing and depths must be based on stock thickness as shown in *Figure 6-5*. Slitting is a somewhat similar operation, but instead of cutting the stock along a straight line, it is often cut around a portion of the periphery. The tab thus formed is bent in subsequent operations.

Piercing, Stamping, and Extruding Holes. In the blanking and related operations previously described, the blank, cut from the stock, is the desired part. In other cutting operations, the stock, cut from the blank, is scrap material.

If holes are required in stamped parts, they are formed by punching, extruding, or piercing (*Figure 6-6*).

152

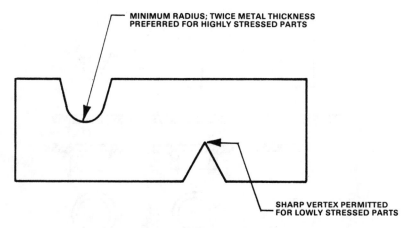

MINIMUM RADIUS; TWICE METAL THICKNESS PREFERRED FOR HIGHLY STRESSED PARTS

SHARP VERTEX PERMITTED FOR LOWLY STRESSED PARTS

Figure 6-4. Notches in highly stressed part should be designed with the largest possible radius. Sharp notches can be used for parts not subjected to stress conditions. (*Courtesy*, Reinhold Publications)

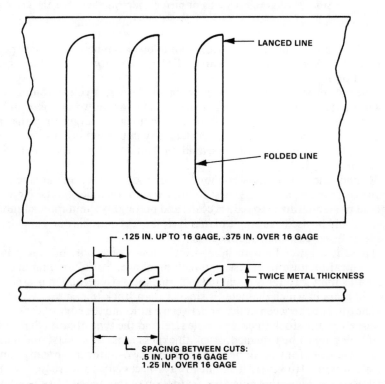

LANCED LINE

FOLDED LINE

.125 IN. UP TO 16 GAGE, .375 IN. OVER 16 GAGE

TWICE METAL THICKNESS

SPACING BETWEEN CUTS:
.5 IN. UP TO 16 GAGE
1.25 IN. OVER 16 GAGE

Figure 6-5. Lanced areas must be designed with spacing and depths bases on stock thickness. (*Courtesy*, Reinhold Publications)

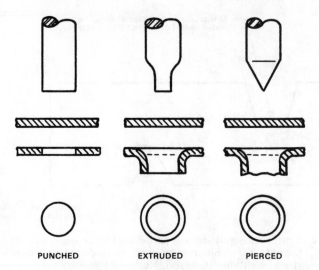

Figure 6-6. Holes are punched, extruded or pierced. Punching does not increase stock thickness; extruding or piercing increases effective thickness at hole. (*Courtesy,* Reinhold Publications)

In designing for punched holes, it should be remembered that only part of the stock thickness is cleanly sheared; the balance is torn out by the pressure exerted on it.

The hole produced by punching has tapered sides. A rule of thumb is that not more than one-half the stock is sheared and, as shown in *Figure 6-7*, the hole diameter below the sheared area is significantly larger than that produced by the punch. This point is particularly important because, if the hole sides are to act as bearing surfaces, a subsequent operation may be required to obtain parallel walls.

Round holes are the most economical to produce, since they are the easiest shape to produce, and the easiest to hold within tolerance limits. Hole sizes should be standardized to reduce costs, and preferably a minimum number of sizes should be used in a single blank. If slots are required, round ends can be made at lower cost than square ends.

There is a lower limit to hole sizes, below which hole punching is not economical because of excessive punch breakage. For aluminum and mild steel, this limit is roughly equal to stock thickness. Generally, it is preferable to drill holes in which diameter is smaller than stock thickness.

The distance between holes, or between a hole and the edge of the stock, is governed by the stock thickness, hole size, and the type of hole (*Figure 6-8*).

If holes are to be threaded, stock thickness must be at least one-half the thread diameter for steel or brass, and at least two-thirds the thread diameter for aluminum. However, it is not always necessary to increase the stock thickness to achieve this objective. Extrusion of the stock (*Figure 6-6*) often increases thickness at the hole to the required value.

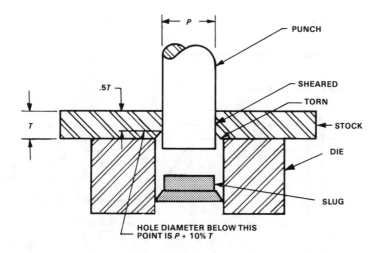

Figure 6-7. In punching a hole, only part of the metal is sheared by the punch; the remainder of the stock is torn out. This causes the hole to taper as indicated. (*Courtesy,* Reinhold Publications)

SHAPE	METAL THICKNESS (INCH)	MINIMUM (A) (INCH)
ROUND	UP TO 0.062	0.12
	OVER 0.062	2T
SQUARE	UP TO 0.090	0.18
	OVER 0.090	2T

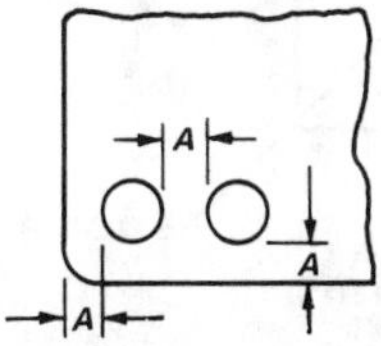

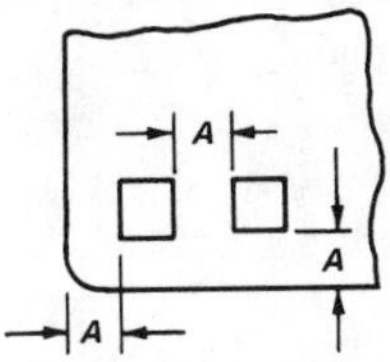

Figure 6-8. Minimum edge distances.

If two stampings are to be fastened together, it is desirable to compensate for inaccuracies which may occur during manufacturing by specifying a round hole in one part and a slot in the other. Slots provide for adjustment in overall length and width dimensions. Slots should be specified as shown in *Figure 6-9*.

155

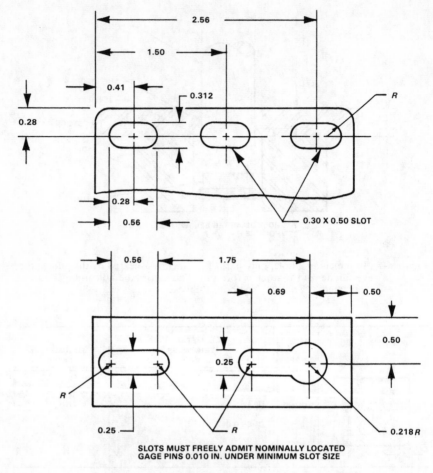

**SLOTS MUST FREELY ADMIT NOMINALLY LOCATED
GAGE PINS 0.010 IN. UNDER MINIMUM SLOT SIZE**

Figure 6-9. Slots should be dimensioned to show requirements plainly.
(*Courtesy,* Reinhold Publications)

Limitations

The minimum tolerances for the form (size and shape) of a detail produced by a cutting operation must be 10 to 15% of stock thickness. Also, the tolerances on the location of those same details cannot be tighter than 10 to 15% of the stock thickness—and often must be looser.

Design vs. Need. The designer should analyze the need for close tolerances in any part designed as a stamping. When only certain dimensions are vital to the function of a part, close tolerances on other dimensions lead to needless expense.

FORMING

Forming includes all operations that produce a desired shape in sheet metal by stressing the metal beyond its yield point to produce a permanent dimensional change. This includes not only stamping and bending, but also drawing and spinning.

Bending

Bending, as used in the stamping process, usually implies bends along a straight line rather than a curve. The extent of the bend is designated by the included angle after bending, and the extent of the sharpness is designated by the radius at the inside corner. Bends should be made across the grain, if possible, or at 45° (0.785 rad) to the grain direction. Bends parallel to the grain should be avoided.

Using the largest possible bend radius is good practice since this permits greater latitude in material selection and often assures better bends. The inside radii at bends should not be less than stock thickness as illustrated in *Figure 6-10*.

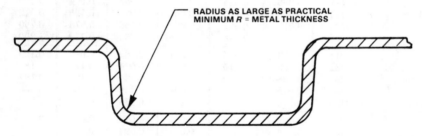

RADIUS AS LARGE AS PRACTICAL
MINIMUM R = METAL THICKNESS

Figure 6-10. Inside radii at bends should not be less than the stock thickness; larger radii are desirable. (*Courtesy,* Reinhold Publications)

Although minimum bend radii have been established for some materials, and suggestions are given in *Tables VI-1* through *VI-4* for bend radii, minimum values must sometimes be developed. For a first approximation, the following rule is suggested:

Multiply the stock thickness (t) by: 0.3 to 0.7 for soft metals, minimum stock thickness 0.020 in. (0.508 mm); 0.6 to 1.2 for hard metals, minimum stock thickness 0.060 in. (1.524 mm); 2.0 to 3.0 for very hard metals.

Modifications must be made if cracking or tearing occurs on bends which are made using the suggested rules or the values in the tables for bend radii. It may be necessary to:
1. Increase the bend radius
2. Barrel finish the blanks to remove rough edges before handling
3. Anneal the blanks
4. Select more ductile material.

Table VI-1. Approximate Bend Radii for 90° (1.57 rad) Cold-bend Aluminum Alloy

Thickness		1/64	1/32	1/16	1/8	3/16	1/4
Alloy	Temper	Bend Radii					
1100	−0	0.008	0.015	0.031	0.062	0.094	0.250
	−H12	0.008	0.015	0.031	0.062	0.094	0.250
	−H14	0.008	0.015	0.031	0.062	0.094	0.250
	−H16	0.008	0.015	0.062	0.078	0.250	0.537
	−H18	0.015	0.031	0.094	0.187	0.462	0.750
Alclad 2014	−0	0.008	0.015	0.031	0.062	0.094	0.250
	−T3	0.025	0.070	0.187	0.375	0.750	1.000
	−T4	0.025	0.070	0.187	0.375	0.750	1.000
	−T6	0.048	0.125	0.250	0.500	0.937	1.500
2024	−0	0.008	0.015	0.031	0.062	0.094	0.250
	−T3	0.031	0.094	0.250	0.500	0.750	1.250
	−T361	0.047	0.125	0.312	0.625	0.937	1.750
	−T4	0.031	0.094	0.250	0.500	0.750	1.250
	−T81	0.062	0.156	0.375	0.812	1.312	2.000
	−T861	0.070	0.187	0.438	0.875	1.500	2.250
3003	−0	0.008	0.015	0.031	0.062	0.094	0.250
	−H12	0.008	0.015	0.031	0.062	0.094	0.250
	−H14	0.008	0.015	0.031	0.094	0.125	0.312
	−H16	0.015	0.031	0.062	0.156	0.375	0.750
	−H18	0.015	0.048	0.093	0.250	0.750	1.250
5050	−0	0.008	0.015	0.031	0.062	0.094	0.125
	−H32	0.008	0.015	0.031	0.094	0.125	0.187
	−H34	0.008	0.015	0.031	0.094	0.125	0.187
	−H36	0.015	0.031	0.094	0.156	0.281	0.500
	−H38	0.015	0.047	0.125	0.375	0.562	1.000
5052	−0	0.008	0.015	0.031	0.062	0.094	0.125
	−H32	0.008	0.015	0.031	0.094	0.125	0.187
	−H34	0.008	0.015	0.047	0.125	0.187	0.250
	−H36	0.008	0.015	0.062	0.187	0.375	0.500
	−H38	0.015	0.047	0.125	0.375	0.437	1.000
6061	−0	0.008	0.015	0.031	0.062	0.094	0.125
	−T4	0.015	0.032	0.062	0.187	0.281	0.500
	−T6	0.015	0.032	0.094	0.250	0.375	0.750
7075	−0	0.008	0.015	0.047	0.125	0.187	0.375
	−T6	0.047	0.125	0.312	0.625	0.937	1.500

Bend Allowance. The total length required for bending is the sum of the two legs plus the bend allowance. Depending on the angle and sharpness of bend, this length can vary considerably. Therefore, it is necessary to consider the effect of stretching the metal at the outside of the bend when developing part size.

Where the radius of a 90° (1.57 rad) bend is less than 0.015 in. (0.38 mm), it is customary to apply an allowance of $0.4t$ to the inside dimensions. For bends having a radius greater than 0.015 in. (0.38 mm), and any angle, the formula is $L = A + B + S (0.4t + R)$, where:

Table VI-2. Minimum Bend Radii for Commonly Formed Stainless Steels

Type	Condition	Thickness (T) in Inches	Bend Radius
301 302 303 304	Annealed	All	1/2 T
	1/4 Hard	To 0.050	1/2 T
		Over 0.050	T
	1/2 Hard	To 0.050	T
		Over 0.050	1.5 T
	Hard	To 0.030	2 T
		0.031–0.050	2.5 T
316	Annealed	All	1/2 T
	1/4 Hard	To 0.050	T
		Over 0.050	1.5 T
	1/2 Hard	To 0.030	2 T
		0.031–0.050	2.5 T
		Over 0.051	3 T
321, 347	Annealed	All	1.5 T
410, 430	Annealed	All	T

L = the length of the developed blank
A and B = the length of the legs
S = a constant taken from *Table VI-5*
R = the bend radius
t = the stock thickness.

The developed length of a blank is computed by considering each bend separately.

Sometimes cost can be reduced by using materials which are thinner than those normally considered practical. Use of reinforcing ribs or curled edges can often increase part strength enough to permit use of thinner stock. Bends for ribs should be made across the grain if possible. Suggested dimensions for ribs are given in *Figure 6-11*.

Flanges. When designing flanges, various precautions should be taken. The minimum height of a flange should range from two to four times the stock thickness, depending on such factors as bend radius, material, and stock thickness.

Tapered flanges should not taper to the face and thus produce a sharp point, but should be cut off so that the narrowest part is about twice the metal thickness. Outside flanges, and flanges around openings, should also have a height of twice the metal thickness.

Hemmed edges should be notched at the corners to eliminate gathering during flanging.

Holes in Bent Parts. The location of a hole near a bend must be carefully planned. If a hole is too close to a bend, distortion results and the shape of the hole may change enough to prevent functioning of the part.

Table VI-3. Minimum Bend Radii for Copper Alloys

Alloy	Temper	Nominal Thickness (inch)	Minimum Bend Radius		
			A	B	C
Copper	Half Hard	0.020	0.031	0.031	0.047
	Extra Hard	0.020	0.047	0.047	0.062
Red Brass (85%)	Drawing Anneal	0.005–0.064	0.010	0.010	0.010
	Half Hard	0.020–0.050	0.010	0.010	0.010
	Full Hard	0.040	0.015	0.032	0.093
	Extra Hard	0.040	0.062	0.094	0.218
	Spring	0.040	0.062	0.187	0.500
Low Brass (80%)	Full Hard	0.020	0.031	0.047	0.062
	Spring	0.020	0.031	0.125	0.187
Cartridge Brass (70%)	Half Hard	0.005–0.050	0.010	0.010	0.010
	Full Hard	0.040	0.015	0.031	0.047
	Extra Hard	0.040	0.031	0.156	0.218
	Spring	0.040	0.062	0.250	0.250
	Extra Spring	0.040	0.125	0.250	0.250
Medium Leaded Brass	Half Hard	0.040	0.010	0.010	0.010
Yellow Brass	Half Hard	0.005–0.090	0.010	0.010	0.010
	Full Hard	0.040	0.015	0.015	0.015
	Extra Hard	0.040	0.047	0.125	0.187
	Spring	0.040	0.047	0.218	0.250
Phosphor Bronze (5%)	Half Hard	0.020–0.070	0.010	0.010	0.010
	Full Hard	0.040	0.063	0.063	0.125
	Extra Hard	0.040	0.063	0.125	—
	Spring	0.040	0.094	—	—
Phosphor Bronze (8%)	Half Hard	0.005–0.064	0.010	0.010	0.010
	Full Hard	0.040	0.031	0.125	—
	Extra Hard	0.040	0.047	0.156	0.250
	Spring	0.040	0.094	0.250	0.500
	Extra Spring	0.064	0.156	0.250	0.500
High-silicon Bronze	Hard	0.020	0.031	0.031	0.063
	Spring	0.020	0.047	0.094	0.187
Nickel Silver (65–18)	Half Hard	0.040	0.010	0.015	0.031
	Full Hard	0.040	0.063	0.063	0.094
	Extra Hard	0.040	0.125	0.125	0.187
	Spring	0.040	0.156	0.187	0.218
	Extra Spring	0.040	0.156	0.218	0.250
Nickel Silver (55–18)	Half Hard	0.040	0.063	0.063	0.094
	Full Hard	0.040	0.063	0.063	0.094
	Extra Hard	0.040	0.125	0.156	0.187

A—Bend perpendicular to grain direction.
B—Bend 45° to grain direction.
C—Bend parallel to grain direction.

Step	**Thickness (inch)**						

Table VI-4. Minimum Bend Radii for Carbon and Low Alloy Steels

Steel	Thickness (inch)						
SAE Steel	0.016	0.025	0.035	0.050	0.062	0.109	0.187
1020–1025	0.030	0.030	0.062	0.062	0.062	0.130	0.190
1070–1095	0.062	0.062	0.094	0.130	0.160	0.312	0.500
4130*	0.030	0.030	0.062	0.094	0.094	0.160	0.312
8630*	0.030	0.030	0.062	0.094	0.094	0.160	0.312

* Annealed.

Table VI-5. Constants for Angle Bends

Angle (deg)	Constant (S)	Angle (deg)	Constant (S)
0° 10′	0.0029	35	0.6109
0° 30′	0.0087	40	0.6981
1	0.0175	45	0.7854
2	0.0349	50	0.8728
3	0.0524	55	0.9599
4	0.0698	60	1.0472
5	0.0873	65	1.1345
10	0.1745	70	1.2217
15	0.2618	75	1.3090
20	0.3491	80	1.3963
25	0.4363	85	1.4835
30	0.5236	90	1.5708

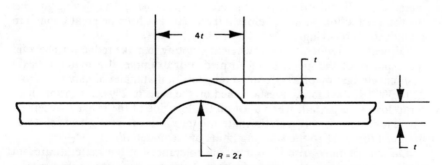

Figure 6-11. Strengthening ribs should be dimensioned as indicated and handled like simple bends. (*Courtesy*, Reinhold Publications)

161

It is preferable to avoid distortion by keeping hole edges at least twice the stock thickness away from the inside radius of the bend. If this is not possible, and the design requires a hole within the area where distortion occurs, the hole can be punched after bending. This secondary operation increases the cost considerably, however.

Springback. During forming operations, the contour of the part matches that of the dies. Upon release of the load, however, the part assumes a different shape because of the release of elastic forces. The distortion that occurs—called springback—is a function of the ratio of part radius to stock thickness (r/t). Springback must be taken into account if the final shape is to correspond to that of the original design.

Tools can be designed to compensate for springback by over-bending the part. If the parts are produced from widely used metals—aluminum, brass, and low-carbon steels—the properties are sufficiently well known to make compensating relatively easy. However, when working with some of the lesser known metals, springback can be responsible for many production difficulties.

Materials

Any metal that can be prefabricated into sheet or strip can be processed further by simple stamping procedures.

Formability. Mechanical properties give some indication of the ability of a metal to form satisfactorily. If there is a relatively large difference between yield and ultimate strengths, and elongation is high, the forming characteristics of a material are good.

However, these characteristics give only partial indication of the actual formability of a material. Rate of workhardening has a profound effect on the reduction that can be given to a material before annealing is required, and it is more important than the mechanical properties of annealed material. Workhardening rates of metals differ greatly, a factor that must be considered in selecting a material for forming operations. As the hardness of a metal increases, its ductility decreases; therefore the rate of workhardening governs the total reduction possible before internal stresses become great enough to require stress relieving.

Difficulties frequently occur when attempting to make reductions beyond the capacity of the metal being formed. For example, if a material has a nominal elongation of 25%, commercial lots of that material may vary from 23 to 30%. If the tooling is established on the basis of 25% elongation, high scrap losses may result when a lot on the low side of the range is received. There is nothing wrong with the material; the tooling is wrong because it was designed too close to the working limits of the material.

Difficulties may arise if commercial tolerances of the material are not taken into account in the designing stage. Thickness variation in sheet metals can cause parts made on the same tooling to be different in shape because of springback or because the pressure applied is either insufficient or excessive for forming the predetermined angles.

162

Breakage in forming operations is not always caused by the quality of the material. Poor die design, improper clearance, and excessive reduction between anneals can all contribute to the failure to form a part satisfactorily.

Ferrous Metals. Stampings are produced from carbon steels ranging from the low-carbon to the high-carbon steels, from various alloy steels, and from stainless steels and heat resisting grades. However, the major production is confined to several modifications of low-carbon steel.

Nonferrous Alloys. A wide range of properties are available in the nonferrous alloys, from very ductile materials that can be formed readily by all of the stamping processes to those that are refractory and formable only by simple operations.

The aluminum alloys are among the most formable of the commonly fabricated metals. There are, of course, differences between aluminum alloys and other metals in the amount of permissible deformation and in some aspect of tool design as well as in details of procedure.

These differences stem primarily from the lower tensile and yield strengths of aluminum alloys, and from their comparatively slow rates of workhardening. The compositions and tempers of aluminum alloys also affect their formability.

Most stampings from aluminum alloys are produced from 1100, 3003, and 5052. The 5052 alloy draws well and gives a considerably stronger part than either of the two other alloys. However, it workhardens more rapidly and consequently a smaller reduction per draw is required.

The heat treatable alloys are used in applications for which a high strength-to-weight ratio is required. These include alloys 6061, 2014, 2024, 7075, and 7178 in approximate order of increasing strength.

Copper and copper alloys are readily formed into complicated shapes, even in foil thickness. The copper alloys commonly formed are characterized by strength and by work-hardening rates between those of steel and the aluminum alloys.

Yellow brass and cartridge brass are the most widely used copper alloys, and second in use only to the low-carbon steels. Red brass is probably the third most commonly used alloy. All three of these alloys have excellent cold working properties, combining optimum ductility and good strength. The nickel silvers (which are brasses containing from 10 to 18% nickel) also belong in this group. Nickel silver 65-18 can be worked almost as well as yellow brass.

Copper, although initially softer than brass, has a lower combination of ductility and strength than brass, and requires more careful handling. However, copper workhardens less rapidly than brass and can be cold worked severely with reductions up to 90%.

Zinc-sheet alloys, nickel, magnesium-alloy sheets, tantalum, and other alloys can be formed during the stamping operation.

The selection of the material for proper function must be carefully analyzed by the designer to achieve the lowest cost stamping.

Stamping Tolerances

When deciding on the tolerances to be required for a given design, careful consideration must be given to the function of the stamping and to the product quality. Also, the closer the tolerance, the greater the cost of production. Proper balance between cost and required accuracy must be determined to achieve the maximum benefit in quality and economy.

An excellent way to keep costs in line is to specify close tolerances only as required for proper function of the part. Use of widest possible tolerances on overall length, width, depth, diameter of formed edges, dimensions of flanges, and distances between holes, increases production rates and lowers cost.

When one part mates with another, the same tolerance should be employed for both.

Although tolerances of ±0.001 in. (±0.025 mm) can be held on holes, hole locations, and outside diameters, such tight requirements call for careful handling and increased production costs; production tolerances of ±0.005 in. (0.13 mm) can be held, but ±0.010 (±0.25 mm) is preferable. Suggested minimum tolerances on punched holes are given in *Table VI-6*.

Table VI-6. Suggested Minimum Tolerances in Punched Holes in Aluminum, Brass, and Low-carbon Steels

Metal Thickness	*Suggested Minimum ± Tolerances (inch)*				
	Nominal Diameter of Hole				
	Up to 1	>1 up to 3	>3 up to 10	>10 up to 20	>20
Up to 0.015	0.0015	0.003	0.004	0.006	0.008
>0.015 to 0.031	0.003	0.004	0.005	0.008	0.010
>0.031 to 0.062	0.004	0.005	0.007	0.010	0.015
>0.062 to 0.125	0.010	0.012	0.015	0.020	0.025
>0.125	0.020	0.025	0.030	0.035	0.040

Parts can generally be held to closer tolerances on a four-slide press than on conventional presses. For example, formed dimensions can be held from ±0.001 to ±0.005 in. (±0.025 to ±0.13 mm), and angles from 0.5 to one degree (0.0087 to 0.0017 rad).

Tolerances allowed on hole locations near bends can have a significant effect on the cost of production. For example, if the tolerance between a bend and a hole center is ±0.015 in. (±0.4 mm), the hole can be punched before bending. But to hold a tolerance of ±0.002 in. (±0.05 mm) would require punching after bending, with higher die cost and increased part cost.

Depth of Formed Parts. A tolerance of ±0.010 in. (±0.25 mm) on depth of formed parts under 0.5 in. (12.7 mm) in depth, and ±0.015 in. (±0.38 mm) up to 1.5 in. (38.1 mm) in depth can be held. Closer limits require extra trimming operations at additional cost.

Flatness. Hard-temper materials retain flatness and parallel surfaces more readily than softer materials, which pull down at the edges during blanking and punching.

Surfaces of a part greater than several inches in area, which must be flat within 0.002 in. (0.05 mm) or less, require additional operations which increase part cost. Generally, parts up to one inch (25.4 mm) in length can be expected within 0.003-in. (0.08-mm) maximum out of flat. For each additional inch in length, 0.002 in. (0.05 mm) should be added for flatness.

Press-brake Forming

Press-brake forming is a process in which the workpiece is placed over an open die and pressed into the die by a punch actuated by the press ram. The process is used primarily for forming long narrow parts that are not adaptable to press forming, and for applications in which production quantities are too small to warrant the tooling cost of other forming processes.

The setup and tooling for press-brake forming (*Figure 6-12*) are relatively simple. The distance the punch enters the die determines the bend angle, and is controlled by the shut height of the press. The span width of the die, or the width of the die opening, affects the force needed to bend the workpiece. The minimum width is determined by the thickness of the material and the bend radii.

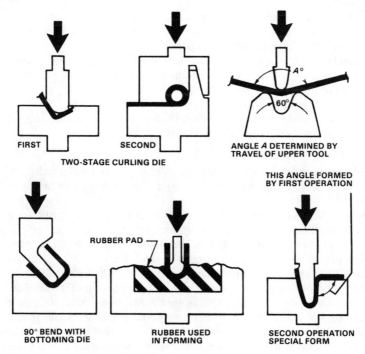

Figure 6-12. Typical brake dies.

165

The minimum flange width (W) for any material which can be obtained in press-brake forming without trimming is noted in *Table VI-7*. Avoid using flange widths less than the minimum values shown in the table. Expensive trimming operations are required to provide smaller flange widths.

Return flanges of parts to be formed on the brake should not be more than 90° (1.5 rad) to the primary flange. The length of plate or sheet that can be bent is limited only by the size of the press brake.

Here is an example of calculating minimum sections for press brake using *Table VI-7*:

Material	2024-T4
Material Thickness	0.050 in. (1.27 mm)
Bend Radius	0.25 in. (6.35 mm)
W (Min) =	0.56 in. (14.0 mm) (from *Table VI-7*)
L (Min) =	$W + R + T$
=	0.56 in. + 0.25 in. + 0.050 in. (14.0 mm + 6.35 mm + 1.27 mm)
=	0.86 in. (22.0 mm) = Minimum Section (L)

The following design practices will aid in designing economical parts for press brake operations.

- Where possible, specify bend radii suitable for tempered material. Doing so helps avoid subsequent heat-treat and straightening operations.
- Parts which require more than one bend should be designed so that all bends have the same radius. Different bend radii in a part cause additional setup operations and expense.
- Bends should not be tangent to each other because of interference with the brake dies. Calculate minimum width from *Table VI-7* if the design requires tangent bends.
- Apply economical tolerances as shown in *Table VI-8*.

Tolerances closer than those shown require extensive reworking of parts, or the use of rolls or other die operations.

Dimensional Accuracy

As in other mechanical operations, tolerances are influenced by design, stock tolerances, blank preparation, and the condition of machine and tooling.

Design. Bends too close to workpiece edges make it difficult to maintain accurate bendlines. Notches and cutouts on the bendline make it difficult to hold accurate bend locations. Offset bends shift unless the distance between bends in the offset is at least six times the stock thickness.

Stock Tolerances. The dimensional accuracy of the finished part is influenced by the stock tolerances, since they use up a portion of the assigned part tolerance. There is a significant difference both in thickness tolerances and cost among hot-rolled strip and sheet, and cold-rolled strip and sheet.

Cold-rolled steel sheet is produced to closer tolerances than hot-rolled sheet, but its cost is higher. Tolerances on steel strip, hot or cold-rolled, are closer than those for corresponding sheet.

Table VI-7A. Minimum Flange Widths Formed on Press Brake

Parts up to 48.0 long

Material Thickness	Bend Radii												
	Widths												
	0.03	0.06	0.09	0.12	0.16	0.19	0.22	0.25	0.28	0.31	0.38	0.44	0.50
0.016	0.080	0.141	0.203	0.266	0.328	0.391	0.453	0.516	0.578	0.641			
0.020	0.091	0.145	0.207	0.270	0.332	0.395	0.457	0.520	0.582	0.645	0.770		
0.025	0.107	0.150	0.212	0.275	0.337	0.400	0.462	0.525	0.587	0.651	0.775	0.900	1.025
0.032	0.128	0.158	0.219	0.282	0.344	0.407	0.469	0.532	0.594	0.657	0.782	0.907	1.032
0.040	0.152	0.182	0.227	0.290	0.352	0.415	0.477	0.540	0.602	0.665	0.790	0.915	1.040
0.051		0.215	0.246	0.301	0.363	0.426	0.488	0.551	0.613	0.676	0.801	0.926	1.051
0.064			0.285	0.316	0.376	0.439	0.501	0.564	0.626	0.689	0.814	0.939	1.064
0.072			0.309	0.340	0.384	0.447	0.509	0.572	0.634	0.697	0.822	0.947	1.072
0.081				0.367	0.398	0.456	0.518	0.581	0.643	0.706	0.831	0.956	1.081
0.091				0.397	0.428	0.466	0.528	0.591	0.653	0.716	0.841	0.966	1.091
0.102					0.462	0.493	0.539	0.602	0.664	0.727	0.852	0.977	1.102
0.125						0.562	0.593	0.625	0.687	0.750	0.875	1.000	1.125
0.156								0.717	0.749	0.781	0.906	1.031	1.156
0.188										0.876	0.938	1.063	1.188
0.250											1.000	1.125	1.250

167

Table VI-7B. Minimum Flange Widths Formed on Press Brake

Parts over 48.0 to 96.0 long

Material Thickness	Bend Radii												
	Widths												
	0.03	0.06	0.09	0.12	0.16	0.19	0.22	0.25	0.28	0.31	0.38	0.44	0.50
0.016	0.142	0.203	0.265	0.328	0.390	0.453	0.515	0.578	0.640	0.703			
0.020	0.154	0.207	0.269	0.332	0.394	0.457	0.519	0.582	0.644	0.707	0.832		
0.025	0.169	0.212	0.274	0.337	0.399	0.462	0.524	0.587	0.649	0.713	0.837	0.962	1.087
0.032	0.190	0.220	0.281	0.344	0.406	0.469	0.531	0.594	0.656	0.719	0.844	0.969	1.094
0.040	0.214	0.244	0.289	0.352	0.414	0.477	0.539	0.602	0.664	0.727	0.852	0.977	1.102
0.051		0.277	0.308	0.363	0.424	0.488	0.550	0.613	0.675	0.738	0.863	0.988	1.113
0.064			0.410	0.441	0.501	0.564	0.626	0.689	0.751	0.814	0.939	1.064	1.189
0.072			0.439	0.465	0.509	0.572	0.634	0.697	0.759	0.822	0.947	1.072	1.197
0.081				0.523	0.554	0.612	0.674	0.737	0.799	0.862	0.987	1.112	1.237
0.091				0.553	0.584	0.622	0.684	0.747	0.809	0.872	0.997	1.122	1.247
0.102					0.618	0.649	0.695	0.758	0.820	0.883	1.008	1.133	1.258
0.125						0.750	0.781	0.813	0.875	0.938	1.063	1.188	1.313
0.156								0.967	0.999	1.031	1.156	1.281	1.406
0.188										1.189	1.251	1.376	1.501
0.250											1.500	1.563	1.625

Table VI-8. Press Brake Tolerances

	Material Thickness (inch)	Tolerance on Flange Width	Angular Tolerance (deg)		Length (inch)
			Attach Flange	Stiffening Flange	
	Up to 0.125	±0.015	±1	±3	48
		±0.030	±1	±3	96
	Over 0.125	±0.040	±3	±5	48
		±0.060	±3	±5	96

Thickness tolerances for steel plate are wider than those for hot-rolled steel sheet or strip. Therefore, when tolerance requirements are such that the material thickness is important, the designer should determine whether the stock can be obtained as strip or sheet rather than as plate.

Blank Preparation. An important effect on tolerances and cost of the finished part is proper blank preparation. A blank merely cut to length from purchased stock is inexpensive, but the width tolerance is that of the mill product. Good shearing increases the cost of the blank, but it provides greater accuracy. The stock from which blanks are cut must be flat enough for the blanks to be properly inserted into tooling and to remain in position during forming. Leveled and resquared sheet costs a little more, but is usually necessary when tolerances are tight.

Table VI-8 shows the economical tolerances that apply to parts designed for press-brake operations. If required, closer tolerances can be held, but at higher cost.

SPINNING

Spinning is a method of forming sheet metal into conical, hemispherical, or cylindrical shapes by combined rotation and force. The forming is done by application of pressure by a roller or spinning tool on the metal piece while it is being rotated by a revolving wood or metal form called the *chuck* in a spinning lathe. Conventional spinning and displacement spinning are the two categories in this method of metal forming.

Conventional Spinning

Conventional spinning involves forming of the metal back along the chuck. The area of the blank must be approximately equal to the shell area; the shell thickness remains constant.

Chuck Spinning. This method refers to the spinning of open shapes with no reentrant contours. The spun shapes can be produced in tiers and by one or more regular spinning operations. This is the most common and oldest method of spinning.

Sectional Chuck Spinning. This method is used mainly on drawn shells to produce shapes having reentrant contours in which the neck or opening is

169

smaller than the body. These chucks must be well matched at the section joints to prevent marks from showing at the finished shell.

Internal Roll Spinning. This improved method of spinning reentrant shapes—bulges and necks—is capable of high-production speeds, since the piece can be quickly removed from the roll without taking the tool apart.

Displacement Spinning

Displacement spinning involves an ironing of the metal back along the chuck. In this process, a smaller thicker blank is used so that the difference between the blank and the shell areas is equalized by thinning out a portion of the thick blank during spinning.

Hydrospin Process. In the hydrospin process, a metal disc-type blank is rotated at high speed while two opposing rollers force the material onto the rotating mandrel. The hydrospin machine is semiautomatic and hydraulically controlled, giving it both power and flexibility.

Hydrospinning can produce strong parts with maximum resistance to fatigue failure. When the metal is hydrospun, it undergoes a shear deformation which greatly elongates the grain structure. This deformation results in workhardening of the metal with a resultant increase in tensile strength.

Floturn Process. Floturn is a trade name that has been applied to a Lodge and Shipley development. It is basically a cold-rolling process in which the metal is displaced parallel to the centerline of a part in a spiral manner. This differs from the application of pressure in a cold-rolling mill only in that displacement in a mill is in a longitudinal direction and the displacement by Floturn is in a spiral manner. This is accomplished by flowing the metal over a mandrel, using a roller that is actuated by mechanical or hydraulic forces.

There is one basic difference between the Floturn method of cold-rolling and spinning. In spinning, a blank considerably larger than the finished piece is used. By exerting pressure, the blank is folded in a circular manner, using a hard tool against a round mold. This requires considerable skill on the part of the operator. In the Floturn method, the metal to form the part is obtained from the thickness of the blank, instead of from the diameter of the blank. The blank diameter is the same as that of the finished part, but its thickness is greater. The additional metal provided by this greater thickness is flowed into the extended shape. The machine controls all operations, and all parts are produced to uniform accuracy.

Because the diameter of the blank is changed in spinning, there is a tendency for the blank to leave or springback from the spin chuck over which it is being formed. For all practical purposes, the problem of springback has been eliminated in the Floturn method. This is due to the fact that the configuration of the blank is not changed with this method. If the blank is round, it remains round, and if it is sheared square, the remaining flanges remain square.

Advantages of Floturn include low tooling costs, increased strength and hardness, and excellent surface finish. A comparison of the conventional and displacement spinning methods is illustrated in *Figure 6-13.*

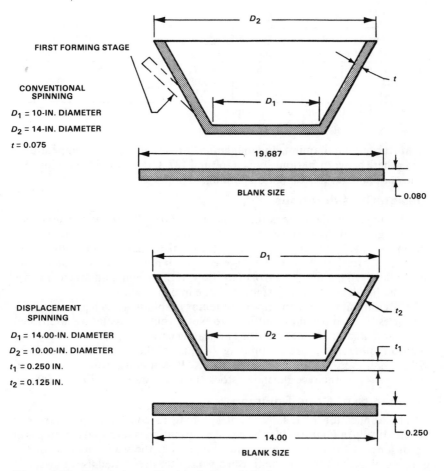

Figure 6-13. Comparison of basic spinning methods. (*Courtesy,* John I. Thompson & Company)

Materials

Almost all metals that are available in sheet form can be spun by either method.

Hand-spinning can be done on aluminum alloys up to 0.25-in. (6.35-mm) thickness, low-carbon steels and brasses up to 0.187-in. (4.75-mm) thickness, and stainless steels up to 0.125-in. (3.17-mm) thickness. Recommended stock thicknesses are shown in *Table VI-9.*

Although most common metals are cold-spun, it is sometimes advantageous to hot-spin them in order to reduce the required forces to move the material. The temperatures for hot-spinning vary with the material, but they must be high enough to maintain good metal flow.

171

Table VI-9. Recommended Stock Thickness for Spinning

Blank Diameter	Aluminum		Steel	
	Min	*Max*	*Min*	*Max*
Less than 4.0	0.025	0.045	0.020	0.040
4.0 to 20.0	0.032	0.080	0.025	0.063
More than 20.0	0.040	0.125	0.032	0.080

(*Courtesy*, John I. Thompson & Company)

Molybdenum, titanium, and magnesium are usually spun at temperatures somewhere between 500 and 800° F (260 and 427° C) above cold-spinning, but at lower temperatures than hot-spinning.

Design Considerations

The height-to-diameter ratio, as shown in *Table VI-10*, may be used as a general guide to the number of operations required, assuming other factors do not add to the difficulty of working the blank to shape. If the ratio is high, the area of metal to be worked is large and one or more breakdown steps may be necessary to maintain control of the flow. If the height-to-diameter ratio is low, the blank can be easily spun to shape in one operation.

Material thickness is an important factor in spinning. As blank thickness increases, it becomes more difficult to work, thus necessitating additional operations and sometimes requiring annealing between operations. Very thin blanks require more careful spinning, because of their tendency to wrinkle. Some may even require extra operations. It is important for economical purposes to use the recommended stock thickness shown in *Table VI-9*.

Mechanics of Cone Spinning

The application of displacement spinning to conical shapes is shown schematically in *Figure 6-14*. The metal deformation is such that forming is in accordance with the sine law, which states that the wall thickness of the starting blank and that of the finished workpiece are related as follows:

Table VI-10. Height-to-Diameter Ratios for Spinning

Alloy	Metal Thickness (inch)		
	Less than 0.032	*0.032 to 0.064*	*More than 0.064*
3003-0	0.60	0.75	0.80
2024-0	0.45	0.60	0.65
5052-0	0.37	0.55	0.62
6061-T4	0.50	0.70	0.75
7075-0	0.60	0.75	0.80
Low Carbon Steel	0.40	0.52	0.60
CRES (Stabilized)	0.37	0.45	—
CRES 302-A	0.32	0.40	—

(*Courtesy*, John I. Thompson & Company)

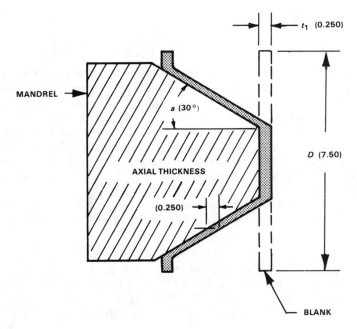

Figure 6-14. Dimensional relations for one-operation power spinning of a cone. (*Courtesy*, the American Society for Metals)

$$t_2 = t_1 (\sin a)$$

t_1 = the thickness of the starting blank
t_2 = the thickness of the spun workpiece
a = one-half the apex angle of the cone.

When spinning in accordance with the sine law, the axial thickness is the same as that of the starting blank.

When spinning cones to small angles (less than 35% included angles), it is best to use more than one spinning pass, with a different cone angle for each pass. When using this technique, the workpiece is annealed or stress relieved between passes.

This practice permits a high total reduction while maintaining a practical limit of 50 to 75% between process anneals. The reduction between successive annealing operations is determined by the maximum acceptable limits of deformation for the metal being spun.

Reducing wall thickness by 50% in accordance with the sine law is illustrated in *Figure 6-14* where:

D = diameter (the same in starting blank and cone)
t_1 = flat-plate thickness
t_2 = wall thickness of spun cone
a = 30°(which is half of the included angle).

173

Using the sine law:

$$t_2 = t_1 (\sin a) = 0.250 \text{ in.} \times 0.500 \text{ in.} = 0.125 \text{ in.}$$
$$= (6.35 \text{ mm} \times 0.500 \text{ mm} = 3.17 \text{ mm})$$

Even in multiple pass spinning, the original blank diameter is retained and the exact volume of material is used in the final part. At any diameter of either the preform or the completed part, the axial thickness equals the thickness of the original blank. For instance, if a flat plate has a diameter of 7.50 in. (190.5 mm) and a thickness of 0.500 in. (12.7 mm), the spun preform has this same 0.500-in. axial thickness, but the wall thickness is only 0.250 in. (6.35 mm) (t_1 in *Figure 6-15*), thus satisfying the sine law. The final part has an axial thickness of 0.500 in. (12.7 mm), but in accordance with the sine law its wall thickness is only 0.125 in. (3.17 mm) (t_3 in *Figure 6-15*).

The sine law applies to multiple-operation spinning as follows, wherein a total reduction of wall thickness of 75% is obtained with exceeding 50% in any one operation:

t_1 = flat-plate thickness = 0.500 in. (12.7 mm)
t_2 = preform wall thickness = 0.250 in. (6.35 mm)
t_3 = final-part wall thickness = 0.125 in. (3.17 mm)
a = half-angle of preform = 30° (.523 rad)
a_1 = half-angle of final part = 14° 29′ (.249 rad)

$$t_1 = t_2 (\sin a_1).$$

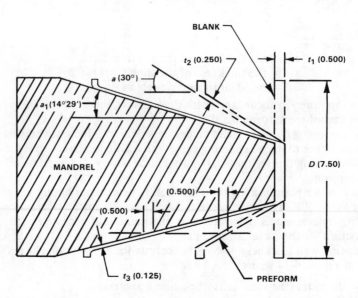

BLANK
t_2 (0.250)
t_1 (0.500)
a (30°)
a_1 (14°29′)
MANDREL
(0.500)
D (7.50)
(0.500)
t_3 (0.125)
PREFORM

Figure 6-15. Dimensional relation for two operation power spinning of a cone to a small angle (less than 35° (.610 rad) included angle). (*Courtesy,* the American Society for Metals)

To find the flat-plate thickness and the preform cone angle and thickness, the following procedure is used:

$$t_1 = \frac{t_3}{\sin a_1} = \frac{0.125}{0.250} = 0.500 \text{ in.} \quad \left(\frac{3.17}{.250} = 12.7 \text{ mm} \right)$$

To satisfy the requirement for a 50% maximum reduction:

$$t_2 = t_1 \times 0.5 = 0.500 \text{ in.} \times 0.5 \text{ in.} = 0.250 \text{ in.}$$
$$= (t_1 \times 0.500 \times 12.7 = 6.35 \text{ mm})$$

The half-angle required to achieve this reduction is found by:

$$\sin a = t_2 / t_1 = \frac{0.250 \text{ in.}}{0.500 \text{ in.}} = 0.500 \text{ or } a = 30°$$

$$= \left(\frac{6.35 \text{ mm}}{12.7 \text{ mm}} = 0.500 \text{ or } a = .523 \text{ rad} \right)$$

Effects of deviation from the sine law are usually expressed in terms of overreduction or underreduction. In overreduction, the final thickness of the workpiece is less than that dictated by the sine law; in underreduction, the thickness is greater. In overreduction, the flange leans forward; in underreduction the flange leans backward. If a thin blank is spun with severe underreduction, the flange wrinkles.

In power-spinning, overreduction has an additional effect on the shape of the workpiece. As the workpiece is overreduced, back extrusion can occur. For a given amount of reduction, the back extrusion increases with decreasing mandrel angle.

The phenomenon of back extrusion in spinning is explained in terms of compressive stress in the spun workpiece. This stress pushes the spun section backward, and curves the shape on a conical mandrel.

Spinning Tolerances. In displacement spinning and most conventional spinning, typical tolerances that may be held are ±0.002 in. (±0.05 mm) on wall thickness, ±0.002 in. (±0.05 mm) on inside diameters up to six inches, ±0.003 in. (±0.08 mm) on diameters over six inches, and ±0.005 in. (±0.13 mm) on length. For economical design, tolerances shown in *Table VI-11* should be used.

Table VI-11. Typical Spinning Tolerances

Nominal Part Diameter (inch)	Minimum Tolerances			
	D(inch)	L(inch)	A(deg)	
Under 1.5	±0.010	±0.015	±1	
1.5 to 5.0	±0.015	±0.030	±3	
5.0 to 20.0	±0.030	±0.030	±3	
20.0 to 36.0	±0.060	±0.045	±5	
36.0 to 72.0	±0.120	±0.060	±5	

(*Courtesy*, John I. Thompson & Company)

FINE-EDGE BLANKING AND PIERCING

What is Fine-Edge Blanking?

Fine-edge blanking is a precisely programmed shearing and extrusion process in which the flow of materials is controlled in the area of the shear. The result is a finished part, flat with smooth edges and only a slight burr along one edge of the blank. If required, holes and slots can be smaller than stock thickness or they do not have to be entirely cut out of the stock.

In conventional blanking or piercing, secondary operations are necessary for close tolerance parts. Generally a shaving operation is added to obtain the close tolerance and fine edge required.

In fine-edge blanking (also known as fine-blanking, smooth-edge blanking, or fine-flow blanking), precise blanks can be produced in a single operation without the fractured edges characteristically produced in conventional blanking and piercing. In fine-edge blanking, a V-shape impingement ring is forced into the stock to lock it tightly against the die and to force the work metal to flow toward the punch. This is done so that the part can be extruded from the strip without fracture or die break. Die clearance is extremely small, and punch speed is much slower than in conventional blanking.

Fine-edge piercing can be done either separately or at the same time as fine-edge blanking. In piercing small holes, an impingement ring may not be needed.

No further finishing or machining operations are necessary to obtain blank or hole edges comparable to machined edges or to those that are conventionally blanked or pierced and then shaved. A quick touch-up on an abrasive belt or a short treatment in a vibratory finisher may be used to remove the small burr on the blank.

Specially designed single-operation or compound blanking and piercing dies are generally used for the process.

Materials

Low-carbon and medium-carbon steels (1018 to 1035), annealed or half-hard, give good blanked edges and normal tool wear. High-carbon steels in the spheroidize-annealed condition can be blanked easily. Blanking of steel with 0.35% carbon or higher is recommended only when it is spheroidized-annealed. Steels quenched and tempered to about R_c 30 are well suited to fine-edge blanking because they do not require subsequent heat treatment which could result in deformation.

High-carbon steels and alloy steels cause considerably higher tool wear than the low-carbon steels, but surface finish of the blanked edge is smoother. Leaded steels are not suitable for fine-edge blanking, because of their low deformability.

Stainless steels 301, 302, 303, 304, 316, 416, and 430 in the form of bright rolled, fully annealed strip, have good blanked edges, but cause higher tool wear than the low- and medium-carbon steels.

Good results have been obtained with most of the aluminum alloys.

Blanked edges on parts made from 2024 alloy generally are rougher than edges on other aluminum alloys.

Brasses containing more than 64% copper are especially suitable. Nickel alloys, nickel silver, beryllium copper, and gold and silver are also easily fine-edge blanked.

Process Capabilities

With this process, holes can be pierced in low-carbon steel with a diameter as small as 50% of stock thickness. In high-carbon steel, the smallest diameter is about 75% of stock thickness. Hole spacing (i.e., between hole edges and between hole edge and blank edge) can be as little as 50 to 70% of stock thickness. No die break shows on the sheared surface of the hole. Blank edges may be rough for a few thousandths of an inch of stock thickness on the burr side of the part, when the width of the part is about twice the stock thickness or less.

Burr formation increases rapidly during a run, necessitating frequent grinding of the cutting elements.

Parts fine-edge blanked from stainless steel have a surface finish of 32 μin. (0.8 μm) or better. Smooth edges also are produced on spheroidize-annealed steel parts. In tests on 60% carbon spring steel with a hardness of R_c 37 to 40, the surface finish on the sheared edges was 32 μin. (0.8 μm) or better, but punch life was only 6000 pieces. The cutting speed for fine-edge blanking is 0.3 to 0.6 in./sec (7.6 to 15.2 mm/min).

Chamfers can be coined around holes and on edges. Forming near the cut edge, or forming offset parts with a bend angle up to 30° (0.523 rad) is possible under restricted conditions.

Metals up to 0.125-in. (3.17-mm) thick having a tensile strength of 85,000 to 115,000 psi (586 to 793 MPa) are easily blanked. Parts up to 0.500-in. (12.7-mm) thick can be blanked if press capacity is available. Material over 0.125-in. (3.17-mm) thick, especially steel having a carbon content of 0.25% or more, requires an impingement ring on the die to prevent part corners from breaking down. The edges of parts made of 1018 steel workharden as much as 7 to 12 points R_c during blanking.

Tolerances

Total tolerances obtainable are: 0.0005 in. (0.013 mm) on hole diameter and accuracy of blank outline; 0.001 in. (0.025 mm) on hole location with respect to a datum surface, and 0.001 in. (0.025 mm) on flatness; 0.002 in. (0.05 mm) on perpendicularity of holes or side walls with respect to a datum surface.

Factors affecting tolerances are stock thickness and material strength. The thinner and softer the material, the closer the tolerances. The sheared edges of the outside contour are not exactly perpendicular to the plane of the stock, but are slightly conical. The die edge dimension is slightly smaller than the punch edge. Inside shapes, especially round holes, are largely cylindrical. Consequently, closer tolerances can be obtained with inner shapes than with outside contours.

Flatness

Because fine-edge blanking exerts large forces on strip or coil material in the tool, the parts rarely need straightening. Parts fabricated from strip will normally have a flatness of 0.0005/in. (0.013/mm). Parts produced from coil will have a flatness of 0.002 in. (0.05 mm). Flatness is more difficult to control on parts with coinings, markings, offsets, bends, and extrusions.

Blank Design

Limitations on blank size depend on stock thickness, tensile strength, metal hardness, and available press capacity. For example, perimeters of approximately 25 in. (63.5 cm) can be blanked in 0.125-in. (3.17-mm) thick low-carbon steel. It is possible to blank smaller parts from low-carbon or medium-carbon steel about 0.500-in. (12.7-mm) thick.

Sharp corner and filled radii should be avoided when possible. A radius of 10 to 20% of stock thickness is preferred, particularly on parts over 0.125-in. (3.17-mm) thick or those made of alloy steel. External angles should be at least 90° (1.57 rad). The radius should be increased on relatively sharp corners or on hard materials.

Parts requiring piercing of tiny holes or narrow slots, or blanking of narrow teeth or projections, may be unsuited to fine-edge blanking. The ratio of hole diameter, slot width, or projection to metal thickness should be at least 0.7 for reasonably efficient blanking, although a ratio as small as 0.5 has been successful with some parts. The spacing, between holes or between a hole and the edge of the blank, should be at least 0.5 to 0.7 times metal thickness in order to maintain the quality of hole-wall and blank-edge surfaces, and to avoid distortion.

THE ECONOMICS OF TRANSFER DIES

According to *Machine and Tool Blue Book*, transfer dies are more expensive than either progressive or manually operated line dies, therefore they can be justified only on the basis of the savings listed below:

- Savings in labor stem from the ability of transfer dies to complete a part in its entirety in one press setup. One person can supervise several transfer dies operating in different presses.
- Savings in material result from eliminating the strip carrier required in progressive dies.
- Savings in press time are derived from the ability of a transfer die to combine stamping operations performed individually in a number of other presses.
- Savings in storage are obtained through the ability of a transfer die to complete all operations on a part in one setup.

A transfer die can be defined as a series of individual stations on a common plate making up a single working tool, and having a transfer unit with the appropriate finger attachment to shuttle the workpiece through the various operations to its completion at the extreme end. Transfer dies are engineered

178

for quick and easy setups. Since both transfer unit and all the separate workstations are integrated on one common plate, it is just as simple and fast to set up or remove a transfer die from the press as it is for a single manually operated die. Any conventional press can be utilized with a transfer die. It must have only the necessary tonnage and stroke.

The economics of transfer dies can be shown with the three main engineering tools:

Speed, because transfer dies have to be directly involved in so many presses of varying speeds, tonnages, strokes and with so many different materials. *Labor savings* are possible with even the so-called low production runs. *Material savings* are possible with a new concept of blank preparation. The dies effect significant savings on labor, material, press time requirements, and parts as well as boosting operating speed and slashing downtime.

Two Important Functions of Speed. With the recognition of speed and its close integration with the die itself, be aware of the introduction of a mechanical die of three physical dimensions into a realm of a fourth dimension speed. What is the speed of a transfer die? A transfer unit is merely a mechanism with grasping finger-bar assemblies which reciprocate with a rectangular motion in a horizontal plane. It, by itself, has no limitations as to the speed of operation. It is only when incorporated with a group of working die stations that certain restraining factors become apparent.

A transfer die can be engineered to run at any speed required except as dictated by the following limiting factors:

- Limitation of the drawing speed of the part material itself.
- Law of inertia: Bodies in motion tend to remain in motion. Bodies at rest tend to remain at rest.

Material Limitations. The first of the limitations is the speed at which the workpiece can be made. Fatigue, shock, and the erosion or wearing of the die components that engage the workpiece also limit the speed, but the realistic limitation is the drawing speed of the material itself.

Every good die and press handbook carries data and charts on the drawing ram speeds of the different metals used.

Schematic points of the ram when the punch comes in contact with the stamping are illustrated in *Figure 6-16*. For automated jobs, the excess stroke, as indicated, is the amount of cycle time left for a transfer unit to envelop the workpiece, shuttle it to the next workstation, and retract the finger bar before the punch reengages the part. The excess stroke should be long enough to allow the transfer cycle to be completed at a safe speed and without interrupting press operations.

Inertia. The second limiting factor is the law of inertia. Inertia of the workpiece may in fact result in a press speed far below that which is permissible by the drawing speed of the material.

Labor Savings. The application of labor saving transfer dies to the so-called low production stampings has been relatively slow, yet it is both feasible and economical to adapt transfer dies to almost any part that requires hard tooling.

179

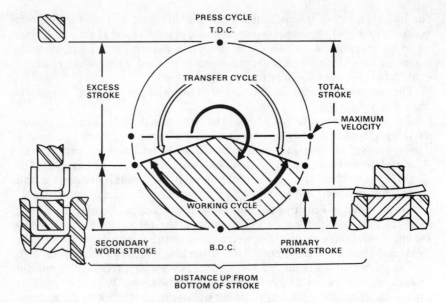

PRESS CYCLE
T.D.C.

TRANSFER CYCLE

EXCESS STROKE

TOTAL STROKE

MAXIMUM VELOCITY

WORKING CYCLE

SECONDARY WORK STROKE

B.D.C.

PRIMARY WORK STROKE

DISTANCE UP FROM BOTTOM OF STROKE

Figure 6-16. The excess stroke of the press must be long enough to allow the transfer device to pick up, move, and deposit the part before the punch makes contact. Hence, long-stroke presses are favored. (*Courtesy, Machine and Tool Blue Book,* December 1966)

To compare methods of producing stampings, the manufacturing engineers must make an analysis to determine at what quantity a higher cost transfer die, with its higher production rate, equals a series of individual manually operated dies with a lower tool cost and a lower production rate. The following factors should be used to determine the break-even quantity X at which to consider going to transfer dies:

- Tool cost of transfer die
- Tool cost of manual die
- Manufacturing cost in transfer die
- Manufacturing cost in manual die.

The blanks in the analysis in *Table VI-12* for the individual and transfer dies are secured from a separate economical operation, the cost of which can be ignored in this analysis. From the tabulation shown in *Table VI-12* transfer the values of 0.075 and 0.00625 (the manufacturing piece costs), and the values of $21,000.00 and $36,000.00 (the total tool cost to the break-even formula

Break-even Computation

$$X = \frac{T - M}{m - t} = \frac{36,000 - 21,000}{0.075 - 0.0062} = 218,023$$

180

Table VI-12. Manual Versus Transfer Cost Analysis for Ball Bearing Retainer

Manual	Press Cost Per Hour		Pieces Per Hour		Manufacturing Piece Cost	Tool Cost
Form	$30.00	÷	1200	=	0.025	$7,000.00
Restrike	30.00	÷	1200	=	0.025	7,000.00
Pierce	30.00	÷	1200	=	0.025	7,000.00
Total Manual	—		—		0.0750	$21,000.00
Transfer	$30.00	÷	4800	=	0.0062	$36,000.00
Diff.	—		—		0.0688	$15,000.00

Double Check Chart

Manual Dies:
$$\frac{\text{Tooling Cost}}{\text{Total Run}} + \text{Piece Cost} = \frac{21,000}{218,023} + 0.075 = 0.1713$$

Transfer Die:
$$\frac{\text{Tooling Cost}}{\text{Total Run}} + \text{Piece Cost} = \frac{36,000}{218,023} + 0.0062 = 0.1713$$

The fringe benefits of using a transfer die in this example are:
- Presses and personnel are released for other profitable work.
- Savings in setup and change over time with only one press involved, not several.
- Only one press and one operator affected when press stoppage occurs.
- Saving of floor space by eliminating bins, chutes, conveyors, and other press handling and storage.

As can be seen in the example (*Table VI-13*), tooling plays a very important role in the economy of producing a part. After making an analysis, the higher cost tooling can be the economical tooling for the low-cost production of a part.

Table VI-13. Cost Savings, Manual vs. Transfer

	Break-even Point 218,023 Run		300,000 Run		400,000 Run		500,000 Run	
	Total Piece Cost	Total Run Cost	Total Piece Cost	Total Run Cost	Total Piece Cost	Total Run Cost	Total Piece Cost	Total Run Cost
Manual	$0.1713	37,347	0.1450	43,500	0.1275	51,000	0.1170	58,500
Transfer	$0.1713	37,347	0.1262	37,860	0.0962	38,480	0.0720	36,000
Diff.	—	—	0.0188	5,640	0.0314	12,520	0.0450	22,500

181

NEW PRODUCTION METHODS

Traditional production methods for stamping and forming metals usually involve the use of a stamping press. Presses can range from small tonnage bench presses to very large single or transfer presses. Stamping presses generally include blanking, piercing, bending, forming, and drawing operations. The disadvantages to using a stamping press are the high cost and the long lead time required to build dies. Also, it is not unusual for a stamping press to require two to six hours of setup time for a typical production run.

Modern computer numerical control (CNC) and numerical control (NC) punch presses are rapidly being employed in production press shops. These CNC machines have found wide application in computer aided design/computer aided manufacturing (CAD/CAM) design systems. Many CAD/CAM drawing systems will produce the CNC programs needed to operate these machines. The advantages of this type of equipment are low tooling costs, short lead time, and relatively short setup time. This type of punch press is particularly cost effective for low volume production of less than 10,000 parts.

Machine tool builders have been making improvements to their machines and peripheral systems. The number of strokes per minute (spm) for a press is dependent upon how the ram is driven, the speed at which the workpiece can be positioned under the punch, and the thickness of material being punched. Generally, the maximum spm made by a punch press is fixed, rated at the maximum material thickness that the press is capable of punching, and cannot be varied by the operator. Based on one inch (25 mm) centers, the speed of the various presses ranges from 55-280 spm. In a continuous punching mode used for nibbling, the press can attain 500 spm.

The workpiece positioning speed is dependent on the weight of the moving parts and the type of carriage drive motors used. The distance that the workpiece must travel during a punching operation is also a factor. Axis positioning speeds up to 3150 ipm (80,010 m/min) are attained if the workpiece is moved in only one direction, and up to 2400 ipm (60.96 m/min) if the workpiece is moved in both directions at the same time.

Punching forces for mechanical and hydraulic punch presses range from 8 to 60 tons (7.4 to 54 tonne). Presses specifically designed for heavy plate and structural steel are capable of producing up to 154 tons (138.6 tonne) of punching force.

Other improvements include the ability to add special tooling if the standard tooling cannot produce the needed features. The special tooling permits milling, tapping, contouring (not nibbling), and louvering operations to be performed. Lasers and plasma arc torches have been added to these CNC presses for either linear cutting or other specialized applications. In addition, special software packages (canned cycles) reduce the part programming work load.

CNC punch presses may be new, but in many respects they have set trends in the area of tool standardization. These new presses have standard dies and punches which are stored in the machine turret magazine. Depending on the size of the press, holes up to 8 in. (203 mm) can be punched with a single punch. The CNC program automatically loads the needed tool into the press workhead to produce the needed feature. These standard tools can be combined to produce a variety of contours and features both externally and internally. If the part produced on this type of machine requires bending, the bends are performed as a secondary operation on a hydraulic brake.

One of the latest advancements in the production of sheet metal parts is the flexible manufacturing system (FMS). This system is based on the transfer of the part from the first to the last operation in a fully automatic sequence. Automatic equipment will take sheared sheet-steel blanks and automatically transfer them to stations for punching, forming, flanging or bending, and then weld them into a variety of completed parts.

Figure 6-17 illustrates a Salvagini programmable-controlled FMS. Blanks entering the FMS are transferred to the notching station for blanking. They are released and turned over en route to the forming station where they are flanged or bent, then released and transferred to the plasma arc welding station where corners are welded. From there, they are transferred to the spot welding station, all in a fully automatic sequence.

The FMS is a special transfer machine and is used for production of electronic and instrument cabinets.

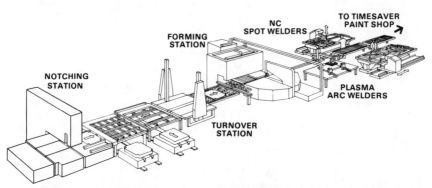

Figure 6-17. Automatic panel forming and welding line. (*Courtesy*, Xerox Corporation and *American Machinist*, December 1985)

7

Powder Metallurgy

This chapter discusses the powder metallurgical process, and the uses, advantages and limitations, design and tolerances of parts made by this process. Powder metallurgy (P/M) offers a new avenue for cost reduction because it is more economical than other metallurgical processes. During the past 30 years, technical innovations have produced many improvements in powders, process controls, and heat-treatments for powder metal fabrication. These improvements have given P/M parts the following attributes:

- High strength
- Low cost with short runs
- Ease of machining
- Ease in replication
- Economy in design of other than intricate parts
- Good magnetic properties
- Low tooling cost
- High impact resistance
- Good elongation in dense or infiltrated parts
- Stresses with definite yield
- Good wear resistance
- Good design flexibility
- Good hardness.

These are only a few of the advantages in using the powder metallurgical process. They have been proven advantages through the use of P/M as a modern method to manufacture automotive, electronic, aircraft, and major structural parts, as well as for components in home appliances and other equipment. In the realization of product improvement at lower cost, powder metallurgy is responsible for shapes, properties, and functions that cannot be achieved in any other way with the same economy.

Powder metal parts can be heat-treated to a particle hardness equivalent to R_c 55-60, and they have good impact resistance. However, R_c hardnesses as high as 65 have been reported. This means that powder metallurgy is actively and successfully competing with other metalforming processes in the production of structural parts.

Progress is continuing at a rapid pace. For example, more recent innovations include new Inconel powders used in turbine engine parts that function in a 1500° F (816° C) environment, and a silicon-iron formulation that offers improved magnetic properties.

Table VII-1 shows a general comparison of the powder metallurgical process with other metalforming processes.

WHAT IS POWDER METALLURGY?

Powder metal parts are made by compacting metal powders in a precision die. The compacted part is subsequently ejected and then sintered in a controlled atmosphere to develop its mechanical and physical properties.

Compacting

Mechanical or hydraulic presses can be used to produce compacting pressures from as low as five tons (4.5 tonne), to as high as 60 tons (54 tonne) with special tooling. In most circumstances, however, the normal pressure range is from 15 to 40 tons (13.5 to 36 tonne). Other techniques employed include isostatic pressing, forging, extruding, roll compacting, high-energy-rate forming, slip casting, and hot pressing.

Many P/M parts are accurately produced at an average rate as high as 1000 parts per hour in conventional automatic presses. Miniature P/M parts are produced at rates up to 200,000 parts per hour.

P/M parts can be pressed and sintered directly to their final shape, size, and surface finish, thus usually eliminating all of the machining required with other metalworking processes.

Table VII-2 shows the tons per square inch and the compression ratio of parts compacted from various metal powders.

Sintering

Sintering is a solid-state phenomenon in which powder particles become metallurgically bonded at temperatures below the melting point of the metal. This bonding develops the desired mechanical properties. Physical and mechanical properties of P/M parts can be made to the designer's functional requirements by alloying, sizing, coining, oil or plastic impregnation, and metal infiltration. Conventional heat-treatment and plating can also be used.

Table VII-3 shows the sintering temperature of the various material.

Infiltration

This is a process of filling the pores of a P/M part with a lower melting temperature metal such as a copper-base alloy. On sintering, the infiltrant material melts and penetrates the pores of the part by capillary action. Mechanical properties such as tensile strength, hardness, wear-resistance and toughness are improved considerably, and a fully dense structure is produced.

Coining and Sizing

Parts can be coined or sized when close dimensional tolerances are required, or when higher properties are desired. This is a repressing operation

186

Table VII-1. General Comparison of Metallurgical Processes

Method as Compared to Powder Metallurgy	Production Rates	Strength of Part	Tooling Cost	Tolerances	Piece Price
Diecast Small Parts	Lower	Lower	Higher	Looser	Generally Lower
Diecast Large Parts	Lower	Lower	Higher	Looser	Lower
Investment Casting	Lower	Equal	Lower	Looser	Higher
Precision Sand Casting	Lower	Equal	Lower	Looser	Higher
Screw Machine Small Parts—No Second Operation	Same	Equal or Higher	Lower	Same	Same
Screw Machine Parts with Second Operation	Lower	Equal or Higher	Lower	Same	Higher
Screw Machine Large Parts	Lower	Equal or Higher	Lower	Same	Higher

Table VII-2. Tonnage Requirements and Compression Ratios for Various Powder Products

Type of Compact	Tons Per Square Inch	Compression Ratio
Brass Parts	30 to 50	2.4 to 2.6:1
Bronze Bearings	15 to 20	2.5 to 2.7:1
Carbon Products	10 to 12	3.0:1
Copper-graphite Brushes	25 to 30	2.0 to 3.0:1
Carbides	10 to 30	2.0 to 3.0:1
Alumina	8 to 10	2.5:1
Steatites	3 to 5	2.8:1
Ferrites	8 to 12	3.0:1
Iron Bearings	15 to 25	2.2:1
Iron Parts:		
Low Density	25 to 35	2.0 to 2.4:1
Medium Density	35 to 40	2.1 to 2.5:1
High Density	35 to 60	2.4 to 2.8:1
Iron Powder Cores	10 to 50	1.5 to 3.5:1
Tungsten	5 to 10	2.5:1
Tantalum	5 to 10	2.5:1

(*Courtesy, Machine and Tool Blue Book*)

Table VII-3. Sintering Temperature and Time in High-Heat Chamber

Material	Temperature °F	Time, Minutes
Bronze	1400 to 1600	10 to 20
Copper	1550 to 1650	12 to 45
Brass	1550 to 1650	10 to 45
Iron, Iron-graphite, etc.	1850 to 2100	8 to 45
Nickel	1850 to 2100	30 to 45
Stainless Steel	2000 to 2350	30 to 60
Alnico Magnets	2200 to 2375	120 to 150
Ferrites	2200 to 2700	10 to 600
90% Tungsten, 6% Nickel, 4% Copper	2450 to 2900	10 to 120
Tungsten Carbide	2600 to 2700	20 to 30
Molybdenum	3730	120 (approx.)
Tungsten	4250	480 (approx.)
Tantalum	4350 (approx.)	480 (approx.)

(*Courtesy, Machine and Tool Blue Book*)

in a die similar to the original compacting die (sometimes the original die is used). An added benefit of coining and sizing is improved surface finish. If higher properties are required, the coining process can be repeated. Resintering also improves properties.

Impregnation

Impregnation is accomplished by filling the pores of a P/M part with a lubricant or other nonmetallic material (i.e., plastic resin). This operation is usually performed by means of a vacuum or by soaking. Low-density, sintered P/M parts are absorbent because of their porosity. Bearings, as well as many structural parts, are oil-impregnated for lubrication purposes. Parts that are to be plated are usually impregnated with plastic resin to avoid plating-salt entrapment.

MATERIALS

Virtually every metallurgical element used by man is available in one or more powder formulations. These formulations include iron, carbon steel, stainless steel, nickel steel, copper steel, nickel silver, copper, brass, aluminum, and bronze, and even the refractory and reactive metals. Each is available in a number of different compositions or special blends which give the designer a wide choice of properties. This range of compositions enables the designer to select the optimum material for each particular application.

ALUMINUM ALLOY COMPOSITION

Studies of numerous aluminum alloys in both prealloyed and blended form led to a preference for blended composition, because lower compacting pressures are required and improved sintering results. Excellent sintered structures are obtained with additions of solid-solution strengthening elements such as magnesium, silicon, copper, and zinc, either individually or in combination.

Dispersion-hardening elements such as manganese, chromium, and iron do not respond well to sintering in the blended form because of low solubility in aluminum. Two blended aluminum powder compositions which exhibit very good compressibility and high mechanical properties after sintering are 601AB and 201AB. Chemical composition of 601AB is close to 6061 wrought aluminum alloy, and 201AB is similar to 2014 alloy except for the absence of manganese.

One of the outstanding characteristics of aluminum powder is its superior compressibility in comparison with common metal powders. Aluminum is compacted to 90% theoretical density at 12 tsi (10886 kg/m^2) and to 95% density at 25 tons/in.^{2} (22680 kg/m^2).

The compression ratio for aluminum powders ranges from 1.5 to 1.9:1, depending on compacting pressure and method of feeding.

Aluminum Powders

According to *Machine and Tool Blue Book,* the selection of aluminum powder particle size, shape, and composition is a key to successful compacting and sintering. If the powder is too fine or in flake form, poor flow will result along with greater tendency for seizing and cold welding in the die. Coarse or spherical powders exhibit good flow, but develop low strength in both green and sintered conditions. Air-atomized 1202 powder has excellent compressibility and improved flow. This powder is nodular or irregular in shape and interlocking of particles improves green strength and facilitates sinterability. In 1202 powder, the iron and silicon elements are controlled to provide a soft, ductile powder that compacts easily.

189

Properties

There are many ways to improve the properties of a powder metal part, one of the latest and very effective treatments is cryogenics. Under this treatment at temperatures below -300° F (184.4° C), a more uniform molecular structure is produced. This process produces a stronger, denser P/M part for longer life and better wear resistance.

The design engineer's primary concern is to create a design that meets the requirements of an application, and still be the most economical solution to that specific design problem. In considering P/M, the best source for advice on a new design and the selection of the best materials for that design is the powder metallurgist. He or she can offer judgment based upon years of experience in meeting design requirements for various applications, parts, and properties of materials, as well as up-to-date knowledge of new materials and process capabilities.

The mechanical property of tensile strength is commonly used in the evaluation of P/M materials, although other properties may also be of prime importance, depending upon intended applications. P/M parts such as bronze bearings can be produced with high porosity, while structural parts can have high density, minimum porosity, and tensile strengths ranging from 150,000 to 180,000 psi (1034 to 1241 MPa)—even approaching 200,000 psi (1379 MPa) in special circumstances. In many cases, properties of P/M parts either equal those of wrought materials or exceed them.

Through selective compacting, parts can be produced with multiple densities. This feature, available only with powder metallurgy, enables the design engineer to specify, for example, a hard, dense, wear-resisting surface and a porous, oil-impregnated running surface.

DESIGNING FOR ECONOMY

Certain considerations during the design of a P/M part can result in cost savings during fabrication as indicated in *Figures 7-1* and *7-2*.

The type of powder used, tolerances, shape, size, physical and mechanical properties required, all have an important bearing on both quality and cost of parts made by the powder metallurgical process.

Advantages

Fabrication by the powder metallurgy process affords the following advantages:

- A way of alloying or blending metals which can be combined in no other way, thus producing new, desirable qualities
- A high-speed, inexpensive means of mass production with close tolerances and short lead time
- New design possibilities, often resulting in the elimination of subassemblies and extra parts by combining mechanical functions
- A high degree of accuracy and uniformity throughout large production runs
- Built-in features for faster assembly and service convenience

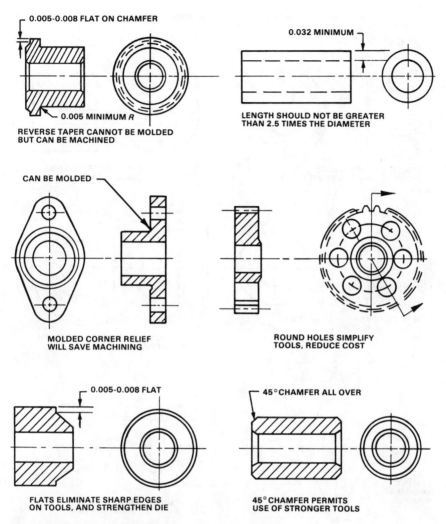

0.005-0.008 FLAT ON CHAMFER

0.005 MINIMUM R

REVERSE TAPER CANNOT BE MOLDED BUT CAN BE MACHINED

0.032 MINIMUM

LENGTH SHOULD NOT BE GREATER THAN 2.5 TIMES THE DIAMETER

CAN BE MOLDED

MOLDED CORNER RELIEF WILL SAVE MACHINING

ROUND HOLES SIMPLIFY TOOLS, REDUCE COST

0.005-0.008 FLAT

FLATS ELIMINATE SHARP EDGES ON TOOLS, AND STRENGTHEN DIE

45° CHAMFER ALL OVER

45° CHAMFER PERMITS USE OF STRONGER TOOLS

Figure 7-1. Preferred P/M design configurations.

- Control of part porosity
- Oil impregnation for lubricating purposes, greater wear-resistance, or corrosion resistance of bearings as well as structural parts
- Economy through the reduction of machining, scrap loss, inventory of metal stock, shop handling, shop inspection, and assembly labor.

Disadvantages

Fabrication by the powder metallurgy process has inherent disadvantages. Some of them are:

191

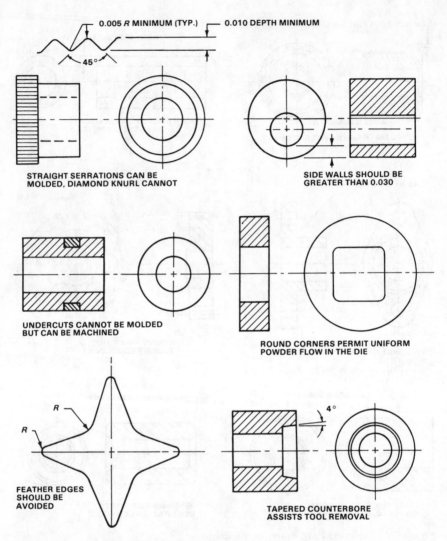

Figure 7-2. Preferred P/M design configurations.

- The shape and size of parts are limited by press capacity and the nature of the molding process itself
- Reentrant angles, side grooves, and similar obstructions to the smooth flow of powder and the pressed part in the direction of applied pressure, cannot be incorporated in the as-pressed design
- Low quantities are usually expensive from a tooling standpoint. (This may be offset, however, if considerable machining is required with other processes.)

Design Considerations

- Design must be such that the part can be ejected from the die. Straight walls are preferred, as draft is not required to facilitate ejection. Undercut and back-draft cannot be tolerated.
- Avoid sharp corners; a generous fillet is preferred. A stronger part will be obtained, and longer tool life will be realized.
- Chamfer external corners whenever possible to avoid objectionable burrs. Chamfers with angles greater than 45° (.785 rad) are preferred. A 0.005 to 0.008-in. (0.13 to 0.2-mm) flat is required, followed by chamfer.
- Provide flats on sharp external edges. Otherwise, edges may crumble during ejection. Also, the flats will allow the use of tooling which does not have sharp edges to wear or distort.
- Avoid thin sections which may rupture when ejection forces are applied. Thin sections also may cause warpage during sintering.
- Uniform wall thickness eliminates possible warpage during sintering.
- Do not stint in powder selection. The basic powder cost may be the least expensive investment in obtaining a quality part.
- Keep the shape simple. Strive for a minimum number of levels.
- Provide wide dimensional tolerances wherever possible. Wide tolerances mean low piece-part cost and long tool life.
- Holes that are parallel to the compression axis can be cored, and should be so specified. Side coring is not possible.
- Holes that are at an oblique angle to the axis of the part cannot be cored.
- Two parts can be assembled together and then sintered. The outside part can be made of a powder that shrinks during sintering; the inside part can be made of a powder that expands.
- Two parts can be bonded during sintering. Two green compacts of like powder can be placed together with a captive brazing ring, and then sintered for satisfactory bonding.
- Perfect spheres cannot be molded. A flat should be provided at the extreme periphery (neutral axis).
- Allowances must be made for the length to which thin-walled cylindrical parts can be compacted. Maximum length is about 2.5 times the diameter.

Shapes. Powdered metal parts can be compressed only in the direction of punch movement. Parts with threads, holes, or undercuts, at angles to the direction of pressure, reentrant angles, and reverse tapers, are either impossible to press or restrict the ejection of the part from the die. These design limitations can frequently be overcome by secondary machining, however.

Inserts should *not* be molded into powdered metal parts.

Sizes. The available press stroke and the compression ratio of the material determine the practical sizes which can be produced by the powder metallurgy process. Parts weighing as much as 50 lb (22 kg) and having a compacting area of 40 in.^{2} (258 cm^2) can be produced with modern presses.

Strengths. Production powdered metal parts generally have elongations, tensile strengths, and impact strengths which are lower than those of production parts made from wrought stock—an exception being heat-treated parts.

Densities. The density of powdered metal parts may vary throughout the sections of the part. Because of poor plastic flow of metal powders under compression, a simple cylinder will have its greatest density at the end in contact with the punch. In practice, there is a necessary compromise on the length-to-diameter ratio of compacts. The most satisfactory ratio generally is not greater than 2.5 to 1. This can be overcome by double-pressing and double-sintering.

Machining. After sintering, undercuts and other features which are not practical for pressing can be machined. Frequently, tool wear in machining sintered parts is lower than tool wear in machining parts from wrought stock.

Heat Treating. The mechanical properties of powdered metal parts can be greatly improved through heat-treatment. However, the process is much more involved than working with conventional wrought stock.

Steel powder metal parts can be hardened by conventional quench and temper or induction practices. However, the heat treater must use a protective atmosphere/quench in order to avoid corrosion. Salt baths (brine) or water cannot be used as quenching media due to entrapment in the pores which results in internal corrosion.

Finishes. Surface finishes of parts made of powdered metal are compatible with normal machine finishes, and should be accepted wherever possible to achieve maximum economy.

Part finish in the as-sintered form is usually smooth and shiny, and, except when impregnations are used, some degree of porosity usually exists. This is not detrimental to operation in service, however.

Where coining is employed as a final operation, surface finish is excellent.

Parts made from powdered metal can be plated, but any surface irregularities will be amplified by the process.

Tolerances. Inasmuch as the economy factor of powder metallurgy is directly influenced by the tolerances to be met, the tolerances should be as liberal as possible. This extends normal die life to the maximum. On parts merely pressed and sintered, it is ordinarily possible to hold radial or side-to-side dimensions from ±0.001 to 0.002 in. (±0.025 to 0.05 mm) per inch, providing that sections are fairly uniform and that shape is not too complicated.

Length tolerances along the axis of pressing can be held to ±0.003 in. (±0.07 mm) on pieces up to about 1.5 in. (38 mm) in length, to ±0.005 in. (±0.13 mm) on pieces up to three inches (76 mm) in length, and ±0.010 in. (±0.25 mm) parts. Flange thicknesses can be held to these length tolerances.

Standard concentricity tolerances for sleeves and bearings are normally 0.003 in. (0.07 mm) total indicator reading to 1.5-in. (38-mm) bore, 0.004 in. (0.1 mm) to three-inch (76 mm) bore, and 0.006 in. (0.15 mm) over three-inch (76 mm) bore.

Hole tolerances, depending on size, can be held from 0.0005 to 0.001 in.

(0.013 to 0.025 mm). Closer tolerances can be held by sizing or coining—but at additional expense.

Gear tolerances can be held to AGMA 8 by special sizing. Normal tolerances are based on AGMA 5 to 7.

Economical Tolerances. The most economical tolerances for use with P/M part design are given in *Table VII-4*, and should be used wherever design permits.

Accuracy. Powder metallurgy dimensional accuracy compares favorably with that of other manufacturing processes.

Wall Thicknesses. Minimum wall thickness for use with maximum lengths and diameters is given in *Table VII-5*.

Table VII-4. Economical Tolerances for Powdered Metal Parts

Diameter or Length (inch)	Length Tolerance (± inch)	Diameter Tolerance (± inch)
Up to 1.0000	0.0050	0.0015
1.0000 to 1.15000	0.0075	0.0020
1.500 to 2.000	0.015	0.003
2.000 to 2.500	0.015	0.004
2.500 to 3.000	0.015	0.005

Flange Diameter		
Diameter (± inch)		Tolerance (± inch)
Up to 1.000		0.004
1.000 to 1.500		0.006
1.500 to 2.000		0.008
2.000 to 2.500		0.010
2.500 to 3.000		0.014
3.000 to 4.000		0.016

Flange Thickness		
Thickness (inch)		Tolerance (± inch)
Up to 0.250		0.004
0.250 to 0.375		0.006
0.375 to 0.500		0.008

Concentricity Tolerance		
Diameter (inch)		Total Indicator Reading (inch)
Up to 1.000		0.003
1.000 to 1.500		0.004
1.500 to 2.000		0.005
2.000 to 2.500		0.006
2.500 to 3.000		0.007

Table VII-5. Ratio of Wall Thickness to Length and Diameter

Minimum Wall Thickness (inch)	Maximum Overall Length (inch)	Maximum Outside Diameter (inch)
0.032	0.500	0.500
0.040	0.625	0.750
0.045	0.750	1.000
0.050	0.875	1.125
0.055	1.000	1.250
0.060	1.250	1.500
0.070	1.375	1.625
0.075	1.500	1.750
0.080	1.625	1.875
0.085	1.750	2.000

TYPICAL PRODUCTION PARTS

Powder metallurgy is no longer limited to simple parts such as bushings or sleeve bearings. The photographs (*Figures 7-3, 7-4,* and *7-5*) show typical production parts produced by the powder metallurgical process.

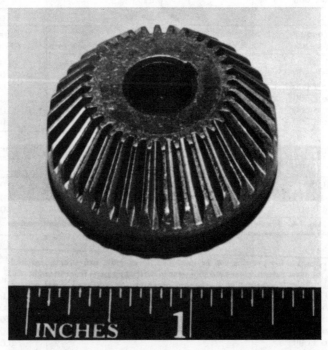

Figure 7-3. Portable engine bevel gear is made of proprietary K-3612 infiltrated steel. (*Courtesy,* Kwikset Powder Metal Products)

Figure 7-4. Tractor engine governor counterweight of proprietary K-3612 infiltrated steel. This is a unique two-level P/M part. (*Courtesy*, Kwikset Powder Metal Products)

Figure 7-5. Plate-magnet of K-4311 nickel steel. (*Courtesy*, Kwikset Powder Metal Products)

8

Limits and Fits for Cylindrical Parts and Antifriction Bearings

This chapter covers standard types and classes of fits, and their functions. The efficiency of assembly and operation of machine elements is controlled by the fits between parts. Fits can be of several types: running fits, locational fits, and force fits.

STANDARD FITS

Tables VIII-1 through *VIII-3* have been developed to give a series of standard types and classes of fits on a unilateral hole basis. The fits produced by mating parts in any class produce approximately the same performance throughout the range of given sizes. The tables prescribe the fits for the given sizes or types of fit. They also prescribe the standard limits for the mating parts which produce the fit.

In developing these tables, it has been recognized that any fit is usually required to perform one of three functions, as indicated by the three general types of fits.

Running Fits

Running fits, for which limits of clearance are given in *Table VIII-1*, represent a typical type of clearance fit. They are intended to provide a running performance, with suitable lubrication allowance, throughout the complete range of sizes. These fits are classified as follows.

Class 1—Close Running Fits. Close running fits are primarily intended for running fits on accurate machinery with moderate surface speeds and journal pressure, where accurate location and minimum play are desired.

Class 2—Medium Running Fits. Medium running fits are intended for higher running speeds, heavy journal pressure, or both.

Class 3—Precision Running Fits. Precision running fits are the closest fits which can run freely. They are intended for precision work at slow speeds and light journal pressures. They are *not* suitable where appreciable temperature differences are likely to be encountered.

199

Table VIII-1. Running Fits

Tolerances for Class 1—Close Running Fits.

Shaft Diam. Nominal Size		Tolerances				Allowable Fits	
		Hole		Shaft		Minimum	Maximum
Over	To	(+)	(−)	(−)	(−)	Clearance	Clearance
0.04	0.12	0.0004	0.0000	0.0003	0.0007	0.0003	0.0011
0.12	0.24	0.0005	0.0000	0.0004	0.0009	0.0004	0.0014
0.24	0.40	0.0006	0.0000	0.0005	0.0011	0.0005	0.0017
0.40	0.71	0.0007	0.0000	0.0006	0.0013	0.0006	0.0020
0.71	1.19	0.0008	0.0000	0.0008	0.0016	0.0008	0.0024
1.19	1.97	0.0010	0.0000	0.0010	0.0020	0.0010	0.0030
1.97	3.15	0.0012	0.0000	0.0012	0.0024	0.0012	0.0036
3.15	4.73	0.0014	0.0000	0.0014	0.0028	0.0014	0.0042

Tolerances for Class 2—Medium Running Fits.

Over	To	(+)	(−)	(−)	(−)	Minimum Clearance	Maximum Clearance
0.04	0.12	0.0004	0.0000	0.0006	0.0010	0.0006	0.0014
0.12	0.24	0.0005	0.0000	0.0008	0.0013	0.0008	0.0018
0.24	0.40	0.0006	0.0000	0.0010	0.0016	0.0010	0.0022
0.40	0.71	0.0007	0.0000	0.0012	0.0019	0.0012	0.0026
0.71	1.19	0.0008	0.0000	0.0016	0.0024	0.0016	0.0032
1.19	1.97	0.0010	0.0000	0.0020	0.0030	0.0020	0.0040
1.97	3.15	0.0012	0.0000	0.0025	0.0037	0.0025	0.0049
3.15	4.73	0.0014	0.0000	0.0030	0.0044	0.0030	0.0058

Tolerances for Class 3—Precision Running Fits.

Over	To	(+)	(−)	(−)	(−)	Minimum Clearance	Maximum Clearance
0.04	0.12	0.00025	0.0000	0.0003	0.00055	0.0003	0.0008
0.12	0.24	0.0003	0.0000	0.0004	0.0007	0.0004	0.0010
0.24	0.40	0.0004	0.0000	0.0005	0.0009	0.0005	0.0013
0.40	0.71	0.0004	0.0000	0.0006	0.0010	0.0006	0.0014
0.71	1.19	0.0005	0.0000	0.0008	0.0013	0.0008	0.0018
1.19	1.97	0.0006	0.0000	0.0010	0.0016	0.0010	0.0022
1.97	3.15	0.0007	0.0000	0.0012	0.0019	0.0012	0.0026
3.15	4.73	0.0009	0.0000	0.0014	0.0023	0.0014	0.0032

Locational Fits

Locational fits are intended solely to determine the location of the mating parts. They may provide rigid or accurate location (as with interference fits), or provide some freedom of location (as with clearance fits). Accordingly, they are divided into three classes as shown in *Table VIII-2*.

Class 1—Locational Clearance Fits. Locational clearance fits are intended for parts which are normally stationary, but which can be freely assembled or disassembled.

Class 2—Locational Transition Fits. Locational transition fits are a compromise between clearance and interference fits, and are suited for applications where accuracy of location is important. However, a small amount of clearance or interference is permissible.

Class 3—Locational Interference Fits. Locational interference fits are used where accuracy of location is of prime importance, and where parts require rigidity and alignment with no special requirements for bore pressure.

Table VIII-2. Locational Fits

Tolerances for Class 1—Clearance Locational Fits.

| Shaft Diam. Nominal Size | | Tolerances | | | | Allowable Fits | |
Over	To	Hole (+)	(−)	Shaft (−)	(−)	Minimum Clearance	Maximum Clearance
0.04	0.12	0.0004	0.0000	0.0001	0.00035	0.0001	0.00075
0.12	0.24	0.0005	0.0000	0.00015	0.00045	0.00015	0.00095
0.24	0.40	0.0006	0.0000	0.0002	0.0006	0.0002	0.00120
0.40	0.71	0.0007	0.0000	0.00025	0.00065	0.00025	0.00135
0.71	1.19	0.0008	0.0000	0.0003	0.0008	0.0003	0.0016
1.19	1.97	0.0010	0.0000	0.0004	0.0010	0.0004	0.0020
1.97	3.15	0.0012	0.0000	0.0004	0.0011	0.0004	0.0023
3.15	4.73	0.0014	0.0000	0.0005	0.0014	0.0005	0.0028

Tolerances for Class 2—Transition Locational Fits.

		(+)	(−)	(+)	(+)	Maximum Interference	Maximum Clearance
0.04	0.12	0.0004	0.0000	0.00025	0.0005	0.0005	0.00015
0.12	0.24	0.0005	0.0000	0.0003	0.0006	0.0006	0.0002
0.24	0.40	0.0006	0.0000	0.0004	0.0008	0.0008	0.0002
0.40	0.71	0.0007	0.0000	0.0005	0.0009	0.0009	0.0002
0.71	1.19	0.0008	0.0000	0.0006	0.0011	0.0011	0.0002
1.19	1.97	0.0010	0.0000	0.0007	0.0013	0.0013	0.0003
1.97	3.15	0.0012	0.0000	0.0008	0.0015	0.0015	0.0004
3.15	4.73	0.0014	0.0000	0.0010	0.0019	0.0019	0.0004

Tolerances for Class 3—Interference Locational Fits.

		(+)	(−)	(+)	(+)		
0.04	0.12	0.0004	0.0000	0.0005	0.00075	0.0001	0.00075
0.12	0.24	0.0005	0.0000	0.0006	0.0009	0.0001	0.0009
0.24	0.40	0.0006	0.0000	0.0008	0.0012	0.0002	0.0012
0.40	0.71	0.0007	0.0000	0.0010	0.0014	0.0003	0.0014
0.71	1.19	0.0008	0.0000	0.0012	0.0017	0.0004	0.0017
1.19	1.97	0.0010	0.0000	0.0014	0.0020	0.0004	0.0020
1.97	3.15	0.0012	0.0000	0.0016	0.0023	0.0004	0.0023
3.15	4.73	0.0014	0.0000	0.0020	0.0029	0.0006	0.0029

Such fits are not intended for parts designed to transmit frictional loads from one part to another by virtue of tightness of fit (See **Force Fits**).

Force Fits

Force (or shrink) fits are a special type of interference fit, normally characterized by maintenance of constant bore pressure throughout the range of sizes. The interference varies almost directly with the diameter to maintain the resulting pressures within reasonable limits. The difference between its minimum and maximum values is small, as can be seen in *Table VIII-3*. Force fits are classified according to the method used in their manufacture.

Class 1—Light Drive Fits. Light drive fits are those requiring light assembly pressures. Their purpose is to provide semipermanent assemblies. They are suitable for thin sections, long fits, or in cast iron external members.

Table VIII-3. Force Fits

Tolerances for Class 1—Light Drive Fits.

Shaft Diam. Nominal Size		Tolerances				Allowable Fits	
		Hole		Shaft		Minimum	Maximum
Over	To	(+)	(−)	(+)	(+)	Interference	Interference
0.04	0.12	0.00025	0.0000	0.0005	0.0003	0.00005	0.0005
0.12	0.24	0.0003	0.0000	0.0006	0.0004	0.0001	0.0006
0.24	0.40	0.0004	0.0000	0.00075	0.0005	0.0001	0.00075
0.40	0.56	0.0004	0.0000	0.0008	0.0005	0.0001	0.0008
0.56	0.71	0.0004	0.0000	0.0009	0.0006	0.0002	0.0009
0.71	0.95	0.0005	0.0000	0.0011	0.0007	0.0002	0.0011
0.95	1.19	0.0005	0.0000	0.0012	0.0008	0.0003	0.0012
1.19	1.58	0.0006	0.0000	0.0013	0.0009	0.0003	0.0013
1.58	1.97	0.0006	0.0000	0.0014	0.0010	0.0004	0.0014
1.97	2.56	0.0007	0.0000	0.0018	0.0013	0.0006	0.0018
2.56	3.15	0.0007	0.0000	0.0019	0.0014	0.0007	0.0019
3.15	3.94	0.0009	0.0000	0.0024	0.0018	0.0009	0.0024
3.94	4.73	0.0009	0.0000	0.0026	0.0020	0.0011	0.0026

Tolerances for Class 2—Medium Drive Fits.

Over	To	(+)	(−)	(+)	(+)	Minimum Interference	Maximum Interference
0.04	0.12	0.0004	0.0000	0.00085	0.0006	0.0002	0.00085
0.12	0.24	0.0005	0.0000	0.0010	0.0007	0.0002	0.0010
0.24	0.40	0.0006	0.0000	0.0014	0.0010	0.0004	0.0014
0.40	0.56	0.0007	0.0000	0.0016	0.0012	0.0005	0.0016
0.56	0.71	0.0007	0.0000	0.0016	0.0012	0.0005	0.0016
0.71	0.95	0.0008	0.0000	0.0019	0.0014	0.0006	0.0019
0.95	1.19	0.0008	0.0000	0.0019	0.0014	0.0006	0.0019
1.19	1.58	0.0010	0.0000	0.0024	0.0018	0.0008	0.0024
1.58	1.97	0.0010	0.0000	0.0024	0.0018	0.0008	0.0024
1.97	2.56	0.0012	0.0000	0.0027	0.0020	0.0008	0.0027
2.56	3.15	0.0012	0.0000	0.0029	0.0022	0.0010	0.0029
3.15	3.94	0.0014	0.0000	0.0037	0.0028	0.0014	0.0037
3.94	4.73	0.0014	0.0000	0.0039	0.0030	0.0016	0.0039

Tolerances for Class 3—Heavy Drive Fits.

Over	To	(+)	(−)	(+)	(+)	Minimum Interference	Maximum Interference
0.95	1.19	0.0008	0.0000	0.0021	0.0016	0.0008	0.0021
1.19	1.58	0.0010	0.0000	0.0024	0.0018	0.0008	0.0024
1.58	1.97	0.0010	0.0000	0.0028	0.0022	0.0012	0.0028
1.97	2.56	0.0012	0.0000	0.0032	0.0025	0.0013	0.0032
2.56	3.15	0.0012	0.0000	0.0037	0.0030	0.0018	0.0037
3.15	3.94	0.0014	0.0000	0.0044	0.0035	0.0021	0.0044
3.94	4.73	0.0014	0.0000	0.0049	0.0040	0.0026	0.0049

Tolerances for Class 4—Press Fit.

Over	To	(+)	(−)	(+)	(+)	Minimum Interference	Maximum Interference
0.04	0.12	0.0004	0.0000	0.0011	0.0008	0.0004	0.0011
0.12	0.24	0.0005	0.0000	0.0014	0.0010	0.0005	0.0014
0.24	0.40	0.0006	0.0000	0.0018	0.0013	0.0007	0.0018
0.40	0.56	0.0007	0.0000	0.0021	0.0015	0.0008	0.0021
0.56	0.71	0.0007	0.0000	0.0023	0.0016	0.0009	0.0023
0.71	0.95	0.0008	0.0000	0.0025	0.0019	0.0011	0.0025
0.95	1.19	0.0008	0.0000	0.0028	0.0022	0.0014	0.0028
1.19	1.58	0.0010	0.0000	0.00355	0.00275	0.00175	0.00355
1.58	1.97	0.0010	0.0000	0.0042	0.0034	0.0024	0.0042
1.97	2.56	0.0012	0.0000	0.0052	0.0042	0.0030	0.0052
2.56	3.15	0.0012	0.0000	0.0060	0.0050	0.0038	0.0060
3.15	3.94	0.0014	0.0000	0.0071	0.0060	0.0046	0.0071
3.94	4.73	0.0014	0.0000	0.0081	0.0070	0.0056	0.0081

Class 2—Medium Drive Fits. Medium drive fits are suitable for ordinary steel parts, or for shrink fits on light sections. They are the tightest fits that can be used with high-grade cast iron external members.

Class 3—Heavy Drive Fits. Heavy drive fits are suitable for heavier steel parts, or for shrink fits in medium sections.

Class 4—Press Fits. Press fits are suitable for parts which can be highly stressed. Where heavy pressing forces are required, yet impractical, a shrink fit may also be used.

Shaft Fits for Antifriction Bearings

It is essential that bearings be mounted in accordance with manufacturer recommendations. In most ball bearing applications, the shaft revolves and the housing remains stationary relative to the direction of radical load, although in some cases, these conditions may be reversed (as for pulleys, wheels). The required fit of the inner ring on the shaft varies with the application and is dependent upon such factors as rotation of the shaft with respect to the direction of radical load, use of lock nuts, light or heavy loads, and fast or slow speeds. Usually, the inner ring must be tight enough to prevent turning under load. This requires a tight fit, or a combination of a tight fit and the use of a lock nut.

When the bearing is tightly fitted on the shaft, the inner race expands and thus reduces the clearance between the ball and the raceway. Ball bearings usually have sufficient radial clearance to compensate for this reduction when fitted according to the manufacturer's recommendations. Should the application require an even tighter fit, the bearing may not have sufficient internal clearance. Expansion of the inner race might squeeze the balls, resulting in overheating and failure. Thus, if the bearing must have a tighter fit than that indicated by the manufacturer, maximum press fit should be specified when ordering.

This will enable the manufacturer to furnish bearings with the amount of clearance needed to offset the extra tightening effect of a more severe press fit. On the other hand, if the fit on the shaft in the bore is too loose, the rotating shaft may cause the inner ring to slip, resulting in continuous wear.

Housing Fits

The ball bearing outer ring should have a push or sliding fit in the housing that is stationary with respect to the radial load, and a light tap fit in the housing that revolves with respect to the radial load. The loose fit in the stationary member is necessary to permit the bearing to move axially and to assume its normal operating position regardless of temperature changes.

In addition, a loose fit for one of the bearing rings is necessary for machine assembly. Where it is essential for the outer ring to freely slide endwise in the housing, the possibility of a tight fit must be eliminated by selection during assembly or else the housing bores must be made larger. Since manufacturers' recommended shaft and housing limits are specified to close tolerances, shafts should be ground round and free from taper. Turned finishes are generally not suitable because they reduce seating area. Shaft shoulders must be machined or ground square with the shaft seat.

Where possible, housings should be ground or bored to precision limits to produce a fine surface and minimal out-of-roundness and taper. Housings should be machined square with the housing bore to prevent misalignment of the outer bearing ring.

Theoretical Fits

Examples of typical shaft and housing fits based on working ranges for both bearing and mounting parts are shown in *Table VIII-4*. These are theoretical and represent extremes of tightness and looseness. The possibility of encountering these extremes is remote, the most common fit will be somewhere in between the numbers. Because of the wide variety of applications, as well as loads, speeds, and environmental conditions, the table can only be a guide to mounting fits. Complete recommendations should be sought from the bearing manufacturer when previous experience does not indicate the type of fit and mounting arrangement that should be used.

Shaft dimensions can be determined as follows:

Maximum shaft size = Minimum bearing bore + tightest fit.
Minimum shaft size = Maximum bearing bore - loosest fit.

Table VIII-4. Theoretical Fits

Miniature and Instrument Bearings			
		Dominant Requirement	*Fit Extremes (inch)**
Shaft Fits	Inner ring clamped	Normal accuracy	0.0000 −0.0004
		Very low runout, high radial rigidity	+0.0001 −0.0003
	Inner ring not clamped	Normal accuracy	+0.0001 −0.0003
		Very low runout, high radial rigidity	+0.0003 −0.0001
		Very high speed service	+0.0002 −0.0002
		Inner ring must float to allow for expansion	0.0000 −0.0004
		Inner ring must hold fast to rotating shaft	+0.0003 −0.0001
Housing Fits		Normal accuracy, low to high speeds. Outer ring can move readily in housing for expansion.	0.0000 −0.0004

Table VIII-4. Theoretical Fits (*Continued*)

		Very low runout, high radial rigidity. Outer ring need not move readily to allow expansion.	+ 0.0001 − 0.0003
		Heavy radial load. Outer ring rotates	+ 0.0001 − 0.0003
		Outer ring must hold fast to rotating housing. Outer ring not clamped.	+ 0.0004 0.0000

Spindle and Turbine Bearings

		Dominant Requirement	Fit Extremes (inch)*
Shaft Fits	Inner ring clamped	Very low runout, high radial rigidity	+ 0.00005 − 0.00025
		Low to high speeds, low to moderate radial loads.	+ 0.0005 − 0.00025
		Heavy radial load. Inner ring rotates	+ 0.00005 − 0.00035
		Heavy radial load. Outer ring rotates	0.0000 − 0.0003
	Inner ring not clamped	Very low runout, high radial rigidity	+ 0.00005 + 0.00035
		Moderate to high speeds, light to moderate radial loads.	+ 0.00005 + 0.00035
		Low to moderate speeds, heavy radial load. Inner ring rotates.	+ 0.00005 + 0.00035
		Low to moderate speeds, heavy radial load. Outer ring rotates.	0.0000 + 0.0003
		Inner ring must float to allow for expansion, low speed only.	− 0.00005 − 0.00035
Housing Fits		Normal accuracy, low to high speeds, Moderate temperature.	0.0000 − 0.0004
		Very low runout, high radial rigidity. Outer ring need not move readily to allow for expansion.	+ 0.0001 − 0.0003
		High temperature, moderate to high speeds. Outer ring can move readily to allow for expansion.	− 0.0001 − 0.0005
		Heavy radial load. Outer ring rotates	+ 0.0002 − 0.0002

* Tight fits are positive (+); loose fits are negative (−)

DETERMINING SHAFT SIZE AND HOUSING BORE

As an example, take an instrument bearing with the inner ring not clamped, normal accuracy, and nominal bore size of 0.18750 in. The tolerance range (ABEC-7) for this bearing is +0.0000 to -0.00015 in. Fit extremes from *Table VIII-4* are +0.0001 in. (tight) and -0.0003 in. (loose).

Nominal bearing bore	0.18750
Subtract: lowest extreme of bore tolerance	- 0.00015
Minimum bearing bore	0.18735
Add: tightest fit extreme	+ 0.00010
Maximum Shaft Size	0.18745
Nominal bearing bore	0.18750
Add: highest extreme of bore tolerance	+ 0.00000
Minimum bearing bore	0.18750
Subtract: loosest fit extreme	- 0.00030
Minimum Shaft Size	0.18720

The nominal OD for this bearing is 0.5000 in. The tolerance range (ABEC-7) is +0.0000 to -0.0002 in. Fit extremes, from *Table VIII-4*, are +0.0001 in. (tight) and -0.0003 in. (loose).

Nominal bearing OD	0.5000
Add: highest extreme of OD tolerance	+ 0.0000
Maximum bearing OD	0.5000
Subtract: tightest fit extreme	+ 0.0001
Minimum Housing Bore	0.4999
Nominal bearing OD	0.5000
Subtract: lowest extreme of OD tolerance	- 0.0002
Minimum bearing OD	0.4998
Subtract: loosest fit extreme	- 0.0003
Maximum Housing Bore	0.4995

Bearing Life

Tables on bearing life expectancies for a number of factors all but assume that the bearing is correctly fitted. If the bearing has an improper fit, either on the shaft or in the housing, its service life will be reduced, and the replacement cost of the product will be increased. Too loose of a fit results in slippage of the bearing inner ring on the shaft and produces fretting corrosion, rapid wear, and pressing of mating parts.

An excessively tight shaft fit causes an expansion of the inner ring, affecting the internal fit of the bearing with resulting overheating, increased power consumption, and early failure.

An excessively tight housing fit prevents axial movement making assembly difficult and resulting in axial preloading of the bearing. A too-loose housing fit may result in poor positioning of the shaft, noisy operation, and pounding out of the housing seat.

For economical production and better reliability, the design engineer must apply the proper tolerances and fits to the shaft and housing.

9

Protective Finishes

Since almost every situation presents the possibility that some form of corrosion will occur, appropriate means of protection must be routinely considered during the design process. The design engineer developing military or commercial equipment that involves metals, must prescribe measures for protecting that equipment from corrosive attack.

This chapter presents the controlling specifications for, and the essential aspects of, various protective finishes for metallic surfaces. The preferred process specification and other applicable specifications are given as a separate part of each protective finish discussion. Coatings are classified into three groups:

- Electrochemical
- Metallurgical
- Mechanical.

The first group depends on electrochemical reactions for application (anodizing, electroplating); the second depends on metallurgical adhesion (flame spraying), and the third depends on mechanical adhesion (paint, elastomeric coatings). The electrochemical coatings discussed are cadmium, chromium, copper, gold, nickel, nickel-phosphorous, rhodium, silver, tin and zinc platings, and protective finishes for aluminum alloys.

The metallurgical coatings discussed are flame-sprayed coatings, weld deposition coatings, diffusion coatings, and the hot dipped metal coating process.

The mechanical coatings are elastomeric coatings, vitreous or porcelain enamel coatings, paint varnish lacquer, and related coatings.

PRACTICES

To the design engineer, thickness, hardness, friction, corrosion resistance, and cost are of prime importance.

Thickness

The thickness of an electrodeposit coating is dependent upon the quantity of electric current used. Thickness, as specified in the applicable specifications, can be reproduced to very close limits.

Hardness

Rhodium, chromium, and nickel plating can be categorized as hard; copper, silver, zinc, and cadmium as medium; gold, tin, and lead are soft. The hardness depends on the plating conditions, which can be varied to favor softer or harder deposits.

Friction

Low-friction surfaces are produced by either soft or extremely hard plating deposits. Lead and tin are used as bearing metals. The harder metals such as chromium have low-friction surfaces and resist galling with steel.

Corrosion Resistance

Corrosion resistance is defined in terms of environment. Chromium is remarkably passive to outdoor environments, but on the electrochemical scale it rates with corrodible iron and cadmium. Silver and copper have good corrosion resistance but poor stain resistance. Many of these engineering requirements are shown in the specifications.

Plating Cost

Plating cost depends upon variables such as the area to be plated, area to be masked off to prevent plating, complexity of the part, hole sizes and depth, and the plating material used. Rhodium is more expensive than gold or silver, and chromium more expensive than nickel and cadmium. If cadmium is a functional protective coating, why use costlier plating materials?

Table IX-1 gives an approximate indication of the cost, friction on steel, wear resistance, and Brinell hardness.

Dissimilar Metals

The designer should prevent surfaces having finishes of dissimilar metals from coming into contact with one another to avoid galvanic action (corrosion). Before using dissimilar metals in an assembly, the designer should check the table of galvanic couples in Mil-STD-186. However, this should not be constructed as being devoid of galvanic action. Permissible couples represent a low galvanic effect.

Table IX-1. Engineering Factors of Plating Deposits

Material	Approximate Brinell Hardness	Wear Resistance	Friction on Steel	Process Cost
Cadmium	35–50	Poor	Fair	Medium
Chromium	800–1000	Excellent	Good	High
Copper	50–150	Fair	Poor	Medium
Gold	5–20	Poor	Good	Very High
Nickel	200–500	Good	Fair	Medium
Rhodium	260–400	Good	Good	Very High
Silver	50–150	Fair	Good	High
Tin	5–15	Poor	Good	Low to Medium
Zinc	35–55	Poor	Poor	Low

GENERAL

In designing a part that requires protective finishes to metal surfaces, the design engineer should use an established order of precedence for equivalent specifications covering materials, processes, or parts. The precedence is established to promote the use of the most economical and widely-accepted plating processes. The specification preference is as follows:

1. Federal
2. Military
3. Nongovernmental standardizing organizations such as AMS (Aerospace Material Specifications), ASA (American Standards Association), ASTM (American Society for Testing and Materials), and NEMA (National Electrical Manufacturers Association)
4. Contractor prepared specifications.

This chapter has been prepared and organized to comply with the required precedence.

PLATING SPECIFICATIONS

Cadmium (Cd) Plating

Cadmium is a soft, white metal which is used primarily for corrosion protection. It is sacrificial (erodes first) to most base metals. Added protection is gained by adding chromate coating over the cadmium plating. The chromate also provides improved adhesion of subsequent organic films such as varnishes and lacquers.

Federal Specification QQ-P-416 (Cadmium Electrodeposited):
Classes (Applicable to all types).
Class 1. 0.00050 in. (0.013 mm) thick minimum
Class 2. 0.00030 in. (0.008 mm) thick minimum
Class 3. 0.00020 in. (0.005 mm) thick minimum
Types
Type I. Without supplementary chromate or phosphate treatment. May be used at elevated temperatures to 450° F (232.2° C).

Type II. With supplementary chromate treatment. For best performance, use to 150° F (65.6° C) for continuous service, or to 300° F (148.9 ° C) for intermittent service.

Type III. With supplementary phosphate treatment. Used as a paint base.

Basis Metal Preparation. Cadmium should be plated directly on basis metal, except in the case of parts made from corrosion resistant steel, on which a nickel strike is permissible.

Other Specifications for Cadmium Plating:
MIL-C-8837, Class _____ ; Type _____ (Vacuum Deposit Cadmium Coating). The classes and types are the same as for *QQ-P*-416. No hydrogen embrittlement relief is required.

AMS 2400, (A number after the specification number indicates minimum thickness except on the threads.)

AMS 2401, Cadmium plating (Low Hydrogen Content Deposit).
ASTM A 165, Type _____ ; for steel only:
Type NS 0.00050 in. (0.013 mm) minimum
Type OS 0.00030 in. (0.008 mm) minimum
Type TS 0.00015 in. (0.004 mm) minimum
*ASTM B*253, for aluminum only.

Chromium (Cr) Plating

Chromium is a bright, hard metal which provides excellent corrosion resistance, wear resistance, and high strength. Brightness and type of finish depend upon preparation of the basis metal.

Federal Specification QQ-C-320 (Chromium Electrodeposited):
Classes.
Class 1. Decorative plating 0.00001 in. (0.00025 mm) thickness minimum.
Class 2. Engineering plating to specified requirements after plating (hardness and thickness).
Types (Applicable to Class 1 only).
Type I. Bright
Type II. Satin

Basis Metal Preparation. The basis metal should be free of visible defects which would be detrimental to the appearance of the protective plating. It will be subjected to such polishing, cleaning, pickling, and plating procedures as necessary to yield deposits as specified in *QQ-C*-320.

Other Specifications for Chromium Plating.
MIL-C-11436, Gray chromium for camouflage
MIL-C-14538, Black chromium for camouflage
MIL-C-23422, Hard chromium (Minimum hardness—DPH 697 Vickers)
AMS 2406, Hard chromium
AMS 2407, Chromium plating (To improve load-carrying and lubricating characteristics of ferrous parts.)
*ASTM A*166, Decorative chromium on steel
*ASTM B*141, Decorative chromium on copper
*ASTM B*142, Decorative chromium on zinc
*ASTM B*177, Hard chromium (Minimum hardness R_c 67 for satisfactory service.)
*ASTM B*253, Decorative chromium on aluminum
*ASTM B*375, Decorative chromium over multilayer nickel plate

Copper (Cu) Plating

Copper is a soft, ductile metal which can be plated from a large number of solutions. Dull to bright finishes are usually obtained. It is principally used as a stopoff for carburizing or brazing operations, as a barrier for subsequent plating layers, and as a substrate for metals that are difficult to plate.

Military Specification MIL-C-14550 (Copper Electrodeposited):
Classes.
Class 1. 0.00100 in. (0.025 mm) minimum thickness for carburizing shield or brazing operations.

Class 2. 0.00050 in. (0.013 mm) minimum thickness as undercoating for nickel or other metals.

Class 3. 0.00020 in. (0.005 mm) minimum thickness to prevent basis metal migration into tin layer to inhibit its solderability.

Class 4. 0.00010 in. (0.0025 mm) minimum thickness. (Use the same as Class 3.)

Types. None

Basis Metal Preparation. Prefabricated joints should be soaked in hot (200-212° F, 93.3-100° C) water for three minutes prior to plating. Any appropriate cleaning procedures can be used.

Other Specifications for Copper Plating:

QQ-A-673, Anodes, copper

Type I. Nondeoxidized

Type II. Oxygen free

Type III. Deoxidized phosphorous bearings.

AMS 2418, provides 0.0005 to 0.0007-in. (0.013 to 0.018-mm) thick deposit for use as an antiseize surface, for use in brazing, and as stopoff.

Gold (Au) Plating

Gold is a soft, yellow metal having a high resistance to corrosion and oxidation. It has excellent electrical conductivity and high reflectivity to visible light. Wear resistance of the deposit may be improved by a nickel strike preceding the gold deposit.

Military Specification MIL-G-45204 (Gold Electrodeposited):

Classes.

Class 1. 0.00005 in. (0.0013 mm) minimum thickness. Minimum gold plating is often used over silver underplating to prevent tarnishing.

Class 2. 0.000010 in. (0.00025 mm) minimum thickness. For waveguides and contacts where nonmigratory material is required.

Class 3. 0.00020 in. (0.005 mm) minimum thickness. Standard coating for engineering use. Same as Class 2 with increased abrasion resistance.

Class 4. 0.00030 in. (0.0076 mm) minimum thickness. For resistance to corrosion and wear by handling.

Class 5. 0.00050 in. (0.013 mm) thickness. Same as Class 4.

Class 6. 0.00150 in. (0.04 mm) minimum thickness. Cathode emission characteristics.

Types.

Type I. 24-carat plate (soft plate), 99.5% gold minimum, no hardness requirements.

Type II. 23-plus-carat (hard plate), 99.5% gold, minimum hardness 110 DPH minimum.

Basis Metal Preparation. Gold will be preceded by a strike as specified. Although a copper strike is preferred, it is not required over high copper alloys. A gold strike is desirable under hard gold; nickel is not as desirable; silver is undesirable. For exterior use on ferrous and other noncopper base alloys, the undercoat should have a minimum thickness of 0.001 in. (0.025 mm).

213

Other Specifications for Gold Plating:
AMS 2422, 0.0005 in. (0.013 mm) minimum thickness
*ASTM B*253, For gold plating on aluminum

Nickel (Ni) Plating

Nickel is a bright, slightly yellow deposit, magnetic, with high passivity. Nickel may be deposited in any condition from a highly stressed to a stress-free state. Because of its excellent bonding characteristics, nickel is often used as a strike deposit.

Federal Specification QQ-N-290 (Nickel Electrodeposited):
Classes.

Class 1. Decorative plating. Bright or matte finish as specified. Class 1 is used for decorative finishes because of its brightness and corrosion resistance.

Class 2. Engineering plating to specified dimensions. Minimum thickness is 0.003 in. (0.07 mm). Class 2 deposits are used for their excellent corrosion and wear resistance.

Types (Applicable to Class 1 only).

Type I. (*DS-ASTM* designation) on steel, 0.002-in. (0.05 mm) copper, 0.0010-in. (0.025 mm) nickel.

Type II. (*FS*) on steel, 0.00125-in. (0.032 mm) copper, 0.0006-in. (0.015 mm) nickel.

Type III. (*KS*) on steel, 0.00075-in. (0.02 mm) copper, 0.0004-in. (0.01 mm) nickel.

Type IV. (*QA*) on steel, 0.0004-in. (0.01 mm) copper, 0.0002-in. (0.005 mm) nickel.

Type V. (*FC*) on copper alloy, 0.0005-in. (0.013 mm) nickel.

Type VI. (*KC*) on copper alloy, 0.0003-in. (0.008 mm) nickel.

Type VII. (*QC*) on copper alloy, 0.0001-in. (0.0025 mm) nickel.

Type VIII. (*FZ*) on zinc alloy, 0.00125-in. (0.032 mm) copper, 0.0005-in. (0.013 mm) nickel.

Type IX. (*KZ*) on zinc alloy, 0.00075-in. (0.02 mm) copper, 0.0003-in. (0.0076 mm) nickel.

Type X. (*QZ*) on zinc alloy, 0.0005-in. (0.013 mm) copper, 0.0003-in. (0.008 mm) nickel.

Basis Metal Preparation. The basis metal should be free of visible defects that would be detrimental to the appearance of the protective plating.

Other Specifications for Nickel Plating:
MIL-P-14535, Black nickel plate
MIL-P-18317, Black nickel plate on brass, bronze, and steel
AMS 2403, Decorative plating, general purpose
AMS 2416, Diffused nickel-cadmium plate
AMS 2417, Nickel-zinc alloy plate
AMS 2423, Hard nickel plating
*ASTM A*166, On steel
*ASTM B*141 On copper
*ASTM B*142 On zinc.

Nickel-Phosphorous (NiP) Plating

Electroless nickel is a bright, medium-hard deposit that can be either magnetic or nonmagnetic. The bath plates appear uniformly on all surfaces. The corrosion resistance is better than that of nickel, and in the hardened state, the deposit offers excellent abrasion and wear resistance. It is used to rebuild worn parts, for reflective coatings, and as an undercoat for gold plating.

Military Specification MIL-C-26074 (Nickel-Phosphorous Electroless Plating):
Classes.
Class 1. As-coated
Class 2. Conditioned for improved hardness (heat-treated), minimum hardness 700 Vickers.
The minimum coating thickness for both classes should be 0.001 in. (0.025 mm) for iron and aluminum-based alloys and 0.0005 in. (0.013 mm) for copper, nickel, and cobalt-based alloys. Unless otherwise specified, the coating is to be used on the above metals only.
Types. None
Basis Metal Preparation. Treat as required to produce a deposit meeting the above requirements. High-stressed steel parts should be shot-peened per *MIL-S*-13165.
Other Specifications for Nickel-Phosphorous Plating.
AMS 2404, Electroless nickel plating.

Palladium (Pd) Plating

Palladium is used as a solderable coating, as a diffusion barrier between copper and gold, and on contacts requiring freedom from oxidation.

Military Specification MIL-P-45209 (Palladium Electrodeposited):
Minimum plating thickness: 0.00005 in. (0.0013 mm).
Classes. None
Types. None
Basis Metal Preparation. The basis metal should be free of visible defects that would be detrimental to the utility, appearance, or protective value of the plating. Articles should be cleaned, pickled, or otherwise pretreated as necessary. Acid pickling on high-strength steels should be avoided.

Rhodium (Rh) Plating

Rhodium is a hard, silvery metal which provides excellent corrosion resistance. The metal has good solderability above 700° F (371.1° C), and has good resistance to wear. Thick coats are very brittle.

Aerospace Material Specification AMS 2413 (Rhodium Electrodeposited):
Minimum plating thickness: 0.00002 in. (0.0005 mm)
Classes. None
Types. None
Basis Metal Preparation. The following strike deposits are required; copper or nickel on corrosion resistant steel, 0.0001 in. (0.0025 mm)

minimum; silver plate, including silver strike, on other metals, 0.0005 in. (0.013 mm) minimum.

Silver (Ag) Plating

Silver may be deposited with a finish which can range from a slightly yellow matte to a lustrous white. It provides fair corrosion protection but tarnishes easily. Solderability and electrical conductivity are excellent. However, the silver tarnish can act as an insulator when low current is used with silver-plated contacts. Its antigalling characteristics make it an excellent bearing material.

Federal Specification QQ-S-365 (Silver Electrodeposited):

Suggested Thickness. For terminals to be soldered, 0.0003 in. (0.0076 mm); for corrosion protection of nonferrous basis metals, 0.0005 in. (0.013 mm); for electrical contacts, 0.0005 to 0.011 in. (0.013 to 0.28 mm). When silver is to be plated on steel, the required thickness, unless otherwise specified, should be 0.0005 in. (0.013 mm), plus 0.0005-in. (0.013 mm) copper or nickel, or any combination of both not to exceed 0.0005 in. (0.013 mm) preplate.

Classes. None

Types.

Type I. Matte

Type II. Semibright

Type III. Bright: Grade A, with supplementary tarnish resistant treatment (chromate treated); Grade B, without supplementary tarnish resistant treatment. These treatments are not intended to improve solderability. Treated parts are solderable, however.

Basis Metal Preparation. An undercoat of nickel and copper may be used providing that, in the case of copper, the part will not be in continuous service at temperatures above 300° F (148.9° C). A silver strike prior to the final silver deposit is mandatory.

Other Specifications for Silver Plating:

AMS 2410, Nickel strike, high bake 950° F (510° C)

AMS 2412, Copper strike, low bake 300° F (148.9° C)

*ASTM B*253, For aluminum alloys

Tin (Sn) Plating

Tin is a soft, white, ductile metal with high luster when flowed onto a suitable surface. It has excellent corrosion resistance and solderability. Tin also has excellent antigalling and antiseizing properties. Pure tin deposits are subject to "tin disease" at temperatures below 32° F (0° C). Small additions of antimony and bismuth prevent this tin disintegration at low temperatures, however.

Military Specification MIL-T-10727 (Tin Electrodeposited or Hot-dipped):

Classes. None

Types.

Type I. Electrodeposited

Type II. Hot-dipped. Thickness as specified. Hot-dipped tin bath is prepared using tin having 99.8% minimum tin content.

Basis Metal Preparation. The basis metal shall be prepared according to the appropriate manufacturing process specification. No preplate is required.

Other Specifications for Tin Plating:

AMS 2408. (A number after the specification number indicates minimum thickness in ten thousandths of an inch.) An electrodeposited tin, 0.0002 in. (0.005 mm) minimum thickness for antigalling, antiseizing, and as a stopoff for nitriting; 0.0003 in. (0.0076 mm) minimum thickness for corrosion resistance.

AMS 2409, Tin Plating, Immersion

Zinc (Zn) Plating

Zinc is a white metal which can be deposited in either a dull or bright coat. Zinc offers excellent corrosion protection since it is sacrificial to most basis metals. Conversion coatings on zinc enhance its corrosion protective properties. These coatings may be applied in a variety of colors from clear to yellow to olive drab.

Federal Specification QQ-Z-325 (Zinc Electrodeposited):
Classes.
Class 1. 0.0010 in. (0.025 mm) minimum thickness
Class 2. 0.0005 in. (0.013 mm) minimum thickness
Class 3. 0.0002 in. (0.005 mm) minimum thickness
Types.
Type I. Without supplementary chromate or phosphate treatment

Type II. With supplementary chromate treatment, for added corrosion protection. Coating should have a minimum of 25 micrograms of hexavalent chromium per square inch of surface. Unless otherwise specified, thickness should be Class 2.

Type III. With supplementary phosphate treatment, for added adhesion for paint base.

Basis Metal Preparation. Zinc can be plated directly on the basis metal except in the case of corrosion-resistant steel on which a nickel strike may be used.

Other Specifications for Zinc Plating:

MIL-T-12879, Zinc, Hot-dip galvanizing plus chromate treatment

MIL-Z-17871, Hot-dip galvanizing

AMS 2402, Zinc plating, General, Type _____ for steel. Type GS, 0.0010 in. (0.025 mm) minimum thickness; Type LS, 0.0005 in. (0.013 mm) minimum thickness, Type RS, 0.00015 in. (0.004 mm) minimum thickness.

AMS 2420, Zincate process for aluminum

AMS 2421, Zinc immersion process for magnesium

*ASTM A*385, Hot-dip galvanizing on assembled parts

*ASTM B*253, For aluminum alloys

Hard-coating Treatment of Aluminum (Al) Alloys (Anodizing)

The primary purpose of the hard-coating treatment is to increase surface hardness and resistance to abrasion and corrosion. The treatment forms a dense aluminum oxide, and is used for aluminum and aluminum alloy parts which contain, in general, less than 5% copper or less than 8% silicon, or a total of 8% of both. Aluminum alloys containing higher than 8% silicon—but no copper, can be satisfactorily coated, provided that proper precautions are taken during the processing.

Careful consideration should be given to the use of the hard-coating treatment on highly stressed parts because of the resultant lowering of the endurance limit. Also, its use should be carefully weighted if the parts have sharp corners and edges where chipping may occur.

Military Specification for Surface Treatments and Finishes Aluminum:

MIL-A-8625, Type I, Anodic film, Chromic acid, Nondyed-dyed

MIL-A-8625, Type II, Anodic film, Sulfuric acid, Nondyed-dyed

MIL-A-8625, Type III, Hard-coating treatment for aluminum alloys

MIL-C-5541, Chemical film for aluminum alloys.

Other Specifications for Surface Treatment of Aluminum:

Aerospace Material Specification *AMS* 2469 (Process and Performance Requirements of Hard-coating treatment for Aluminum Alloys).

Classes. None

Types. None

AMS 2468, Hard-coating treatment for aluminum alloys

Basis Metal Preparation. The surface finish of the part to be hard-coated must be better than that required after hard-coating. Allowance must be made for the coating thickness.

Surface Finish. The designer should specify that the surface finish be determined after the hard-coating treatment.

Thickness. AMS 2469 designates 0.002 ± 0.0005 in. (0.05 ± 0.013 mm) as a standard finish coating thickness. However, other coating thicknesses may be specified using the *AMS* specification number and a suffix number designating the nominal thickness in thousandths of an inch. A tolerance of ±0.0005 in. (±0.013 mm) will be allowed, unless otherwise specified on the drawing. Thus, *AMS* 2469-3 designates a finish coating of 0.003 ±0.0005 in. (0.07 ±0.013 mm).

Hard-coating treatment for aluminum and its alloys is expensive. If not required for the intended purpose, other coatings should be used. Chemical film treatment for aluminum and its alloys is the most economical protective finish.

GENERAL PROPERTIES OF ELASTOMERIC COATINGS

The general properties of elastomeric coatings are shown in *Table X-1*, the Gross Selection and Service Guide in Chapter 10, "Elastomers".

Flame-sprayed coatings are applied by spraying molten metal material onto a previously prepared surface. Their principal value is in increasing the wear-resistance of metal parts; however, they are useful in building up worn or damaged parts, as well as in providing corrosion protection and heat oxidation resistance. Flame-sprayed coatings can be applied to cast iron, steel, aluminum, copper, brass, bronze, molybdenum, titanium, magnesium, nickel, and beryllium. The coating materials that can be used with flame-spraying include metals, ceramics, carbides, borides, and silicides.

Weld deposition coatings are applied to produce a hard, wear-resistant facing on less expensive base metals or on ones with special engineering properties, e.g., toughness. These facings are applied in thicknesses between 0.0625 and 0.25 in. (1.58 and 6.35 mm) by any standard fussion welding process. More than 100 facing materials for use with weld deposition coatings are available. They have been classified by the American Welding Society and the American Society for Metals in order of increasing toughness or in order of decreasing abrasion resistance.

Despite their name, hard facings are often applied for corrosion or thermal applications. *Table IX-2* lists the major facing materials and their properties.

Diffusion coating is a surface alloying treatment for metal produced by changing the surface composition of the metal and thereby improving its properties. It is accomplished by heating metals to high temperatures while the surface is in contact with some appropriate substance. Diffusion coatings result in wear and abrasion-resistant surfaces; however, they are also used to obtain corrosion and heat-resistant surfaces.

The *hot-dipped metal coating process*, generally applied to iron and steel, consists of dipping the material to be protected in a molten bath of a more corrosion-resistant metal. Aluminum, zinc, lead, tin, and lead-tin alloy are the principal materials applied by hot dipping as indicated in *Table IX-2*.

Mechanical Coatings

Elastomeric, vitreous enamel, and paint coatings are among the commonly used mechanical coatings. Elastomeric coatings may be applied to most metals. In addition to being elastic, they offer a wide range of interesting protective properties. The five major elastomer types used in coating are polychloroprene (neoprene), chlorosulfonated polyethylene (hypalon), urethane, polysulfide, and fluoroelastomer. Combinations of these are

Table IX-2. Properties and Use of Coatings

Metals That Can Be Flame Sprayed and Principal Applications	
Metal	*Applications*
Aluminum	Corrosion protection in industrial and salt atmospheres, electrical applications
Babbitt	For bearing buildup
Boron	Neutron absorber
Cadminum	Corrosion resistance
Cobalt	For hard facing
Copper	Electrical applications, aluminum, bronze, and phosphor bronze are used for general-purpose wear applications
Carbon Steel	UNS G10100, G10250, and G10800 are used for rebuilding worn parts and wear resistance

219

Table IX-2. Properties and Use of Coatings (*Continued*)

Hafnium	Neutron flux depressor
Iron	Magnetic applications
Lead	Nuclear shielding, resistance against acids
Magnesium	Corrosion resistance
Manganese	Hard facing and wear
Molybdenum	Hard wearing surfaces, bonding between substrate and sprayed ceramic coatings, buildup material
Nickel	Hard facing, corrosion-resistant coating
Platinum	Electrical contacts, high temperature electrical connectors
Silicon	Wear-resistant coating
Silver	Electrical contacts
Stainless Steel	Corrosion protection, wear-resistant applications
Tantalum	High temperature applications
Tin	Electrical contact coating, food container coating
Titanium	Corrosion and oxidation resistance at high temperature 360°F (182.2°C).
Tungsten	Metal and nonmetallic parts to high temperature as a means of fabricating intricate parts from tungsten
Zinc	General atmospheric corrosion resistance
Zirconium	Nuclear application

Hard Facing Materials Used For Weld Deposition

Material	Properties
Tungsten Carbide	Greatest hardness and best wear resistance
High Chromium Iron	Best for metal to metal wear, inexpensive
Martensitic Iron	Good abrasion resistance, subject to internal stresses, and a tendency to crack
Austenitic Iron	Less abrasion resistance than martensitic, less tendency to crack
Cobalt Base Alloys	Used where wear and abrasion resistance must be combined with resistance to heat and oxidation corrosion

Hot Dip Coating

Coating	Base Metal	Properties	Uses
Aluminum	Steel, cast iron	Protects equipment subject to corrosion and heat up to 1000°F (538°C). Minimizes high temperature oxidation and permits use of inexpensive materials for use in corrosive or high temperature applications	Oil refinery pro-piping, appliance parts, furnace heater tubes, brazing fixtures
Zinc	Steel	Combines high corrosion resistance with low cost. Effective life generally is in proportion to thickness	Nails, wire, tanks, boilers, pails, hardware, lighting standards

Table IX-2. Properties and Use of Coatings (*Continued*)

Lead	Steel, copper	High resistance to atmospheric corrosion and chemicals. Protective oxide film regenerates itself when damaged	Wire, pole-line hardware, bolts, tanks, barrels, cans, air ducts, outdoor hardware
Tin	Steel, cast iron copper	Good resistance to tarnishing and staining indoors and in contact with foods. Sheet lends itself to stamping, drawing, rolling; readily soldered	Milk cans, food grinders, cooking pans, kitchen utensils, and electronic parts (Food cans generally are electrolytically tin-plated.)
Lead-tin alloy (terne)	Steel, copper	Provides some advantage of tin coatings at lower cost; ductility and good adhesion allow deep drawing; excellent paint-holding properties; good solderability	Roofing, gasoline tanks, oil filters, capacitor and condenser cans, connectors, and printed circuits

Diffusion Coating Processes			
Process	*Base Metal*	*Surface Mixture*	*Use*
Calorized	Carbon and low alloy steel	Aluminum compound or AlCl vapor	Resistance to high temperature oxidation makes useful for furnace parts, chemical pots, air heater tubes
Chromized	Carbon steels, alloy steel, cast iron, stainless steel, iron powder parts	Chromium	High resistance to wear, abrasion and corrosion; high hardness
Nickel-Phosphorous	Ferrous metal	Nickel phosphorus	Pipe fittings because of high corrosion resistance
Sherardized	Ferrous metal	Zinc	Small parts that must resist atmospheric corrosion, electrical conduit

sometimes used, one as a primer and the other as a top coating. This enables the designer to take advantage of the best properties of each.

The typical properties of elastomeric coating materials are listed in *Table X-1*. Elastomers are usually applied manually by spraying, brushing, or rolling. For production line use of the process, they can be applied by dipping.

Vitreous or Porcelain Enamel Coatings. These coatings may be applied to metals including cast iron. They provide a hard, glass-like surface with excellent resistance to atmospheric corrosion and most acids. A variety of colors, color combinations (speckled, stippled), and a variety of finishes are available. These coatings are applied by a process of spraying the coating on and then baking.

Paint, Varnish Lacquer, and Related Coatings. Paint probably offers the most versatile type of coating for protecting metals against corrosion. Generally, a properly applied paint coating offers much higher corrosion

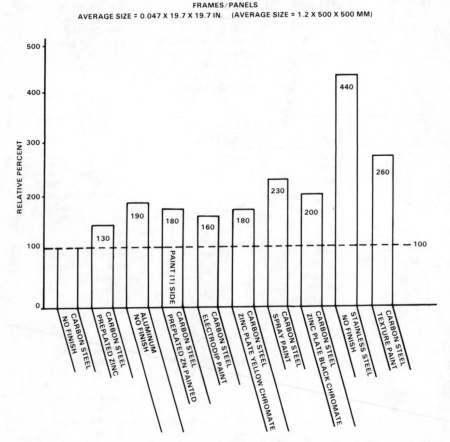

FRAMES/PANELS
AVERAGE SIZE = 0.047 X 19.7 X 19.7 IN. (AVERAGE SIZE = 1.2 X 500 X 500 MM)

Figure 9-1. Relative Cost of Brackets and Supports (*Courtesy, Xerox Corporation*)

222

resistance than an inorganic finish, such as a plated coating or a bare surface coating. Therefore, whenever the nature of a part and its intended usage allow, it should be painted. Four types of transparent coatings in use are varnish, shellac, lacquer, and linseed oil. Pigmented coatings include oil-type paints, varnish enamels, lacquer enamels, sealers, undercoatings, and some stains.

In the area of sheet metal fabrication, the most widely used finishes are organic paints and lacquers. Paints provide protection and give product-appealing color and appearance. It must be recognized that applying these finishes can substantially add to the total cost of producing a part. *Figure 9-1* illustrates the relative cost of producing a simple frame or panel which might be found in any business machine. Plain carbon 0.047 in. (1.2 mm) steel with no finish is the base for all other material and finish calculations. Fabrication processes are virtually the same for all material shown in the figure, but the finishing process varies. Specifying the proper finish is critical in designing for economical production.

10

Elastomers

This chapter provides a glossary of terms used in the rubber industry with descriptions and applications for a few high-usage elastomers. It also includes economical design considerations.

DEFINITIONS

Elastomer is a material, which at room temperature can be stretched repeatedly to at least twice its original length. Upon release of stress it immediately returns with force to approximately its original length.

Tensile strength is the force per unit of original cross section sufficient to rupture a specimen.

Ultimate elongation is the elongation at moment of rupture. (Vulcanized natural rubber can be extended to ten times its original length before it breaks.)

Modulus (or tensile stress) is the stress in pounds per square inch (MPa), of original cross section, required to produce a certain elongation. In rubber, as opposed to steel, the stress-strain relationship is not proportional. The modulus of an elastomer refers only to a single point on the stress curve (strain at a certain stress).

Hardness is a measure of the resistance of elastomer to deformation. Hardness readings are approximate, and should not be specified closer than ±5 durometer points.

Resilience is the ratio of energy given up on recovery from deformation to the energy required to produce the deformation. Resilience is usually expressed in percent.

Hysteresis is the percent energy lost per cycle of deformation, or 100% minus the resilience percentage. Hysteresis is usually manifested by the conversion of mechanical energy into heat.

Heat buildup is a term used to express temperature rise in an elastomer product resulting from hysteresis. Resilience is significant to the designer as an indication of the bounce in a piece of elastomer. Low resilience, however, may be useful where certain damping characteristics are required. Heat buildup in the part, if excessive, is evidence of the need for more resilient material.

Permanent set is the deformation of an elastomer part that remains after a load has been released. It is usual to specify whether the set has resulted from forces in tension, compression, or shear. Set is expressed as a percentage of increase (when loaded in tension) or a decrease (when loaded in compression) of the original thickness.

Stress relaxation is a loss in stress when the part is held at constant strain over a period of time.

Creep is a change in strain when the stress is held constant. Both stress relaxation and creep are expressed as percent change in deformation.

Abrasion resistance is the resistance of an elastomer composition to wear, which is measured by the loss of material when an elastomer is brought into contact with a moving abrasive surface. It is specified as percent of volume loss of sample as compared with an established standard elastomer composition.

Tear strength is a measure of the force required to propagate a cut in a direction normal to that of the applied stress. The tear resistance of elastomers is greater at higher temperatures than at room temperature.

Flex fatigue is the inability of an elastomer to withstand repeated distortion by bending, extension, or compression. Flex resistance is the ability of a resilient material to withstand these forces.

In elastomers, as in steels, the *modulus of elasticity* is the ratio of stress to the strain produced by that stress. since these values are not proportional in elastomers, the modulus is not constant. However, the elastomer's stress-strain curve is almost straight within the region less than 15% strain, and therefore valid calculations which assume stress proportional to strain may be made with tolerable error.

Modulus measurements in elastomers are made in compression or shear, rather than in tension.

Elastomers in general have two moduli of elasticity (static and dynamic) inasmuch as they have the peculiar property of becoming stiffer when vibrated. In highly resilient compounds the dynamic modulus is only slightly greater. In compounds of low resilience (high hysteresis), the dynamic modulus may be twice as much as the static modulus.

Shape factors are changes in the compression-deflection relationship because of the shape of the part. For pieces having parallel loading faces and sides normal to these, the ratio of the load face to the side area provides a measure for degree of compressibility. The ability of a rubber part to compress depends on the amount of side area that is unrestricted.

Adhesion is the strength of the bond between an elastomer and another material. It can be measured by applying a force to peel or strip the material, a force normal to the plane of the bond, or a force applied in shear. Adhesion does not depend entirely upon the elastomer, since metal or fabric also contribute to the strength of the bond.

Thermal properties of natural synthetic elastomers include coefficient of expansion, thermal conductivity, and what is known as the Joule Effect. The coefficient of expansion of elastomers varies, depending upon the kind and amount of filler added to the base elastomer. The more filler added, the lower the coefficient. The expansion of rubber is about ten times that of steel. The means that mold shrinkage is considerable and close tolerances on molded parts become quite costly.

Thermal conductivity is the time rate of heat transfer by conduction for a unit thickness over a unit area for a temperature differential. The thermal conductivity of rubber is important to the designer where heat dissipation is a factor.

The *Joule Effect* is a phenomenon based on the fact that the modulus of elasticity of an elastomer increases with a rise in temperature. If an elastomer is stretched and then heated, it tries to contract. Elastomers must be in strain before this effect occurs. This apparent curiosity is important to the designer if the elastomer products being used are subject to both strain and heat. An example of this would be the use of O-rings on rotating shafts; as they become heated because of friction, they try to contract, and as they contract, more heat is generated, eventually resulting in failure.

Chemical resistance is a measure of the ability of the elastomer to withstand a chemical environment. There are no standards for this property, since the conditions encountered are so variable. Chemical tables are published by most producers of natural and synthetic elastomers and should be consulted for specific information.

Age sensitivity is that characteristic of an elastomer which makes it subject to deterioration by oxygen, ozone, sunlight, heat, rain, and similar factors experienced in the normal course of manufacture, storage, or use.

PRACTICES

The selection and application of elastomers is not without problems. Familiar terminology, when applied to natural or synthetic elastomers, often means something other than when used with structural materials. In order to apply the terminology to elastomers, it is necessary that the characteristics of the material be understood. Elastomers are organic materials and unlike metals, often react in a completely different manner than would be expected.

Design Considerations

Costs. When designing with elastomers, it should be a prime consideration to design the item in such a manner that it can be used in the as-molded and trimmed condition. Machining of elastomers is possible, but adds considerable cost to the product. Relative costs of each composition, as compared to SRB (styrene butadiene) = 1.00, are shown in *Table X-1*.

Age Control. Age control is an important factor when designing with elastomers. It is defined as the designation of a specific maximum period of age after cure date or assembly date that will assure desired conformance characteristics. Requirements for age limitations, cure and assembly date marking, shelf life, and storage conditions are defined further in military specifications for elastomers, and American Society for Testing and Materials (ASTM) specifications.

227

Table X-1. Gross Selection and Service Guide

	Specific Gravity	Durometer Hardness	Tensile Strength (psi at room temperature)	Elongation (percent)	Service Temperature Range	Relative Costs*
Natural Rubber (NR)	0.93	20–100	1000–4000	100–700	−35 to 212 F	1.14
Polyisoprene (IR)	0.94	20–100	1000–4000	100–750	−35 to 212 F	1.00
Styrene Butadiene (SBR)	0.94	40–100	1000–3500	100–700	−25 to 225 F	1.00
Polyisobutylene (IIR)	0.92	30–100	1000–3000	100–700	−35 to 250 F	1.25
Polybutadiene (BR)	1.93	30–100	1000–3000	100–700	−45 to 212 F	1.15
Ethlyene Propylene (EPM)	0.85	30–100	1000–3000	100–300	−25 to 300 F	1.00
Neoprene-Chloroprene (CR)	1.23	20–90	1000–4000	100–700	−20 to 212 F	1.25
Nitrile Butadiene (NBR)	1.00	30–100	1000–4000	100–600	−20 to 250 F	1.40
Polysulfide	1.35	20–80	500–1250	100–400	−30 to 212 F	2.50
Polyurethane	0.85	62–95	1000–8000	100–700	−20 to 200 F	4–10
Silicone	0.98	20–95	500–1500	50–800	−120 to 500 F	12
Chlorosulfonated Polyethylene (Hypalon)	1.10	50–95	1000–2800	100–500	−40 to 250 F	1.30
Polyacrylic	1.10	40–100	500–2200	100–400	+20 to 300 F	3.50
Fluoroelastomers	1.4–1.95	60–90	1000–2400	100–350	−30 to 500 F	30–50

* Relative costs are compared to SBR. A—Most desirable, B—Good, C—Fair to Good, D—Fair to Poor.

Table X-1. Gross Selection and Service Guide (*Continued*)

Weather Resistance	Ozone Resistance	Water/Steam Resistance	Petroleum Fuel & Oil Resis.	Animal & Vegetable Oils Resis.	Chemical Resistance	Acid Resistance-Dilute	Impermeability to Gases	Flame Resistance	Tear Resistance	Abrasion Resistance	Set Resistance	Electrical Properties	Adhesion to Metal	Principal Advantages
D	D	C	D	C	C	A	B	D	A	A	B	A	A	High resilience, good abrasion resistance
D	D	C	D	C	C	A	B	D	A	A	B	A	A	Same as rubber, plus resistance to discoloration and staining
D	D	C	D	C	C	C	B	D	B	A	B	A	A	Good bonding capabilities
B	B	B	D	A	A	A	A	D	B	B	C	B	B	Low permeability to air
C	D	C	D	C	C	B	B	D	D	A	B	A	A	Low temperature, good abrasion resistance
A	A	A	D	D	A	B	B	D	B	B	B	B	D	Aging resistance, Ozone, oxygen, and weather resistance
B	B	D	B	B	C	A	A	B	B	A	C	D	A	Ozone, oil, and water resistance
D	D	C	A	A	C	B	B	D	D	B	B	D	A	Resistance to all oils
A	B	D	A	A	B	D	A	D	D	D	D	D	A	Excellent weather and oil resistance
A	A	D	A	A	D	D	B	D	A	A	D	D	A	Abrasion resistance shock absorption, flexibility and elasticity
A	B	C	D	A	B	A	D	D	D	D	A	B	A	High and low temperature, weathering resistance
A	A	D	D	D	A	A	A	B	D	B	C	D	B	Outstanding ozone and weather resistance
A	B	D	A	A	D	D	A	D	D	D	D	D	B	Oil and heat resistance
A	A	B	A	A	A	A	C	A	B	B	C	D	B	Maximum resistance to dry heat, oils

229

Design Notes

Design Shapes. The elasticity of an elastomer can be used to advantage in designing for economical production. Odd-shaped rings can be made circular and curved parts straight, lending to ease of adaptability. Undercuts can usually be produced by using simple molds, unless parts are reinforced with fabric.

Reinforcements. Reinforcements may be of various materials. The most widely used materials are glass, nylon, or orlon fabrics. These materials provide good abrasion resistance and age sensitivity. An exception is nylon which deteriorates when exposed in sunlight. It is possible to entirely enclose the elastomer in the fabric. This is expensive, however, and should be avoided.

Inserts. Metal inserts, when molded in an elastomer, should be designed to withstand loosening. This can be accomplished by using inserts that have knurls, serrations, or shoulders to provide better adhesion. The maximum material volume should be used around the inserts to provide extra strength. *Figure 10-1* shows some typical molded parts.

Figure 10-1. Molded inserts.

Wall Thickness. Walls of molded parts should be as thick and uniform as possible and consistent with design requirements to prevent distortion and facilitate curing.

Walls of extrusions should not be too thin, nor should they be tapered to a feather edge, as such sections present poor extruding characteristics. In particular, extrusions such as those shown in *Figure 10-2* should have thick walls, with durometer hardness as high as possible to prevent distortion during cure.

Fillet and Corner Radii. Fillet and corner radii on molded parts should be as large as possible to facilitate removal from the mold and to economize in the manufacture of the mold. Allow radii (usually one-half the thickness) on all outside corners of extruded parts to eliminate rough corner edges and decrease the possibility of tearing.

230

GOOD PRACTICE   POOR PRACTICE   POOR PRACTICE
                       (THIN WALLS)   (TAPERED WALLS)

Figure 10-2. Wall extrusions.

Draft. Draft is not necessary when molding elastomers. This allows the designer to place the entire impression in one-half of the mold, thereby permitting the optional use of either sharp or round corners at the parting line.

Tolerances. As on all products, tolerances should be as large as possible. They are more easily held on harder materials. As a rule of thumb, molded parts smaller than one inch in cross section may be held to ±0.010 in. (±0.25 mm). The tolerances on molded parts larger than one inch should be increased accordingly. Tolerances on extruded parts, in general, should be more generous.

Parts can be made to tighter tolerances than mentioned, but this is not recommended because of the expense associated with more precise molds.

Forming Processes. Various processing steps such as compounding, mastication, calendering, and slabbing precede the actual forming of elastomer products. The designer of elastomer parts is concerned with two major forming processes—molding and extruding.

Molding. Molded elastomer parts are formed and vulcanized in a single operation by the simultaneous application of pressure and heat. A quantity of the stock, slightly in excess of the article to be molded, is weighed, preformed, and placed in the mold cavity. The mold is then put under pressure between the heated platens of a hydraulic press.

The mold for an elastomer article determines the shape, size, dimensional accuracy, and surface finish of the final product. Product cavities can be machined directly in solid steel plates in the case of simple shapes. In the case of complicated mold designs, the cavity can be partially formed by several steel inserts which are fitted together to form the entire mold cavity. Design and preparation of the molds are usually the responsibility of the manufacturer, who determines—depending on the number of parts ordered—whether single or multiple-cavity molds are to be built.

Extrusion. Extrusion is an economical method of forming rods, tubes, channels, gaskets, and other parts which have a constant cross section. By means of a screw, a continuous strip of compound is forced through a die orifice to produce the desired shape. It should be noted that most elastomers expand when emerging from the extruding dies, and the percentage of expansion varies with each type of compound. Silicone is an exception in that it tends to shrink. This phenomenon causes the diemaker to make a slightly different die for each compound in order to achieve the same size part.

A large number of extruded parts are available as standards which require no new tooling. Catalogs of rubber manufacturers contain hundreds of these standard extrusions. When designing new parts, the use of these standards should be considered as much as possible.

Machining. In cases where the volume or quantity of work involved is very small, and shape and size permit, machining sometimes provides a satisfactory method of fabrication. As most elastomer parts make use of low durometer (soft) compounds, it is necessary to freeze the part before machining. This method is not suitable for silicone because of its outstanding low-temperature flexibility.

Die-cutting. Die-cutting provides a quick and inexpensive way to make flat parts, and should be considered whenever possible. On a per 1000-part basis, it is approximately 50% less expensive than molding. Square corners can be die-cut, but round corners must be molded. (See *Figure 10-3.*)

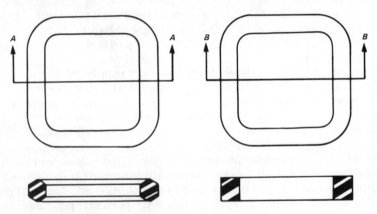

Figure 10-3. Molding vs. machining.

Adhesion Characteristics. Inserts of metal, fabric, plastics, wood, and other materials are successfully bonded to elastomers with an adhesive strength often exceeding the ultimate tensile strength of the parent compound itself. To assure adhesion, metal surfaces are treated by sand or abrasive slurry blasting, and coated with a primer best suited for the compound to be used for molding.

LOW-TEMPERATURE CHARACTERISTICS

All elastomers undergo several kinds of changes when exposed to low temperatures. Some of the changes occur immediately, others after prolonged exposure.

Stiffness

Figure 10-4 shows how stiffness of two different elastomers is affected by exposing them to successive lower temperatures. As the elastomer is cooled, it gradually loses its flexibility until it reaches what is known as the *Second Order Transition*. During this period, the item rapidly becomes stiffer until it reaches a point of stiffness that is no longer affected by lower temperatures. The curve is generally the same shape for each elastomer, but varies transversely with the service temperature range of the specific elastomer.

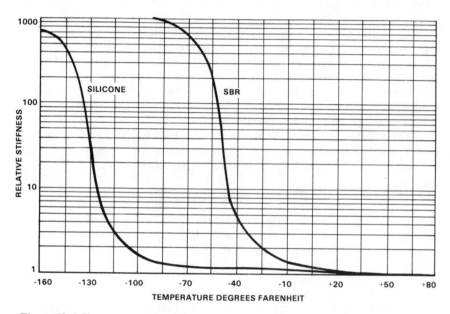

Figure 10-4. Temperature vs. stiffness (short duration).

Brittleness

At some temperature during the *Second Order Transition* period, the elastomer becomes brittle and shatters on sudden bending or impact. The temperature at which this occurs depends on the rate of application of load. Tests prescribed in the ASTM standards determine the actual brittle point of the material.

The brittle point bears no relationship to the stiffness curve. For example, stiffness measurements may indicate a high degree of flexibility at a certain temperature, while impact tests show the composition to be brittle at the same or higher temperature. Actually, stiffness measurements involve loading at low speed and low deflection, while brittleness tests involve impact loading at high speed and high deflection.

233

Brittleness and stiffness occur quite rapidly during a low-temperature cycle. However, other phenomena take place only when the composition is exposed to low temperatures over a long period of time.

Crystallization

Crystallization occurs in natural rubber, butyl, and most types of neoprene. It results in stiffening which is only evident after prolong exposure (days, weeks, or even months, depending on the composition and temperature). Crystallization does not necessarily result in brittleness nor does it affect the brittle point. The rate of crystallization is increased when the elastomer is under strain.

Crystallization is a phenomenon whereby the molecules of an elastomer assume a crystal-like relationship to one another and do not have the thermal energy (because of reduced temperature) to break loose from one another. If the temperature is too low, the molecules do not form into this crystal-like relationship because of insufficient thermal energy. At higher and lower temperatures crystallization takes place less rapidly, and at temperature extremes the phenomenon is practically nil.

The critical temperature for neoprene is 32° F (0° C). At this temperature, the crystal-like structures form more rapidly and grow in size and number. The elastomer increases in stiffness with the passage of time.

Plasticizer-time Effects

Almost all compounds designed for low-temperature service contain substantial quantities of special plasticizers which are used to improve low-temperature flexibility and to depress the brittle point of the composition. Under ordinary temperature conditions, such plasticizers are soluble in the elastomer. Upon prolonged exposure to low temperatures, however, the compatibility of the plasticizer is reduced and a portion of it is thrown out of solution. This portion is no longer effective.

Consequently, the rubber is stiffer at temperatures above the brittle point, and its brittle point may be raised several degrees. Generally speaking, plasticizer-time effects are apparent only after prolonged exposure at extremely low temperatures, such as -40° F (-40° C) and are noted only when large quantities of certain plasticizers are used.

Classification System for Elastomers. The American Society for Testing and Materials has prepared a classification system (*ASTM* D2000) to provide a method for specifying elastomeric materials by use of simple line callout designations. These designations will not be discussed, however, as the majority of usages do not require such callouts.

MATERIAL SELECTION

When selecting materials for a particular application, the designer can usually find more than one elastomer to meet particular requirements. He or she can then choose the material based on price and delivery. The designer should never be satisfied with finding only one material for the application.

Natural Rubber (NR)—Natural Polyisoprene

Natural rubber refers specifically to a polymer of isoprene that has the chemical composition $(C_5H_8)n$.

Natural rubber should not be used where it will be exposed to chemicals or oils, and is not recommended for outdoor use. Exposure to ozone, sunlight, or heat causes deterioration.

Major Advantages. A good balance of high resilience, tensile strength, and tear resistance are characteristics of natural rubber, as are good wear resistance, low permanent set, and good flex qualities at low temperatures. It also has superior tear and out-growth resistance.

Applications: Boots, bumpers, belts, seals, acid tank liners, and mounting devices.

Synthetic Polyisoprene (IR)

The development of synthetic polyisoprene has resulted in a commercially available elastomer that can be used to replace natural rubber in many applications. Polyisoprene has the distinction of being a synthetic elastomer whose chemical composition is identical to that of natural rubber.

Major Advantages. One of the major advantages of synthetic polyisoprene is its purity compared to that of natural rubber. This is an important factor in its nonstaining and nondiscoloring properties. Other advantages are outstanding resilience, good resistance to tear abrasion and heat, and relatively high tensile strength.

Applications: The same as natural rubber.

Styrene Butadiene (SBR)-Buna-S. GR-S

SBR is a workhorse among the synthetics, accounting for a large percentage of all synthetic elastomers. It is the lowest priced polymer on the market today.

Resistance to oils and chemicals is generally poor, but can be improved by proper compounding. Resistance to ozone, sunlight, and heat can also be improved, but is generally fair overall.

Major Advantages. Butadiene has good mechanical properties that range slightly below those of natural rubber. It can be compounded to give good abrasion, wear, and tensile properties. The ability to be bonded to other materials is good.

Applications: The same as natural rubber except for acid tank liners.

Stereo (SBR)

Conventional SBR rubbers are emulsion-polymerized. Improved properties can be realized through the use of a stereo catalyst in a solution-polymerized SBR. This method of polymerization permits greater control of the elastomer structure. Resistance to oils, chemicals, ozone, and heat is not as high in SBRs as in other elastomers, but is acceptable when other characteristics are of primary importance.

235

Major Advantages. Stereo has better strength and resistance to wear, abrasion, and flex, as well as lower heat buildup than standard emulsion-polymerized SBR.

Butyl (IIR)—Isobutylene Isoprene

Butyl, an all-petroleum product, is a vulcanizable copolymer of isobutylene and isoprene. Only a small amount of isoprene is used.

Butyl varies in degree of unsaturation, which is referred to as mole percent unsaturation. This usually varies from 0.6 to 2.5 molecules of isoprene per 100 molecules of copolymer.

The polymers of lowest unsaturation cure the slowest and need fast acceleration. Medium unsaturation grades cure faster, while polymers with greatest saturation have the fastest cure rate.

The butyl elastomer is *not* recommended for use in petroleum oils, or di-ester base lubricants. It is recommended for phosphate-ester-type hydraulic fluids, ketones (MEK, acetone), silicone fluids, and greases.

Major Advantages. IIR has low permeability to gases and vapors, excellent damping characteristics, resistance to aging due to weather, ozone, heat, abrasion, flexing and chemicals, and has high strength.

Butyl is heat treated to improve its physical properties and to reduce cold flow. Heat-treated stocks exhibit greater flexibility, less damping, and less heat buildup when flexed. Heat-treatment also improves the electrical and chemical resistance of butyl vulcanizates.

The most important property of butyl is its permeability to air, which is 1/10 that of natural rubber. Because of the lack of double bonds, butyl is chemically inert. It has approximately the same strength as natural rubber.

Applications: Flexible electrical insulation, shock bumpers, and vibration absorption.

Chlorobutyl

Chlorobutyls are isobutylene-isoprene copolymers containing reactive chlorine. Chlorine provides additional functionability for vulcanization. It readily responds to heat-treatment, and cures at a more rapid rate than the unhalogenated butyls. Chlorobutyl can resist heat up to 400° F (204.4° C).

Major Advantages. These vulcanizates are usually stable when subjected to heat and other environmental attacks. They have good resistance to aging, oxidation, and ozone, as well as acids, gases, and oxygenated solvents. They also have good stability in flexing, low-compression set, good tear strength, and low permeability.

Applications: Same as butyl, but including steam hoses, hydraulic hose fittings, and gaskets.

Polybutadiene (BR)

Polybutadiene is basically similar to natural rubber and synthetic polyisoprene, but has been subjected to sophisticated compounding. Polybutadiene is a controlled-structure polymer. In its pure form it is difficult to

236

handle on conventional equipment, so it is used primarily in blends with natural rubber, SBR or nitrile, and neoprene. This improves its processing ability and imparts some desirable properties to the blend. Tensile strength and elongation characteristics are not as good as those of natural rubber.

Stereo polybutadiene is available in three commercial types according to CIS content (fixed position of molecular units). There is a low CIS (about 40%), a high CIS (about 90%) and a very high CIS (about 98%) polymer, all requiring the use of a special catalyst.

Major Advantages. Polybutadiene has excellent resilience, high abrasion and out-growth resistance, and low-temperature flexibility.

Applications: Gaskets and seals, blends for other elastomers to increase resilience, and abrasion resistant applications.

Ethylene Propylene (EP)

Ethylene propylene is an elastomer prepared from ethylene and propylene monomers (EPM-Ethylene Propylene Copolymers) and at times with a small amount of a third monomer (EPDM-Ethylene Propylene Therpolymers). The EP elastomer has a high coefficient of friction and exhibits excellent aging characteristics, even at high temperatures. Fillers can be added to reduce material costs without loss of desirable properties.

The elastomer is not recommended for applications involving petroleum derivatives, and is not flame-resistant unless compounded for the property.

Major Advantages. The EP elastomer has excellent ozone, oxygen, and weather resistance, good color stability, heat resistance, and dielectric qualities. EPM is peroxide-cured and EPDM sulfur-cured, making the latter more desirable from the standpoint of handling in conventional elastomer processing.

Applications: Seals, weatherstripping, snubbers, electrical insulation, boots, dust covers, sleeves, mounts, and bumpers.

Neoprene (CR) Chloroprene

Neoprene is an all-purpose elastomer with a good balance of properties.

There are two main types of neoprene. The G types which are sulfur-modified: GN, the general-purpose polymer; Gna, which is identical to GN except for a staining stabilizer; and GRT, which has good crystallization resistance and can be used for colored materials.

The W types (lowest priced neoprene polymers) are nonsulfur-modified. Type WHV has a high molecular weight designed for extending with oils. Type WB has excellent processing characteristics and improved heat resistance.

Major Advantages. Neoprene has very good resistance to ozone, sunlight, and oxidation. It performs well in contact with oils, water, and some chemicals. It also is heat and flame-resistant, and has good tensile strength and resilience.

Applications: Wire and cable insulation, gaskets, adhesives, and petroleum and chemical tank liners.

Nitrile (NRB) Butadiene Acrylonitrile

Nitrile is used extensively in the automotive and aircraft industries where its resistance to gasoline and oils is important.

Major Advantages. Nitrile has excellent resistance to solvents, fats, oils, and aromatic hydrocarbons. Good natural and heat aging properties, good abrasion resistance, flexibility, and low-compression set are other significant Nitrile characteristics.

Applications: Diaphragms, hoses, gaskets, tubing, cups, seals, valves, O-rings, packings, flexible couplings, and rubber rollers.

Polysulfide

Generally referred to as Thiokol, a trade name for a series of polysulfide elastomers, polysulfide is resistant to common solvents such as alcohols, ketones, esters and crude oils, as well as lubricating oils, diesel fuel, jet fuel, nonoxidizing acids, and strongly alkaline inorganic compounds. Some swelling occurs on contact with aromatic hydrocarbons, but elastomeric properties are not seriously affected.

Thiokol is highly impermeable to gases, water vapor, and many volatile organic liquids and their gases. This polymer, when suitably compounded, can perform at temperatures up to 200° F (93.3° C) or better, and maintain flexibility at temperatures as low as -65° F (-54° C).

Major Advantages. Thiokol has outstanding resistance to a wide range of oils, solvents, petroleum-based fuels, and other chemicals. It also exhibits a permanent resilience or flexibility over a wide temperature range, and is resistant to weather, sunlight, and ozone. It adheres to a variety of materials with minimal surface preparation.

Applications: Hose liners, tubing for gasoline and oil systems, gaskets, O-rings, and cups and seals. Some of the primary uses of polysulfide compounds is in sealants, potting compounds, adhesives, putties, and certain types of cement.

Polyurethane-Di-Isocyanate

Polyurethane is a rather remarkable elastomer with excellent physical properties. There are two primary types of polyurethane elastomers—cast and millable. The cast type, solidified and vulcanized in a mold, has high tensile strength and excellent oil resistance. Fillers do not increase its strength, but in fact can have a harmful effect.

The millable type polyurethane elastomer can be milled in the same manner as natural rubber and either cured by heat after adding more isocyanate or, if made as a double-bond product, cured with sulfur.

Millable polyurethanes do not have the outstanding properties of cast polymers, but can be made on conventional machinery. The sulfur-cured elastomers can have their properties improved by fillers.

Polyurethane has a most useful combination of hardness with elasticity, as demonstrated by mallets that will drive nails but will not mar a desk surface.

Limitations of the polyurethane are poor resistance to high temperatures, hot water, steam, and hydrolytic agents.

Polyurethanes are the result of the reaction of various di-isocyanates and polyesters or a polyether glycol. The chemistry is complicated, and specific properties should be checked with the producer or molder, since there can be slight variations.

Major Advantages. Polyurethanes have high abrasion resistance, tear strength, and tensile strength; good elongation, excellent shock absorption with a wide range of flexibility and elasticity. They have good resistance to solvents, oxygen and ozone.

Applications: Bumpers, shock pads, drive wheels, impellers, bushings, stripper springs, wear plates, abrasive contact wheels, duct lining, and ball joint seals.

Silicone-Polysiloxane

Silicone elastomers are among the most stable elastomers known. The remarkable feature of silicone is its ability to retain its properties through temperature extremes. The tensile strength of silicone is relatively modest at room temperature, but much of its strength can be retained at elevated temperatures, making this elastomer stronger than most under these conditions.

Silicone, throughout its wide temperature range (up to 600° F (315.6° C)) has superior resistance to compression set. This is a valuable property in the design of seals and gaskets.

The types of silicone are usually grouped into grades according to performance. A general-purpose grade may have a hardness range of from 40 to 80 Shore A; tensile strength up to 1000 psi (6.9 MPa); and a 300% elongation. Silicones have good dielectric characteristics and also resistance to oils and other chemicals, depending on condition of exposure.

Special high-temperature and low-temperature grades can be compounded for these types of service. Special silicone elastomers for compression-set resistance can be compounded for seals and O-rings. There are also high-strength silicones with tensiles in the 1500 to 1700 psi (10 to 12 MPa) range, and extremely high tear strength and ultimate elongation exceeding 700%.

Major Advantages. Silicone is able to withstand extremely high and low temperatures, and it has good dielectric properties as well as good resistance to oils, weathering, compression set, fatigue, and flex.

Applications: O-rings, seals, gaskets, diaphragms, shock mounts, bushings, cushions, ducts, and tubing.

Chlorosulfonated Polyethylene (CSM)

Hypalon is a trade name for this elastomer of E.I. DuPont de Nemours and Co., Inc. When properly compounded, Hypalon possesses a high resistance to ozone. Hypalon vulcanizates are unaffected by concentrations as high as one part ozone in 100 parts air. This resistance to ozone is inherent and not a result of additives.

This elastomer also has a slow rate of oxygen degradation, and high ultraviolet and sunlight resistance. Hypalon weathers extremely well and can be buried or immersed with satisfactory life and performance, since water pickup does not seem to affect its other properties seriously.

Hypalon can be used from as high as 375° F (190 ° C) to as low as -80° F (-62.2° C) (brittle point). Other desirable properties include resistance to abrasion and crack growth, and good color stability. The raw polymer is white and does not contribute to fading or discoloration of pigments.

Hypalon does not propagate flame; it is self-extinguishing. Electrical characteristics are good. Tensile strength and resilience are lower than those of natural rubber. Compression set is fair to good.

Major Advantages. Hypalon has excellent resistance to ozone, weather, heat, and oil. A low rate of oxygen degradation, and good chemical resistance to many acids and alkalies are other advantages.

Applications: Electrical insulation, acid hose, belting, pump diaphragms and seals, O-rings and packings.

Polyacrylic

Polyacrylic elastomers are saturated polyesters of acrylic acid that are vulcanized by special techniques. They show very good heat resistance and good heat aging characteristics, not only in air but also when exposed to various oils and solvents.

The oil resistance of this elastomer, in conjunction with the heat resistance, has made it useful in many automotive and hydraulic applications.

Strength, compression set, and water resistance are not as good as the other polymers. Polyacrylic is not recommended for dynamic seals unless they are spring loaded.

Major Advantages. Polyacrylic has high heat resistance; it can operate from 300 to 400° F (148.9 to 204.4° C) for extended periods without loss of chemical properties; has good oil resistance at high temperatures; good resistance to oxygen; good resistance to heat aging, and good flex life.

Applications: Seals, gaskets, O-rings, hose, wire insulation, belting, and tank liners.

Fluoroelastomers

The fluoroelastomers consist of a fluorinated elastomer developed for specialized severe temperature and corrosion applications.

There are various methods of synthesizing an elastomer containing a large amount of fluorine. The results are polymers with a great tolerance to heat, petroleum products, and chemical attack. The stability of the fluoroelastomer at high temperatures without degradation of structure or mechanical properties makes seals of this material very desirable in the aircraft industry.

Major Advantages. Fluoroelastomers possess high-temperature resistance while retaining good mechanical properties; resistance to oils, solvents, fuels and corrosive industrial chemicals; and good compression-set properties at high temperatures.

Applications: Seals, seats, and gasket materials.

ENGINEERING PROPERTIES OF ELASTOMERS

According to Uniroyal Tire from the text, *Engineering Properties of Rubber,* elastomers are used for a very broad field of mechanical applications which may be divided into two types, structural use and nonstructural use. The structural characteristics of the material allow for such applications as vibrations or shock insulation, couplings, and bearings. The nonstructural uses take advantage of such characteristics as are applied to seals, protective coverings, frictional control, and electrical insulation.

This section is basically concerned with the elastomers applicable to the structural use of the product. The data on stress and rigidity calculations and general design details are applicable to natural elastomers; and within reasonable limits, to the rubber-like synthetics. Nevertheless, caution must be taken not to apply the contained drift, hysteresis, or fatigue data to the various types of synthetics or their blends. The proper selection of a synthetic and the correct design for the product should be supplemented by consulting *Table X-1* and the supplier of the elastomer.

There are two valid methods of designing a new mechanical elastomer part. One method deals with the design of parts in small production numbers. In this situation, consideration of material cost is generally subordinated to demands for adequacy since service failure is not permissible. Formal methods of design depend on *safe stress* or *factors of safety* and must sufficiently control the quantity of material in the part because there are not enough parts to bear the cost of refinement by laboratory or ground testing.

The second method has to do with mass production of a large number of parts. Considerations of material cost are equally as important as adequacy. Laboratory or proving ground testing to control the quality of the material in a part is not only justified, but actually pays big dividends in economies. A small percentage of service failures can be permissible, and indeed, even desirable as an indication of the balance between adequacy and economy. The large majority of elastomer parts (rubber parts) are in mass production. It is, therefore, to the designer of mass production parts that the following is addressed.

ELASTOMERS IN STATIC COMPRESSION

Definition of an Elastic Modulus in Compression

Unlike most structural materials, elastomers may undergo relatively large deformation, and Hooke's law of elasticity is not followed. However, an elastic modulus under compression may be defined for small compressions by the following approximate relation, which is Hooke's law with the compression stress based on the actual elastomer's area.

$$E = \frac{F}{a} \left(\frac{H}{H-h} \right) \tag{1}$$

Where:

E = the elastic modulus in compression in pounds per square inch of actual area

F = the compression load in pounds

a = the actual cross-sectional area of the elastomer block in square inches when compressed into the height h

H = the original height in inches

h = the compressed height in inches

Within the approximation that the volume of the elastomer remains constant under compression, Formula (1) can be written:

$$E = \frac{F}{A} \left(\frac{h}{H-h} \right) \tag{2}$$

where A = the original, no load, cross-sectional area in square inches.

The above definition of E is correct only if the block being compressed is allowed to expand freely in directions perpendicular to that of the applied load; that is, the definition of E applies only to those blocks of elastomer whose pressure faces have been lubricated with a good soap solution so that the sides bulge but expand freely laterally, as shown in *Figure 10-5*.

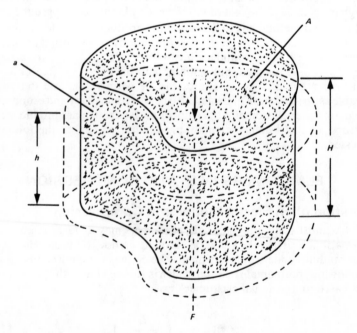

Figure 10-5. An elastomer under compression. (*Courtesy*, Uniroyal Tire Company)

For soft stocks (30-Shore durometer) the linear relationships may hold up to 50% compression; for hard stocks (80-Shore durometer) they probably will not be good past 15% compression. For compression greater than those specified for the particular durometers, the deflection for a given load per unit actual area is less than that indicated in Formula (1).

In determining the elastic modulus of a block under compression, as defined here, the block must first be subjected to ten or fifteen complete compression cycles before data is taken.

A relationship connecting durometer hardness with the compression elastic modulus can at best be only approximate. The compression modulus is an integrated property of the whole volume of the elastomer body, whereas the durometer reading is a property of a small region in and near the elastomer's surface, namely the local surface hardness. *Table X-2* shows the durometer hardness and the corresponding elastic modulus in compression of various elastomers. In addition, *Table X-2* also shows the approximate elastic modulus in compression for various durometer hardness for elastomers at 70° F (21° C).

Table X-2. Elastic Moduli in Compression

Durometer Hardness (Shore)	Elastic Modulus in Compression (lbs/in.², Actual Area)
30 ± 3	185 ± 30
40 ± 4	270 ± 40
50 ± 4	375 ± 50
60 ± 4	550 ± 70
70 ± 4	750 ± 125
80 ± 5	1200 ± 300

Elastic Moduli in Tension

If the force per unit actual area (rather than original area) is plotted against percentage elongation, the resulting curves are approximate straight lines for stresses less than 100 lbs/in.² (45 kg/m²) actual area. The ratio of the force per unit of the actual cross-sectional area to the change in length per unit length, is defined as the *tension modulus*. The formulas of the tension modulus reads:

$$Y = \frac{F}{a} \left(\frac{L}{l - L} \right) \tag{3}$$

In Formula (3),

L = the free unstrained length of the elastomer in inches
l = the corresponding length of the elastomer in inches
a = the actual cross-sectional area of the elastomer in square inches when it is extended by a force F in pounds
Y = the tension modulus in lbs/in.² (kg/m²), actual area.

243

The difference between the values of the tension and compression moduli for a given stock becomes greater the harder the stock—the two moduli being approximately equal for the soft stock (30-Shore durometer). The difference between the compression modulus and the tension modulus is not to be interpreted as meaning that the stress-strain curve is discontinuous at the origin.

Table X-3 shows the approximate elastic moduli in tension for various durometer hardness for elastomers at 70° F (21° C).

Table X-3. Elastic Moduli in Tension

Durometer Hardness (Shore)	Elastic Modulus in Tension (lbs/in.², Actual Area)
30 ± 3	175 ± 30
40 ± 4	230 ± 40
50 ± 4	305 ± 50
60 ± 4	450 ± 70
70 ± 4	610 ± 125
80 ± 5	1025 ± 300

PRODUCTION DETAILS

This section details information concerning manufacturing procedures and specifications. A knowledge of such practical information is necessary for the final planning and designing of an elastomer part.

Metal Parts for Bonding to Elastomers

As a matter of policy, most rubber companies prefer to furnish the metal parts to which the elastomer is to be bonded. In general, SAE 1010 hot-rolled full-pickled steel is the most suitable metal for bonding; moreover, the bonding of elastomers to this metal can be furnished at lower prices than bonding to other metals which may require special processing. If a metal other than 1010 hot-rolled steel is under consideration, it is advisable to submit a sample of the metal (with the metallurgical analysis and treatment) for an adhesion test to the type of elastomer to be bonded.

Specifications. The following specifications must be met by metal to which an elastomer is to be bonded:

- The metal must be free from acid black.
- The metal must be free from rust, scale, slag inclusions, and other foreign substances.
- If grease is used in making stampings, the grease should be saponifiable.
- All tapping should be done with soda solution. If possible, no heavy oil should come in contact with the metals. In case this cannot be avoided, the oil must be removed by a pickling and cleaning process.

Tolerances. Tolerances on the outside dimensions of metal parts should never be plus (+).

244

The usual tolerance in sizes up to 12 in. (305 mm) is plus (+) 0.000, minus (-) 0.015 (+0.000, -0.381 mm). For pieces larger than 12 in. (305 mm), the allowable minus tolerance may be as high as 0.030 in. (0.762 mm). If metals are used with too much tolerance and with no means of definitely locating their position in the mold cavity, they may float into undesirable positions.

Holes in metal parts through which molding cores or pins in the mold must pass, either to prevent metal parts from floating during cure or to provide voids in the elastomer, should be 0.03 in. (0.76 mm) larger in diameter than the nominal size desired and should be furnished to a tolerance of minus (-) 0.000, (+) plus 0.032 in. (0.813 mm).

Clearance hole tolerances of this type should never be minus. In cases where subsequent processing and assembling necessitates precision dimensions on metal parts, such as locating or mounting holes, these can be processed by allowing suitable clearances in the old parts.

Tolerances on Cured Elastomer Parts

Rubber overflow from the cavity is called *flash*. The flash grooves serve as receptacles for the excess rubber flowing from the cavity. Where dimensional precision is required, the flash grooves are more than sufficiently large to accommodate all of the excess, thereby preventing the molds from being held open by rubber between the plates. The thickness of the flash is variable and is a factor which must be taken into consideration for thickness tolerances of finished parts.

Typical commercial tolerances of precision-finish parts are shown in *Table X-4*. These tolerances are established on the basis of the metal parts being flat and relatively rigid.

Table X-4. Tolerances of Precision-Finished Parts Made in a Two-Plate Mold

Thickness	Tolerance (Inches)	
	Adhered Metal	No Adhered Metal
Less than 0.5 inch	± 0.015	± 0.010
0.5 to 1 inch	± 0.020	± 0.010
1 to 2 inches	± 0.030	± 0.015
2 to 3 inches	± 0.040	± 0.020

11

Plastics

This chapter is structured to provide the design engineer with guidance on producibility that may be used in the design of plastic components. The discussion of materials considers the basic selection process, available material forms for processing, and cost considerations. It also deals with the materials most commonly used by custom injection, compression, and transfer molders, and with the properties, applications, and design guidelines for economical design.

Outstanding performances of plastic over long periods of time have been demonstrated in innumerable applications, yet some users of plastic products still continue to encounter difficulties.

Most incidences of malfunction are caused by a lack of knowledge concerning the characteristics and potentials of various plastics rather than by any material's shortcomings. This, in turn, leads to material misapplication.

PRACTICES

Plastics can be molded, cast, extruded, and formed into any number of required shapes. The nature of the plastic material (thermoplastic or thermosetting) largely determines the form in which plastic parts should be specified.

Thermoplastic resins soften when heated, and harden when cooled. Thermosetting plastics do not soften when heated, but gradually lose properties as temperature increases until they char and disintegrate. Thermosetting resins used for molding are usually supplied in a partially polymerized granular form, usually with some type of fibrous reinforcement. They flow to a limited degree on initial heating, but as heating continues they polymerize completely and irreversibly into a hardened state.

For molding parts from thermoplastic resins, the polymer is usually supplied in a granular form. After being heated to the fluid state it is injected into the mold or die, where it cools and solidifies.

247

Materials

The following charts and the plastic material guide are quick references to the most commonly used materials. For materials not listed, the designer should consult the plastic manufacturer as to the selection of the most economical and functional material for the design. Approximately 22 generic resins are commercially available, most of which have several variations. The number of compounds formed by combining resins with fillers is therefore large and diverse, and numerous advantages are to be realized by use of these compounds. Important physical features include:

- Low density and high strength-to-weight ratio (STWR)
- Resistance to shock loading
- Resistance to atmospheric corrosion and chemical attack
- Electrical insulation properties
- Thermal insulation

Perhaps the most significant advantage of plastics compared to metals is their formability.

Not all plastic designs are successful, and failures are often attributed to the material. In actuality, however, they are more likely due to misapplication of a material, inadequate evaluation of properties, or defects in the processing. A thorough analysis of material capabilities before final selection and a close coordination of the component design with the designated fabrication process are essential in preventing failures and in attaining satisfactory performance.

Cost Considerations

Raw material cost and manufacturing cost are the major factors determining the overall cost of a component. Therefore, the total material cost must be carefully considered, and the use of a more expensive material must be justified by improved and necessary performance characteristics. Because manufacturing costs depend on numerous factors as well as on the design of a specific component, the complexity, and tolerances, suggestions are offered to aid the designer in reaching a rough estimate of the fabrication costs.

Raw Material Costs. The list prices, based on unit weight and on unit volume, of a representative group of plastics are shown in *Table XI-1*. Since the specific gravities of plastics range from 0.90 to 2.00, the cost per unit volume is of greatest significance in comparing materials.

Resin prices have shown marked increase since 1980 and are subject to frequent change. Therefore, the prices listed in *Table XI-1* are intended to serve only as a guide. Relative material prices tend to remain fairly constant, so they are most useful for comparative purposes.

Table XI-1 is based on the following calculations as an example to find the cost of plastic materials per unit volume (in.^{3}):

(a) .577 (oz of H_2O per in.^{3}) x Specific Gravity of material = Weight of material in oz per in.^{3}
.577 x 1.05 (Specific Gravity of ABS) = .60585 oz per in.^{3}

Table XI-1. Bulk List Price of Plastic Materials

Material	$/lb	¢/in.³	Comparative Price
Fluorocarbon (FEP)	8.25	63.8	42.53
Fluorocarbon (PTFE)	5.00	38.7	25.80
Silicone	4.17	28.0	18.67
Nylon 6/12	2.33	9.0	6.00
33% glass	2.27	16.3	10.87
Nylon 6/6	1.44	5.9	3.93
30% glass	1.50	7.4	4.93
Polysulfone	3.57	15.9	10.60
Polyurethane	1.54	6.6	4.40
Diallyl phthalate	1.90	12.6	8.40
Polycarbonate	1.44	6.3	4.20
30% glass	2.02	10.4	6.93
Cellulose acetate	1.07	4.9	3.27
Acetal	1.18	6.0	4.00
20% glass	1.43	8.2	5.47
Acrylic	0.73	3.1	2.07
Melamine	0.73	3.9	2.60
Alkyd	0.58	4.2	2.80
Polyester	1.16	5.5	3.67
ABS	0.76	2.9	1.93
10% glass	0.95	3.8	2.53
Polypropylene	0.44	1.5	1.00
30% glass	0.74	3.0	2.00
Phenolic	0.54	2.7	1.80
Urea	0.53	2.9	1.93
Polyethylene Low Density	0.46	1.5	1.00
High Density	0.45	1.5	1.00
Polystyrene	0.46	1.7	1.13

(b) 16 oz ÷ oz per in.³ = in.³ of material per lb
16 ÷ .60585 (oz of ABS per in.³) = 26.4 in.³ of ABS per lb
(c) Cost of material per lb ÷ in.³ of material per lb = Cost per in.³
$0.76 (Cost of ABS per lb) ÷ 26.4 = 2.9¢ per in.³

Manufacturing Costs. Manufacturing costs are influenced by the number of parts being produced, the material being processed, tooling costs, the specific process, cycle times, the amount of scrap generated, how many times the scrap material can be reprocessed or if the design calls for the use of virgin material only. Before releasing the design for production, it is recommended that the designer receive from the fabricators and/or material suppliers the estimated cost and recommended changes to reduce the cost of the product.

A rough estimate of manufacturing costs can be made by multiplying the total material cost by a factor related to the process. Examples of such factors are given in *Table XI-2.*

Generally, when the material costs are low, as with phenolics, polystyrene, polyethylene, and polypropylene, the factors will be greater. Low factors apply to large volume production without finishing operations; the larger

249

Table XI-2. Material Cost Factors

Process	Material Cost Factor	
	Overall Range	Probable Average Range
Compression molding	2-10	3-5
Injection molding	1.5-5	2-3
Blow molding	1.5-5	2-3
Extrusion	2-5	3-4
Thermoforming	2-10	3-5

factors are applicable to low volume runs, low equipment productivity, and some finishing. When material prices are higher, the factor range is narrower. However, the probable average range can be used in most cases.

Scrap losses are usually low with thermoplastic injection molding, blow molding, and extrusion, and are estimated to be less than 10% in the majority of cases. Scrap generation in thermoforming thermoplastic sheet or in molding thermoset resins is greater and may be as high as 30%.

PLASTIC MATERIAL GUIDE

ABS (Acrylonitrile-Butadiene-Styrene) Resins

ABS polymers are available in injection molding, blow molding, and extrusion grades (*Table XI-3*). These materials provide a unique balance of toughness, rigidity, chemical resistance, and cost, that qualifies them for a broad range of applications. They have been successfully used in such commercial application as automobile grills and instrument clusters, television cabinets, tubes, refrigerator panels, and luggage shells. They are also known for their wide range of colorability.

ABS molding materials are easily processed and offer both a relatively broad range of moldability and an excellent thermal stability. They are designed to minimize development of strains in molded parts. Injection molded parts exhibit excellent surface finish and gloss, and usually do not require buffing or trimming.

The extrusion grades are available in a broad range of toughness and rigidity combinations. They provide excellent gage control, surface finish, and chemical resistance. Their unusually good resistance to thermal degradation minimizes problems with color uniformity and scrap rework during extrusion of sheet and profile shapes.

ABS sheet offers outstanding thermoforming characteristics, particularly in difficult deep draw parts.

Properties.

Strength. Good tensile strength, outstanding combinations of rigidity and toughness, and good fabrication characteristics.

Toughness is generally characterized by high impact and high tensile elongation. One of the most important characteristics of ABS is good impact strength or ability to resist shock. This strength is temperature dependent—as

250

Table XI-3. ABS (Acrylonitrile-Butadiene-Styrene)

Properties	Type of ABS				
	Medium Impact	High Impact	Very High Impact	Low Temp. Impact	Heat Resistant
Molding Qualities			Good to Excellent		
Mold Shrinkage (inch/inch)	0.004–0.006	0.004–0.007	0.006–0.007	0.005–0.008	0.003–0.007
Physical Properties					
Specific Gravity	1.05–1.07	1.02–1.04	1.01–1.06	1.02–1.04	1.06–1.08
Thermal Expansion (10^{-5} per deg F)	3.2–4.8	5.5–6.0	5.0–6.0	5.0–6.0	3.0–4.0
Thermal Conductivity (Btu/hr/sq ft/deg F/ft)	0.08–0.18	0.12–0.16	0.01–0.14	0.08–0.14	0.12–0.20
Deflection Temp. (deg F) (264 psi Fiber Stress)	185–223	180–215	180–218	185–224	220–245
Mechanical Properties					
Tensile Strength (psi)	6500	5500	5250	5000	7500
Elongation (%)	5–20	5–50	20–50	30–200	3–20
Tensile Modulus (10^5 psi)	3.3–4.0	2.6–3.1	2.0–3.1	2.0–3.1	3.5–4.2
Flexural Strength (psi)	11000	8500	8000	6500	11500
Compressive Strength (psi)	10500	8000	5500	5800	1000
Hardness (R$_R$)	108–115	95–105	85–105	75–95	107–115
Impact Strength (Izod) (ft-lb/inch notch)	2.0–4.0	3.0–5.0	5.0–7.0	6–10	2.0–4.0
Electrical Properties					
Volume Resistivity (ohm/cm)	2.7 × 10^{16}	1–4 × 10^{16}	1–4 × 10^{16}	1–4 × 10^{16}	1–5 × 10^{16}
Dielectric Strength (Short Time, volts/mil)	385	350–440	300–375	300–415	360–400
Dielectric Constant					
60 Hz	2.8–3.2	2.8–3.2	2.8–3.5	2.5–3.5	2.7–3.5
10^6 Hz	2.75–3.0	2.7–3.0	2.4–3.0	2.4–3.0	2.8–3.2
Dissipation Factor					
60 Hz	0.003–0.006	0.005–0.007	0.005–0.010	0.005–0.010	0.030–0.040
10^6 Hz	0.008–0.009	0.007–0.015	0.008–0.016	0.008–0.016	0.005–0.015

temperature decreases, impact strength decreases. ABS polymers can be formulated to exhibit ductile behavior at temperatures as low as -40° F (-40° C).

Chemical Resistance. ABS families of thermoplastics are highly resistant to aqueous acids, alkalies, salts, concentrated phosphoric and hydrochloric acids, and animal, vegetable, and mineral oils. They disintegrate when in contact with concentrated sulfuric or nitric acids. They are soluble in esters, ketones, and ethylene dichloride. A low water absorption gives ABS polymers high resistance to staining.

Electrical. ABS plastics have excellent electrical insulation properties with dielectric strength of 300 to 450 volts/mil.

Applications: Household appliances, business machines, and computer housings, lawn and garden equipment, chrome-plated parts, highway safety devices, and extruded profiles. ABS plastics are also available as formable sheets for such uses as cases, luggage, refrigerator linings, fume hoods, and ducts.

Polycarbonate

Polycarbonate's properties make it a key member of the group of engineering or high performance plastics. This resin spans a wide range of physical properties that combine to make it one of the toughest, most versatile of all engineering thermoplastics. This combination of properties provides the design engineer with exceptional freedom in creating functional, attractive, cost effective products. Applications include automotive components, optical lenses, medical and business machines, and new communication technology.

Properties. In general, polycarbonate exhibits high impact strength and good ductility, broad use temperature limits, high creep resistance, good electrical properties, and low water absorption. (See *Table XI-4.*) In many cases, all of these properties can be combined with the material's glass-like transparency. The material also is modified by adding thermal stabilizers, UV stabilizers, and flame retardancy additives. All of the usual thermoplastic processing methods can be used with polycarbonate. Of greatest commercial significance are injection molding, sheet and profile extrusion, structural foam molding and blow molding.

Modified PPO (Polyphenylene Oxide)

PPO is a thermoplastic engineering resin which is available in a variety of molding and extrusion grades. (See *Table XI-5.*) It combines high heat, flame retardance, and high impact properties with low moisture absorption. Mineral-filled grades offer a combination of good appearance, flame retardancy, impact strength, higher modulus, and heat deflection temperatures from 190 to 270° F (87.8 to 132.2° C). Standard unfilled and glass filled grades are available with heat deflection temperatures from 180 to 300° F (82 to 149° C). Applications include telecommunications, appliance parts, and computer and business equipment.

Table XI-4. Polycarbonate

Properties	Types of Polycarbonates		
	General Purpose	*Glass 10% Reinforced*	*Glass 30% Reinforced*
Molding Qualities	Good-Excellent	Very Good	Good
Mold Shrinkage (inch/inch)	0.005-0.007	0.002-0.005	0.0015-0.0025
Physical Properties			
Specific Gravity	1.2	1.24-1.32	1.43
Thermal Expansion	3.75	1.77	1.21
(10^{-5} per °F)			
Thermal Conductivity	1.35	1.44	1.50
(Btu-in./hr/sq. ft./°F)			
Deflection Temp. (°F)	260-280	295	295
(264 psi Fiber Stress)			
Mechanical Properties			
Tensile Strength (psi)	9,000	12,000-14,000	19,000
Elongation (%)	6-8	5	3-5
Tensile Modulus (10^5 psi)	3.45	5.00	12.5
Flexural Strength (psi)	13,500	15,000	23,000
Compressive Strength (psi)	12,500	—	18,000
Hardness (R_R)	118	119	120
Impact Strength (Izod)	1.2	1.2	2
(ft-lb/inch notch)			
Electrical Properties			
Volume Resistivity	8.2×10^{16}	$> 10^{16}$	$> 10^{16}$
(ohm/cm)			
Dielectric Strength	380	490	450
(Short Time, volts/mil)			
Dielectric Constant			
60 Hz	3.17	3.17	3.53
10^6 Hz	2.96	3.13	3.48
Dissipation Factor			
60 Hz	—	—	0.0013
10^6 Hz	—	—	0.0067

Properties. The material is fairly nonpolar, and dimensionally stable with resistance to aqueous solutions, acids, bases, and salt solutions. Blends of this material with polystyrene form true alloys and retain much of their base resin properties. By alloying, the resin gains better moldability and a wide range of physical properties become available.

This material has only a fair resistance to greases and oils. There are several grades which are UL listed from HB to V-O ratings. Specialty grades include a nonglass-filled family of products, and foamable grades for added rigidity and dimensional stability in large parts. Processing is achieved through a variety of equipment such as screw type injection molding, extrusion, blow molding and vacuum or thermoforming machines. Chemical blowing agents can be used with some grades of this material for structural foam applications.

Table XI-5. Polyphenylene Oxide Modified (PPO)

Properties	Types of Polyethylene Oxide Modified	
	General Purpose	Computer and Business Equipment
Molding Qualities		
Mold Shrinkage (inch/inch)	0.006	0.005-0.007
Physical Properties		
Specific Gravity	1.25	1.09
Thermal Expansion		
10^{-5} (inch/inch°F	3.0	3.08
Deflection Temp. (°F)		
(264 psi Fiber Stress)	190	180
Mechanical Properties		
Tensile Strength (psi)	9,500	7,000
Flexural Strength (psi)	14,000	8,300
Hardness (R_R)	112	111
Impact Strength (Izod)	3.0-4.0	5.0
(ft-lb/inch notch)		
Electrical Properties		
Dielectric Strength	420	495
(Short Time, volts/mil)		
Dielectric Constant	3.00	2.74
60 Hz		
Dissipation Factor	0.0047	0.0043
60 Hz		

Acetal Homopolymer

The regular structure and high crystallinity of acetal homopolymers—made by the polymerization of formaldehyde—give parts an unusual combination of physical properties that bridge the gap between those of metals and plastics. Some of the desirable engineering properties are: high strength and rigidity, excellent dimensional stability, and resilience over a wide range of service temperatures, humidities, and solvent exposures. It is an easily processed thermoplastic that has been designed for injection molding and for extrusion (See *Table XI-6*).

Properties.

Mechanical. One of the strongest and stiffest thermoplastics, acetal polymers possess a tensile strength of 10,000 psi (69 MPa) at room temperature, with no true yield point, and a flexural modulus of 410,000 psi (2.87 GPa).

Chemical Resistance. Acetal resin is unusual among thermoplastics in its resistance to organic solvents. The polymer is not recommended for use with strong acids or strong bases, however.

Dimensional Stability. The low moisture absorption of this material gives it excellent stability. At 50% relative humidity at room temperature, the

Table XI-6. Acetals

Properties	Types	
	Homopolymer	*Copolymer*
Molding Qualities	Excellent	
Mold Shrinkage (inch/inch)	0.020–0.025	0.020 (avg)
Physical Properties		
Specific Gravity	1.42	1.41
Thermal Expansion (10^{-5} per deg F)	4.2	4.2
Thermal Conductivity		
(Btu/hr/sq ft/deg F/ft)	0.13	0.16
Deflection Temp. (deg F)		
(264 psi Fiber Stress)	255	230
Mechanical Properties		
Tensile Strength (psi)	10,000	8800
Elongation (%)	25	60–75
Tensile Modulus (10^5 psi)	5.2	4.1
Flexural Strength (psi)	14,100	13,000
Comprehessive Strength* (psi)	5200	4500
Hardness	$R_M 94$, $R_R 120$	$R_M 80$
Impact Strength (Izod)		
(ft-lb/inch notch)	1.4	1.2
Electrical Properties		
Volume Resistivity (ohm/cm)	1×10^{15}	1×10^{14}
Dielectric Strength		
(Short Time, volts/mil)	500	400
Dielectric Constant		
60 Hz	3.7	3.7 @ 100
10^6 Hz	3.7	3.7
Dissipation Factor		
60 Hz	0.0048	0.001 @ 100
10^6 Hz	0.0048	0.006

* One-percent deformation

polymer increases in dimension one mil/inch, and only four mil/inch, when totally immersed in water.

Abrasion and Frictional Resistance. The abrasion resistance of the polymer is excellent, and superior to that of other thermoplastics with the exception of nylon. Hardness (Rockwell M-94) and resistance to scratching are outstanding.

The hard, smooth surface of the finished product has a slippery feel. Its coefficient of friction is very low, and shows very little variation from 73 to 250° F (23 to 121° C), and under loads up to 2500 psi (17 MPa).

Electrical. Acetal homopolymer resin has excellent electrical properties. A low dissipation factor and dielectric constant prevail over a wide range of frequencies, and temperatures up to 250° F (121° C). The polymer maintains its good electrical properties even while exposed to high temperatures and humidity.

Applications. The broad range of engineering properties, ease of fabrication, and adaptability to many assembly techniques have led to the continued expansion of applications calling for acetal homopolymers, particularly where there is a need for economically attractive multifunction parts.

In the automotive industry, acetal homopolymer has made possible many design improvements and cost savings. In the plumbing industry, ballcocks, shower heads, valves, and fittings made of the homopolymer are replacing brass and zinc parts.

Acetal Copolymer

Acetal copolymer's high stability at elevated temperatures, in comparison with other plastics even over extended periods of time, is one of the outstanding characteristics of the material.

Parts molded of the copolymer maintain their high strength and stiffness along with other properties such as resilience and toughness, even through long-term exposure to elevated temperatures. Resistance to creep under load and elevated temperatures compares with that of diecast metal. In addition, the copolymer has excellent electrical properties, low moisture sensitivity, and high solvent and alkali resistance compared to other plastics.

Acetal copolymers are supplied in injection molding grades to a high-molecular extrusion grade. The extrusion grade offers greater toughness than the molding grade, with other properties being basically the same.

The natural copolymer is translucent to opaque, and colors are available in a wide range.

Properties.

Mechanical. Minimum creep under load, and resistance to degradation of properties upon long-term exposure to elevated temperatures in a broad range of environments have been demonstrated in automotive carburetor parts and body trim clips, as well as appliance and chemical industry pump impellers and gears.

Acetal copolymer's tensile strength of 8800 psi (60 MPa) is retained for long periods at elevated temperatures of 180 and 240° F (82 and 115°C).

Stress and strain tests have shown that the acetal copolymer has metal-like characteristics, good hardness, and rigidity. Thus when overloaded, the material will distort or deform rather than fail by an abrupt break. Low temperatures have little effect on the copolymer. Izod impact strength is essentially the same at -40° F (-40° C) as it is at room temperature.

Heat Aging. Acetal copolymers retain high levels of mechanical properties through long-term exposure to elevated temperatures. Long-term exposure at 180° F (82° C) has almost no effect on tensile strength.

Chemical Resistance. Exceptional resistance to alkalies and solvents at temperatures to 220° F (104° C) is another quality of acetal copolymers.

Strong oxidizing agents and acids do affect the copolymer, and applications involving these media should be thoroughly checked before designing with acetal copolymers.

Electrical. The electrical properties of the copolymer are good in comparison with other plastics. It has a low dielectric constant and dissipation factor even over a wide range of frequencies, coupled with excellent mechanical strength, particularly at elevated temperatures (220° F (104° C)).

Processing. Acetal copolymer can readily be processed by injection molding, extrusion, or blow molding. Injection-molded parts weighing from a few ounces up to 10 lb (4.5 kg) have been successfully produced.

Applications. Industrial parts include components for domestic appliance machines of all types. The material has the necessary strength and stamina to do the job, and the parts are generally ready to use as-molded.

Automotive components made up of acetal copolymer range from tiny trim clips to gears to fuel-emission systems.

The plumbing industry has many uses for acetal copolymer since it is noncorrosive when in contact with other metals, even in long term hot water exposure. It has been approved by the National Sanitation Foundation (NSF) for use in contact with drinking water.

The toy industry uses acetal copolymer for mechanical components such as gears, bearings, and other parts that must run smoothly.

Aerosol containers made of acetal copolymer bring new styling flair to a field formerly limited to metal and glass. Its use in containers under continuous pressure dramatizes its resistance to creep.

Acrylic

Crystal clear transparency and resistance to deterioration in all types of outdoor environments are outstanding characteristics of the acrylic plastics. They also offer exceptional stiffness and intermediate toughness, as well as low smoke generation during combustion.

Based on polymethylacrylates, the acrylics are used primarily in the aircraft, appliance, automotive, building, dental, embedment, lighting, packaging, and sign industries. This thermoplastic material, first introduced as cast sheet, now is offered in molding and extrusion cubes, fine powders, film, rods, tubes, blocks, and light-conducting filaments (see *Table XI-7*.)

There are two basic classes of acrylics—unmodified and modified. In addition, cast sheet with abrasion-resistant coating was introduced in developmental quantities in 1970.

Unmodified Acrylics. The unmodified acrylics are clear and transparent and are characterized by outstanding resistance to weather degradation. They have almost unlimited color possibilities, are stiff and tough compared to glass, but are brittle compared to many other plastics. They are slow burning and evolve essentially no smoke during combustion. They have outstanding resistance against radiation from mercury-vapor, fluorescent, and incandescent lamps. Service temperatures range from -40 to 240° F (-40 to 115° C).

Modified Acrylics. Properties of greater toughness, its self-extinguishing characteristic, and better solvent resistance are imparted to acrylics by modification of the basic material. Impact-modified acrylics have impact

Table XI-7. Acrylics

Properties	Molding Grades	
	Grades 5, 6, 8	High Impact Grades
Molding Qualities	Excellent	
Mold Shrinkage (inch/inch)	0.002–0.008	0.004–0.008
Physical Properties		
Specific Gravity	1.18–1.19	1.12–1.16
Thermal Expansion (10^{-5} per deg F)	3–4	4–6
Thermal Conductivity		
(Btu/hr/sq ft/deg F/ft)	0.12	0.12
Deflection Temp. deg F		
(264 psi Fiber Stress)	185	190
Mechanical Properties		
Tensile Strength (psi)	7000–11,000	5000–9000
Elongation (%)	3–10	20–40
Tensile Modulus (10^5 psi)	3.5–5.0	2.3–3.3
Flexural Strength (psi)	15,000–16,000	8700–12,000
Compressive Strength* (psi)	14,500–17,000	7300–12,000
Hardness	R_M85–105	R_R105–120
Impact Strength (Izod)		
(ft-lb/inch notch)	0.3–0.5	0.8–2.5
Electrical Properties		
Volume Resistivity (ohm/cm)	10^{14}	2.0×10^{16}
Dielectric Strength		
(Short Time, volts/mil)	400–500	400–500
Dielectric Constant		
60 Hz	3.5–3.9	3.5–4.0
10^6 Hz	2.7–2.9	2.5–3.0
Dissipation Factor		
60 Hz	0.04–0.06	0.03–0.04
10^6 Hz	0.02–0.03	0.01–0.02

* One-percent deformation
Note: For properties of cast resin sheets and rods, consult the fabricator

strengths up to 10 times that of general purpose unmodified acrylics. One family of tough acrylic polymers is transparent, has a slight haze, and is employed primarily in blow molding. A second family offered is usually opaque colors and is employed in injection-molding applications. Both families are less stiff than the unmodified acrylics and have lower service temperatures, as well as substantially poorer resistance to weathering and to radiation from various light sources. These modified polymers have low water absorption and good resistance to staining.

Properties.

Mechanical. Izod impact strength for cast acrylic is 0.4 to 0.5 ft. lb/in. (21.3 to 26.6 J/m) of notch. General-purpose molded acrylics range from 0.3 to 0.5 ft. lb/in. (15.9 to 26.6 J/m) of notch. Tensile strengths for cast acrylics run from 8000 to 11,000 psi (55 to 76 MPa); for general molding material from 7000 to 11,000 psi (48 to 76 MPa). Modulus of elasticity ranges from 350,000 to 470,000 psi (2.4 to 3.3 GPa). Unmodified acrylic compositions are not embrittled by temperatures of -40° F (-40° C).

Dimensional Stability. Prolonged exposure of acrylics to temperatures slightly below their softening points may cause some loss of shape in formed parts. However, acrylics exhibit excellent dimensional stability within their useful temperature ranges. Deformation resulting from solar heat absorption has not been encountered.

Thermal Expansion. Like most thermoplastics, the acrylics have relatively large coefficients of thermal expansion. Therefore, adequate provision must be made for expansion and contraction of the material, particularly when it is used in very large applications or under temperature extremes.

Chemical Resistance. Acrylics are not affected by alkalies, nonoxidizing acids, salt water photographic solutions, or chemicals used in treating water. They are also unaffected by petroleum oils and grease, salt spray, and household cleaning products. However, they are attacked by alcohols, strong solvents, and many aromatic hydrocarbons.

Applications. The largest single use of acrylics is in the sign industry where the cast-sheet products have been established for many years because of their extraordinary resistance to weather deterioration. The building industry is using modified acrylics in the form of cast sheet, extruded sheet, and film.

Acrylic sheet is used for glazing in industrial plants, school buildings, and buildings in high-vandalism areas, replacing glass where breakage is a costly factor. Acrylic cast sheet, first used in the aircraft industry, continues to be an important material of construction in windows, instrument panels, radar plotting boards, and canopies.

Automotive and highway industries have long used acrylics as lenses because of the light-control capabilities, toughness, and weather resistance.

Cellulosic Plastics

Unlike other common synthetic plastics, cellulosic plastics are not manufactured by polymerizing a monomer; they are produced by chemical modification of cellulose, a natural polymer.

Cellulose itself is not a thermoplastic, since it does not melt. Nevertheless, it is made into products that compete with products made from its thermoplastic derivatives.

Competitors are most frequently produced by treating the cellulose with sodium hydroxide (caustic) and carbon disulfide to produce cellulose xanthate, which is soluble in weak caustic. If the solution so formed is extruded into an acid bath, the cellulose is regenerated and solidifies into a transparent solid having the shape of the die through which it was extruded. This is the viscose process, and it is one that is used to produce film (cellophane) and fiber (Rayon).

The first cellulose derivative to be used for a commercial plastic was cellulose nitrate. Nitrates of cellulose were prepared in Europe as early as 1833; but it was not until 1869 when John Wesly Hyatt patented Celluloid that the material was used to produce a plastic. Celluloid was a mixture of cellulose nitrate and camphor. It was the first synthetic thermoplastic.

Cellulose Nitrate. Prepared by the direct nitration of chemical cellulose, with sulfuric acid as the catalyst and dehydrating agent, cellulose nitrate has a nitrogen content that increases as the degree of substitution increases, and the ester is generally characterized by its nitrogen content. (See *Table XI-8*).

The standard plasticizer in cellulose nitrate is camphor, although other materials may be used, either in conjunction with camphor or as a replacement for it.

Characteristics. The outstanding characteristics of nitrate are its dimensional stability, low water absorption, and toughness. It is one of the toughest thermoplastics and the most dimensionally stable of the cellulosics. It has excellent machining characteristics and is easy to use in the fabrication of various items.

The chief disadvantages of nitrate are its flammability and its lack of stability in heat and sunlight. It is too heat-sensitive to be used in standard molding and extrusion operations in heated equipment, but it is readily formed into hollow articles by the application of pressure between heated sheets. In sunlight, nitrate discolors and becomes brittle.

Table XI-8. Cellulosic Molding Compounds and Sheet (Part 1)

Properties	Cellulose Nitrate	Ethyl Cellulose Moldings
Molding Qualities	Good	Excellent
Mold Shrinkage (inch/inch)	—	0.005–0.009
Physical Properties		
Specific Gravity	1.35–1.40	1.10–1.16
Thermal Expansion (10^{-5} per deg F)	4.4–6.6	5.5–11
Thermal Conductivity		
(Btu/hr/sq ft/deg F/ft)	0.133	0.092–0.167
Deflection Temp. deg F		
(264 psi Fiber Stress)	140–160	120–160
Mechanical Properties		
Tensile Strength (psi)	7000–8000	3000–7000
Elongation (%)	40–45	5–40
Tensile Modulus (10^5 psi)	1.9–2.2	1.0–3.0
Flexural Strength (psi)	9000–11,000	4000–12,000
Compressive Strength (psi)	22,000–35,000	10,000–35,000
Hardness (R_R)	96–115	50–115
Impact Strength (Izod)		
(ft-lb/inch notch)	5–7	3.5–6.0
Electrical Properties		
Volume Resistivity (ohm/cm)	$10–15 \times 10^{10}$	$10^{12}–10^{14}$
Dielectric Strength		
(Short Time, volts/mil)	300–600	350–500
Dielectric Constant		
60 Hz	7.0–7.5	3.5–4.2
10^6 Hz	6.4	3.0–4.1
Dissipation Factor		
60 Hz	0.09–0.12	0.005–0.020
10^6 Hz	0.06–0.09	0.010–0.060

Organic Cellulose Esters

The organic cellulose ester plastics constitute a closely related subgroup in the cellulosics family of plastics. This subgroup consist of triacetate, acetate, butyrate, and propionate. Triacetate is considered separately from acetate because it is not a true thermoplastic.

Triacetate. Like cellulose itself, triacetate plastic must be processed in solution because its high softening temperature is not greatly reduced by the incorporation of plasticizers. Plasticizers added in solution, however, will remain in the plastic after the solvent is removed. Thin sheeting and fibers are made from triacetate by casting or extruding and evaporating the solvent.

Sheeting cast from triacetate has better dimensional stability than that made of plastic-grade acetate and is more resistant to water, both absorbing and transmitting less. It also has better folding endurance, better burst strength, and less tendency to change in dimensions and properties with age. Most triacetate film is formulated to meet the self-extinguishing requirements of Underwriters' Laboratories.

Acetate, Butyrate, and Propionate. Cellulose acetate, butyrate, and propionate are true thermoplastics. The cellulose esters from which they are made fuse with plasticizers under heat and pressure to form a homogenous material whose softening temperature decreases as more plasticizer is added. Plasticization of these three esters is possible because they contain large numbers of hydroxyl groups. These groups are polar and have an affinity for other polar materials such as the ester groups on most plasticizers. (See *Tables XI-9* and *XI-10*).

The cellulose ester plastics are produced in different grades for molding and extrusion, and extrusion grade should always be specified for this type of processing. All three plastics can be furnished upon request in formulations lawful for use in contact with food under the regulations of the U.S. Food and Drug Administration.

Characteristics. The cellulose ester plastics, in general, are hard, stiff, strong materials that are unique in their price class in being both tough and transparent.

Properties.

Mechanical. Mechanical properties of the cellulose ester plastics vary with the particular plastic, the formula, and the flow. Hard flow of plastic has high hardness, high stiffness, and high tensile strength. As the flow becomes softer, hardness, tensile strength, and stiffness decrease and impact strength increases. At any given flow, the properties of the plastic vary slightly between formulas. In general, within the flow range normally used for processing, acetate tends to be the hardest and stiffest of the three, while butyrate and propionate have better toughness.

Dimensional Stability. Butyrate and propionate have excellent dimensional stability. Both plastics contain high-boiling plasticizers that do not evaporate significantly, and are practically immune to extraction by water. The plasticizers in acetate are more subject to evaporation and water

261

Table XI-9. Cellulosic Molding Compounds and Sheet (Part 2)

Properties	Cellulose Acetate	
	Sheet	*Molding*
Molding Qualities	Excellent	
Molding Shrinkage (inch/inch)	—	0.003–0.006
Physical Properties		
Specific Gravity	1.28–1.32	1.22–1.34
Thermal Expansion		
(10^{-5} per deg F)	4.4–9.0	4.4–9.0
Thermal Conductivity		
Bt/hr/sq ft/deg F/ft)	0.10–0.19	0.10–0.19
Deflection Temp. deg F		
(264 psi Fiber Stress)	120–180	120–180
Mechanical Properties		
Tensile Strength (psi)	4500–8000	1900–9000
Elongation (%)	20–50	6–70
Tensile Modulus (10^5 psi)	3.0–6.0	0.65–4.0
Flexural Strength (psi)	6000–10,000	2000–16,000
Compressive Strength (psi)	—	2000–36,000
Hardness (R_R)	85–120	34–125
Impact Strength (Izod)		
(ft-lb/inch notch)	—	0.4–5.2
Electrical Properties		
Volume Resistivity (ohm/cm)	10^{11}–10^{14}	10^{10}–10^{14}
Dielectric Strength		
(Short Time, volts/mil)	250–600	250–600
Dielectric Constant		
60 Hz	4.0–5.0	3.5–5.7
10^6 Hz	4.0–5.0	3.2–7.0
Dissipation Factor		
60 Hz	0.01–0.02	0.01–0.06
10^6 Hz	0.03–0.04	0.01–0.10

extraction. Nevertheless, the dimensional stability of acetate is adequate for a great many applications.

Electrical Properties. All cellulose ester plastics have a high dielectric constant, good dielectric strength, and good volume resistivity. All have a rather high dissipation factor, which permits films to be sealed with dielectric heating, but excludes the plastics from such applications as radar coil forms.

Chemical Resistance. Butyrate and propionate are highly resistant to water and most aqueous solutions except strong acids and strong bases. They resist nonpolar materials such as aliphatic hydrocarbons and ethers, but they are swelled or dissolved by low-molecular weight polar compounds such as alcohols, esters, and ketones, as well as by aromatic and chlorinated hydrocarbons.

Processing. All of the cellulose ester plastics are easily processed, but large differences in processing characteristics exist because of the large number of formulas and flows available. Very hard flows are generally not used for

262

Table XI-10. Cellulosic Molding Compounds and Sheet (Part 3)

Properties	Cellulose Acetate	
	Butyrate	Propionate
Molding Qualities	Excellent	
Molding Shrinkage (inch/inch)	0.003–0.006	0.003–0.006
Physical Properties		
Specific Gravity	1.15–1.22	1.17–1.24
Thermal Expansion (10^{-5} per deg F)	6–9	6–9
Thermal Conductivity		
(Btu/hr/sq ft/deg F/ft)	0.10–0.19	0.10–0.19
Deflection Temp. (deg F)		
(264 psi Fiber Stress)	118–196	129–172
Mechanical Properties		
Tensile Strength (psi)	2600–6900	2000–7800
Elongation (%)	29.0–100.0	40.0–88.0
Tensile Modulus (10^5 psi)	0.6–2.15	0.5–2.0
Flexural Strength (psi)	1800–9300	2900–11,400
Compressive Strength (psi)	2100–22,000	2400–22,000
Hardness (R_R)	31–116	10–122
Impact Strength (Izod)		
(ft-lb/inch notch)	3.0–10.0	1.7–9.4
Electrical Properties		
Volume Resistivity (ohm/cm)	10^{11}–10^{15}	10^{12}–10^{16}
Dielectric Strength		
(Short Time, volts/mil)	250–400	300–450
Dielectric Constant		
60 Hz	3.5–6.4	3.7–4.3
10^6 Hz	3.2–6.2	3.3–3.8
Dissipation Factor		
60 Hz	0.01–0.04	0.01–0.04
10^6 Hz	0.02–0.05	0.02–0.05

injection molding, but extruders can easily process the hardest flows manufactured. Butyrate and propionate are generally considered easier to process than acetate.

Applications. The cellulose plastics are fabricated into many decorative and functional products, such as personal accessories, toilet articles, and various items for industrial use.

Ethyl Cellulose

There is a distinct difference between ethyl cellulose and the cellulose derivatives discussed previously. While all the others are esters, ethyl cellulose is an ether. It is manufactured by the reaction of chemical cellulose with caustic to form alkali cellulose, which then reacts with ethyl chloride to form ethyl cellulose.

Ethyl cellulose plastic is produced in pellet forms for molding and extrusion, and in sheet form for fabrication and miscellaneous uses. Sheet is transparent, tough, and moderately flexible. It can be drawn, crimped, folded, or scored even through a beaded edge.

Characteristics. Ethyl cellulose has the lowest density of all cellulosics. It is light amber in color and slightly hazy; it cannot be obtained in crystal but it is available in many transparent, translucent, and opaque colors. It has good processibility and is manufactured in special heat-resistant formulations, high-impact formulations, and formulations suitable for use in contact with food under the regulations of the U.S. Food and Drug Administration. Its outstanding characteristic is its great toughness at low temperatures.

Properties.

Mechanical. Mechanical properties of ethyl cellulose, like those of the cellulose ester plastics, vary with flow, and except for low-temperature toughness, they are quite comparable to those of acetate, butyrate, and propionate. In general, the plastic has good hardness, stiffness, tensile strength, impact strength, and dimensional stability. It is available in soft flows, but not very good ones.

Electrical. Electrical properties of ethyl cellulose are influenced by the fact that the ether group is relatively nonpolar. The dielectric constant and dissipation factor of ethyl cellulose are lower than those of the organic cellulose esters, whereas its dielectric strength is higher.

Chemical Resistance. Ethyl cellulose, as an ether, has chemical properties different from those of cellulose esters. It is not as resistant as cellulose ester to acids, but it is much more resistant to bases—even strong bases. It dissolves in all the common solvents for cellulose esters as well as in materials such as hydrocarbons and ethers which are not solvents for cellulose esters. It is compatible with a wide range of resins, waxes, and oils which are frequently used to modify its properties for specialized end use.

Processing. Ethyl cellulose is suitable for either molding or extruding but, like the cellulose esters, is slightly hygroscopic and must be dried before it is processed. It should be molded in a warm mold—commonly 120 to 160° F (49 to 71° C).

Applications. Ethyl cellulose is used in the manufacture of fountain pens, pen and pencil barrels, radio housings, drawing instruments, and other useful items.

Chlorinated Polyether

Chlorinated polyether is an engineering thermoplastic having an unusual combination of mechanical, electrical, and chemical-resistant properties that make it possible to fabricate parts that remain extremely stable even under severe service conditions. (See *Table XI-11*.)

Because of its highly crystalline nature, chlorinated polyether has a narrow melting range and low mold shrinkage. Melt viscosities are low. These properties facilitate design and production of precision moldings to accuracies which approach those of machined metal parts.

Characteristics. Chlorinated polyether is available as a molding material and in powder form for use in coating. The molding material is supplied as unfilled resin or filled with graphite as well as graphite plus wollastonite.

264

Table XI-11. The Properties of Chlorinated Polyether

Molding Quality	Excellent
Mold Shrinkage (inch/inch)	0.004–0.008
Physical Properties	
Specific Gravity	1.4
Thermal Expansion (10^{-5} per deg F)	6.6
Thermal Conductivity (Btu/hr/sq ft/deg F/ft)	0.91
Deflection Temp. deg F (264 psi Fiber Stress)	210
Mechanical Properties	
Tensile Strength (psi)	6000
Elongation (%)	60.0–160.0
Tensile Modulus (10^5 psi)	1.6
Flexural Strength (psi)	5000 (0.1 % offset)
Compressive Strength (psi)	9000
Hardness	$R_R 100$
Impact Strength (Izod) (ft-lb/inch notch)	0.4
Electrical Properties	
Volume Resistivity (ohm/cm)	1.5×10^{16}
Dielectric Strength (Short Time, volts/mil)	400
Dielectric Constant	
60 Hz	3.10
10^6 Hz	2.90
Dissipation Factor	
60 Hz	0.011
10^6 Hz	0.011

Low-mold shrinkage can be expected with chlorinated polyether because of its low-volume change from a melt to a solid state; its low-melt viscosity accounts for its easy mold filling.

Chlorinated polyether crystallizes rapidly, resulting in the production of essentially strain-free components stable over many chemically active environments.

Properties.

Mechanical. The mechanical properties of the chlorinated polyether are good, the mechanical creep properties are particularly good.

Electrical. Electrical properties of the chlorinated polyether further expand its area of usefulness. Although loss factors are somewhat higher than for styrene, fluoroplastics, and polyethylene, they are still lower than for many other thermoplastic materials.

Chemical Resistance. The corrosion resistance of chlorinated polyether to more than 300 chemicals and reagents makes this plastic an outstanding material for use in the chemical industry. It resists organic and inorganic agents (with the exception of strong oxidizing agents) at temperatures up to 250° F (121° C) or higher, depending upon the type of environment.

Processing. Chlorinated polyether can be fabricated as a solid, a lining, or as a coating material in functional and low-cost components for chemical processing.

265

A wide assortment of corrosion-resistant processing components are fabricated from chlorinated polyether by injection molding and extrusion. Sheet, rod, tube, or block stock so formed can be precision machined.

Applications. Many leading manufacturers of processing equipment now offer complete lines of injection-molded valves and pump heads, of extruded pipe in standard lengths and diameters with threaded or socked connection, and of precision-machined gears, pins, bushings and similar items.

Linings for valves, pumps, and metal parts can be extruded, injection or transfer molded. Parts lined with chlorinated polyether offer improved performance.

Continuous pinhole-free coatings of chlorinated polyether can be applied to pipe and fittings, valves, pumps, vessels, and other chemical processing components by a number of coating techniques.

Epoxy

Generally speaking, the end-use technology of epoxy resins is based on the conversion, by the user, of a low-molecular weight di- or polyepoxy compound to a network of crosslinked molecules having a high degree of structural integrity. This conversion is most often accomplished by a coreaction with other compounds usually referred to as curing agents; although a crosslinked network can also be achieved by homopolymerization of the resin in the presence of certain catalysts. With a given epoxy resin the properties of the final product can be influenced by the choice and amount of curing agent, curing conditions, and the modifiers added. (See *Table XI-12.*)

Characteristics. The many possible combinations of coreactants, resin types, resin grades, and modifiers give epoxy technology its wide product and process versatility. These combinations extend the useful range of properties to higher strengths, better heat resistance, and improved electrical and weathering properties.

Properties.

Mechanical. Epoxies are specially characterized by good flexibility, mechanical strength, impact strength, and low shrinkage during cure.

Electrical. Epoxies exhibit good electrical properties.

Chemical Resistance. The standard epoxies (Diglycidyl Ethers of Bisphenol A), cast, molded, and reinforced, are highly resistant to water and strong alkaline environments; less resistant to sulfuric and acetic acids and oxidizing agents. The epoxy novolacs, cast rigid, molded, and glass cloth laminates, are resistant to water and strong alkalies; and more resistant to sulfuric acids and oxidizing agents than the standard epoxies. The high-performance resins (Cycloaliphatic Diepoxides), have outstanding resistance to weather; high resistance to water and strong alkaline environments; and less resistance to sulfuric and acetic acids, and oxidizing agents.

Processing. Epoxies can be cast for potting and encapsulation of electronic components, molded and extruded.

Applications. Typical applications for epoxy resin systems include laminated plastics for printed circuit boards, reinforced plastics for aircraft

Table XI-12. Standard Epoxies

Properties	Cast rigid	Molded
Molding Qualities	—	Excellent
Mold Shrinkage (inch/inch)	—	0.002–0.003
Physical Properties		
Specific Gravity	1.15	1.80–2.0
Thermal Expansion		
(10^{-5} per deg F)	3.3	1–2
Thermal Conductivity		
(Btu/hr/sq ft/deg F/ft)	0.1–0.3	0.1–0.5
Deflection Temp. deg F		
(264 psi Fiber Stress)	23ɔ	340–400
Mechanical Properties		
Tensile Strength (psi)	9500–11,500	8000–11,000
Elongation (%)	4.4	—
Tensile Modulus (10^5 psi)	4.5	—
Flexural Strength (psi)	14,000–18,000	19,000–22,000
Compressive Strength (psi)	16,500–24,000	34,000–38,000
Hardness	R_M 106	75–80 (Barcol)
Impact Strength (Izod)		
(ft-lb/inch notch)	0.2–0.5	0.4–0.5
Electrical Properties		
Volume Resistivity (ohm/cm)	6.1×10^{15}	1–5×10^{15}
Dielectric Strength		
(Short Time, volts/mil)	400	360–400
Dielectric Constant		
60 Hz	4.02	4.4–5.4
10^6 Hz	3.42	4.1–4.6
Dissipation Factor		
60 Hz	0.0074	0.011–0.018
10^6 Hz	0.032	0.013–0.020

and space vehicles, filament-wound structures for rocket bodies, and potting and encapsulating.

Nylon

Marketed under the generic name of nylon, the polyamide polymers are forecast to continue steady growth through wide acceptance in extrusion and injection-molding applications.

Of immediate interest are the commercially available nylons synthesized from dibasic acids and diamines or from amino acids. These homopolymers constitute the major types of nylons available. However, nylons possessing specific end-use properties or processing characteristics formed by copolymerizing the various amide-producing ingredients are receiving considerable attention for specialty uses.

Theoretically, because many different dibasic acids, diamines, and amino acids can be produced, a substantial number of nylons are possible. In practice, however, the availability and cost of various amide-forming ingredients and the finished-product properties determine which nylons are economically and commercially acceptable. Currently there are three nylon homopolymers in widest use: Nylon 6 (*Table XI-13*), Nylon 6/6 (*Table XI-14*), and Nylon 6/10 (*Table XI-15*).

Nylon 6/6 and 6/10, developed in the United States and introduced as molding resins in the early 1940s have gained good acceptance as engineering materials. In the early 1950s Nylon 6, first commercialized in Europe, was introduced in this country.

Characteristics. Both Nylon 6/6 and Nylon 6 are considered general-purpose nylons and are offered in a wide range of formulations for injection molding and extrusion. Improved thermal stability, rapid crystallization, and other desirable characteristics are derived through various modifications and additive systems.

Nylon 6/10 is considered a specialty nylon, is more expensive, and is generally used where the good engineering and design properties of nylon are needed and where the lower moisture sensitivity of Nylon 6/10 is required.

Table XI-13. Nylons—Type 6

Properties	Types	
	General Purpose	30% Glass Fiber Reinforced
Molding Qualities	Excellent	
Mold Shrinkage (inch/inch)	0.006–0.014	0.003
Physical Properties		
Specific Gravity	1.15–1.17	1.37
Thermal Expansion (10^{-5} per deg F)	4.8	1.2
Thermal Conductivity (Btu/hr/sq ft/deg F/ft)	1.2	1.2–1.7
Deflection Temp. deg F (264 psi Fiber Stress)	155–160	420–429
Mechanical Properties		
Tensile Strength (psi)	9500–12,500	21,000–23,000
Elongation (%)	30.0–220.0	2.0–4.0
Tensile Modulus (10^5 psi)	3.7–4.5	10.0–12.0
Flexural Strength (psi)	Unbreakable	26,000–34,000
Compressive Strength* (psi)	6700–13,000	19,000–20,000
Hardness (R_R)	118–120	118–121
Impact Strength (Izod) (ft-lb/inch notch)	0.8–1.2	2.3–3.0
Electrical Properties		
Volume Resistivity (ohm/cm)	4.5×10^{13}	1.5×10^{15}
Dielectric Strength (Short Time, volts/mil)	385–410	400–450
Dielectric Constant		
60 Hz	4.0–5.3	4.6–5.6
10^6 Hz	3.6–3.8	3.9–5.4
Dissipation Factor		
60 Hz	0.06–0.014	0.022–0.008
10^6 Hz	0.03–0.04	0.019–0.015

* One-percent deformation

Table XI-14. Nylons—Type 6/6

Properties	Types	
	General Purpose	30% Glass Filled
Molding qualities	Excellent	
Mold Shrinkage (inch/inch)	0.015	0.002–0.007
Physical Properties		
Specific Gravity	1.13–1.15	1.34–1.37
Thermal Expansion	4.5	1.4–2.1
(10^{-5} per deg F)		
Thermal Conductivity	1.7	1.5–3.3
(Btu/hr/sq ft/deg F/ft)		
Deflection Temp. deg F	150–220	495–500
(264 psi Fiber Stress)		
Mechanical Properties		
Tensile Strength (psi)	9000–12,000	20,000–25,000
Elongation (%)	60.0–300.0	5.0–10.0
Tensile Modulus (10^5 psi)	1.75–4.15	10.0–12.5
Flexural Strength (psi)	Unbreakable	28,000–30,000
Compressive Strength* (psi)	6700–12,500	18,500–20,000
Hardness (R_R)	108–120	118–121
Impact Strength (Izod)	1.0–2.0	2.0–3.4
(ft-lb/inch notch)		
Electrical Properties		
Volume Resistivity (ohm/cm)	10^{14}–10^{15}	5.5×10^{15}
Dielectric Strength	385–470	400–480
(Short Time, volts/mil)		
Dielectric Constant		
60 Hz	4.0	4.0–4.4
10^6 Hz	3.6	3.5–4.1
Dissipation Factor		
60 Hz	0.14–0.40	0.006
10^6 Hz	0.040	0.017–0.018

* One-percent deformation

Properties.

Mechanical. Nylon's principal advantage over competing resins is generally considered to be its toughness. Its resistance to repeated blows such as those received by automobile-door striker blocks is well known. While it is somewhat notch sensitive (Izod impact is about 1.0 ft lb/ in. (53 J/ m) of notch in dry state), the design of the part, the amount of moisture absorbed, contamination, and mold-in stress have a much greater influence on the impact performance of a nylon part than does the resin identity.

Electrical. Nylons are generally considered to be good electrical insulators but are not recommended for high-dielectric applications where polyolefins and fluorocarbons are normally used.

Chemical Resistance. The commercial nylons are not susceptible to attack by chemicals such as the alkyl halides, thiols, esters, glycols, organic solvents, oil fuels, and aldehydes (except formaldehyde). All nylons, however, are sensitive in varying degrees to polar solvents such as water and alcohol.

Table XI-15. Nylons—Type 6/10

Properties	Types	
	General Purpose	30% Glass Fiber Reinforced
Molding Qualities	Excellent	
Mold Shrinkage (inch/inch)	0.010–0.015	0.0035–0.0045
Physical Properties		
Specific Gravity	1.07–1.09	1.30
Thermal Expansion (10^{-5} per deg F)	5	2.5
Thermal Conductivity (Btu/hr/sq ft/deg F/ft)	1.5	3.5
Deflection Temp. deg F (264 psi Fiber Stress)	135	420
Mechanical Properties		
Tensile Strength (psi)	8500–8600	12,000–25,000
Elongation (%)	85.0–220.0	1.5–1.9
Tensile Modulus (10^5 psi)	2.8–3.0	5.0–15.0
Flexural Strength (psi)	Unbreakable	15,000–23,000
Compressive Strength* (psi)	3000	13,000–18,000
Hardness	$R_R 111$	$R_E 40$–50
Impact Strength (Izod) (ft-lb/inch notch)	1.2	3.4
Electrical Properties		
Volume Resistivity (ohm/cm)	10^{12}–10^{15}	1.53–5.5 × 10^{15}
Dielectric Strength (Short Time, volts/mil)	470	400–500
Dielectric Constant		
60 Hz	3.9	4.0–4.5
10^6 Hz	3.5	3.4–3.7
Dissipation Factor		
60 Hz	0.04	0.001–0.002
10^6 Hz	0.04	0.011–0.020

* One-percent deformation

The hygroscopic nature of the nylons must be carefully considered when designing with these materials. The rate and amount of moisture absorbed depends not only on the temperature and relative humidity of the environment, but also on the geometry (thickness and surface area/volume ratio) of the part. Fortunately, these changes can be predicted if the service environment is known. *Table XI-16* shows the dimensional and flexural modulus changes of Nylon 6/6, 6, and 6/10, at various relative humidities.

Processes. Nylons can be injection molded and extruded.

Applications. The low coefficient of friction and excellent lubricity of nylon, coupled with the good abrasion resistance, make it an ideal material for bearings, cams, and bushings, particularly in applications where lubricants are undesirable. (The textile, food-processing, and home-appliance fields are examples.)

270

Table XI-16. Physical Changes in Nylons at Various Relative Humidities

Nylon Types	Relative Humidities			
	Dry	20%	50%	75%
Type 6/6				
Moisture gain (%)	—	0.95	2.50	4.75
Dimensional change (%)	—	0.25	0.60	1.15
Flexural modulus (psi)	410,000	300,000	175,000	110,000
Type 6				
Moisture gain (%)	—	1.05	2.70	5.10
Dimensional change (%)	—	0.30	0.70	1.35
Flexural modulus (psi)	395,000	275,000	140,000	85,000
Type 6/10				
Moisture gain (%)	—	0.65	1.50	2.31
Dimensional change (%)	—	0.08	0.20	0.40
Flexural modulus (psi)	280,000	230,000	160,000	115,000

(*Courtesy*, McGraw-Hill Publishing Company)

The nylons are frequently used in applications where their low flammability is desirable. Many formulations, particularly of the mechanical type, are rated self-extinguishing according to ASTM D635.

The unmodified homopolymers—those not possessing unacceptable stabilizers or modifiers—can be used in food and milk processing and in packaging applications, as they are nontoxic and acceptable to the FDA.

Phenolic

The phenolic family has long been recognized as the industry workhorse. Now, with injection molding of phenolics an established reality, designers are taking a fresh look at a material that has an impressive and well-documented history. (See *Table XI-17*.)

Versatile and durable phenolic molding compounds, first of the modern engineering plastics, still rank number one for heat and chemical resistance, modulus at elevated temperatures, and overall dimensional stability. Cost is lower than that of any other engineering material.

Characteristics. The general-purpose materials with wood-flour as the main filler are used in most applications where the basic property profile of phenolics is adequate. These materials provide a good balance of performance, moldability, and appearance at the lowest cost. Where higher heat resistance is required, mineral-filled compounds (such as asbestos) are usually specified.

Improved impact grades with cotton flock or glass fillers cost more, but are able to withstand much greater abuse.

Properties.

Mechanical. Phenolics have good mechanical properties. Dimensional stability is maintained over a wide temperature range and they possess the best creep resistance of any plastic. Certain impact grades have Izod impact values as high as 20 ft-lb. (1068 J/m).

271

Table XI-17. Molded Phenolics

Properties	Type and Filler	
	General Type Woodflour and flock	Heat Resistant type Asbestos
Molding Qualities	Fair to good	
Mold Shrinkage (inch/inch)	0.005–0.008	0.002–0.006
Physical Properties		
Specific Gravity	1.32–1.46	1.57–1.65
Thermal Expansion (10^{-5} per deg F)	1.66–2.50	1.17
Thermal conductivity (Btu/hr/sq ft/deg F/ft)	0.097–0.3	0.19–0.39
Deflection Temp. deg F (264 psi Fiber Stress)	260–360	350–400
Mechanical Properties		
Tensile Strength (psi)	5000–8500	4000–6500
Elongation (%)	0.4–0.8	—
Tensile Modulus (10^5 psi)	8–13	10–20
Flexural Strength (psi)	8500–12,000	3000–10,500
Compressive Strength (psi)	22,000–36,000	12,000–22,000
Hardness	R_E85–100	R_M50
Impact Strength (Izod) (ft-lb/inch notch)	0.24–0.50	0.3–0.4
Electrical Properties		
Volume Resistivity (ohm/cm)	10^9–10^{12}	10^{11}
Dielectric Strength (Short Time, volts/mil)	200–425	275–350
Dielectric Constant		
60 Hz	5.0–9.0	15
10^6 Hz	4.0–7.0	5.0
Dissipation Factor		
60 Hz	0.05–0.30	0.15
10^6 Hz	0.03–0.07	0.13

Electrical. Good electrical properties are retained through extreme environmental conditions.

Chemical Resistance. Phenolics are attacked by strong acids and strong alkalies. Effects of dilute acids, alkalies, and organic solvents vary with the reagent. Chemical resistance varies with the particular formulation, and not all materials of a type are equally resistant.

Processes. The phenolic molding compounds can be compression molded, transfer molded, and injection molded.

Application. There is a tremendous market growth in the use of phenolics for mechanical applications because of injection-molding economy. Significant gains should come from metal-replacement applications, as has already happened in the automotive and various other industries. Power-brake and automatic-transmission components in phenolics have now moved into full-scale production.

Other mechanical applications include pulleys, wheels, motor housings, and handles. Electrical uses include coil forms, ignition parts, condenser housings, fuse blocks, and instrument panels. Thermal applications include handles and appliance connector plugs.

Phenolics also have found new applications in the toy industry and in photography; in both areas, metals have been replaced and injection-molding economies were the deciding factors.

There are many other plastic materials available to the designer, too numerous to detail in one chapter. The *Modern Plastics Encyclopedia,* McGraw-Hill, Inc., and *Materials Selector by Materials Engineering,* Reinhold Publishing Corporation, are recommended for plastic material selection.

MOLDED PARTS

Injection-molded Parts

The injection-molding process for plastics is similar in nature to the diecasting process for metals. A thermoplastic molding compound is heated to plasticity in a cylinder at controlled temperature and forced under high pressure into a single or multiple-cavity mold. The resin solidifies rapidly, the mold is opened, and the part or parts are ejected. The primary advantage of this process, as also is the case with diecastings, is the relatively low cost per part.

In some cases, modifications of the injection-molding processes can be used to mold small parts of thermosetting resins. These processes are called jet, flow, or offset injection molding. They make use of the fluid state of thermosetting molding materials before complete polymerization. The process is suitable only for relatively small parts, and is one that requires careful temperature control. It can be easily used to make one-pound parts and has the advantage of having fast cycles.

Compression-molded Parts

Compression molding is primarily used to mold thermosetting plastics, though in some instances it can be used economically to mold thermoplastics. Thermoplastic materials cannot usually be preformed, but can be charged as powder or granules.

In compression molding, a partially polymerized thermosetting resin, usually in the form of a preform made from powder or granules, is placed in the heated mold cavity. The heat fully polymerizes the material before the mold is opened and the part is removed.

In the case of thermoplastic materials, heating softens the polymer, which flows and fills the mold. Then the mold is cooled and the part solidifies.

Less material is required for compression molding than for injection or transfer molding, since the material is placed directly in the mold and no sprues, runners, or gates are required. With thermosetting resins, the cycle is longer than in injection molding, since the part must be cured in the mold.

Cold-molded Parts

Cold molding is similar to compression molding in that it makes use of a split, or open mold in which the material is charged. It differs from compression molding in that it uses no heat—only high pressure. After the part is removed from the mold it is cured in an oven to its final state.

Transfer-molded Parts

Transfer molding of thermosetting materials is roughly analogous to injection molding of thermoplastics. The thermosetting molding compound is heated to plasticity in a transfer chamber, and is then fed to the mold cavity (or cavities) through sprues, runners, and gates. After the mold is filled, heat is maintained for a predetermined period of time to fully polymerize and cure the part.

In comparison with compression molding, transfer molding is particularly advantageous where thin sections or delicate inserts are used. Since runner and gate design permits some control over where the material is to be fed into the mold, material flow can be closely controlled. Close tolerances can also be held on transfer-molded parts. Part size, however, is somewhat limited. Physical properties of transfer-molded parts are less than compression-molded parts.

Design Factors

Although generalizations concerning the design factors for injection, compression, and transfer moldings are difficult to formulate, the following factors should be considered.

Shrinkage. Allowance must be made for shrinkage of the molding compound in design of the part. In addition to affecting dimensional accuracy of the part, shrinkage can introduce internal stresses which may make the part unserviceable. Shrinkage values for the various plastics are given by the manufacturers of the plastic molding compounds and should be used in the design of a plastic part.

Wall Thickness. Strength required both in service and during manufacture must be considered in designing wall thickness. Wall thicknesses for thermosetting and thermoplastic parts are given in *Table XI-18.*

Draft. A draft taper in deep drawn parts creates a wedging action as the mold is closed, in addition to making it easier to remove the part from the mold. When thermosetting materials are compression molded, converging tapers increase the density of the plastic in the upper sections. There are no precise formulas for taper, but the design should allow for the maximum taper possible. Tapers of less than one degree can be used for deep parts. Large cabinets of up to 24-in. (609-mm) deep have been molded with tapers as small as 0.001 inch per in. (0.02 mm).

Tolerances. Small parts of one inch (25.4 mm) or under can be molded to tolerances as small as ±0.002 in. (±0.05 mm). When size is increased to a few inches, overall tolerances increase to approximately ±0.005 in. (±0.13 mm). On large parts, tolerances of about ±0.001 to 0.002 in. (±0.025 to 0.05 mm)

Table XI-18. Wall Thickness of Molded Parts (Inches)

Materials	Part Sizes			
	Minimum Thickness	*Small Parts*	*Average Thickness*	*Large Parts*
Thermosetting				
Phenolics				
General Purpose and Flock-filled	0.050	0.062	0.125	0.187–1.000
Fabric-filled	0.062	0.125	0.187	0.187–0.375
Mineral-filled	0.125	0.125	0.187	0.200–1.000
Alkyd				
Glass-filled	0.040	0.093	0.125	0.187–0.500
Mineral-filled	0.040	0.125	0.187	0.187–0.375
Ureas, Melamines				
Cellulose-filled	0.035	0.062	0.100	0.125–0.187
Fabric-filled	0.050	0.125	0.125	0.125–0.187
Mineral-filled	0.040	0.093	0.187	0.187–0.375
Thermoplastics				
Acrylics	0.025	0.035	0.093	0.125–0.250
Cellulose Acetate	0.025	0.050	0.075	0.125–0.187
Cellulose Acetate Butyrate	0.025	0.050	0.075	0.125–0.187
Ethyl Cellulose	0.035	0.050	0.062	0.093–0.125
Polyamide	0.015	0.025	0.060	0.093–0.125
Polyethylene	0.035	0.050	0.062	0.093–0.125
Polystyrene	0.030	0.050	0.062	0.125–0.250
Polyvinyl Chloride	0.062	0.093	0.093	0.125–0.250

(*Courtesy*, Reinhold Publications)

per inch are obtainable. Tolerances closer than functional requirements should not be specified. As specified accuracy increases, cost also increases, but disproportionately.

Design Rules

1. Use sufficient draft on long thin shapes to permit their withdrawal from the mold.
2. Minimize coring. When cores are used they should be easy to withdraw.
3. Avoid internal and external undercuts. They make withdrawal of parts difficult and require considerably more expensive molds.
4. Provide ample fillets on inside corners, and avoid sharp external edges and corners except at the parting line of the die.
5. Avoid large flat areas. Dappling or otherwise breaking up the surface is recommended.
6. Keep tolerances as liberal as possible. Excessively close tolerances add to the cost because of increased die costs and high rejection rates.
7. Avoid abrupt changes in wall thickness. Use fillets or angle into thinner areas.

8. Locate parting lines so that flash can be removed easily without marring surrounding areas.
9. Locate holes for easy coring.
10. Use rigs to achieve desired strength and stiffness. Ribs permit material savings by reducing section thickness. Rib thickness should be 60% of base wall thickness.
11. Use inserts for threaded holes where high stresses are anticipated or where considerable wear is to be encountered. Round inserts are preferred.

CASTINGS

Any resin available in liquid form can be cast. Castable resins include phenolics, polyesters, epoxies, silicones, and acrylics.

Types of Molds

The type of mold used depends on the plastic, the size and shape of the part, and other design considerations.

Draw Mold. No undercut is possible. Flutes and scallops must run in the direction of removal. Taper must be provided to break the vacuum and reduce friction. Castings are removed by ejection, and minimum wall thickness is critical, running from 0.125 in. (3.2 mm) on small parts to 0.188 in. (4.8 mm) on larger parts.

Split Mold. Undercuts may be provided if they do not prevent release from the separate mold parts. Minimum wall thickness is 0.188 in. (4.7 mm), and parts less than 0.1 lb (0.04 kg) are not commonly produced economically.

Cored Mold. This type allows complexity of design, but is not feasible from a cost standpoint for small parts. Molds require no taper. Minimum wall thickness is 0.188 in. (4.77 mm). Mold shrinkage allowance must be considered.

Flexible Mold. This plaster mold offers a lining of rubber latex or an elastomeric plastic. Epoxy materials may be cast in flexible molds, but most polyesters react with the lining material. Parts cast in rubber molds cannot be held to the tolerances possible with matched metal molds. A reasonable degree of accuracy, however, is reproducible. On cast phenolic parts, dimensions can be held to about ±0.004 in. (±0.10 mm) per inch. The degree of accuracy obtainable on any part depends on the oversize allowance used in making the master pattern, the care with which the pattern is made, and the degree of accuracy attained in calculating the amount of shrinkage during cure of the rubber mold and the cast resin.

EXTRUSIONS

In many cases, extruded parts are competitive with molded parts. Where many parts are required with complicated cross sections in one plane, the cross section can be produced by extrusion.

Thermoplastics

In extruding a thermoplastic, the molding powder is fed through a hopper into a chamber which is heated to plasticity at controlled temperatures. The plastic powder is then driven, usually by a rotating screw, through a die having the shape of the desired cross section. The process is continuous and is used to produce tube, rod, film, and sheet, as well as other continuous shapes.

Thermosets

Reinforced thermosetting tube and rod can be produced by an extrusion process. The reinforcing fibers are fed continuously through a bath of liquid thermosetting resin and then through a die of the desired cross section. The extruded shapes pass through a cylinder held at a controlled temperature to polymerize and cure the thermosetting resin. Extrusion speed must be relatively slow to provide time for complete cure.

Tolerances

Extrusion tolerances should be as liberal as possible. Excessively close tolerances add to the die cost and high rejection rate, and this in turn will increase the part cost.

RECOMMENDED DESIGN CONSIDERATIONS

Threads. Molded threads should be coarse. For good molding design, take care to chamfer, counterbore, or recess at least the depth of one thread. Minimum size should be No. 6-32, Class 1 or 2.

Cut threads should be of larger sizes, coarse pitch, and thread classes. Minimum size should be No. 6-32, Class 1 or 2, and 60% thread depth.

Inserts are preferred for threads when possible, especially where fine pitch, small diameter, and tight tolerance classes are required.

Inserts Molded-in. Where inserts must be molded in place, problems could develop due to plastic flashing in the hole or on the up-side of metal. Secondary removal operations may be necessary.

Insert Assembly. Inserts and holes in plastic can be designed in some cases to assemble the insert at the press while the plastic is hot. Further, many screw-machine type inserts can be assembled by expanding metal into plastic when parts are cold.

Fillets and Radii. Avoid sharp corners where possible; add maximum radii for strength; minimize strains; assist flow in mold; and strenghthen mold members.

Tapers. Tapers are necessary in plastic parts. Pins, projections, holes, and cavities (where possible) should have taper sides. The amount of taper or draft per side depends on the shape of the part. In general, for parts less than one inch in length, the taper should be one degree (0.017 rad) per side; over one inch (25.4 mm) in length, 0.5° (0.08 rad) per side.

Concentricity. Part concentricity must allow for maximum TIR tolerance. Part geometry governs tolerances. However, a minimum of 0.005 in. (0.13 mm) TIR for one-inch (25.4-mm) diameter parts, with others in the same proportion, should be considered.

Out-of-roundness. Many shell, cup, and ring designs will distort and go out-of-round. But part geometry and gating methods are controlling factors. Design for 0.007 in. (0.17 mm) on one-inch (25.4-mm) diameters. Keep other sizes of the part proportional.

Gates. Gates are necessary for most plastic moldings. However, some type gates, through necessity, are objectionably positioned and must be removed. Secondary operations can become costly.

A drawing note indicating the type of gate removal can reduce the cost of this operation. Wherever possible, allow the gates to be broken to ±0.025 in. (±0.6 mm), or trimmed to ±0.010 in. (±0.2 mm), or if necessary, machined to ±0.005 in. (±0.13 mm).

Mismatch Designs. Design mating parts with a planned mismatch to prevent problems.

Wall Sections. Design uniform sections and walls. Heavy and nonuniform sections are subject to sinks in thermoplastic material. Minimum and maximum wall sections will depend upon the part geometry.

Ribs and adjoining walls should be 60% of a normal wall to prevent sink.

Flatness and Warpage. Warpage or distortion vary with plastics. Allow 0.010 in. (0.25 mm) for a three-inch (76-mm) part. Other lengths of parts should be kept proportional.

ASSEMBLY AND JOINING TECHNIQUES

Joining plastics to themselves or to other materials is frequently necessary to complete an assembly. The various techniques currently in use include adhesive bonding, mechanical fastening, and melt processes in which the plastic is heated and subject to pressure to effect a bond. Plastics also lend themselves to snap fit assembly features. The more important methods of bonding or assemblies are as follows:

Adhesive/Solvent Bonding

Adhesive/solvent bonding is an efficient and economical method for joining plastics to themselves or to other materials. Adhesives are classified as elastomeric, thermoplastic, or thermosetting types. The *elastomerics* are used to impart flexibility in the joint. The *thermoplastic* adhesives are easy to use, readily adapted to high-speed production, and are applied as resin melts or as solvent solutions of the resin. However, the *thermosetting* types are the most durable and versatile. Best results are obtained by curing under pressure at elevated temperatures, but some thermosetting and elastomeric systems are curable at room temperature.

For effective bonding, both surfaces must be compatible with the adhesive. The polyethylenes, polypropylenes, and fluorocarbons are difficult to bond, and require surface treatments, such as etching or oxidation, to insure adherence to the plastic. Surface treatments for other materials involve removal of mold release agents and all foreign matter. The strengths of adhesive bonds are influenced strongly by the joint design as well as the adhesive. Typical joint designs for adhesives are shown in *Figure 11-1.*

278

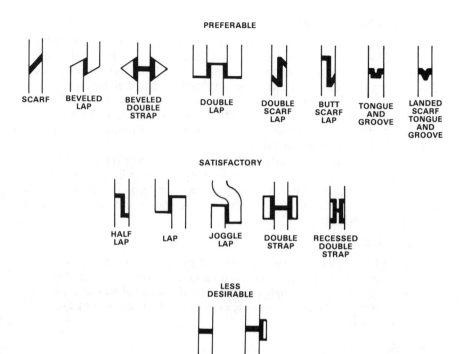

PREFERABLE

| SCARF | BEVELED LAP | BEVELED DOUBLE STRAP | DOUBLE LAP | DOUBLE SCARF LAP | BUTT SCARF LAP | TONGUE AND GROOVE | LANDED SCARF TONGUE AND GROOVE |

SATISFACTORY

| HALF LAP | LAP | JOGGLE LAP | DOUBLE STRAP | RECESSED DOUBLE STRAP |

LESS DESIRABLE

| BUTT | SINGLE STRAP |

Figure 11-1. Bonded joint configurations. (*Courtesy, Modern Plastics Encyclopedia,* MIL-HDBK-727)

Mechanical Fastening

Mechanical fasteners are widely used to secure plastics to other materials. The advantages of this method are fast installation, low cost, minimal tooling, and reliability. The choice of fastener depends on the plastic type, loading condition at the joint, the environment to which the assembly will be exposed, and whether disassembly is a requirement.

The most common fastener types are common machine screws made to National Coarse and National Fine Thread Standards. They are employed in conjunction with threaded metal inserts. Pretapped holes are suited only to extremely hard plastics. Thread-forming screws are specified for ductile plastics having an elastic modulus below 400,000 psi (2.8 GPa), and thread-cutting screws for more brittle materials. When holes are located on bosses, the diameter of the boss should be from 2.5 to 3 times the hole diameter.

Stripping torques can be increased by reducing hole size, increasing the length of thread engagement, and increasing screw diameter. A common failure is cracking of the plastic boss; corrective measures are to increase the boss radius where it joins the base material or to increase the boss hole diameter to decrease screw diameter or thread engagement.

Threaded Metal Inserts

Internally, metal inserts have tapped threads, and externally, they have configurations of various designs to anchor into plastics. Inserts are frequently added to the mold and integrally molded into the part. Although this is a costly method, the insert becomes well anchored and stresses in the plastic are normally kept to a minimum. However, in extreme environments the inserts can induce stresses due to differing shrinkage rates. Other types of inserts are pressed into bosses, threaded in place, ultrasonically inserted, expanded in place, or bonded in place.

The installed cost of a metal insert and a machine screw is greater than it is for tapping screws, but the advantage over tapping screws is of having greater load distribution areas. The screw can also be assembled and disassembled a greater number of times. It is also possible to incorporate thread locking features in the insert.

Drive Pin Fasteners

Solid drive pins with knurls or splines are pressed in place or ultrasonically inserted. They are designed to fasten components without the use of screws. The pins are either solid, single pieces, or solid with a tubular receiver. The tubular pins can be inserted to provide interference fits or can be flared over for positive retention.

Heat Sealing

Heat sealing is a method for joining two layers of plastic film by applying heat and pressure. Sufficient heat is furnished to fuse the layers into a single mass. The process if known as *RF sealing* or *thermal sealing*, depending on the heat source. RF heating brings the plastic to melting temperature rapidly, but it is possible only with those materials having high dielectric losses. These include cellulose, acetate, nylon, polyurethane, PVC, and other vinyl polymers. Electrical elements supply the heat for thermal sealing. In both cases, pressure is applied by pneumatic or hydraulic activation of sealing bars or plates.

Ultrasonic Bonding

Ultrasonic techniques are based on the fact that material subjected to high-frequency mechanical vibrations absorb energy and rise in temperature. Most thermoplastics can be melted and bonded by ultrasonic means. The equipment for this process is automated and capable of handling high-volume runs at fast rates.

Performance in bonding depends on the material type and the joint configuration. Rigid thermoplastics readily transmit vibrations and are easy to melt, but flexible materials require higher amplitude vibrations for melting and bonding. Materials with low melting points and specific heats are easier to process. The crystalline resins, acetal nylon, polyethylene, polypropylene, polyester, and polyphenylene sulfide require additional heat to account for the heat of fusion at melting, and consequently are more difficult to bond.

Higher energy input and higher amplitudes are necessary with these materials.

The *amorphous resins*, particularly ABS, polycarbonate, and polystyrene, are easier to bond. Materials that absorb moisture, nylon, and polycarbonate for example, must be dried prior to bonding. Material with glass or mineral fillers up to 30 to 35% can be bonded. Dissimilar materials can be bonded together provided their melting points are in the same range and they are chemically compatible.

The design of joints for ultrasonic bonding depends on the type of plastic, the geometry of the part, and the function of the bond. A basic requirement of all joints is a small uniform contact area. In the most common design, a triangular section, known as an energy director, concentrates the vibration for a rapid heat buildup at the bond line. (See *Figure 11-2*.)

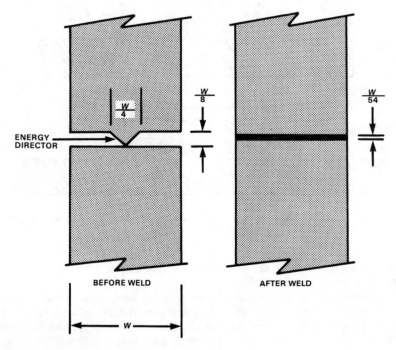

Figure 11-2. Modified butt joint with energy director. (*Courtesy*, Branson Sonic Power Company, MIL-HDBK-727)

Ultrasonic Staking

Ultrasonic staking is a method for joining plastics to metals or other dissimilar materials. A typical staking joint is shown in *Figure 11-3*. A hole is drilled in the material to be joined to the plastic. A stud or boss previously molded into the plastic part is fitted into the hole. Vibrations are transmitted

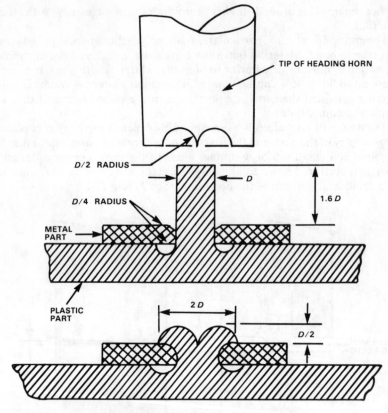

Figure 11-3. Typical ultrasonic staking. (*Courtesy*, Branson Sonic Power Company, MIL-HDBK-727)

through the horn, which shapes the melted plastic and maintains pressure until the joint is cooled.

Various stud and cavity designs are used in ultrasonic staking. These include hollow, domed, knurled, and flush stakes as depicted in *Figure 11-4*. There are other assembly methods that can be used such as spin welding, spot welding, vibration welding, hot gas welding, and electromagnetic bonding.

Finishing Processes

The surface of molded or formed components normally do not need further treatment. There are some applications, however, for which surface finishing is used to improve properties or overcome deficiencies. Of the existing finishing methods, electroplating, vacuum metallizing, and painting may offer specific advantages. These and other surface finishing processes should be considered and applied only when a functional purpose would be served.

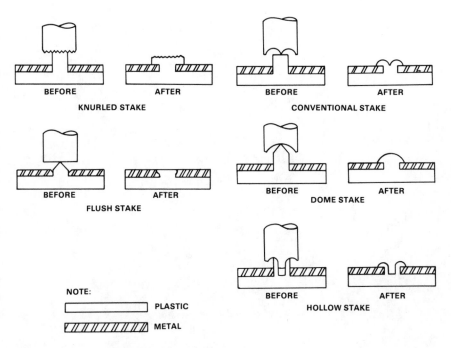

BEFORE · AFTER

KNURLED STAKE

BEFORE · AFTER

CONVENTIONAL STAKE

BEFORE · AFTER

FLUSH STAKE

BEFORE · AFTER

DOME STAKE

BEFORE · AFTER

HOLLOW STAKE

NOTE:

☐ PLASTIC

▨ METAL

Figure 11-4. Stud cavity designs for staking. (*Courtesy*, Branson Sonic Power Company, MIL-HDBK-727)

12

Cost Reduction Programs

PRODUCIBILITY ACTIVITIES

There are various cost reduction programs that can be implemented to reduce manufacturing costs and produce a functional part. Some of these programs are in use with good results, such as: value engineering, design review, plain cost reduction programs, and zero defects programs. Zero defects and plain cost reduction programs are effective, but they are put into operation during production. Accordingly, they sometimes require expensive changes of the product in order to reduce the cost. Management must decide what type of program or programs are best suited for their contract. A well organized program, backed by management and started during the design and experimental stage, and backed up during production by a strong zero defects program, should result in satisfactory cost reduction.

A well organized producibility design review program is well suited for the cost reduction of a new product. Generally, it is the most flexible since it uses value engineering techniques, design review, and manufacturing method studies.

Many companies have implemented a producibility design review program to assure full utilization of design, development, and manufacturing capabilities.

The conducting of a producibility design review, chaired by the value engineering group of the engineering department, assures adequate management planning, control of design, development, and manufacturing.

Team Organization

To function properly, the producibility review team must have representation from the engineering as well as the manufacturing departments. After each design is carefully reviewed and comments and recommendations are made as to the changes that should be incorporated to reduce the production cost of each electronic, electromechanical and mechanical item, value engineering edits the comments and compiles these findings into log sheets to be used by the responsible design groups for appropriate action. *Figure 12-1* shows a typical organization chart for a producibility design review team.

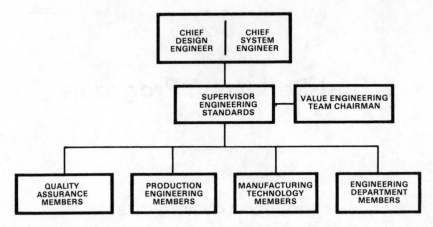

Figure 12-1. Producibility design-review team organization chart.

Team Function

The basic functions of the team can be broken down to:

- Review the design for economical producibility for in-house or outside production as to tolerances, surface finishes, standard parts in the electronic component design, and production methods as to castings, forgings, or extrusions. This is done to determine which is the most economical method to produce a functional part. In the case of castings, for example, if the part is designed for a sand casting that requires additional machining and an adjustment of tolerance settings, a diecasting with no machining would be the most economical method.
- Assure that the assembly of the items can be accomplished economically.
- Assure that the item can be produced economically on present equipment, and make recommendations for a design change that permits the item to be produced on present equipment. If the design is such that new equipment is needed, a study should be made by the team as to the economy of purchasing such equipment, or of having the item manufactured by a supplier of such equipment.
- Provide technical assistance to design engineering, thereby promoting development of designs that can be optimized with respect to ease of production and reduction of cost.
- Provide additional means for management's periodic evaluation of the progress and adequacy of the producibility aspects of the design.
- Provide effective documentation of design problems that affect producibility and planning of corrective action.
- Identify marginal design and isolate marginal parts and material applications.
- Identify potential manufacturing control and process problems, and make recommendations to correct these problems.

- Reduce the probability of repeating past mistakes.
- If, after careful study as to producibility, the design itself is a costly item to produce, a tradeoff study should be conducted using value engineering techniques to assure that the most economical design is released for production.
- If so required, the maintainability of the product should be analyzed by the team. This includes life-cycle cost studies over the given number of years the product is to be maintained.

These are the eleven basic functions that must guide the team. The resulting recommendations must be technically sound so that there will be no question in the designer's mind as to the function of the recommended change. The team must be careful not be become super checkers, however, for this can destroy the program before its effect can be known.

Since schedules are important and expensive if not met, the team should not record dollar savings. Estimates would have to be made of the design before and after the study, and this is time-consuming. But it can be seen that, if the design is such that it can be economically produced, the cost of the product is favorably affected. When the drawings have been changed according to the team's recommendations and are released for production, other cost reduction programs should also be implemented to avoid costly over tooling and production planning which may be good for high production runs, but may not be best for the production quantity required.

VALUE ANALYSIS

Historically, normal cost reduction activity concentrates on reducing the cost of parts or assemblies and does not address function. This type of cost reduction activity results in material and assembly savings and usually yields cost reductions of about 10%. Value analysis, on the other hand, talks of function costs, challenges the specifications, and represents a deeper, more comprehensive look at the real problems. Value analysis usually yields potential cost reductions of 25-40%.

Value analysis should be used on new product designs as early as possible, preferably in the concept or feasibility phase of the new design. In this way, all recommended alterations to a soft design will result in a paper change and not a hardware change.

Value analysis is not a substitute for good design practices, it is a tool that can be applied to improve the design process. *Value analysis* is an intense creative study of every item of cost in every part or material of the design. Value analysis relates a cost to the function of every part in the case study, thus allowing the product development team an insight into the cost of every function performed by the team's design.

To be effective, value analysis must be performed by a interdisciplinary team of highly motivated people who are willing to participate and contribute to this effort. The value analysis team should consist of representatives from the design, development, manufacturing, service and product cost engineering, and drafting departments, in addition to other subject matter experts needed to support the team. The cross talk between the varied disciplines provides a broader view of the problems, usually resulting in innovative solutions.

Of critical importance is the value analysis leader who must guide the team through the value analysis exercise and assure full participation of all members. The leader must keep the team focused on the objective and record the group's ideas. The value analysis team leader explains the value analysis techniques and tries to make sure that the team adheres to the principles of the value analysis plan.

The application of value analysis principles will result in the development of goods and services which perform the required functions at the lowest possible cost. Because value analysis is function-oriented, it often increases the value of the product while lowering the cost of producing it. Maximum value is obtained when essential function is achieved for minimum cost.

Value analysis is defined as the systematic application of recognized techniques that identify the function of the product or service and describe how those functions are interrelated; establishes a value for that function of service; and provides that service at the lowest possible cost without diminishing performance or quality.

VALUE ENGINEERING PLAN

The chronological steps to be performed on any value analysis task are incorporated in the value engineering plan which should consist of the following five phases.

Information Phase

Review and understand the design specifications and your customer requirements. Raise the team level of understanding of the total design so every member is working at the same level. All available information pertinent to the design is gathered, analyzed, and organized. This includes:

- Customer requirements
- Manufacturing processes
- Materials
- Preliminary cost estimates and targets
- Volume to be produced.

On the basis of this information, the basic and secondary functions of every part is determined as the new design is reviewed with the team, thereby allowing a cost to be assigned to each required function of the design.

Creative Phase

Creative thinking is applied to devise alternate ways of performing the required functions defined in the information phase. Strive to generate as many ideas as possible, encourage off-the-wall ideas. Judgment is suspended until the evaluation phase. Generate solutions to case study problems using known creative techniques such as brainstorming and synectics. (Synectics is a method of problemsolving similar to brainstorming.)

The value engineering team should follow the rules of brainstorming to develop their ideas. The discipline of brainstorming is maintained by four basic rules which create an atmosphere of freedom. The rules are:

- Don't allow criticism or evaluation of ideas; defer this until later
- Encourage wild ideas
- Build on the ideas of others (hitchhiking)
- Strive for quantity of ideas (hundreds).

The group leader presents the problem for which ideas are sought. The wording should encourage specific, tangible ideas, not abstract ideas or opinions. The leader must make sure that all the members understand the problem. There are three methods of brainstorming. The most familiar is *free-wheeling*. This is where team members call out their ideas spontaneously and the leader records the ideas. Another method is *round-robin* brainstorming. The leader asks each member, in turn, for an idea. A member may pass on any round. The session continues until all members have passed during the round. Ideas are recorded as with free-wheeling. The third method is the *slip* method which differs markedly from the other two approaches. The leader asks each team member to write down ideas on small slips of paper or index cards. The ideas are then collected and organized.

Each approach has its advantages and disadvantages. Regardless of the approach used, the output of the brainstorming session must be reviewed and evaluated. *Figure 12-2* represents what a possible list of ideas might look like after a brainstorming session was held on a hypothetical problem of dispensing soap powder in an automatic dishwasher.

DISPENSING CONTAINERS FOR SOAP IN DISHWASHERS
1. BOX
2. LUNCH BOX
3. PAPER BOX
4. IRON BOX
5. CYLINDER
6. HOURGLASS
7. CEMENT MIXER
8. GLASS CYLINDER
9. SEALED TOMB
10. AIR BUBBLE
11. THIMBLE
12. EYE DROPPER
13. SWEATER
14. POCKET
15. SHOE

Figure 12-2. Ideas from brainstorming session.

As you can see by this list, many far-fetched ideas were generated which just might stimulate some other member of the team to think of a innovative idea.

After the brainstorming phase has been completed, each of the ideas are reviewed by the team. Team members are asked if the idea is good and worthy of development into a concept. If the consensus is positive and if a team member voluntarily offers to develop the idea, it is then developed into a concept. Concept development is done away from the team by individuals or small groups. The concept is sketched, described, and evaluated by noting its technical, financial, and development schedule advantages and disadvantages. See *Figure 12-3* for an example of the level of detail necessary for the sketched layout of the concept.

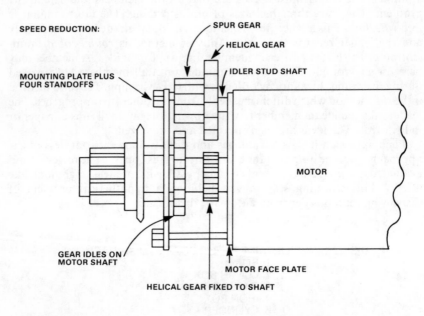

ADVANTAGES
* UMC Reduction
* Very Low Developmental Risk
* Eliminates Long Lead Items
* Improved Service Visibility
* Parts Can Be Fabricated Quickly In Model Shop

DISADVANTAGES
* Noise Due To Vibration
* Manual Field Backlash Setup
* Increased Assembly Labor Time
* May Be More Prone To Contamination

Figure 12-3. Level of detail necessary for sketched concept layout.

The originator presents his or her concept with its advantages and disadvantages to the team for review. After a fuller understanding of the concept has been attained, the team is asked to optimize the concept by minimizing or eliminating the disadvantages. Again, this is done by consensus. Each individual is made to feel that it is his or her job to make sure all of the proposed concepts are feasible and optimal regardless of who came up with the idea. Each team should try to develop as many feasible concepts as possible.

Integration Phase

Identify performance specifications within the design case study to insure that any possible solutions are able to be integrated within the total product design. The functional performance of the present and proposed concepts must be measured to insure that they are within the minimum and maximum function specification. Identify interfacing performance specifications between other product subsystems. The team must understand the critical path functions which are required to perform basic functions in other subsystems as well as the functions in the team's own subsystem.

Great care must be used to insure the total integrity of the product. Don't let your zeal to reduce cost cause you to use bad engineering judgement. This requires the impacted engineers of other areas of the design to meet with each other to agree on the appropriate solutions.

Any unresolved questions must be raised to the engineering program manager for resolution. It is very important that total solutions are found which will benefit the total product, not just one small area. One of the basic rules to follow is: If a problem can be more efficiently solved within some other area of the design, it should be given to that engineer only after both engineers agree to transfer the problem.

Evaluation Phase

Ideas generated in the creative phase are evaluated through comparison of function, cost, and industrial design criteria. Concepts which do not meet these performance criteria are immediately rejected. The remaining concepts which survive this screening process are then financially evaluated against the following criteria: reliability, maintainability, service cost in the field, tooling cost, development cost, and manufacturing cost and schedule. The data reflecting the expert judgment of the evaluation team is then listed in order of apparent value.

Implementation Phase

The concepts are then rank-ordered by return on investment or some other financial criterion. The team then presents the concepts to the design management team which reviews all of the concepts and categorizes them as approved (funded), approved (unfunded), and rejected.

It is important that the design management team goes through this phase with the value analysis team to show support for the process and to insure there will be follow-up to the team's recommendations. Many value analysis teams have been demoralized by a lack of support of the management team to fund or provide the needed time to implement the team's recommendations.

The concepts which meet the performance and interface specifications and financial criteria will then be implemented. A written report should be distributed to all team members and management.

Value Engineering Techniques

Value engineering techniques are tools to be applied (as required) to each phase of the job plan. Some of these techniques are:

Get All the Facts. Gather and organize, from the best sources, all design, material, manufacturing, cost, and customer requirements.

Define the Function. List the required function to be performed. What does the user really want? Use verb-noun definitions ("transmits torque," "protects surface," "conducts current.") Segregate parts of the function into a series of functional areas.

Work on Specifics—Not Generalities. Check every part, every radius, every tolerance, and every increment of cost. Eliminate those generalities which serve only to protect the status quo.

Analyze Costs. Associate specific increments of cost with specific increments of function. Know the cost of each component, manufacturing process, step of assembly, tolerance, special finish, and inspection. Consider recurring costs of raw material, direct labor, overhead, inspection, purchased part, rejection, rework, retest, shipping and packing.

Use Your Own Judgement. Accept an authority's opinion only if it makes sense to you.

Create, then Refine. Consider basic functions of complex equipment, create as many alternates as possible, refine the results.

Use Standards. Make use of what is already available if it can perform for a lower cost.

Use Specialty Products—Materials, Processes, Vendors. Take advantage of specialized knowledge and avoid expensive "do-it-ourselves" approaches. Don't re-invent something already available.

Use Company and Industry Experts. Obtain the best available technical and manufacturing information and experience.

Think Creatively. Develop as many ideas as possible; the more ideas you can produce, the greater chance of obtaining maximum value.

Put a Dollar Sign on Tolerances. Be sure there is valid reason for each tolerance and finish. Question the necessity for close tolerance radius callouts that are difficult and expensive to achieve; give tooling and manufacturing as much flexibility as possible—increasing tolerances decreases rejections.

Overcome Roadblocks. Anticipate roadblocks and devise ways of circumventing them.

Use Effective Employee Relations. Treat people with the dignity and consideration they deserve, and avoid the appearance of being critical. Give willing and enthusiastic credit to others, but remember, a better way can always be found even though a good job has been done.

Determine Engineering Value. Endeavor to get the most function for your money. Every material, every part, every operation must contribute value. Shop around and decide: If it were your money, how would you spend it? Your goal is to provide reliable function at the lowest cost.

The basic techniques of value engineering are identical whether applied to design, development, production, hardware, or software. However, maximum savings are achieved when value engineering is applied in the early design/development phases of the design development/production cycle.

Value engineering is performed by an analysis of function. There may be more than one basic function to an item. Secondary functions must be kept at a minimum to obtain best values.

An elementary example of value engineering follows:

PART	FUNCTION	BASIC	SECONDARY	UNIT COST
Cup	Contain Liquid	X		$1.25
Handle	Provide Grip		X	.50
Decoration	Provide Attractiveness		X	3.00
			Overall Cost	$4.75

The basic function of the coffee cup is to contain liquid or a substance. The handle and decorations provide secondary functions not needed to perform the *basic* function. The handle provides convenience, firm grip, and may prevent burning of the fingers. While the basic function must remain, and for convenience and safety the handle should remain, the decoration is not needed for the required function to be performed. It is considered "gold-plating" and may be eliminated, thereby reducing the unit cost to $1.75—a reduction of 63%.

Note that value analysis is a function of value engineering techniques, not a separate cost reduction program.

Engineering management concerned with product design, fabrication, or support should develop the value engineering approach. Designs, procedures, and techniques should be correlated with value through consideration of the following six basic questions:

1. What is it?
2. What does it cost?
3. What does it do?
4. What is the value of the essential function?
5. What else will do the job?
6. What will that cost?

In the final analysis, value engineering is an attitude—a desire on the part of the individual to want to design, to want to manufacture, and to want to purchase with value in mind.

Useful Techniques for Manufacturing Engineers

Numerous methods exist for analysis and quantitative decision making by the manufacturing engineer to reduce the cost of a product. Brief descriptions of several of the methodologies are provided, and knowledge of these by the manufacturing engineer will permit an analysis of one's own producibility problems. They also may be used as a tool for verifying a contractor's analysis. The following techniques discussed are cost estimating, break-even analysis, tolerance analysis, and learning curves. Value engineering plays an important role in the cost analysis of a product.

Cost Estimating. Product costs include the cost of material, labor, and equipment. There can be trade-offs between the various costs. For example, a more expensive material with better machinability may reduce the machining cost, or a low-cost material may be functional for the intended product. In order to develop the least costly product design, the designer and manufacturing engineer must have a way of estimating those costs. Estimating material costs is reasonably straightforward. It is necessary to consider the cost of the raw material minus the value of the scrap. Volume buying may influence the cost per price.

Estimating labor requirements such as manning per production line or per machine is less straightforward. Given the operations that must be performed, one must estimate the time required to perform those operations and the skill level required. It is also important to estimate the tooling cost, and determine by a break-even analysis if the tooling cost can be reduced or if higher cost tooling is more economical to use.

There is a variety of methods for estimating time requirements in advance of production. The methods to be used will be different during different stages of the design process. Coarser estimates are adequate during the earlier stages while more precise estimates are needed at the later stages. Four basic methods are described: technical estimates, historical data, predetermined time standards, and elemental standard data.

Technical Estimates. As the title implies, this is an estimate provided by a person technically qualified to recognize the various phases of the work to be accomplished. The job is broken down into phases, and time is estimated for each phase. This person is normally the manufacturing engineer.

Historical Data. This data relies on a statistical standard and has been developed to a high degree. This standard establishes a statistical relationship between gross work units such as tons handled and man-hours expended. Data is required on the past performance of individual jobs producing similar products. Data is expressed in man-hours expended and units produced.

Predetermined Time Standards. These standards, often called microdata, are derived from tables of time values for fundamental types of motions. The method for performing the job must first be described in terms of elements. The elements are then broken down into basic motions pertinent to the particular predetermined time systems. Widely used systems include methods-time measurement (MTM), work factors, and basic motion/time studies. The result provided by these synthetic standards is an estimate of normal time for the task.

With MTM for each type of motion element, the standard time is dependent on certain physical variables, such as distance, and on classifications of the sensory control required. For example, for the element reach, the major variable is distance, but there are five classifications of reach that specify the condition of the object to which one is reaching, such as an object in a fixed location or an object jumbled with others in a group.

In developing the motion analysis for the task, the appropriate reaches, grasps, and moves are matched to fit the general situation of required sensory control. For example, to obtain a part from a supply bin and place it in a fixture, one would first reach to an object jumbled with others in the bin. For grasping the object, the tables indicate that the grasp time will depend on the part size classification.

Moving the part to the fixture requires close control because the fixture is placed in an exact location. The time required to position the part in the fixture depends on the closeness of the fit between the part and fixture, the symmetry (how much orientation is required to align the mating parts), and the ease of handling (characteristics of the material, its size and flexibility). Once positioned in the fixture, the part must be released.

Elemental Standard Data. This data (often called macrodata) gives normal time values for major elements of jobs. Time values for machine setup and for different manual elements are given, so a normal time for an entirely new job can be constructed by an analysis of blueprints to see what materials are specified, what cuts must be made, and how the workpiece can be held in the machine. This data must include the machinability rating of the material, the feeds and speeds that should be used for a given cutting tool material, and the most economical tool life for a total economical production.

Macrostandard data is commonly used especially in machine shops where distinct job families have a long standing tradition. However, the occurrence of this kind of standard data is by no means limited to machine shops. It is likely to exist wherever job families exist or when parts or products occur in many sizes and types.

Methods of Determining Machining Cost. In milling operations, as in any other machining operation, surface quality conditions are called out on the drawing that must first be met. These conditions include dimensional accuracy, surface roughness, and freedom from damage in the surface layer. The proper machine tool, fixtures for accuracy, fast loading and unloading, machine conditions which include speed, feed, cutting tool and fluid combinations are all important factors in determining cost and production rates.

A series of equations has been developed to determine the cost per piece and production rate and detailed items, such as the machine tool and the cutting tool reconditioning cost factors which make up the total cost. If a computer is available and is to be used to determine the cost and production rates for milling and other machining operations, the transactions of the American Society of Mechanical Engineers (ASME) paper No. 68-WA/Prod-17 is highly recommended for the use of such computer programs.

However, a computer is not always available; therefore, a simple equation must be used to determine the total milling cost. The following is suggested:

Total cost to mill one piece =
Milling cost + Initial cost of cutter per piece + Cutter reconditioning cost.

The milling cost must include the following:
- Labor plus overhead on the milling machine in dollars per minute
- Total time in minutes to mill one piece; this equals feeding time, plus rapid traverse time, plus loading and unloading time
- Setup time per piece per minute

- Time to change or reset cutter in minutes
- Number of pieces milled per cutter sharpening.

Cutter recondition costs must include:
- Labor plus overhead on the cutter-grinder in dollars per minute
- Time required to resharpen the cutter in minutes
- Number of pieces milled per cutter sharpening
- Time in minutes to rebraze teeth or reset blades (for carbides or cast alloys)
- Blade cost or wheel cost per sharpening in dollars.

This formula not only yields total milling costs, but also indicates to the alert user the relative importance of the three main variables—tool cost, cost of upkeep, and cost of production, as they contribute to the total cost. It shows where the manufacturing engineer can make the largest gain in lowering total cost.

Learning Curve. The number of units to be produced should be considered in estimating labor requirements because the learning curve comes into play. The learning curve assumes that practice leads to improvement; therefore, as learning takes place, workers need fewer hours to produce a given quantity of work. Learning with its reduced man-hour input implications, is always at work in manufacturing. Experience at making anything can almost always lead to more economical methods.

Airplane and electronics manufacturers have found that the learning curve operates when they make products in large numbers. Knowing about the curve and expected rates of improvement allows the managers to project the need for fewer man-hours per unit of product as well as lower costs per unit. All airplane and electronic manufacturers, therefore, use the learning curve to estimate the cost of direct labor, scheduling, planning, budgeting, purchasing, and pricing.

The Government requires industry, on all Government contracts, to anticipate lower unit costs as quantities increase. Usually these companies use an 80% learning curve or something very close to it. An 80% curve means that every time the production quantity doubles, the average amount of direct labor for all units produced up to that point goes down to 80% of its former level. This is an average for all units and not just the direct labor hours put into the last unit.

Thus, if the first 10 units require an average of 100 direct labor hours per product, the first 20 units (including the first 10) will average 80 direct labor hours per unit of product. Airplane companies plot their figures on double logarithmic graph paper so that the curve depicting the relationship appears as a straight line.

The equation for the line is:

$$\log Y = -S \log X + \log C$$

where:
S = slope
X = number of units of product

C = direct labor hours required by the first unit of product

Y = average number of direct labor hours per unit of product.

The equation for the slope of the line is:

$$S = \frac{\log L}{\log 2}$$

where:

L = learning curve

For an 80% curve the equation becomes:

$$S = \frac{\log 0.8}{\log 2}$$

$$S = \frac{-0.09691}{0.30103}$$

$$S = -0.322.$$

Since L will always be less than one, the logarithm of L will be negative; therefore, the slope will be negative. A negative slope is expected since cost goes down as quantity goes up. To get the slope of a value other than 80%, the procedure is the same.

There are instances in which the curve should be expected to differ from 80%. If the product to be produced is very similar to ones that have previously been produced in large quantities, costs should not be expected to go down as rapidly as they would on an 80% curve. On the other hand, on crash programs without enough time for adequate planning before manufacturing begins, it can be expected that costs will decrease more rapidly than predicted by an 80% curve.

A limitation of this procedure is that the curves are concerned only with manual work; where machines are involved, an 80% curve calls for more improvement than can be realized because the learning curve may not apply to machine time.

Still another problem is that curves exaggerate the savings somewhat. To achieve reduction in direct labor costs, it is necessary to put manufacturing engineers, tool engineers, supervisors, and value engineers to work trying to make improvements. These are indirect labor, and their costs are not shown as offsets against the gains in direct labor costs.

For more information of cost estimating, it is recommended that the estimating department use the book, *Realistic Cost Estimating for Manufacturing*, by I.E. Vernon, published by the Society of Manufacturing Engineers.

13

Management Tools for Value Control and Cost Control

Management must consider the following questions before an effective value control and cost reduction program can be implemented. Management must take action to establish a sound and reliable value control and cost reduction program.

QUESTIONS FOR CONSIDERATION BY MANAGEMENT

Value Control

- What techniques are used by the design engineer to consider all possible designs in order to arrive at the best and most reliable value from a design and production cost viewpoint?
- Are procurement releases value-analyzed to insure that reasonable prices are being paid and that maximum value is being received?
- Are the make-or-buy decisions reviewed on a continual basis to insure that the part or assembly is produced by the lowest cost source—in-plant or outside production?
- Are there adequate procurement review procedures to insure that low-cost producers are selected for the manufacture of outside produced items?
- Is there a continuing market review plan to enable us to procure from low-cost and reliable suppliers consistent with program requirements?
- Is there a program for analysis of design and performance data to insure the most economical and reliable production?

Direct Hours Control

- Is there a working application of direct work measurement such as manning per machine or production line, work standards, and job loading to assure manufacturing costs are reduced?
- Is there an effective method of production crew assignment and reporting manufacturing progress in the production shop?

299

Quality Cost Control

- Is there a system to review inspection test procedures for improvements, and is this review scheduled frequently enough?
- Is there control over scrap rate and rework costs?

Indirect Cost Control

- Is there an effective system of budgetary control in use to control and reduce direct and indirect costs?
- Are budget goals set at the working level and reporting of performance required along with an explanation of variances on a timely basis?
- Are travel and shipping costs monitored to insure minimum costs in these areas?

Management Control

- Are procedures established to assure that engineering changes are handled so as to consolidate changes into packages where possible, and obtain the earliest effectiveness consistent with minimum cost?
- Are improvement type changes controlled so as to reduce the number of changes and hold costs to a minimum?
- Are the production control procedures adequate to assure that parts are available on schedule at a minimum of cost?
- Are the advantages of computerized production control applications considered to provide location of parts, inventory status, and shop ordering on a timely basis?
- Is there a computer system for programming and accomplishing improvements in management techniques and controls?
- Is there a system for reviewing the organization as programs change to assure that there is the most effective organization to accomplish the current task?

Management controls are based on a three-step operation:

- Preplan
- Activate the plan
- Monitor the plan

A system of management controls based on specific plans can be managed by the exception principle. Management attention is required only on those exceptions to the predetermined plan.

Advanced Preparation

Long before a new product proposal is submitted, policy decisions and fundamental planning are completed, and continuously reviewed. These policy decisions and planning reviews, which make possible a rapid and realistic evaluation of a new product proposal, include:

- Current product policy
- Established fields of interest
- New product policy

- Organization concept and plans
- Systematic long-range plans—actual and potential
- Periodic planning review

Planning a New Program

A firm control should be maintained—no new task can be brought in without the specific approval of the plant manager. Within the framework of established policy, and after thorough evaluation of the effect of a proposed new program on existing and potential programs, plans for a new program can be established. The long-range planning department, representing management, coordinates the efforts in establishing that a task can be accomplished on schedule at a mutually satisfactory cost and consonant with current research or production programs.

All functions that would be affected by the new program participate in this determination. An official document is issued by management giving ground rules and assumptions for the study. The design engineering department supplies as complete a statement of work as the known facts, assumptions, and schedule will permit. Based on the statement of work, a manufacturing plan is developed by the manufacturing engineer which includes the following:

- Component breakdown and assembly sequence
- Equipment and space requirements
- Workstations and fixtures
- Procurement plan
- Load and capacity study
- Manufacturing schedules
- Organization and manpower requirements.

A *should*-cost estimate is compiled to cover the task. Each functional area is again affected by the proposed program participants in the preparation of the bid estimate. Final compilation and reconciliation of the estimate is made by the estimating department. This department will make the final *should*-cost analysis for review by the finance committee and approval by management.

Upon timely acceptance by the customer, the contracts group issues a document authorizing the go-ahead to the operating departments. If the date of acceptance or other changes are not in keeping with the proposal, the long-range planning group reviews its effect on the program and determines the need for reappraisal by the manufacturing engineers and the operating department. Once the go-ahead is established, the financial organization develops an operating budget based on the proposed estimate.

Product Design — Release and Control

After acceptance of the proposal by the customer (military or industrial), the product is progressively designed and released in conformance with the manufacturing plan and master schedule.

During initial design decisions, the tooling section of the manufacturing engineering department and factory supervision are called upon to help preplan and coordinate producibility, tooling, and manufacturing problems.

A detailed computer release system is maintained to assure that the design has been released on all areas of the product for the final assembly, and that subsequent changes are documented, recorded, coordinated, and released.

Engineering Design Change Control

A developing product is subject to frequent improvements and changes. Therefore, a tight control is maintained to assure that all proposed changes are thoroughly evaluated by an engineering review board as to necessity, effect, and possible alternatives. After approval by the engineering board, the change is further evaluated by a change control group on such factors as scheduling, effectiveness, and other factors affecting cost. The change control group is composed of all functions primarily affected by an engineering change.

All approved changes are documented in the computer system and released in the form of a revised drawing or an engineering change order to be attached to an existing drawing. The engineering department prepares a summary list of all revised drawings and engineering change orders released to accomplish the change. To facilitate control, a change control number is assigned to each summary list.

Manufacturing Engineering, Tool Design, Operation Planning

As the product design is progressively released, the question at hand is how to build the product. What tools are needed? How are detailed parts to be fabricated? What is the sequence of operation?

The manufacturing engineering group issued instructions to the shop in the form of a detailed sequence of operations, showing the tooling required for each operation and the manufacturing equipment to be used for these operations. The complete planning sheet will show how to fabricate and assemble the product.

A central computer group control is maintained over all planning. The central planning group receives all engineering information, accumulates it into planning packages, and releases it to the manufacturing engineering planning group. The central planning control group also maintains scheduling and follow-up within the manufacturing engineering planning group to insure timely completion.

For economy of operation, the planning task is split between clerical and technical planners. The list of operation sequences, tooling, production equipment, and other manufacturing information is prepared by the technical planners. The clerical personnel (computer programmers) will record the technical planning, the engineering authorization that establishes the requirements for the part, and usage information such as quantity per next assembly and effectiveness. Since some of the engineering changes affect usage and authorization, the computer personnel can perform a large bulk of planning revisions.

Types of Planning

Most operations in a manufacturing function fit into three basic categories:
- Fabrication of detail parts.
- Assembly of detail parts into assemblies.
- Installation of detail parts and assemblies into the finished product.

Detail Parts Planning. Planning for the manufacture of detail parts is best performed by the manufacturing engineering planning group. This basically calls out the detailed steps required to make the part from the first operation to the final operation. It also contains the material required, the tools, finish specifications, and reference information needed to make the part.

To reduce the cost of detail planning, preprinted operation sheets can be used for a number of basic processes such as machine shop, sheet metalwork, welding, and plating. The planner merely adds or deletes certain operations, and adds part number, tool number, etc.

Assembly and Installation Planning. This planning consists primarily of:
- Operation sheets for each assembly calling out the parts to be used and their sequence of installation.
- A computerized installation log listing all the operations required to assemble or install a particular component.
- Installation or inspection check sheets listing the inspections required during installation or operation of a component.

The assembly and installation task is usually set up by station; that is, the task is broken down into groups of operations to be performed in progressive stations within an assembly line.

Tool Control

Tool orders are released according to schedule by the tooling release group. The condition of the tools is determined daily by personnel assigned to follow tools through the production shop. This system allows easy location of priority tool orders that require expediting or special handling.

This personnel is also responsible for the timely change of cutting tools, and to make certain that the required quantity of reconditioned cutting tools are on hand so that there will be no delay in tooling changes.

Procurement

During the same time that the product is being designed and the operation planning being developed, procurement action is taking place. Requirements for long lead time items are released ahead of official design release in order to gain as much procurement time as possible.

As a check and balance control, requirements are developed by the material control group. The buying groups purchase only those items and quantities that are authorized by procurement releases issued by the control group.

The material control group develops requirements from several sources. The engineering drawing calls out the basic requirements in a bill of material. This is modified to a degree by how the product is planned and built. Test requirements, spare requirements, subcontract requirements, and special

303

requirements add on needs. Whether an item is to be built in-plant or will be subcontracted out is determined by the make-or-buy committee. If the decision is in-plant, the raw materials must be procured; if it is subcontracted, an outside production authorization is submitted to the material control group or by the make-or-buy group.

After the needs are determined and made known to the procurement groups, it is their responsibility to locate satisfactory sources and negotiate contracts at fair prices for the delivery of material and parts in accordance with required delivery schedules. Buyers compile industrial, financial, capabilities, quality, and other information about possible sources as a means of determining qualified bidders. On highly complex items, management participates in selecting qualified bidders.

Follow-Up

A copy of each purchase order goes to the follow-up function. An up-to-date status is maintained through the computer to assure that prompt action is taken to solve any problem that would delay on-schedule delivery.

Subsystems Procurement

A specialized procurement group negotiates and administers the complicated subsystems for research and development programs. Due to the unusual importance of such procurements, management participates in both the selection of qualified bidders and in the final award.

The vendor evaluation unit is a group specially formed that reports functionally to the assistant manager responsible for procurement. This group performs the basic functions such as data-gathering and proposal and vendor evaluations including survey visits and coordination. It incorporates its findings into fully computer-documented recommendations. This group is composed of the:

- Subsystems procurement management
- Subsystems procurement buyer
- Subsystems procurement cost analyst
- Project engineer
- General accounting department representative.

Quality Control representatives and manufacturing engineers are included as required.

The Procurement Committee

The procurement committee is a management group reporting to the manager. The committee receives and reviews the comprehensive reports, findings, and recommendations of the vendor evaluation unit. Upon approving a course of action, the committee forwards its recommendations to the manager. The procurement committee consists of the:

- Assistant manager, contracts and procurement chairman
- Assistant manager, operations
- Assistant chief engineer, product design

- Controller
- Manager, long-range planning
- Manager, manufacturing engineering

The manager takes final action on the recommendations submitted by the procurement committee. The participation of management in the selection of subsystem vendors elevates the character of the action. Instead of relying on the decision of an individual buyer, or even a procurement department, it draws upon the best talents of all departments and becomes a plant-wise judgement.

Value Engineering

Buyers, with the aid of the value engineering group, continuously analyze past and present procurements to determine and document ways to reduce costs by procuring items that cost less, but still meet all functional requirements. They also investigate the possibilities of using standard items rather than specially designed items. (See the Value Engineering section in *Chapter 12*.)

Manufacturing Control

The manufacturing (or production) control group ties all of the related design, planning, procurement, and production into a comprehensive master schedule. Such a schedule points out the trouble spots where expedited action must be taken to meet the end requirements.

Component schedules are prepared from the master schedule to show specific lead times for the components making up the complete assembly. The component schedule is then broken down into items which are the major portions of the components to be manufactured. An item and indenture system further breaks down the schedule into details and assemblies.

Shop Loading

To provide an even flow of work to the manufacturing areas, a computer-integrated load control system is used to control the release of orders. The shop control group of manufacturing production control maintains charts which graphically show the shop conditions relative to backlogs, orders issued, and forecasted loads.

Shop loading is integrated with the order release function. Data is developed pertinent to estimates for setup and run on all critical machines. Data is then processed through the computer which provides necessary information regarding types of orders to be released which will maintain an even work load for the shop. Control charts for each department, group of machines, and critical machines are maintained on a weekly basis.

Fabrication Control

A manufacturing control system is used to inform the assembly and parts departments where every order is in the manufacturing process and what orders must be worked next to relieve a shortage or potential shortage. The manufacturing control system provides a complete file of manufacturing work-in-process with current order location continuously maintained by the computer-integrated system. With this first-in first-out concept, orders are issued in the correct schedule sequence.

Manpower Controls—Direct Departments

The factory has been given the design, tools, plans, materials, and schedules needed to build the product. They must also be given the tools to enable them to use their manpower efficiently in order to manufacture a quality product with the lowest possible cost.

Work measurement is one of the most important controls available to modern management. A management technique successfully applied is *manpower loading*. Manpower loading is a single tool of first line supervision providing each employee with a specific preplanned task and a time target graphically arranged in an effective manner. All manufacturing areas are manpower loaded and analyzed in detail for the most economical manning, and each person or crew is assigned eight hours of tasks per person per day.

The first line supervisor and employee are motivated through participation. The supervisor's participation is in developing the manpower load and reporting daily performance. The manpower loading is the supervisor's plan for accomplishing the assigned task. The worker's participation is in posting tasks and reviewing the daily accomplishments. This lets them know how they fit into the overall picture. The manning system provides the basis for determining cost and schedule status, and performance measurement.

Work Measurement—Indirect Departments

The work measurement program is also extended to certain indirect departments where the task in the various sections is repetitive in nature. Work measurement is carried on in certain areas of the engineering, plant engineering, traffic, procurements, office services, tooling, and manufacturing production control departments, and in other indirect areas. In these departments record standards are used as the basis of measurement. Historical records are audited for statistical purposes in the development of the standard or target.

After the program is developed and installed, a weekly performance report is compiled to show effectiveness of each employee and section of each department. The weekly report is a summary of daily reports turned in by each employee showing quantity of units completed and hours worked against the targets. The weekly report is reviewed by supervision to determine how well each employee and section is performing.

Quality Control

The quality control department has the responsibility of seeing that quality requirements established by specification are met during manufacturing. Product specifications negotiated with the customer are interpreted by the product engineering and manufacturing engineering groups and set forth in engineering documents and prints. Quality control criteria, procedures, and processing standards are established during production and testing of prototypes and early units.

Tooling requirements are established by tool design specifications, tool planning, and manufacturing engineering.

As the product is being manufactured, continuous surveillance of quality is maintained through inspection procedures, rejection reviews, and statistical reports.

Quality control has a very significant place in cost control. Quality control exerts its efforts by watching costs closely. Unnecessarily high quality standards which cannot be met realistically should be reviewed for revisions to requirements in order to stay within the negotiated limits. In cases where quality standards are extremely high and difficult to meet, but mandatory, immediate action should be taken to improve methods which will reduce cost.

Accounting

Current and accurate identification of actual costs is necessary to determine how performance compares with the predetermined plan. This adequate accounting is essential in monitoring the plan and in keeping management aware of potential trouble areas that require corrective action. Each major project is assigned a series of work order numbers by the industrial accounting group so that actual direct labor hours, material, and other direct costs can be identified to the greatest degree practical.

Costs are accumulated and identified down to the major components. By the use of the computer in the accounting department, detailed part costs are recorded and summarized. Costs are identified by:

- Contract and project
- Type of cost: engineering, tooling, manufacturing
- Area: fabrication assembly, field operations, and testing
- Organization: manufacturing, assembly, and quality control.

The work order pattern for cost accumulation purposes is also correlated with the project budget so that a direct comparison can be made between actual cost and budgeted cost.

Budgetary Control

In the cost area, it is desirable to establish a plan, activate the plan, and monitor it on a current and continuous basis. In this case, the plan is the budget covering both direct and overhead activities. The budget department establishes a project budget base on the bid covering the direct costs on each major project. The project budget is broken down into major functions such as: engineering, tooling, manufacturing, and material.

The project budget covering manufacturing is broken down into department levels. The operating departments receive periodic performance reports showing actual versus budget costs and other pertinent operating data. This report is issued directly from the computer in the accounting department. The report distributed to the manufacturing departments is expressed in terms of hours of work completed against the budget. Hours in lieu of dollars are used because hours and people are the units most operating supervisors use in controlling tasks.

Overhead labor and expenses are forecasted for a fiscal year. The same direct labor ground rules are interpreted for the next budget year and issued with other general instructions by the budget department, including an estimated number of direct labor employees as a fixed point for indirect forecasting. The department head is responsible for determining the requirements for each budget period and for controlling overhead expenditures to budget.

Each department manager participates fully in the budget program by indicating the needs for the budget period and furnishing complete justification for the plan. The manager is given staff assistance by the budget department in preparing the budget.

Plant-wide Control Program

In addition to daily operating management controls over manpower, materials, and machines, specific planned programs of improvement on a plant-wide basis are a valuable tool to assist in improving operations and reducing cost. The following are some examples of such programs.

Value Control. The value control or value engineering (see *Chapter 12*) program is used to excite the imagination of all levels of decision makers to think in terms of the effect of their decisions on the overall cost.

Management Analysis. The management analysis section of the manufacturing engineering industrial engineering group is responsible for analyzing controls needed at each management level. In attaining continual improvements, most of the efforts of the section are centered around applications of the computer system. Before installation of any job in the computer, applications are evaluated from the economic standpoint. Offsetting reductions are forecasted by the affected departments in their budgets.

Methods Improvements. The methods section of manufacturing engineering is responsible for furnishing technical assistance to all areas for continually improving management and operating techniques to attain lower cost. The prime responsibility for all improvements is with supervision. Assistance is given by developing, promoting, and installing programs for methods improvements and cost reduction to achieve production goals and program objectives.

The methods section establishes requirements for manpower, tools, space, machinery, equipment, and production aids. The assigned manufacturing engineers study and develop manpower loading and individual work measurement systems. They assist supervision to determine how the methods improvements and cost reduction objectives can be achieved. They call on other sections of the manufacturing engineering department for specialized services.

STANDARDIZED COST CONTROL—
A SPECIAL ADVANTAGE

The many advantages of cost controls such as manning, performance reports, and the like, are well known. When these controls are sufficiently standardized throughout the company, there is one major advantage that is often overlooked. One supervisor can take another's place on immediate notice. No mystery exists as to the work assignments of the employees or the current cost and schedule status of any operation or the sum total. The open task can be known in a few minutes as well as that which can be expected from each employee. The replacement supervisor can assume full control without delay.

Products will be manufactured at a much lower unit cost by offering greater value for the money—an important advantage in a world of global competition.

14

Producibility Considerations for Mechanical Assemblies

Automation of the assembly process can be difficult unless the product designer takes producibility into consideration. This chapter introduces the general considerations relating to automated assembly. Design considerations relating to the total assembly are considered first with emphasis on design simplifcation, human and mechanical constraints, and the assembly sequence. Next, the producibility considerations for the individual components of an assembly are examined. Included here are factors which will ease assembly along with approaches for feeding, orienting, and loading components for automated assembly.

The subsequent paragraphs cover fastening and joining, including mechanical fasteners, mechanical connections, and a variety of heat-type joining methods, such as soldering, brazing, and welding. The basic rules for producibility in assembly along with rules for product design and the design of components are discussed. In addition, nontraditional techniques introducing industrial robots and inspection and testing are detailed.

THE PRODUCT DESIGN/MANUFACTURING INTERFACE

One of the most significant opportunities to reduce the direct labor content in assembly will come from the selected application of automated assembly. To capture the benefits of these assembly methods, product designs that are compatible with these techniques are required. The results will benefit manual assembly in the short term and flow through to the introduction of products that can be built using various methods of flexible automation.

The challenge we face today is how to improve the producibility of the product. The design/manufacturing interface offers tremendous opportunities to improve design efficiency, manufacturability, reliability, and serviceability.

The design of a product determines its method of assembly, component tolerance, number of adjustments, and type of fabrication tooling used. As more and more competitive pressure is felt from world class manufacturers, it becomes important to take a critical look at the product development process. The manufacturing engineer and the design engineer must understand each other's job and work closely to reduce the product/manufacturing development cost and satisfy the expectations of the customer. Each one of us must ask ourselves, "What can I do to improve the product design and manufacturing interface?"

One approach to improving the design/manufacturing interface is to develop a design for assembly (DFA) process within the product development team. The DFA process should consist of two steps. First, develop a list of principles which will guide the product development team. This can include guidelines and a catalog of clever ideas which can stimulate people's imaginations.

Second, use a formal DFA system, design for assembly software, or a producibility index. These systems are used to evaluate the design and point out labor intensified assembly operations. These systems will also drive the design to reduce part counts within the assembly or combine parts.

Design for assembly is not a mystical process, it is nothing more than a tool which design and manufacturing engineers can use to organize the assembly process. It does not replace ability, knowledge, imagination, creativity, attitude, and good work habits. It will only work if it is recognized that some extra time during the early development stage of a new product will be needed to get the process started off on the right foot.

The manufacturing process begins with a concept—usually a mental picture of a product. The process ends with parts flowing off of the production line. It is the role of the manufacturing engineer to develop the production process whereby the designer's concept is translated into manufactured goods at the lowest possible cost. The manufacturing engineer must have early input into product design in order to insure the proper selection of cost-effective materials and assembly processes. The product design and manufacturing engineers must work together as a team in the concept development phase of all new products.

At this point, the process limitations of the selected materials and the normal tolerances associated with the materials manufacturing processing capabilities should be understood by the design engineer. Standardization should include reducing the amount and size of fasteners allowed. Standardization should also include the approach to tooling used to form the materials into the components of the assembly.

There must be control of the design and fabrication of component tooling to insure quality and to insure that cost targets can be met. This area of understanding fabrication tooling is probably the most ignored area in design for assembly today.

Selecting the proper manufacturing process to produce the components of the design for economical assembly becomes critical. Or, put another way, choosing the proper method of designing the components so the most economical manufacturing method is employed to meet fit, form, and function of the components becomes critical. The designer must provide features in the components to facilitate handling and insertion during assembly.

Assembly requires control of component tolerance, so the process capabilities being dealt with need to be understood. Assembly is a management problem that must be considered from the beginning of the program. The product design must be compatible with the assembly methods one has control over in order to meet quality and cost targets. Design teams must understand these capabilities. Only then will the design/manufacturing interface be optimized.

Effective design for assembly comes from a commitment and understanding by all members of a design team to drive toward the highest possible producibility, lowest part count, and highest quality. These goals then will lead to the lowest assembly hours/cost, multifunctional parts, and the ability to automate.

Producibility is the ability for parts to come together efficiently. In addition, producibility, the heart of good design for assembly, is also being certain that reducing part counts will lead to efficiency, but won't top-down assembly. It will only work if management recognizes that some extra time during the early development stage of the new product will be needed to get the process started.

DESIGN FOR ASSEMBLY PRINCIPLES

- Develop a sound base component or modular design
- Stack assembly is best, but all assembly operations should be in one direction
- Drive the uses of multifunctional parts
- Eliminate assembly adjustment where possible
- Provide self-locating features where possible to aid the assembly operation
- Provide direct accessibility to all subassemblies
- Standardize fasteners, components, and materials whenever possible
- Minimize levels of assembly
- Facilitate handling of parts, avoid orientation; make parts symmetrical; avoid tangling and nesting problems.

General Considerations

To exploit manual or automated assembly to the fullest extent, the product to be assembled must be inherently suited to and designed for the assembly method. It is safe to say that what is difficult for the human assembler to do is probably also difficult for an automatic assembly machine. The product designer must understand the interface between human movements and equipment design. The design of the product, its component parts, and the means used to fasten it together exert a powerful influence on determining its ease of assembly.

313

Automatic Machine Assembly

With the current trend toward greater use of automatic machinery for assembly, product designers must change their thinking to suit the requirements of automated equipment. The human hand can move in a wide range of combined motions; it has sense to touch, and it is controlled by all the senses. Product designers, when designing to suit automatic mechanical assembly, will be dependent upon mechanical functions, all of which are designed to perform a set cycle of events. Any decisions the machine may have to make must be anticipated and built in. This requires rethinking by the product designer to eliminate as much machine decision making as possible.

Considerations for Assembly by Machine

The majority of currently produced products are not designed for automated assembly. This new technique has raised a whole range of problems. Obviously, the function and reliability must never suffer, but designing for automated assembly may well dictate the uses of different materials. In the manual assembly process, the assembly operator normally did not care how parts were delivered to the assembly line. However, with automated assembly this becomes a critical parameter.

Also, the product may be designed to be thrown away. This has been an accepted principle for some electrical equipment and for some types of watches and clocks. Conversely, the product may, for economic reasons, be designed for disassembly and repair during its life cycle. In either case, the designer must eventually consider this in the initial product design.

Designing for Assembly

The real problem lies in the techniques of designing for automatic assembly. The rules and guidelines can be given, but real knowledge of their use comes from applying them in practice.

If all product designers were to develop a philosophy where they would design for robotic assembly, greater savings would be found in manual assembly. Many times, if a product is designed for robotic assembly, it will turn out that the manual assembly process becomes the most economical method. One simple rule of thumb to follow is: Does the design facilitate handling and insertion of the parts into the assembly?

For example, can the parts be assembled by a right-handed worker who:
- Must work with the left hand only?
- Must wear a glove on the left hand?
- Can use only the thumb and index finger of the left hand to do all work?
- Must do all work with eyes closed?

If you can answer yes to these questions, then and only then can you use the steel collar assembler (*Figure 14-1*)

It is not difficult to design components for manufacture on automatic machines and presses. These are common tools (automatic screw machines, CNC machining centers) for all industries, and what applies in the manufacture of one product also applies in the manufacture of others. In assembly

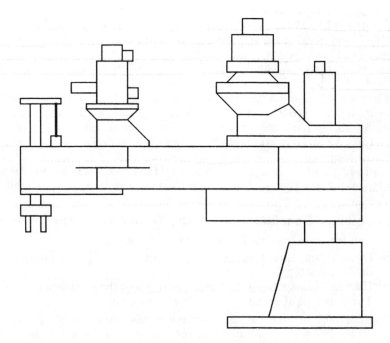

Figure 14-1. Steel collar assembler.

work, however, different shapes, materials, tolerances, and sizes have to be considered. Parts that tangle or become damaged and contaminated require special consideration on the automated assembly line.

Apart from designing for economical production, designing for easy orientation, selection, and feeding makes the problem quite different. With the advent of standard assembly machines, the product designer must have knowledge of their capabilities and limitations. In the initial stages, until full experience has been gained, the best way for the product designer to learn is by working with the machine tool designer and the manufacturing engineer on the project.

In most engineering projects, compromise is necessary; the same is true in products designed for automatic assembly. The product designer has to meet the requirements of function, reliability, appearance, and normal production techniques. The marketable price is determined by management and dictated to the product designer. To add to this existing burden may seem unreasonable, but to achieve maximum producibility, the designer must also consider the limitations of assembly techniques, whether automatic or manual.

Experience indicates that it is difficult to make large savings in cost merely by the introduction of automated assembly. Where large savings are claimed, examination often shows that the savings are really due to changes in the design of the product to facilitate the introduction of the new automation process.

Undoubtedly, the greatest cost savings are to be made by careful consideration of the design of the product and its individual component parts. Generally, when a product is designed, consideration is given to the ease of manufacture of its individual parts and to the function and appearance of the final product.

For obvious reasons, it must be possible to assemble the product; however, little thought is given to those aspects of the design that will facilitate assembly of the parts, and great reliance often is placed on the assembly operators. A trained operator is able to make logical decisions and assemble the most complicated parts based on those decisions. One of the first steps in the introduction of automation to the assembly process is to reconsider the design of the product so that mechanical, rather than human logic is applicable.

Producibility Considerations in the Total Assembly

Design for assembly should always consider basic items:

- Design simplification as a means of reducing the complexity of the assembly
- Human factors and mechanical constraints of the assembly
- The sequence of assembly regardless of volume.

In designing for high-volume assembly, consideration must be given to progressive assembly. Additional factors, such as division of labor and transfer of units, must also be considered.

Design Simplification

The most obvious way in which the assembly process can be facilitated by the product designer is by reducing the number of different parts to a minimum. The assembly should be value analyzed to reduce the number of parts.

An analysis would show if it is more economical to redesign the part for simplicity of assembly and for reducing the number of parts with the same function and better reliability than the old design.

Simplification by Manufacturing

It is sometimes possible to simplify a product by preparing it as a net shape using one of the new processes that enables a group of complex contacting parts to be produced as a single entity (multifunctional part). These parts can sometimes replace complete subassemblies and hence eliminate many assembly operations. Powder metallurgy, warm and hot forgings, and squeeze castings are examples of processes that may help in this respect.

Simplification in the Assembly Process

One or more important factors may arise during the redesign of a product. For instance, it might be suggested in a particular situation that a screw, nut, and washer be replaced by a rivet or, alternatively, that the parts be joined by welding or by use of adhesives. The suggestion would eliminate at least two assembly operations, but would result in a product that would be more

316

difficult to repair. This illustrates a common trend in which the introduction mechanization may result in a cheaper product but one that is uneconomical to maintain.

Guidelines for Simplification

There are no rigorous guidelines for product simplification across all product lines. There are only two checklist questions that can be used universally to achieve design simplicity: 1) Is this component necessary? Each component of an assembly should be examined to determine whether it can be eliminated and its function built into an existing component. Components should be examined jointly and individually. 2) Can these components be combined? In this situation, the designer is seeking net shape manufacturing processes that can be used to manufacture, as an integral component, a series of mating or contacting components that do not move independently of each other.

WHAT DESIGN FOR ASSEMBLY CAN DO

The principles of design for assembly are concerned with minimizing the cost of assembly within the constraints imposed by the need to meet fit, form, and function of the assembly. The best way to achieve this minimization is first to value analyze the assembly to reduce the number of parts to be assembled, thus reducing material cost and next to ensure that the remaining parts are easy to assemble and produce, thus reducing assembly time and cost and increasing assembly flexibility. This analysis will show if it is more economical to redesign the part for simplicity of assembly and for reducing the number of parts with the same function and better reliability than the old design.

Mechanical Decision Making

Lack of logical decision making capabilities in machines must also be considered. When a person is instructed to insert a shaft into a bearing, he or she has the ability to feel and position the shaft into the bearing. A simple machine doing the same task lacks the ability to adjust the location based on feel and, therefore, must have the parts precisely located and oriented. Proper fixturing is the key here. Just as in machining operations, assembly operations need accurate locations and flat surfaces for fixturing. Knowledge of these conditions in assembly will allow the product designer to make compensations in design which will eliminate high forces and tight tolerances.

Assembly Motions

The next logical step is inserting motions. Can the parts be placed in the main body of the assembly with simple, short, straight line motions? If not, can clearances be provided to assist the assembly tool motions? Avoid combined rotary and straight line motions if possible because these usually will require two or more assembly stations. Also, compound motions usually require a separate special motion or even a separate machine. The assembly of turbine vanes is a good example of a compound assembly motion.

In addition to inserting motions, tooling clearances require some thought. Think in terms of disassembly. If there is not room to grasp or push the parts out of position, it may be difficult loading it into that position. If precision alignments are required, locating points for the tooling will be required in addition to clearances.

APPLYING THE PRINCIPLES OF DFA

Develop a Base or Modular Design for the Assembly Process. To achieve the most efficient assembly method it is best to build on a sound base component. The base part must be fitted with guide surfaces or nesting features which make assembly of the other components subassemblies easy to locate. This base part will often have snap features which will secure the mating parts as they are put in place. A base component will greatly improve the manual assembly process and is almost an absolute necessity for automation.

It is always necessary in mechanical assembly to have a base part on which the assembly can be built. This base part must have features that make it suitable for accurate location on the work carrier. *Figure 14-2* shows a base part for which it would be difficult to design a suitable work carrier. In this case, if a force were applied at *X*, the part would rotate unless adequate clamping were provided.

One method of insuring that the base part is stable is to arrange it so that its center of gravity is contained within flat, horizontal surfaces. For example, a small ledge machined into the part will allow a simple and effective work carrier to be designed as shown in *Figure 14-2*. Location of the base part in the horizontal plane is often achieved by dowel pins mounted in the work carrier. To simplify placing the base part on the work carrier, the dowel pins can be tapered to provide guidance as in the example shown in *Figure 14-3*.

Use of Multifuctional Parts. The use of multifunctional parts represents the combination of parts/functions into one part. One of the basic rules of DFA is to combine parts whenever possible. In *Figure 14-4*, the engineer redesigned a latch mechanism that contained 56 parts and took 7.06 minutes to assemble, so that it could be assembled with only 18 parts. The redesign latch mechanism took only 1.10 minutes to build, thus reducing the assembly time by 5.96 minutes with a reduction to cost of 15.5%.

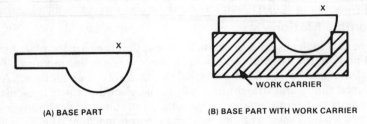

(A) BASE PART   (B) BASE PART WITH WORK CARRIER

Figure 14-2. Design of base part for mounting on a work carrier.

318

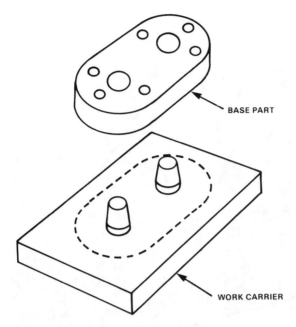

BASE PART

WORK CARRIER

Figure 14-3. Tapered pegs to facilitate assembly.

The redesigned latch would better enable automatic assembly as well as a reduction in manual assembly time. Multifuctional parts can often replace complete subassemblies and hence eliminate many assembly operations. Powder metallurgy, plastic moldings, sheet metal, forgings, and castings are examples of processes that may help achieve part reductions or multifunctional parts.

Eliminate Assembly Adjustments. Whenever possible, eliminate adjustments. Equipment that goes out of adjustment is the biggest cause of customer dissatisfaction. Eliminating adjustments can reduce assembly cost and improve maintainability of the product. *Figure 14-5* shows one approach, whereby hard mounting one shaft and spring mounting the mating shaft, no adjustment is required. Providing a key-shaped hole allows for ease of assembly as well as improved access for service. This spring loading concept can also be used to eliminate interface adjustments between subassemblies to achieve modularity.

Provide Self-locating Features in Components. By designing locational features into the parts, the designer can greatly influence both the quality of the assembly as well as the assembly time. The engineer needs to understand the manufacturing process used to fabricate the component parts. Most often, locational features such as tab-in-slot, dimples, and chamfers can be provided at no increase to part cost.

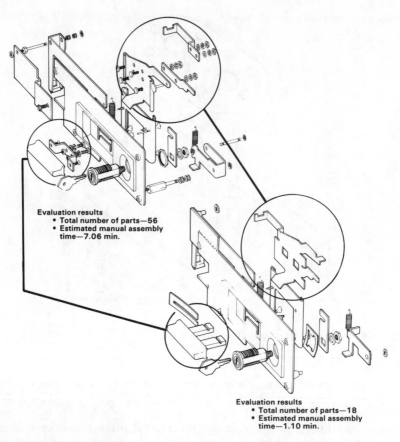

Evaluation results
• Total number of parts—56
• Estimated manual assembly
  time—7.06 min.

Evaluation results
• Total number of parts—18
• Estimated manual assembly
  time—1.10 min.

Figure 14-4. Latch mechanism. (*Courtesy*, Xerox Corporation)

Assemble from One Direction. Stack assembly is best, but all the assembly operations should be in one direction. The product design should allow for ease of insertion or removal of assemblies or parts. Product designers must realize that the geometry of a part in assembly is important. If the parts have to be rotated, biased, or held in place during the assembly operation, this is all wasted time.

Facilitate Handling of Parts. When designing a part, ask yourself how this part can be fed to simple automatic parts feeding equipment. Many times, parts can be designed so that orientation is not important.

STANDARDIZATION OF FASTENERS, COMPONENTS AND MATERIALS

There is no greater opportunity in applying design for assembly than that of standardization of fasteners, materials, and components (electrical/

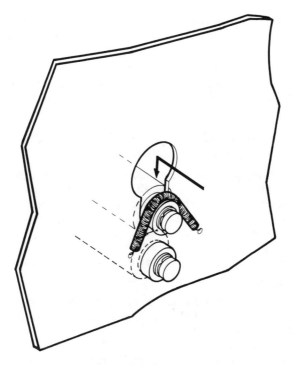

Figure 14-5. Spring loaded shaft assembly.

electronic/mechanical). The benefits will yield lower assembly cost, reduced component cost, reduced need for unique tooling, and good common sense. The product development team should select standards at the start of the development cycle and any deviation should be an exception rather than the rule.

Component parts are often difficult to differentiate, especially on small electrical assemblies. For example, rivets should be standardized to the same length, diameter, and material. Washers and screws are other possible candidates for commonality. It is easy for the assembly machine to become jammed if the wrong parts are introduced.

This difficulty can be overcome by coloring the components and painting the hopper feeder the same color, or by using some distinguishing feature, such as a type of rivet head. However, these are moves to be considered only when tooling an existing product for mechanized assembly. A little thought on new products can generally eliminate these expensive additions to storage, ordering, and administration.

Eliminate as many components as possible from the assembly. Examine the parts carefully in light of the production processes described in other chapters to determine what parts can be combined. Finally, examine all parts to determine their essentiality to the intended design function.

321

Assembly Sequence for In-Process Inspection and Repair

Excessive disassembly and resulting damaged component cost can be avoided if test and inspection of the partially assembled unit is performed early in the assembly process. The objective is to have a working assembly unit prior to the assembly of covers and cases. Therefore, the product designer should, wherever possible, segregate the working components before they are hidden from view and inaccessible.

DESIGN CONSIDERATIONS FOR HIGH-VOLUME ASSEMBLY

With a few exceptions, high-volume assembly means progressive assembly in which assembly operations are divided among several workstations. Progressive assembly can also be found in low-volume operations. Progressive assembly does, however, place additional constraints on the product designer. Two obvious factors must be considered:

- Dividing the work of the assembly
- Transferring the in-process unit from one assembly station to the next.

Work Division

Assume an operator has time to place two awkwardly shaped components into the assembly build. At the next workstation, a riveting operation is performed on one of the components with the possibility of dislodging the other. There are three alternatives:

- Clamp the part which is likely to be dislodged while riveting takes place.
- Use two operators. The first operator places one component, and at the next station riveting takes place. The second operator then places component number two, which is riveted at the following station.
- The last alternative is to design the product with the help of the manufacturing engineer so that both parts can be held and riveted at the same time.

This example shows to some degree the depth of thinking necessary for product design and the need for a sound knowledge of assembly line balancing techniques.

Assembly Line Balancing

The sequence in which parts can be assembled can be determined by logic, but more often a graphical approach is better, and should show all alternatives. One such graphical approach is a precedence diagram. *Figure 14-6* shows the steps in getting dressed. This is a simplistic example to aid in the understanding of a precedence diagram. Most assembly operations are more restrictive since the first loading operation is usually a single choice—a main casting or stamping. However, in this simplistic example, there are several alternatives for the first operation.

Any of the events in column I may occur first; there is no required precedence. But the events in column II require that those events in column I, with a connecting arrow, precede them in order of accomplishment. For

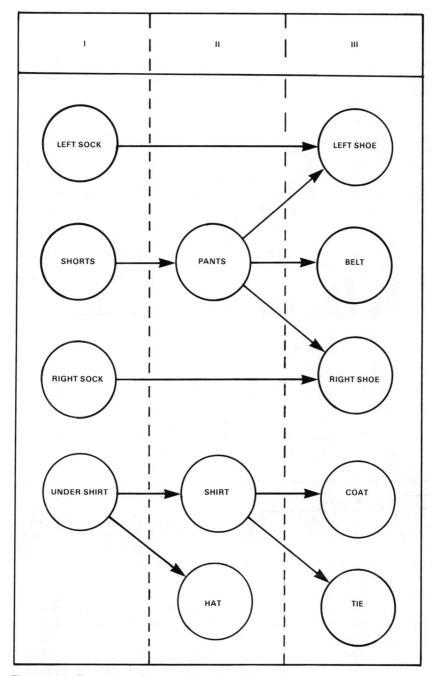

Figure 14-6. Precedence diagram of how to get dressed.

example, you cannot put on your pants until after you have put on your shorts.

Likewise, in column III, you cannot put on your coat until after you have put on your shirt and undershirt. This is a *precedence diagram*—it describes only the events that must precede other events. Do not be misled into believing that you must put you hat on before you put on your tie. All this chart says about the sequence of putting on your hat is that it must be preceded by putting on your undershirt. Everything else can be put on after putting on your hat; only the undershirt must precede it. This chart is not an ordering of succeeding events.

During the design phase, a precedence diagram may be helpful in designing the product for maximum flexibility during the assembly process. This flexibility provides the assembly machine manufacturer with a means of optimizing the machine configuration for placement of the operator's minimum floor space, accessibility for maintenance and operation, and the feeding and unloading position of parts. The precedence diagram can also prevent designing something which cannot be assembled or which can be assembled but only with great difficulty.

DESIGN GUIDANCE FOR TOTAL ASSEMBLY

A set of helpful hints follows to assist the designer in achieving maximum producibility from the standpoint of total assembly.

Datum Surface

The product should be designed so that it has a datum surface or datum point on which to build the assembly. This provides a known vertical height for the automatic placing of components. As each component is placed in position, new location points are established. Close control of tolerances may be necessary to insure that when many parts are fitted together, the buildup of maximum or minimum limits is within the capacity of the automatic workheads.

Location Points

The product should have locating points for assembly to provide a known horizontal position for the automatic placing of components. If no salient features of the component can be used, tooling holes or projections of the component may be necessary. Datum and location points are commonly used in metal-removing machinery. Therefore, it is reasonable to expect this practice to apply on assembly machinery.

The words *vertical* and *horizontal* for positioning the components should be considered only as an explanation. The majority of products are assembled one part on top of another, but datum and location points are just as important where this is not the case. It is essential that as each component is placed into the assembly build, it is held in such a way that it cannot move out of position. The ideal is to have it held in position by surrounding parts

324

(nested). This is most readily achieved if the assembly build is of the layer type, i.e., vertical build.

Vertical Build Assembly

Design the product so that one component can be placed on top of another. It is difficult to feed parts into the assembly from the side. For example, if a component is designed to be assembled into a vertical build assembly after the part above it and the part below it are in place, it must be fed into the assembly from the side. The alternative to this side feeding process is to previously attach the component to either the part above it or the part below it to facilitate automatic assembly.

Single Assembly Orientation

Never turn the assembly over if it can be avoided. At best, a mechanical or manual workstation will be needed to perform the operation. Complications can arise from a new datum and location, and the work carrier becomes more complex. The most important reason is that, if the previously placed components have not been fastened together, turning the assembly over may cause them to move out of position. Even so, experience has shown that it is far better to turn the part assembly over than to assemble components from below. Feeding components from underneath complicates the workhead, especially if accessibility is to be maintained for tool changing and for clearing of jams.

Accessibility of Important Components

Any component whose position cannot be seen or readily checked by a mechanical probe after the assembly is complete must be checked during assembly prior to the positioning of other parts, or it must suffer the cost of remote sensing. Remote sensing can be accomplished through the use of X ray or components containing low level radiation. Remote sensing can add extra workheads to the machine.

On electrical equipment manufactured in large quantities—such as that found in automobiles, telephones, and domestic appliances—simple components are used. Small paper bushings are often used for insulation. These are difficult for an operator to handle and almost impossible for a machine to handle. Insulated screws or rivets could be used instead. An electrical continuity check will show whether or not the assembly is correct.

PRODUCIBILITY CONSIDERATIONS FOR INDIVIDUAL COMPONENTS OF AN ASSEMBLY

Previous paragraphs in this chapter have addressed producibility considerations of the total assembly. A primary concern is to improve producibility in the assembly of an end item by considering the individual components. There are many things the designer can do to the individual components that will enhance producibility of the assembly. The problem is simplified if these are categorized under their major objectives, i.e., ease of assembly of parts; and feeding, orienting, and loading of parts.

Ease of Assembly

The designer can contribute greatly to the producibility of a mechanical assembly through the design of special features of components to facilitate their assembly. The approach should be to design all components so that they will fall together and can be oriented with either side up, i.e., with no preferred orientation. The basic rule should be to design the component for easy manual assembly. It naturally follows that if the product is easy to assemble by hand, it is probably easy to assemble with automation.

Elimination of Sharp Corners

To ease assembly, it is always a good practice to allow generous chamfers or radii to eliminate sharp corners that can cause parts to cross lock. Human operators often resort to selective assembly when parts do not fit; if necessary, they discard a part and pick up another. This cannot happen on machine assembly.

Generous Radii and Chamfers Help Assembly

Good examples of the need for chamfers are screw point forms. The point form of a screw is the feature that dictates more than any other whether it can be located in true relationship to the mating threads ready for driving. If one attempts to drive a screw automatically into a tapped hole that is not easily accessible (for example, at the bottom of a counterbored hole), it is often impossible to control the screw so that it positively centers in the tapped hole. Under these conditions it is necessary that the form of the screw point is such that the screw centers itself.

This example is particularly difficult, but self-centering screws should be used at all times, if possible. In the example of screw point forms shown in *Figure 14-7*, the cone and oval points tend to be self-centering. Evaluation of the various types of thread points follows:

- **Rolled Thread Point.** Very poor in locating hole—will not center without outside diameter positive control.

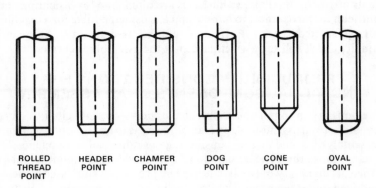

ROLLED	HEADER	CHAMFER	DOG	CONE	OVAL
THREAD	POINT	POINT	POINT	POINT	POINT
POINT					

Figure 14-7. Types of thread points commonly encountered in assembly operations.

326

- **Header Point.** Only slightly better and then only if guaranteed to be forged square and clean.
- **Chamfer Point.** Fair in locating hole since the chamfer angle is larger than the header angle.
- **Dog Point.** Fair in locating hole.
- **Cone Point.** Very good in locating hole.
- **Oval Point.** Very good in locating hole.

The approach used with screws applies equally well to all components, i.e., if the parts will fall together, it is impossible to do better. *Figure 14-8* shows the line of approach that should be adopted if possible; let the parts fall naturally into place.

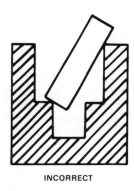 

INCORRECT   CORRECT

Figure 14-8. Sharp corners removed so that parts will fall naturally into place.

Self-Guiding Assemblies

Apart from eliminating sharp corners on screws and pins, great improvements often can be made by the introduction of guides and tapers that directly facilitate assembly. An example of this is given in *Figure 14-9*. Sharp corners are removed so that the part to be assembled is guided into its correct position during assembly.

Component Design to Facilitate Assembly

The designer's primary objective is to create a design that satisfies the performance characteristics of the product. Of secondary concern are the producibility aspects of the components in that design. All too often, the concern stops there without considering the assembly aspects of the finished part. Frequently, it is assumed that if the components can be assembled in the prototype shop, the item is adequately designed for producibility.

A second look at the design with the manufacturing engineer would reveal that some basic redesign with the proper guides, or chamfers, would ease the assembly operation and maximize the producibility of the item. This second look can be doubly rewarding because it facilitates assembly and provides the

327

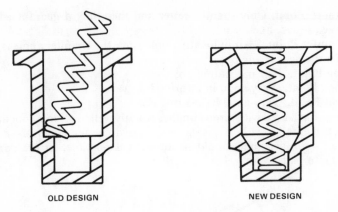

OLD DESIGN   NEW DESIGN

Figure 14-9. Redesign of product for ease of assembly.

added benefit of assuring that the design will be properly assembled into a functioning end item with a minimum of rework and rejects. This maximizes the producibility aspects. This second look at the design can also provide the necessary design features to permit the use of common parts in the assembly process.

Feeding, Orienting, and Loading

With the help of the manufacturing engineer, the necessity for feeding components so that they can be separated, oriented, fed, and placed by an automatic device is another basic reason for designers to take a second look at their designs. Most problems of feeding, orienting, and loading originate in the design of the component. The product designer must consider the various ways components are delivered to the assembly station.

Feeding Methods

Parts arriving at the assembly machine are usually delivered in bulk and are typically placed in a hopper and then tracked to a loading station. Whether the hopper is vibratory, rotary, or oscillatory, it relies on gravity and/or friction to move the parts past gating or orienting features. These features only allow parts in the proper orientation to pass to the next orienting feature and ultimately out of the bowl into a track.

Typically, nonvibratory feeders are limited in the number of orientations they can perform. There are several feeding problems. The first problem is the number of orientations required. The odds of the part going out of the bowl on the first try decrease with the number of orientations required. The way to increase the odds is to reduce the number of orientations by part symmetry.

Hard-to-sense features, such as off-center holes or cavities, are another problem, and sometimes may require extra tooling outside the bowl to sense and orient. The obvious solution to this dilemma is to change dimensions, add an external feature, or possibly change the center of gravity of the part.

328

Tangling is another common problem. A protrusion on the part can enter an opening in another part. Here again the solution is obvious—eliminate the protrusion, close the opening, or both. The compression-type coil spring is the most common part that has this problem. Close coiling the ends, increasing wire diameter, and increasing the pitch all help alleviate the condition.

Another part configuration that can lead to poor hopper efficiency and can severely limit feed rates is instability caused by the tracking surface and center of gravity. If the part is unstable in the sense that its center of gravity is high relative to its tracking surface dimension, the part will fall over. Also related to this is having the part land wrong side up when it is returned to the bowl. The design change here may be to move the center of gravity or increase the tracking surface.

Soft or rubber parts cause still another problem. They may tangle in the hopper, but more seriously, the bowl driving forces may distort the part to the point that orienting in the bowl is impossible. Distortion of the parts caused by stacking and handling can create serious problems. Plastics, rubber, and thin metal parts are susceptible to these adversities. Additionally, parting line flash from molded parts can be easily overlooked since it does not appear on the drawings. This is analogous to burrs and cutoff tabs in stampings. The designer of feeding mechanisms should keep in mind that drawings may show a perfectly clean part, but the actual part from the manufacturing process may have minor imperfections that can cause feeding difficulty unless they receive adequate consideration early in the process.

Once an orientation has been paid for, why discard it? One method of retention is to use trays or magazines to transport parts and to feed the assembly machine loading stations. Another method is to feed directly into the next machine. Direct in-line feeders are commonly used for this purpose.

Orienting Methods

There are two types of easily oriented component configurations. The ideal is the completely symmetrical part, which by its very nature, is always in an oriented condition. Examples are a sphere (e.g., a ball bearing), cube, and cylinder.

The second type is a component with marked polar properties, of either shape or weight. If it is the shape that creates the difference, some mechanical means of orientation is usually possible. The greater the difference, the easier orientation becomes. If the difference is weight, the location of the center of gravity to one end of the component produces a natural tendency to feed and be oriented in one direction. Quite often both shape and weight apply on such components. From the foregoing, there are two simple rules:

- Components should be symmetrical, if possible.
- Components should have distinct polar properties by geometry and/or weight if they are not symmetrical.

Statistical Technique. The statistical technique, so called because it is reliant on the statistical probability that the parts will arrive properly oriented, is usually performed on tracks in a vibratory bowl feeder. This technique uses the silhouette or profile of the part to determine correct orientation. Some form of mechanical filter is used for this operation.

Polarizing Technique. This system is very similar to the statistical technique. The difference is that with the statistical technique, shape is the principal means of selecting correctly and incorrectly oriented parts while the polarizing technique is used where both shape and weight differences occur. Mechanical filters are also used in the vibratory bowl feeder in this technique.

Design to Minimize Orientation Problems

There are numerous everyday examples of nearly symmetrical, simple parts that, due to minor differences, cause considerable problems with orientation. Consider a round pin such as a dowel pin. It is spherical on one end and has a chamfer on the other—no marked polar difference to assist in easy orientation. Why could it not be either chamfered or spherical at both ends? Functionally, it does not matter, and the only object of the spherical end is appearance. To have a spherical form at both ends may be too costly, but these are the sorts of questions the product engineer must ask. If in doubt, the engineer can and should discuss the problem with the machine designer and manufacturing engineer who will be faced eventually with the task of automatically handling the part.

Critical Assembly Dimensions

Consistency in the dimensions used to feed, orient, and locate the component is essential. With manual assembly certain dimensions are not important. Operators can make adjustments, and the components are not mechanically handled in hopper feeders, along chutes and into slides where jams can occur through inconsistency of manufacture. The assembly machine, on the other hand, is accurate and has dimensional limits on its work carriers, workheads, hoppers, and chutes. It is also inflexible and cannot learn to cope with components outside these limits.

The designer must consider the tolerances that the assembly machine can accomodate, and the shop producing the components must not exceed them, or else the assembly machine will fail. Of course, the added cost of improving component quality and consistency may not be worthwhile under certain circumstances. This again is where complete cooperation is essential among product design, machine design, and the manufacturing engineer.

Loading Methods

The most efficient type of loading station is one at which the part can be dropped into the assembly over a pilot pin from either open tracks or from a tube and then followed down with tooling to insure part placement. This free-fall, self-loading method is most efficient because of its simplicity.

This loading method will also provide high efficiency. For loading in this manner, pilot holes are required in the part as is a location feature in the mating part. The short, straight line motion is also an asset in obtaining high station efficiency.

330

Unfortunately, not all parts can be loaded into the assembly build using a self-locating, free-fall method. Some parts will require that they be grasped, lifted, and moved into the assembly build. There are three possible methods for grasping parts to load them into the assembly build: mechanical clamping, vacuum, and magnetic forces.

Mechanical Clamping. This requires the mechanical actuation of a clamp. It is usually accomplished with a pneumatic device and, therefore, involves the use of timed signals, solenoid valves, and complex tool motions, all of which tend to decrease efficiency of assembly. However, parts can be designed to minimize the decrease in efficiency by providing good clamping surfaces, pilot holes and pins for assembly alignment, generous chamfers for easy entry, and short, easily controlled loading motions. Remember, if you have difficulty loading the part, the machine will too.

Vacuum Loading. This method should be considered if mechanically clamping the part is impractical. To use the vacuum method, the designer must provide large, flat, smooth surfaces on the component to facilitate pickup, and should also add locating features if possible.

Magnetic Forces. This method is occasionally used, but most assembly machine manufacturers avoid the method because holding forces decrease rapidly with small amounts of dirt and oil on the contacting surfaces. Also, residual magnetism is usually strictly forbidden in the final assembly.

In general, the rules for loading are:

- Provide good grasping surfaces for the part length and weight, or provide locating surfaces or holes to guide the part into position.
- Keep loading strokes as straight and as short as possible.
- Keep external features for radial locations in mind for use if needed.
- Avoid a vacuum if possible; if not, keep surfaces large and flat. For flat disks provide a locating feature, such as a circular ridge.

FASTENING AND JOINING

There are three principal ways in which component parts can be joined to the final assembly build: threaded fasteners, pressure, and heat.

Threaded Fasteners

In component design, screws are considered based on their ability to align within a tapped hole. Nuts are more difficult to feed and assemble automatically than screws. If it is intended to feed and drive a nut onto a screw, the problem is holding the nut square while starting the thread (danger of cross threading). Removing the first thread to give some seating helps, but this is not absolutely reliable.

The machine designer can help by arranging the feeding and driving of a nut onto the screw with two operations—very light pressure at one station to give the nut an initial start followed by final tightening at the next station. If it is possible, it is always better to feed the nut into the assembly build first and then drive the screw into it. The examples of screw points shown in *Figure 14-7* should be considered.

331

Fastening by Pressure

Pressure fastening is one of the better methods for automatic assembly. The more common pressure fastening methods include riveting, swaging, staking, crimping, and force fitting. Certain pressure fastening methods need specific times for metal flow. This may require an in-line transfer where the first station will not allow time for completion of an operation, the work is transferred, and the work is completed at the next station. This may be necessary on certain pressure fastening systems and will be dictated by production output.

As an example, for a production rate of 800 assemblies/hour (4.5 seconds each), assume all parts placing operations plus transfer can be performed in this time, but a swaging operation takes 6 seconds to complete. There are two alternatives: Use two workstations; partly swage at one and finish swage at the next (indexing machine). Swaging can be accomplished using two machines to achieve overall cycle time.

The first method can be used provided that this two-step forming is free from work hardening to an extent likely to affect such a procedure. Swaging, spin riveting, and vibratory riveting are the most likely operations to require step-wise forming. Normally with manual assembly, two operators would be used for this work, each taking alternate assemblies and completing the operation. This can be done automatically provided the transfer line for automatic assembly is of the free transfer type or is individual operator paced.

Riveting. This is perhaps the least desirable of the pressure fastening methods because a separate component is required. By eliminating the rivet, obvious savings can be obtained in material and component consistency.

Swaging. Swaging is a method of shaping the material, reducing the diameter of a tubular part, and pressure bonding it to a smaller tube, rod, or to other parts inside the tube. The process is performed by a machine that causes the work to be struck a number of successive blows by hammers contoured to match the surface of the part.

Staking. This process is used to lock two pieces of material together by upsetting the two materials at one or more points along a common contact line. As an example, a threaded plug screwed into a tapped hole can be locked into place by centerpunching along the joint line, after the plug is threaded into place.

Crimping. Crimping is a process used to join two pieces of material by crimping or folding their edges together. It is most commonly used in the tin can industry for assembling ends of cans.

Force Fitting. Force fits, or interference fits, are generally used on cylindrical parts and depend on closely controlled dimensions for the outer and inner diameters of the parts. These dimensions are designed so that the inside and outside parts have diameters that overlap each other slightly and result in an interference fit. (See *Table VIII-3* for tolerances of these fits.) This type of pressure fastening is obviously expensive due to the precision machining required on the matching surfaces and the hazards of creating swarf.

332

However, the efficiency of the resulting assembly process sometimes offsets the cost of the precision machining. The element of critical concern to the designer is the amount of pressure required to press the two parts together. There must be assurance that the parts and the assembly build can withstand the pressure. *Table XIV-1* provides some information relative to the pressure factors encountered in press fitting steel parts of different diameters with an interference fit range of from 0.001 to 0.0015 in. (0.025 to 0.038 mm).

Table XIV-1. Press Fit Loads

Part Diameter	Total Load to Press 1.0 Inch Depth
Inch	*Tons*
4.0	1.38
3.0	1.40
2.0	1.44
1.0	1.50

Fastening by Heat

These processes will result in metallurgical bonds that are considered permanent and are generally not disassembled except for repair. Specific processes included under this category are welding, brazing, and soldering. Soldering requires the application of heat to the parts to be joined and the addition of a nonferrous filler metal with a melting point less than that of the base metal but never more than 800° F (427° C). Brazing also requires the application of heat to the parts to be joined and the addition of a nonferrous filler metal with a melting point less than that of the base metal; however, the melting point is more than 800° F (427° C).

Welding requires sufficient application of heat to cause the surfaces to be joined to become molten; while molten, they are joined together and allowed to cool. The use of filler metal and pressure in the welding process is optional.

The three metallurgical bonds of joining parts and assemblies by heat require trained and certified operators. The quality of the process is dependent on the correct application of the production techniques. The manufacturing engineer must determine what process should be used for a particular application. Soldering is primarily used by the electronics industry.

There are five brazing operations that could be used for assembly work. They are: torch brazing, furnace brazing, induction brazing, dip brazing, and resistance brazing.

There are numerous welding processes in use by industry today. The capabilities of the processes overlap in some areas; usually, one will have a specific advantage over another in a particular application. In some cases, several welding processes can do the job, although one will probably do it better.

The welding processes are: coated electrode arc welding, inert gas metal arc consumable electrode welding, inert gas tungsten arc welding, submerged arc welding, atomic hydrogen welding, and plasma arc welding. Other methods are: resistance welding, thermite welding, electron beam welding, and ultrasonic welding.

Selecting the optimum method requires analysis of the joint requirements, metal to be joined, configuration of parts, production quantity involved, production rates desired, and equipment available. *Table XIV-2* is a guide containing information to assist in making the selection. More comprehensive guides to recommended practices are published in most welding handbooks.

Design Considerations

- Heavy structural parts being assembled by welding should be welded from the center out toward the edges to let the stresses work out to an edge to avoid or minimize locking stresses into the work.
- Welded joints must be accessible to the welder to minimize welding time and maximize quality.
- Joints must be clean to avoid contamination, porosity, and cracking.
- Very heavy material, in excess of one inch (25.4 mm), and very light material, less than 0.036 in. (0.91 mm), will require special welding procedures.
- The most producible welds are achieved by using steel with a carbon range of 0.13 to 0.20%, manganese at 0.4 to 0.6%, silicon at 0.1% maximum, sulphur at 0.035% maximum, and phosphorus at 0.035% maximum. Higher alloy steels will require special treatment, such as preheating to produce sound welds.
- Material 0.1875 in. (4.76 mm) thick or thicker is welded best in a flat position, whereas thinner material is welded best in a 45° (.785 rad) downhill position.

NONTRADITIONAL ASSEMBLY TECHNIQUES

Probably one of the most significant developments to appear on the assembly scene in recent years has been the emergence of the industrial robot.

New Tools for Assembly

More than 17 types and 100 styles of assembly robots are now available in the United States, at least 12 of which are manufactured in this country. They range from minirobots, with payloads of only a few ounces and reaches of less than 3.3 ft (1.0 m), to the larger universal robots, which can transport payloads of up to 150 lbs (68 kg), over a reach distance of 2.5 ft (0.76 m), and can move at speeds up to 3 ft/sec (0.9 m/sec).

Besides the differences in payloads and reach capabilities, many other variations exist among industrial robots today. The most simple robots, limited to pick-and-place operations over relatively fixed distances, are capable of a few primary and secondary movements and are limited to one or two input/output signals. On the other end of the spectrum, the highly

334

Table XIV-2. Recommended Welding Processes

	Shielded Metal Arc[1]	Submerged Arc	Atomic Hydrogen	Inert Gas-Tungsten Arc	Inert Gas-Metal Arc	Flash Welding	Spot Welding	Seam Welding[2]	Gas Welding	Brazing Furnace	Brazing Torch	Thermit
Based on Welded Material												
Low Carbon, mild steel types	R	R	S	S	S	R	R	R	R	R	S	S
Medium carbon steel types	R	R	S	S	S	R	R	S	R	R	S	S
Wrought alloy engineering steels	R	R	S	S	S	R	R	NR	S	S	NR	S
High alloy stainless steels,	R	R	R	R	R	R	R	R	S	S	S	NR
austenitic types stainless steels	R	R	R	R	R	R	R	R	S	S	S	NR
Ferritic and martensitic types	R	S	S	S	S	S	S	S	S	S	S	NR
High temperature alloys	R	S	S	S	S	S	S	R	S	NR	NR	NR
Cast iron, gray iron	S	NR	NR	S	NR	NR	NA	NA	R	NR	R	S
Aluminum and aluminum alloys	S	NR	S	R	R	S	R	S	S	R	R	NA
Nickel and nickel alloys	R	S	S	R	R	S	R	S	S	S	R	NR
Copper and copper alloys	NR	NR	NR	R	R	S	S	NR	S	S	R	NR
Magnesium and magnesium alloys	NA	NA	NR	R	S	NR	S	NR	NR	NR	NR	NA
Silver	NR	NR	R	R	S	S	NR	NR	R	S	R	NR
Gold, platinum, iridium	NR	NR	R	R	S	S	S	NR	R	S	R	NR
Titanium and titanium alloys	NA	NA	NA	R	NR	S	S	NR	NA	NR	S	NA
Uranium, molybdenum, vanadium, zirconium, tungsten	NA	NA	NR	R	NR	S	S	S	NR	NR	NR	NR
Based on Joint Design												
Butt joint — Light section[3]	S	S	R	R	NR	NR	NA	NA	R	NR	S	NA
Butt joint — Heavy section[4]	R	R	S	S	R	R	NA	NA	S	NR	S	R
Lap joint — Light section	R	S	S	R	NR	NR	R	R	R	R	R	NA
Lap joint — Heavy section	R	R	S	S	R	R	R	S	R	R	R	NA
Fillet joint — Light section	R	S	S	R	NR	NR	NA	NA	R	R	R	NA
Fillet joint — Heavy section	R	R	R	S	R	R	NA	NA	S	R	R	NA
Edge joint — Light section	NR	NR	R	R	NR	NR	NA	R	R	NA	S	NA
Edge joint — Heavy section	R	S	S	S	S	S	NA	R	S	NA	S	NA
Overlay welding	R	R	R	R	R	R	NA	NA	R	NR	S	NR

Notes: [1]—Shielded metal arc (coated electrode)
[2]—Gas welding (oxyacetylene)
[3]—Light section (0.005 to 0.125 in.)
[4]—Heavy section (0.125 in. and over)
Key: R—recommended; S—satisfactory; NR—not recommended; NA—not applicable

sophisticated machines have several primary and secondary movements, have work envelopes in excess of 100 ft³ (2.83 m³), and move in complicated paths controlled by programs of up to a 30-minute duration.

Another important difference among the robots is their ability or lack of ability to stop movements at intermediate positions. In this quality, the least sophisticated robots have fixed strokes and may be positioned only at either end. The next level of sophistication—into which most of the robots fall— allows adjustment of both the minimum and maximum positions of all movements, but the movements are also limited to either one position or the other. Robots with the most sophisticated control systems can position all movements at several intermediate positions—the number being a function of the program capabilities.

All of the programming methods available today for robots fall into two classes: point-to-point (P-to-P) or continuous path (CP). In the P-to-P programs, which are the most common, movements of the robots are from one distinct point in space to another distinct point. At any point, the robot may delay for a predetermined period of time, wait for a signal from associated equipment, then grip or release a part. The number of points available in any program is a function of the sophistication of the robot and the time duration of the program.

In the CP form of program, the robot gripper can move in a straight or a curved path for the entire length of the program, which may extend to a 30-minute duration. This type of movement is advantageous for operations such as welding, paint spraying, or laying a bead of adhesive along a complex path. Initial CP programming is normally accomplished by *teaching the path* to the robot which stores it in magnetic memory. In this type of programming the robot is manually led through the desired motions.

Every industrial robot is available with one or more standard grippers to hold and release the parts being transported. In general, the grippers roughly simulate the movement of two fingers on a human hand, but robots are not nearly as limited as humans in this respect. They may be equipped with multiple grippers to hold several parts simultaneously, extended length grippers to hold large parts, grippers with built-in switches to detect the presence of parts, or vacuum or electromagnetic pickups in place of grippers. Most robots are designed for a variety of special grippers that hold specific parts, for ease of gripper removal and replacement, and for quick changeover from job to job. Some even include a screwdriver to complete assembly operations.

Applications

Industrial robots are reprogrammable, operatorless handling devices that can perform simple, respective jobs requiring few alternative actions and minimum communication with the work environment. They are well suited to handling parts that are extremely hot or cold, and they can function in corrosive, noisy, noxious, or extremely dusty atmospheres that would be injurious to human beings.

Passage in the U.S. of the Occupational Safety and Health Act (OSHA) in 1970 has provided strong impetus for the use of industrial robots. The act states that a human being cannot place his or her hand within punch press dies to load or remove parts. It is imminent that OSHA standards will be extended to cover other fabricating and assembly operations, such as staking, spot welding, riveting, holding, clamping, electronic component insertion, and automatic screwdriving.

In many cases, the cost in time to retool an existing operation to conform to the standards will be prohibitive compared to the cost and time required to purchase and program an industrial robot to perform the potentially dangerous operations.

15

Electromechanical Parts Assembly: An Example

The material in this chapter presents an example of how a design for assembly (DFA) analysis is performed. Although a small electromechanical assembly is used to illustrate the steps one might use to perform a DFA analysis, it must be pointed out that this process is applicable to most any type of mechanical, electrical, or electromechanical assembly. What is important is that all product designers must take the time early during a new design to insure that the product can be assembled in the most efficient manner, thus allowing the use of your company's manufacturing capabilities as a strategic weapon against the competition.

Switch Assemblies

Figure 15-1 illustrates a typical switch assembly which could be used in a variety of products. This switch assembly consists of eight parts with an approximate assembly time of 61 seconds. The results of analyzing this switch assembly are shown in *Figures 15-2* and *15-3*. *Figure 15-2* identifies the design for manual assembly sequence that would be followed to assemble the lever switch. It is a simple assembly process which could be given to the shop floor. This is an important step because it forces the user to think about how the assembly will be put together (assembly sequence).

Figure 15-3 illustrates the final results which present a wrap-up of all information fed into the computer. Assembly efficiency is expressed by the formula:

$$\text{Assembly Efficiency (\%)} = \frac{3 \times \text{Theoretical Minimum Number of Parts}}{\text{Total Assembly Time (Seconds)}} \quad (1)$$

$$\text{Design Efficiency} = \frac{3 \times 2}{61} = .098 \text{ or } 10\%$$

The rationale for this formula is as follows. The 3 in the formula is based on the assumption that each part should take a total of three seconds to handle and insert into an ideal assembly. This ideal time is based on the assumption

339

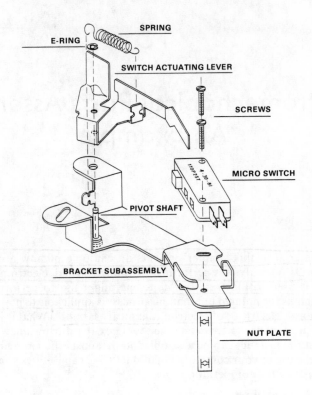

Figure 15-1. Lever switch assembly. (*Courtesy*, Xerox Corporation)

LEVER SWITCH ASSEMBLY

NO.	PART NAME	PART OPERATION
1.	NUT PLATE	PART IS PLACED INTO WORK FIXTURE
2.	BRACKET SUBASSEMBLY	PART IS NOT SECURED IMMEDIATELY ON INSERTION
3.	SWITCH	PART IS NOT SECURED IMMEDIATELY ON INSERTION
4.	SCREWS	PARTS ARE SECURED BY SCREW FASTENING (TWO CONSECUTIVE OPERATIONS)
5.	SWITCH ACT. LEVER	PART IS NOT SECURED IMMEDIATELY ON INSERTION
6.	E-RING	PART IS SECURED BY SNAP/PRESS FIT OR SIMILAR OPERATION
7.	SPRING	PART IS SECURED BY SNAP/PRESS FIT OR SIMILAR OPERATION

Figure 15-2. Design for manual assembly sequence.
(*Courtesy*, Xerox Corporation and Boothroyd & Dewhurst, Inc.)

340

LEVER SWITCH ASSEMBLY

ASSEMBLY EFFICIENCY (PERCENT)	10%
TOTAL ASSEMBLY TIME (SECONDS)	61
NUMBER OF DIFFERENT OPERATIONS	8
TOTAL NUMBER OF PARTS	8
THEORETICAL MINIMUM NUMBER OF PARTS	2

Figure 15-3. Summary of analysis for manual assembly.
(*Courtesy*, Xerox Corporation and Boothroyd & Dewhurst, Inc.)

that each part is easy to handle and insert, and that about one third of the parts are secured immediately on insertion with well-designed snap-fit fasteners.

Number of Parts

The theoretical minimum number of parts is determined by honestly answering *yes* or *no* to the following statement.

This part must be separate from all those parts already placed in the assembly...

...because it moves during the operation of the assembly (and that movement cannot be achieved through combination of parts in a flexible material).

...because a different material is required or the part must be isolated for electrical or heat insulation purposes.

...because it must allow for assembly or disassembly of other parts, such as service in the field.

If the response can be *no* to all three statements above, then that part is a "candidate for elimination" and a zero is placed in that column. At this point, apply some creativity to rethink the function of this part in the design. This is probably the most important part of design for assembly (DFA), however, it is a subtle point.

If the response to any of the statements is *yes,* a 1 is placed in the "candidate for elimination" column. Part #5 (the microswitch) must be separate because it provides the basic electrical function of the assembly. Therefore, answer *yes* to the second statement above. The screws (part #4) need not be a separate part because you can reply *no* to all three, so the screws are candidates for elimination.

Assembly Time

Total assembly time in seconds is generated from the designing for assembly software which is based on research data, developing a relationship between design features and handling, or assembly time for component parts. By developing data showing each part of the assembly and stating how long it takes to handle and insert each part into the assembly early in the design process, the product designer will have an insight as to how much time it takes to put the product together and what the assembly sequence is. By studying

341

this information, the product designer will have the opportunity to reduce assembly time by eliminating inefficient assembly operations and by reducing total part count in the assembly.

Applying Design for Assembly

After the design for assembly analysis was performed on the lever switch assembly and data was reviewed, the designer applied some creative solutions to improving the producibility of the old design. *Figure 15-4* is an example of applying DFA. This new assembly is made up of two parts and takes approximately six seconds to assemble. Not only has producibility been improved, an assembly containing only two parts will be more reliable and will improve serviceability.

Producibility Index

Another method of analyzing a design is the producibility index guide (*Figure 15-5*). This guide provides a quick and easy method to quantitatively evaluate each part in an assembly for producibility. It is recommended that the design engineer use this type of assembly analysis sheet to determine if the design is economical for good assembly.

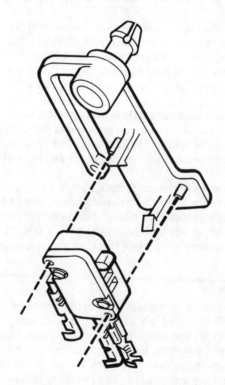

Figure 15-4. Redesign lever switch assembly. (*Courtesy*, Xerox Corporation)

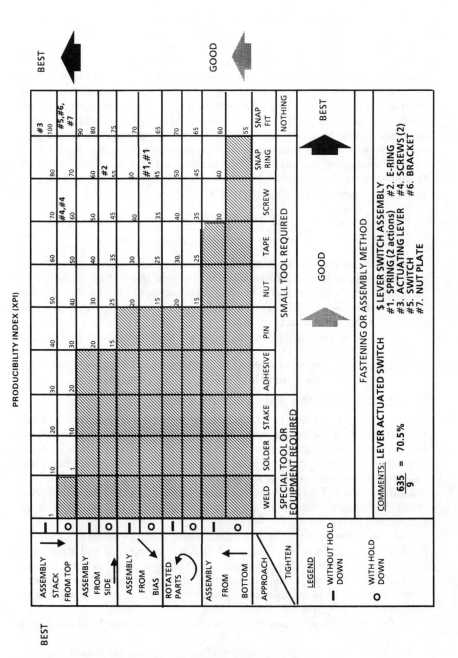

PRODUCIBILITY INDEX (XPI)

BEST

APPROACH	WELD	SOLDER	STAKE	ADHESIVE	PIN	NUT	TAPE	SCREW	SNAP RING	SNAP FIT
ASSEMBLY STACK FROM TOP	1	10	20	30	40	50	60	70	80	#3 100
ASSEMBLY FROM SIDE	1	10	20	30	20	40	50	#4,#4 60	70	#5,#6, #7 90 80
ASSEMBLY FROM BIAS				20	15	30	40	50	60	75
ROTATED PARTS						20	30	45	#2 55	70
ASSEMBLY FROM BOTTOM						15	25	40	#1,#1 45	70
TIGHTEN						20	30	40	50	65
						15	25	35	45	65
								30	40	60
										55

SPECIAL TOOL OR EQUIPMENT REQUIRED | **SMALL TOOL REQUIRED** | **NOTHING**

FASTENING OR ASSEMBLY METHOD

GOOD ← **GOOD** ← **BEST**

LEGEND
| WITHOUT HOLD DOWN
○ WITH HOLD DOWN

COMMENTS: LEVER ACTUATED SWITCH

$$\frac{635}{9} = 70.5\%$$

$ LEVER SWITCH ASSEMBLY
#1. SPRING (2 actions)   #2. E-RING
#3. ACTUATING LEVER   #4. SCREWS (2)
#5. SWITCH   #6. BRACKET
#7. NUT PLATE

Figure 15-5. Producibility index for lever switch assembly.
(*Courtesy*, Xerox Corporation)

343

The approach to assembly along the vertical axis is shown. Assembly from the top down is best and assembly from the bottom is the worst. The dash indicates that a part can be placed in the assembly without a hold down.

The zero indicates that two hands would be required to perform this assembly operation because a hold down or some other assembly process to be used is shown. This can be changed to represent any other assembly method or process which might be used for a specific manufacturing process. Select the approach to assembly on the vertical column, and method of assembly on the horizontal column. Read to the right and up to the point where the two columns intersect to find the producibility score (*Figure 15-5*).

After evaluating all parts in the assembly, add up the total points and divide the sum by the number of parts or assembly operations in the assembly. This results in the producibility rating.

$$\text{Producibility Index (\%)} = \frac{\text{Total Points in Boxes}}{\text{Number of Parts in Assembly}} = \frac{750 \text{ Points}}{10 \text{ Parts}} = 75\%$$

The lever switch assembly is evaluated in this example. A good rule of thumb to follow is that an assembly must score out at 65% or better for manual assembly. If it is less than 65%, it should not be released to the shop floor. *Figure 15-6* displays the results of the redesigned switch assembly analyzed with the producibility index.

Figure 15-7 shows the inputs and outputs to the manufacturing process. In the past, a model like this did not have design for economical production as one of the manufacturing processes. Today, however, it must be considered as primary because of the competitive pressure felt by everyone.

Simplification in the Assembly Process

One or more important factors may arise during the redesign of a product. For instance, it might be suggested in a particular situation that a screw, nut, and washer be replaced by a rivet or, alternatively, that the parts be joined by welding or by the use of adhesives. The suggestion would eliminate at least two assembly operations, but would result in a product that would be more difficult to repair. This illustrates a common trend in which the introduction of mechanization may result in a cheaper product, but one that is uneconomical to service.

This problem might have been eliminated if the product designer had developed a snap-fit joint. The use of engineering plastics and sheet metal materials offers great opportunities to develop a wide range of design possibilities with snap joints. This method of securing parts has a number of inherent assembly advantages associated with it. These include, but are not limited to, the following:

- The use of snap features allows parts, especially hardware to be eliminated.
- Direct material cost is reduced and assembly time is lowered, minimizing necessary expenditures for material handling equipment. Manufacturing overhead rates are ultimately impacted.

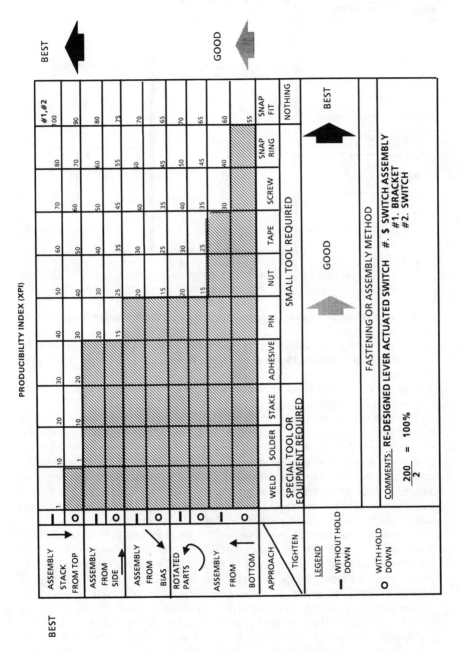

Figure 15-6. Redesign switch production index. (*Courtesy*, Xerox Corporation)

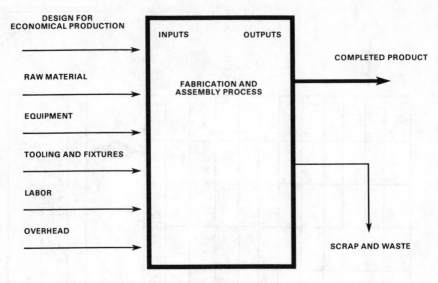

Figure 15-7. Manufacturing process model.

- Snap features can be designed to provide positive location as well as securing parts.
- The number of adjustments necessary on an assembly line can be lessened thereby reducing the number of potential problems which may occur.

This type of assembly is not recommended for aircraft or missile parts due to the vibration problems.

Parts subject to wear and or abuse can be easily replaced when they are assembled and secured with snap features. This can lower service time and cost and may also allow a reduction in the total number of parts which must be available in the field for service. A design utilizing snap features typically contains less parts than a traditional approach. Therefore, it is easier to assemble since it reduces the number of parts that must be handled as a part of any one operation. The simplification of tasks needed to complete a product will result in lower assembly costs and higher outgoing quality.

The advantages cited above allow for, to a great extent, the increased use of automated assembly techniques. Therefore, the potential benefits from incorporating snap features into a product go far beyond those which are immediately evident. Snap fits provide a simple, cost effective means of joining parts. There are numerous opportunities for their application. Although plastic is the most common material used, sheet metal may also lend itself to this type of application. Because of the inherent assembly advantages associated with them, the use of snap features should always be considered as a possibility. Here, again, these assembly methods with snap features apply to sheet metal, plastic, and small electrical components.

Appendix

Production time tables are generated for the cost estimator and manufacturing engineer to use in making an analysis and to determine if the estimate used is an economical one. Material, cost of functional material, feeds and speeds, type of tooling and tooling material, tolerances, and surface roughness determine the time and expense of production costs.

If the estimate of part production shows that it takes 13.2 seconds to produce the part in a production run of 100,000 parts, and the *should-cost* analysis shows that the part could be produced in 10 seconds, the savings for the 100,000 quantity would be 88.8 hours. Added to this is the possible savings on material cost, tooling cost, and setup cost if the economical quantity has been determined.

For other production time tables not shown in this Appendix, use the following equations:

If the time to produce a part has been estimated at 110 seconds, Gross production per hour = 32.7 parts

$$3600 \div 110 = 32.7$$

To change the time in seconds, divide the seconds by 60

$$110 \div 60 = 1.83 \text{ minutes}$$

To convert to decimal hours, divide the time in seconds by 3600

$$110 \div 3600 = 0.0305 \text{ hours}$$

After 1.2 seconds, the table increases by 0.6 seconds.

Production Time Table

Minutes	Seconds	Production Per Hour	Decimal Hours
.0083	.5	7200	.00014
.0100	.6	6000	.00016
.0116	.7	5143	.00019
.0133	.8	4500	.00022
.0150	.9	4000	.00025
.0166	1.0	3600	.00028
.0200	1.2	3000	.00033
.0300	1.8	2000	.00050
.0400	2.4	1500	.00066
.0500	3.0	1200	.00083

Minutes	Seconds	Production Per Hour	Decimal Hours
.0600	3.6	1000	.00100
.0700	4.2	857.143	.00116
.0800	4.8	750	.00133
.0900	5.4	666.667	.00150
.1000	6.0	600	.00166
.1100	6.6	545.454	.00183
.1200	7.2	500	.00200
.1300	7.8	461.538	.00216
.1400	8.4	428.571	.00233
.1500	9.0	400	.00250
.1600	9.6	375	.00266
.1700	10.2	352.941	.00283
.1800	10.8	333.334	.00300
.1900	11.4	315.789	.00316
.2000	12.0	300	.00333
.2100	12.6	285.714	.00350
.2200	13.2	272.727	.00366
.2300	13.8	260.860	.00383
.2400	14.4	250	.00400
.2500	15.0	240	.00416
.2600	15.6	230.769	.00433
.2700	16.2	222.222	.00450
.2800	16.8	214.289	.00466
.2900	17.4	206.896	.00483
.3000	18.0	200	.00500
.3100	18.6	193.548	.00516
.3200	19.2	187.5	.00533
.3300	19.8	181.818	.00550
.3400	20.4	176.470	.00566
.3500	21.0	171.428	.00583
.3600	21.6	166.667	.00600
.3700	22.2	162.162	.00616
.3800	22.8	157.894	.00633
.3900	23.4	153.846	.00650
.4000	24.0	150	.00666
.4100	24.6	146.341	.00683
.4200	25.2	142.875	.00700
.4300	25.8	139.534	.00716
.4400	26.4	136.363	.00733
.4500	27.0	133.333	.00750
.4600	27.6	130.424	.00766
.4700	28.2	127.659	.00783
.4800	28.8	125	.00800
.4900	29.4	122.448	.00816

Production Time Table (*Continued*)

Minutes	Seconds	Production Per Hour	Decimal Hours
.5000	30.0	120	.00833
.5100	30.6	117.647	.00850
.5200	31.2	115.384	.00866
.5300	31.8	113.207	.00833
.5400	32.4	111.111	.00900
.5500	33.0	109.090	.00916
.5600	33.6	107.142	.00933
.5700	34.2	105.263	.00950
.5800	34.8	103.448	.00966
.5900	35.4	101.694	.00983
.6000	36.0	100	.01000
.6100	36.6	98.360	.01016
.6200	37.2	96.774	.01033
.6300	37.8	95.237	.01050
.6400	38.4	93.750	.01066
.6500	39.0	92.307	.01083
.6600	39.6	90.909	.01100
.6700	40.2	89.552	.01116
.6800	40.8	88.235	.01133
.6900	41.4	86.956	.01150
.7000	42.0	85.714	.01166
.7100	42.6	84.507	.01183
.7200	43.2	83.333	.01200
.7300	43.8	82.191	.01216
.7400	44.4	81.080	.01233
.7500	45.0	80	.01250
.7600	45.6	78.947	.01266
.7700	46.2	77.909	.01283
.7800	46.8	76.923	.01300
.7900	47.4	75.936	.01316
.8000	48.0	75	.01333
.8100	48.6	74.074	.01350
.8200	49.2	73.170	.01366
.8300	49.8	72.289	.01383
.8400	50.4	71.428	.01400
.8500	51.0	70.588	.01416
.8600	51.6	69.768	.01433
.8700	52.2	68.965	.01450
.8800	52.8	68.181	.01466
.8900	53.4	67.415	.01483
.9000	54.0	66.666	.01500
.9100	54.6	65.934	.01516
.9200	55.2	65.217	.01533
.9300	55.8	64.516	.01550

Production Time Table (*Continued*)

Minutes	Seconds	Production Per Hour	Decimal Hours
.9400	56.4	63.827	.01566
.9500	57.0	63.157	.01583
.9600	57.6	62.500	.01600
.9700	58.2	61.855	.01616
.9800	58.8	61.224	.01633
.9900	59.4	60.606	.01650
1.0000	60.0	60	.01666
1.0100	60.6	59.405	.01683
1.0200	61.2	58.823	.01700
1.0300	61.8	58.252	.01716
1.0400	62.4	57.692	.01733
1.0500	63.0	57.142	.01750
1.0600	63.6	56.603	.01766
1.0700	64.2	56.074	.01783
1.0800	64.8	55.555	.01800
1.0900	65.4	55.045	.01816
1.1000	66.0	54.545	.01833
1.1100	66.6	54.054	.01850
1.1200	67.2	53.571	.01866
1.1300	67.8	53.097	.01883
1.1400	68.4	52.631	.01900
1.1500	69.0	52.174	.01916
1.1600	69.6	51.724	.01933
1.1700	70.2	51.205	.01950
1.1800	70.8	50.847	.01966
1.1900	71.4	50.420	.01983
1.2000	72.0	50	.02000
1.2100	72.6	49.586	.02016
1.2200	73.2	49.180	.02033
1.2300	73.8	48.780	.02050
1.2400	74.4	48.387	.02066
1.2500	75.0	48	.02083
1.2600	75.6	47.619	.02100
1.2700	76.2	47.244	.02116
1.2800	76.8	46.875	.02133
1.2900	77.4	46.511	.02150
1.3000	78.0	46.133	.02166
1.3100	78.6	45.801	.02183
1.3200	79.2	45.454	.02200
1.3300	79.8	45.112	.02216
1.3400	80.4	44.776	.02233
1.3500	81.0	44.444	.02250
1.3600	81.6	44.117	.02266
1.3700	82.2	43.795	.02283
1.3800	82.8	43.479	.02300
1.3900	83.4	43.165	.02316

350

Production Time Table (*Continued*)

Minutes	Seconds	Production Per Hour	Decimal Hours
1.4000	84.0	42.857	.02333
1.4100	84.6	42.553	.02350
1.4200	85.2	42.253	.02366
1.4300	85.8	41.958	.02383
1.4400	86.4	41.666	.02400
1.4500	87.0	41.310	.02416
1.4600	87.6	41.095	.02433
1.4700	88.2	40.816	.02450
1.4800	88.8	40.450	.02466
1.4900	89.4	40.268	.02483
1.5000	90.0	40	.02500
1.5100	90.6	39.734	.02516
1.5200	91.2	39.473	.02533
1.5300	91.8	39.209	.02550
1.5400	92.4	38.961	.02566
1.5500	93.0	38.709	.02583
1.5600	93.6	38.461	.02600
1.5700	94.2	38.216	.02616
1.5800	94.8	37.974	.02633
1.5900	95.4	37.735	.02650
1.6000	96.0	37.500	.02666
1.6100	96.6	37.267	.02683
1.6200	97.2	37.037	.02700
1.6300	97.8	36.871	.02716
1.6400	98.4	36.585	.02733
1.6500	99.0	36.363	.02750
1.6600	99.6	36.144	.02766
1.6700	100.2	35.928	.02783
1.6800	100.8	35.714	.02800
1.6900	101.4	35.502	.02816
1.7000	102.0	35.293	.02833
1.7100	102.6	35.087	.02850
1.7200	103.2	34.883	.02866
1.7300	103.8	34.682	.02883
1.7400	104.4	34.482	.02900
1.7500	105.0	34.285	.02916
1.7600	105.6	34.091	.02933
1.7700	106.2	33.898	.02950
1.7800	106.8	33.702	.02966
1.7900	107.4	33.519	.02983
1.8000	108.0	33.333	.03000

Select Bibliography

Aluminum Forging Design Manual, 4th ed. Washington, D.C.: Forging Division, Aluminum Association, 1980.

ARDC Production Design Handbook. Washington, D.C.: John I. Thompson & Company, 1958.

Bayer, Lad J. *Analysis of Manufacturing Costs Relative to Product Design*, ASME Paper No. 56-SA-9. New York, NY: American Society of Mechanical Engineers, 1956.

Design Drafting Manual. Pomona, CA: General Dynamics, Electro Dynamic Division, 1986.

Design for Assembly, Wakefield, RI: Boothroyd Dewhurst, Inc., 1983.

Dimensioning and Tolerancing for Engineering Drawings, USASI Y14.5-1966. New York, NY: American Society of Mechanical Engineers, 1966.

Engineering "E" Series Standard. Des Plaines, IL: American Die Casting Institute, 1983.

Everhart, John L., ed. *Handbook of Parts, Forms and Processes, Materials in Design Engineering*. New York, NY: Van-Nostrand-Reinhold, 1960.

Extruded Shapes Technical Bulletin. ITT Harper, Inc.

Gross, Sidney, ed. *Modern Plastics Encyclopedia, 1970-1971*, Volume 47, No. 10-A, New York, NY: McGraw-Hill, October 1970.

Jenson, Jon E., ed. *Forging Industry Handbook*. Cleveland, OH: Forging Industry Association, 1970.

LeGrand, Rupert, ed. *New American Machinist's Handbook*, Section 17, "Cold Working of Metals." New York, NY: McGraw-Hill, 1955.

Liggett, John V. *Fundamentals of Position Tolerance*. Dearborn, MI: Society of Manufacturing Engineers, 1970.

Lyman, Taylor, ed. *Metals Handbook*, Volume 4, "Forming," 8th ed. Metals Park, OH: American Society for Metals, 1969.

Ready Spec No. 1. Los Angeles, CA: Ready Spec Associates, 1964.

Soderholm, Lars G. "Elastomers, Tailor-Made Design Materials." *Design News Supplement*. Boston, MA: Cahners Publishing Co., Inc., March 31, 1965.

Standards for Aluminum Sand and Permanent Mold Castings. Washington, D.C.: Aluminum Association, 1985.

Trucks, H. E., "Which Casting Method is Best," *Precision Metal.* Cleveland, OH: Penton-IPC, November, 1969.

---. "Design Flexibility with Powder Metallurgy," *Machine and Tool Blue Book.* Wheaton, IL: Hitchcock Publication, April, 1971.

Wick, Charles, et al., ed. *Tool and Manufacturing Engineers Handbook*, Volume 2, "Forming," 4th ed., Dearborn, MI: Society of Manufacturing Engineers, 1984.

Index

357

specific, 228, 248
Grinding, 36
 centerless, 36, 41
 costs, 36-40
 cylindrical, 41
 internal, 41
 production, 35
 surface, 41
 thread, 41
 tolerances, 35, 41

H

Hard coating treatments, 218
Hard facing materials, 219-220
Hardness, 132, 185, 210, 225
 durometer, 228, 230, 243-244
Heat
 aging, 256
 buildup, 225
 fastening, 333
 resistance, 251
 sealing, 280
 transfer, 227
Historical data, 294
Holes, 60, 63-64, 79, 154. 159, 162
 depths, 24, 80
 sizes, 154
 spacing, 177
 tolerances, 32-33, 245
Hollows, 136
Homopolymers, 267
 properties of, 255
Hooker process, 127-128
Hooke's law, 241
Hot forging, 101
Housing
 bores, 206
 fits, 203-205
Hydrospinning, 170
Hypalon, 239
Hysteresis, 225

I

Impact
 extrusions, 127, 142
 pressure, 102
 resistance, 185
 strength, 252
Industrial robots, 334, 336
Inertia, 179
Infiltration, 186
Injection molding, 250, 272-274
In-process inspection, 322
Inspection costs, 48
Inserts, 230, 276-277

Installation planning, 303
Insulation
 electrical, 248
 thermal, 248
Integration, 291
Integrity, 291
Inventory, 42
 costs, 44, 46
Investment castings, 47, 50, 88, 91, 94
 costs, 88, 92
 molds, 90
 tolerances, 92

J

Jigs, 121
Joining, 311, 331, 346
 methods, 146
 techniques, 278
Joint configurations, 279
Joints, 334
 lap, 146
Joule effect, 227

K

Key slots, 144
Knurling, 91

L

Labor, 295-296, 308, 346
 costs, 122, 297
 direct, 311
 requirements, 294, 296
 savings, 179
Lasers, 182
Latch mechanisms, 320
Lathes, 31, 33
Learning curves, 296
Limits, 199-207
Linear tolerances, 56
Loading, 328
 methods, 330
Locational
 features, 319
 fits, 200-201
 points, 324
 tolerances, 24
Lost wax process, 89
Lot sizes, 39
Low-carbon steels, 3, 8, 164

M

Machinability, 294
 ratings, 1-10

plans, 288
techniques, 291
Vents, 47
Vitreous coatings, 222

W

Wall
extrusions, 231
sections, 83, 87, 278
thicknesses, 230, 274
Warpage, 113, 117, 278
Wax patterns, 90
Wear resistance, 210
Weather
degradation, 257
resistance, 229, 259
Webs, 109, 112

Welding, 333
deposition, 220
lines, 183
processes, 333-335
Work
carriers, 318
division, 322
factors, 294
hardening, 132, 134, 162
measurement, 299, 306
Work-in-process, 306
Workstations, 322, 325

Z

Zinc, 70, 72, 79-80, 82
plating, 217